The PrivateBank Guide
2011-2012 Edition

A Scholl Corporate Guide®

Major publicly held corporations and financial institutions
headquartered in Illinois

JAN   2012

Published by:
Scholl Communications Incorporated
P.O. Box 560
Deerfield, IL 60015

Telephone: 847.945.1891

ISBN: 978-0-912519-43-2

Printed in U.S.A.

THE PRIVATE BANK

The Bank for Business · The Bank for Life

Dear Friends,

We are pleased to bring you the 2011-2012 edition of *The PrivateBank Guide*, with company profiles, financial data and information on executive leadership for 166 publicly traded companies in Illinois.

The PrivateBank Guide puts a who's who of Illinois companies and company leaders at your fingertips. In times like these, a trusted and reliable source of information is critical to any business. The principals at Scholl Communications have been compiling data on Illinois companies for over 40 years. We are proud to partner with Scholl Communications, just as we are proud to serve the banking needs of hundreds of Illinois companies.

The PrivateBank is known as "The Bank for Business and The Bank for Life." To us, that is more than just a catchy phrase in our advertising. It is a commitment. A promise to all of the companies we serve to bring thoughtful, creative banking solutions delivered by our relationship bankers.

The next several pages will give you a brief overview of our company. To learn more, we invite you to call us at (312) 564-2000, visit any of our 19 Illinois locations or see our website at www.theprivatebank.com.

Sincerely,

Larry D. Richman
President and Chief Executive Officer
PrivateBancorp, Inc.

THE PRIVATE BANK
The Bank for Business · The Bank for Life

HISTORY

The PrivateBank was founded on the belief that personal service is the key to delivering success for our clients. Today, that commitment to knowing our clients and earning their trust remains a hallmark of how we do business.

The PrivateBank opened for business in 1991 in a vintage building at 10 N. Dearborn Street in Chicago. Known for our distinctive approach to banking, we understand our clients want something more from their financial institution. Our clients value continuity and strong personal relationships with their bankers. The PrivateBank has long turned to seasoned professionals committed to knowing each client and delivering exceptionally personalized service.

Today we have a clear vision: To be the bank of choice for middle market commercial and commercial real estate companies, as well as business owners, executives, entrepreneurs and families in all of the communities we serve. We will achieve our vision by providing our clients with a comprehensive suite of personal and commercial banking, treasury management, investment products, capital markets, private banking and wealth management services. And we will deliver these services the same way we always have—by building strong relationships with our clients.

SERVING OUR CLIENTS

We believe our commitment to know our clients, to know what matters most to them, and to help them realize their goals, helps to differentiate us in all of our markets and business segments.

Knowing our clients means we become a trusted advisor to them. When coupled with the entrepreneurial spirit in our company, our professionals are thoughtful, responsive, creative and dedicated when working with our clients to deliver customized solutions. The importance we place in teamwork and collaboration means we can deepen existing relationships by leveraging the full scope of our products and services we offer.

THE PRIVATE BANK

Commercial Banking

Our Commercial Banking professionals concentrate on clients with $10 million to $2 billion in annual sales volume. We also have Specialty Banking Groups with particular expertise in Healthcare, Construction & Engineering, Security Alarm Finance and Asset-based Lending.

Commercial Real Estate

The PrivateBank's Commercial Real Estate team is dedicated to working with professional real estate developers and our focus is on commercial construction, retail, industrial and office property lending.

Community Banking

We have a network of bank branches in key communities in and around Chicago to serve individuals, families, small businesses and community organizations with everyday banking, mortgage and business banking services. These locations provide convenience and easy access for our clients, while ensuring we are active and engaged in making the towns and neighborhoods in which we operate strong and vibrant.

Private Wealth

Our Private Wealth team delivers private banking, investment management and trust services designed to help clients manage, grow, use and transfer wealth. Our professionals serve clients with a commitment to lifetime relationships by combining a passion for personal service with exceptional expertise. Private Wealth services have been a part of The PrivateBank since its founding and remain a cornerstone of our business today.

Specialized Services

Our emphasis is on delivering the products and services our clients need to manage their businesses and achieve results. To that end, we have developed specialized capabilities in Treasury Management, Capital Markets, Corporate Liquidity Advisory, Syndications and Letters of Credit.

OUR COMMITMENT TO OUR COMMUNITIES

We believe strongly in our responsibility to support our communities and to use the expertise of our professionals to help when we are able. The commitment to being an active and engaged corporate citizen runs deep throughout our company. Volunteer service is an important part of the performance objectives for each of our employees.

As we grow our company, we are working closely with key community groups to ensure our programs and philanthropic activities align with what our neighborhoods and their residents need.

We have placed a particular emphasis on education, especially financial literacy, and have forged a number of partnerships that allow us to support programs that teach the importance of responsible financial management.

OFFICES IN ILLINOIS

CHICAGO
120 South LaSalle Street
312.564.2000

70 West Madison Street
312.564.2000

Gold Coast Office
149 East Walton Place
312.238.8500

Lodestar Investment Counsel, LLC
150 South Wacker Drive
312.630.9666

NORTH SHORE
920 South Waukegan Road,
Lake Forest
847.615.3030

5260 Old Orchard Road, Skokie
847.853.3900

1000 Green Bay Road, Winnetka
847.441.4400

DUPAGE COUNTY
1110 Jorie Boulevard, Oak Brook
630.516.0900

KANE COUNTY
24 South Second Street, St. Charles
630.762.0092

501 West State Street, Geneva
630.845.4830

SOUTHERN COOK COUNTY
3052 West 111th Street, Chicago
(Mt. Greenwood)
773.445.4500

10515 South Cicero Avenue, OakLawn
708.448.6500

14497 John Humphrey Drive,
Orland Park
708.448.6500

11850 South Harlem Avenue,
Palos Heights
708.448.6500

17865 South 80th Avenue, Tinley Park
708.448.6500

6825 West 111th Street, Worth
708.448.6500

WILL COUNTY
23840 West Eames Street, Channahon
815.467.5321

14102 South Bell Road, Homer Glen
708.448.6500

1500 Essington Road, Joliet
815.467.5321

GRUNDY COUNTY
502 West Mondamin Road, Minooka
815.467.5321

Foreword

Welcome to the 46th edition of the Guide. The book is sponsored by PrivateBancorp, Inc. and published by Scholl Communications Incorporated. Originally published in 1965 by A.G. Becker & Co. Incorporated, the book was acquired in 1984 by Scholl Communications Incorporated and has been published annually, except for 2008, with the sponsorships of First Chicago Corporation and its successor, LaSalle Bank, and currently PrivateBancorp, Inc. Editorial management has remained unchanged throughout the book's history.

This edition profiles 166 industrial, commercial, and financial corporations headquartered in Illinois. These organizations were selected principally on the basis of their total revenues and total assets, and the information presented is intended to be of general interest.

Directory Organization

Companies and financial institutions are listed in alphabetical order. Beginning on page 168 is a listing of companies indexed according to the North American Industry Classification System (NAICS). The NAICS business code numbers were developed by Statistics Canada, Mexico's Instituto Nacional de Estadística, Geografía e Informática, and the U.S. Economic Classification Policy Committee to provide standard industry definitions for Canada, Mexico, and the United States. The NAICS codes listed in this edition are based on the 1997 edition of the NAICS manual published by the Office of Management and Budget of the Executive Office of the President.

An ordinal ranking of industrial, retail, transportation, utility, and diversified financial companies by revenues and total assets begins on page 175. Bank and savings institution holding companies are ranked separately.

A glossary of abbreviations used in the directory can be found on page 179. Number of stockholders is identified as either (R) stockholders of record or (B) stockholders with beneficial interest. A list of company changes, including new listings, name changes, and companies no longer listed, can be found on page 180.

Sources and Presentation of Information

The information contained in this book was obtained principally from the companies included, and from annual reports, proxy statements, websites, prospectuses, and other Securities and Exchange Commission filings.

The information contained in this book was collected from sources believed to be reliable, and the editor and publisher have exercised due care and caution in preparing and producing this book, but its accuracy and completeness are not guaranteed, and liability cannot be assumed for the correctness of the data contained herein. The descriptions are not to be construed as an offer to sell or the solicitation of an offer to buy any of the securities of these companies. Because of the abbreviated nature of the data, the Guide is designed as a general source of reference and is not a basis for investment decisions.

Businesses are constantly changing. Therefore, some of the data, particularly lists of directors and officers, may have changed since compilation.

Contents

Company	Page	Company	Page

Publicly Held Corporations and Financial Institutions Headquartered in Illinois

AAR CORP.

One AAR Place, 1100 North Wood Dale Road, Wood Dale, Illinois 60191
Telephone: (630) 227-2000   **www.aarcorp.com**

AAR is a leading provider of products and value-added services to the worldwide aerospace and government/defense industry. AAR provides commercial airlines and defense customers with a wide range of products and services in four areas: Aviation Supply Chain, which includes end-to-end supply chain programs as well as parts supply, repair, redistribution, and information technology systems integration; Government and Defense Services, which provides flight operations, personnel transport, and cargo in support of government deployments, and performs engineering and design modifications on rotary-wing aircraft for government customers; Maintenance, Repair and Overhaul, which includes the overhaul and modification of aircraft and landing gear; and Structures and Systems, which includes specialized mobility products, cargo systems, and composites. The company has facilities at more than 60 locations in 13 countries. Incorporated in Illinois in 1955; reincorporated in Delaware in 1966.

Directors (In addition to indicated officers)

Norman R. Bobins	Ronald R. Fogleman	Peter Paul
Michael R. Boyce	James E. Goodwin	Marc J. Walfish
James G. Brocksmith, Jr.	Patrick J. Kelly	Ronald B. Woodard

Officers (Directors*)

*David P. Storch, Chm. & C.E.O.
*Timothy J. Romenesko, Pres. & C.O.O.
Richard J. Poulton, V.P., C.F.O. & Treas.
Robert J. Regan, V.P., Gen. Coun. & Secy.
Michael J. Sharp, V.P., Cont. & Chf. Acct. Off.
Dany Kleiman, Grp. V.P.—Maintenance, Repair & Overhaul
Randy J. Martinez, Grp. V.P.—Govt. & Defense Svcs.
Terry D. Stinson, Grp. V.P.—Structures & Sys.

Donald J. Wetekam, Sr. V.P.—Govt. & Defense Bus. Dev.
Michael K. Carr, V.P.—Tax & Asst. Treas.
Peter K. Chapman, V.P. & Chf. Commer. Off.
James J. Clark, V.P.—Commer. Strat. & Bus. Dev.
Cheryle R. Jackson, V.P.—Govt. Affs. & Corp. Dev.
Kevin M. Larson, V.P. & C.I.O.
David E. Prusiecki, V.P.—Defense Programs
Timothy O. Skelly, V.P.—Hum. Res.

Consolidated Balance Sheet As of May 31, 2011 (000 omitted)

Assets		Liabilities & Stockholders' Equity	
Current assets	$ 913,985	Current liabilities	
Net property, plant & equipment	324,377	Long-term debt	$ 416,010
Other assets	465,365	Other liabilities	313,981
		*Stockholders' equity	138,447
			835,289
Total	$1,703,727	Total	$1,703,727

*39,781,000 shares common stock outstanding.

Consolidated Income Statement

Years Ended May 31	Thousands — — — —		Per Share — — — —		Common Stock Price Range Fiscal Year
	Net Sales[a]	Net Income	Diluted Earnings	Cash Dividends	
2011	$1,775,782	$69,826	$1.73	$0.075	$ 29.03—15.23
2010	1,316,416	44,628	1.16	0.00	25.90—14.44
2009	1,380,529	56,772[b]	1.45[b]	0.00	19.71—10.37
2008	1,327,512	68,158[b]	1.71[b]	0.00	38.54—18.94
2007	1,004,557	54,474[b]	1.40[b]	0.00	33.55—19.50

[a] From continuing operations.
[b] Restated to reflect change in accounting standard.

Transfer Agent & Registrar: Computershare Investor Services

Special Counsel:	Schiff Hardin LLP	Traded (Symbol):	NYSE, CSE (AIR)
Investor Relations:	Tom Udovich, Dir.	Stockholders:	1,250 (R)
Human Resources:	Timothy O. Skelly, V.P.	Employees:	6,100
Info. Tech.:	Kevin M. Larson, V.P.	Annual Meeting:	In October
Auditors:	KPMG LLP		

Abbott Laboratories

100 Abbott Park Road, Abbott Park, Illinois 60064-6400

Telephone: (847) 937-6100   www.abbott.com

Abbott Laboratories is a global, broad-based health care company devoted to the discovery, development, manufacture, and marketing of pharmaceuticals and medical products, including nutritionals, devices, and diagnostics. The company has three diverse business segments—Durable Growth, Innovation-Driven Devices, and Proprietary Pharmaceuticals—with leadership positions in the world's fastest-growing markets. The Durable Growth segment includes established pharmaceuticals, nutritionals, and diabetes care as well as the company's core and point of care diagnostics businesses. The Innovation-Driven Devices segment includes molecular diagnostics, vision care, and vascular businesses. This segment requires a higher level of R&D investment to deliver innovative technologies and can generate significant financial contributions. Proprietary Pharmaceuticals includes global patented pharmaceuticals with leadership positions in autoimmune disease, HIV, cystic fibrosis, testosterone replacement, and lipid management. In February 2010, Abbott acquired Belgium-based Solvay Pharmaceuticals, expanding Abbott's presence in key global emerging markets. In April 2010, Abbott acquired Facet Biotech Corporation to enhance the company's early- and mid-stage pharmaceutical pipeline. In October 2011, Abbott announced plans to separate into two publicly traded companies, one in diversified medical products and the other in research-based pharmaceuticals. Incorporated in Illinois in 1900.

Directors (In addition to indicated officers)

Robert J. Alpern, M.D.	H. Laurance Fuller	William A. Osborn
Roxanne S. Austin	Edward M. Liddy	Samuel C. Scott III
W. James Farrell	Phebe N. Novakovic	Glenn F. Tilton

Officers (Directors*)

*Miles D. White, Chm. & C.E.O.
Richard W. Ashley, Exec. V.P.—Corp. Dev.
John M. Capek, Exec. V.P.—Med. Devices
Thomas C. Freyman, Exec. V.P.—Fin. & C.F.O.
Richard Gonzalez, Exec. V.P.—Pharmaceutical Prods.
John C. Landgraf, Exec. V.P.—Nutritional Products
Edward L. Michael, Exec. V.P.—Diagnostics
Laura J. Schumacher, Exec. V.P., Gen. Coun. & Secy.
Carlos Alban, Sr. V.P.—Proprietary Pharmaceutical Prods.
Brian J. Blaser, Sr. V.P.—Diagnostics

A. David Forrest, Sr. V.P.—Intl. Nutrition
Stephen R. Fussell, Sr. V.P.—Hum. Res.
Robert B. Hance, Sr. V.P.—Vascular
Heather L. Mason, Sr. V.P.—Diabetes Care
James V. Mazzo, Sr. V.P.—Med. Optics
Donald V. Patton, Jr., Sr. V.P.—U.S. Pharmaceuticals
Mary T. Szela, Sr. V.P.—Gbl. Strat. Mktg. & Svcs.
Michael J. Warmuth, Sr. V.P.—Established Prods., Pharmaceutical Prods. Grp.
J. Scott White, Sr. V.P.—U.S. Nutrition

Consolidated Balance Sheet As of December 31, 2010 (000 omitted)

Assets		Liabilities & Stockholders' Equity	
Current assets	$23,317,529	Current liabilities	$17,262,434
Net property, plant & equipment	7,970,956	Long-term debt	12,523,517
Intangibles, net	12,151,628	Other liabilities	7,199,851
Goodwill	15,930,077	*Stockholders' equity	22,476,464
Other assets	1,092,076		
Total	$59,462,266	Total	$59,462,266

*1,546,983,948 shares common stock outstanding.

Consolidated Income Statement

Years Ended Dec. 31	Thousands — — — — —		Per Share — — — — —		Common Stock Price Range Calendar Year
	Net Sales	Net Income	Basic Earnings	Cash Dividends	
2010	$35,166,721	$4,626,172	$2.98	$1.76	$56.79—44.59
2009	30,764,707	5,745,838	3.71	1.60	57.39—41.27
2008	29,527,552	4,734,200	3.06	1.44	61.09—45.75
2007	25,914,238	3,606,314	2.34	1.30	59.50—48.75
2006	22,476,322	1,716,755 [a]	1.12 [a]	1.18	49.87—39.18

[a] Includes pre-tax charges of $2,014,000 for acquired in-process and collaborations research and development.

Transfer Agent & Registrar: Computershare Investor Services

General Counsel:	Laura Schumacher, Exec. V.P.	Traded (Symbol):	NYSE, CSE, LON, SWISS
Investor Relations:	John B. Thomas, V.P.		(ABT)
Human Resources:	Stephen R. Fussell, Sr. V.P.	Stockholders:	64,413 (R)
Info. Tech.:	Preston T. Simons, V.P.	Employees:	90,000
Auditors:	Deloitte & Touche LLP	Annual Meeting:	In April

THE PRIVATEBANK GUIDE

ACCO Brands Corporation

300 Tower Parkway, Lincolnshire, Illinois 60069

Telephone: (847) 541-9500   www.accobrands.com

ACCO Brands Corporation supplies branded office products to the office products resale industry, primarily to markets located in North America, Europe, and Australia. The company is organized into three business segments: ACCO Brands Americas, ACCO Brands International, and the Computer Products Group. ACCO Brands America and ACCO Brands International source and sell traditional office products and supplies. The Computer Products Group designs, distributes, markets, and sells accessories for computers and Apple® iPod®, iPad®, and iPhone® products. The company's brands include Swingline®, Kensington®, Wilson Jones®, Quartet®, GBC®, Rexel, NOBO, Marbig, and Day-Timer®. ACCO Brands markets its products to office products wholesalers, resellers, commercial contract stationers, retail superstores, mail order and internet catalogs, mass merchandisers, club stores, dealers, commercial and industrial end-users and to the educational market. In June 2009, the company completed the sale of its commercial print finishing business. Incorporated in Delaware in 2005.

Directors (In addition to indicated officers)

George V. Bayly	Thomas Kroeger
Kathleen S. Dvorak	Michael Norkus
G. Thomas Hargrove	Sheila G. Talton
Robert H. Jenkins	Norman H. Wesley

Officers (Directors*)

*Robert J. Keller, Chm. & C.E.O.
Boris Elisman, Pres. & C.O.O,
Neal V. Fenwick, Exec. V.P. & C.F.O.
Christopher Franey, Exec. V.P. & Pres.—ACCO Brands Int'l. & Computer Products Group
Thomas H. Shortt, Exec. V.P. & Pres.—Product Strategy & Development

Thomas W. Tedford, Exec V.P. & Pres.—ACCO Brands America Mark C. Anderson, Sr. V.P.—Corp. Dev.
David L. Kaput, Sr. V.P. & Chf. Hum. Res. Off.
Tom O'Neill, Sr. V.P.—Fin. & Acct.
Steven Rubin, Sr. V.P., Secy. & Gen. Coun.

Consolidated Balance Sheet As of December 31, 2010 (000 omitted)

Assets		Liabilities & Stockholders' Deficit	
Current assets	$ 620,700	Current liabilities	$ 327,900
Net property, plant & equipment	163,500	Long-term debt	727,400
Goodwill, net	144,400	Other liabilities	174,100
Identifiable intangibles, net of amortization	138,200	*Stockholders' deficit	(79,800)
Other assets	82,800		
Total	$1,149.600	Total	$1,149,600

*54,572,191 shares common stock outstanding.

Consolidated Income Statement

Years Ended Abt. Dec. 31	Thousands — — — —		Per Share — — — —		
	Net Sales	Net Income	Diluted Earnings	Cash Dividends	Common Stock Price Range Calendar Year
2010	$1,330,500	$ 11,500	$ 0.20	$0.00	$ 9.47— 4.63
2009 a	1,272,500	(115,800)	(2.13)	0.00	7.80— 0.67
2008	1,578,200	(263,000)	(4.85)	0.00	16.49— 0.65
2007	1,834,800	34,000	0.62	0.00	26.83—15.50
2006	1,847,000	2,100	0.04	0.00	27.45—17.95

a Includes non-cash charge of $108.1 million to establish a valuation allowance against U.S. deferred taxes.

Transfer Agent & Registrar: Wells Fargo Bank, N.A.

General Counsel:	Steven Rubin, Sr. V.P.	Traded (Symbol):	NYSE (ABD)
Investor Relations:	Jennifer Rice, V.P.	Stockholders:	12,115 (R)
Human Resources:	David L. Kaput, Sr. V.P.	Employees:	4,200
Info. Tech.:	Royce Heaney, V.P. Global I.T.	Annual Meeting:	In May
Auditors:	KPMG LLP		

Accretive Health, Inc.

401 North Michigan Avenue, Suite 2700, Chicago, Illinois 60611

Telephone: (312) 324-7820   www.accretivehealth.com

Accretive Health, Inc. provides services to healthcare providers that are designed to generate sustainable improvements in their operating margins and healthcare quality while also improving patient, physician, and staff satisfaction. Core services help U.S. healthcare providers to more efficiently manage their revenue cycles which encompass patient registration, insurance and benefit verification, medical treatment documentation and coding, bill preparation, and collections. Customers include multi-hospital systems, including faith-based or community healthcare systems, academic medical centers and independent ambulatory clinics, and their affiliated physician practice groups. The company's integrated technology and services offering helps its customers realize sustainable improvements in their operating margins and improve the satisfaction of their patients, physicians, and staff. As of December 31, 2010, the company provided revenue cycle service to 26 customers representing 66 hospitals, as well as quality and total cost of care service to one customer representing seven hospitals and 42 clinics. Incorporated in Delaware in 2003; present name adopted in 2009.

Directors (In addition to indicated officers)

Edgar M. Bronfman, Jr.
Steven N. Kaplan
Stanley N. Logan
Denis J. Nayden

George P. Shultz
Arthur H. Spiegel, III
Mark A. Wolfson

Officers (Directors*)

*J. Michael Cline, Founder & Chm.
*Mary A. Tolan, Founder, Pres. & C.E.O.
Etienne H. Deffarges, Exec. V.P.

Gregory N. Kazarian, Sr. V.P.
John T. Staton, C.F.O. & Treas.

Consolidated Balance Sheet As of December 31, 2010 (000 omitted)

Assets		Liabilities & Stockholders' Equity	
Current assets	$225,745	Current liabilities	$ 115,988
Net furniture & equipment	21,698	Other liabilities	3,912
Other assets	15,176	*Stockholders' equity	142,719
Total	$262,619	Total	$262,619

*94,826,509 shares common stock outstanding.

Consolidated Income Statement

Years Ended Dec. 31	Thousands — — — —		Per Share — — — —		Common Stock
	Net Revenue	Net Income [b]	Diluted Earnings [b]	Cash Dividends	Price Range [a] Calendar Year
2010	$606,294	$12,618	$0.13	0.00	$16.25—8.30
2009	510,192	6,546	0.15	0.18	
2008	398,469	(6,805)	(0.19)	0.18	
2007	240,725	774	0.01	0.00	
2006	160,741	(7,319)	(0.28)	0.00	

[a] Initial public offering May 20, 2010 at $12.00 per share.
[b] Applicable to common shareholders.

Transfer Agent & Registrar: American Stock Transfer & Trust Co.. LLC
Corporate Counsel: Wilmer Cutler Pickering Hale & Dorr LLP
Investor Relations   Gary Rubin
Human Resources: Jeff Bucklew
Info. Tech.:   Paul Cottey

Auditors: Ernst & Young LLP
Traded (Symbol): NYSE (AH)
Stockholders   79 (R)
Employees   1,991
Annual Meeting: In June

Acura Pharmaceuticals, Inc.

616 North North Court, Suite 120, Palatine, Illinois 60067

Telephone: (847) 705-7709   www.acurapharm.com

Acura Pharmaceuticals, Inc. is a specialty pharmaceutical company engaged in research, development, and manufacture of product candidates providing abuse deterrent features and benefits utilizing its proprietary Aversion® and Impede™ Technologies. Its portfolio of product candidates includes opioid analgesics intended to effectively relieve pain while simultaneously discouraging common methods of pharmaceutical product misuse and abuse including: intravenous injection of dissolved tablets or capsules; nasal snorting of crushed tablets or capsules; and intentional swallowing of excess quantities of tablets or capsules. The company conducts research, development, laboratory, manufacturing, and warehousing activities at its operations facility in Culver, Indiana. In October 2007, Acura entered into a license, development, and commercialization agreement with King Pharmaceuticals Research and Development, Inc., a subsidiary of Pfizer, Inc.. Under this agreement, Acura and King are now jointly developing Acurox® tablets and additional opioid analgesic product candidates utilizing Aversion® Technology. The company has three issues U.S. patents covering Aversion® technology with numerous U.S. and international patent applications pending. On February 14, 2011, The Food and Drug Administration notified Pfizer and Acura that the New Drug Application for Acurox® tablets was accepted for filing with an priority review classification. Incorporated in New York in 1934; present name adopted in 2004.

Directors (In addition to indicated officers)

Richard J. Markham, Chm.	William G. Skelly
David F. Azad	Immanuel Thangaraj
George K. Ross	Bruce F. Wesson

Officers (Directors*)

*Robert B. Jones, Pres. & C.E.O.	Ronald L. Leech, Sr. Dir.—Qual. &
Peter A. Clemens, Sr. V.P., C.F.O. & Secy.	Analytical Chemistry
Albert W. Brzeczko, Ph.D., V.P.—Tech. Affs	John G. Gilkay, Dir.—EHS & Eng.
James F. Emigh, V.P.—Mktg. & Admin.	Gregory A. Spinner, Dir.—Logistics & Spec. Projs.
Robert A. Seiser, V.P., Corp. Cont. & Treas.	

Consolidated Balance Sheet   As of December 31, 10 (000 omitted)

Assets		Liabilities & Stockholders' Equity	
Current assets	$24,441	Current liabilities	$ 1,152
Net property & equipment	1,052	*Stockholders' equity	24,341
Total	$25,493	Total	$25,493

*43,894,000 shares common stock outstanding.

Consolidated Income Statement

Years Ended Dec. 31	Thousands — — — — —		Per Share [a]— — — — —		Common Stock Price Range [ab] Calendar Year
	Net Revenues	Net Income	Diluted Earnings	Cash Dividends	
2010	$ 3,311	$(12,707)	(0.27)	0.00	$ 9.13—2.20
2009	3,835	(15,835)	(0.35)	0.00	9.00—4.00
2008	44,437	14,474	0.29	0.00	10.50—3.43
2007	6,404	(4,314)[c]	(0.11)[c]	0.00	28.40—6.00
2006	—	(5,967)	(0.75)	0.00	10.90—2.50

[a] Adjusted to reflect a 1-for-10 reverse stock split effected on December 5, 2007.
[b] Traded on OTC Bulletin Board through February 1, 2008. Commenced trading on NASDAQ Capital Markets February 4, 2008.
[c] Reflects impact of $30 million received from King Pharmaceuticals Inc. in December 2007.

Transfer Agent & Registrar: Broadridge Corporate Issuers Solutions, Inc.

General Counsel:	LeClair Ryan	Traded (Symbol):	NASDAQ CM (ACUR)
Investor Relations:	Peter A. Clemens, C.F.O.	Stockholders:	600 (R)
Human Resources:	James F. Emigh, V.P.	Employees:	15
Info. Tech.:	Robert A. Seiser, V.P.	Annual Meeting:	In June
Auditors:	BDO USA, LLP		

Addus HomeCare Corporation

2401 South Plum Grove Road, Palatine, Illinois 60067

Telephone: (847) 303-5300   **www.addus.com**

Addus HomeCare Corporation, through its subsidiary Addus HealthCare, is a comprehensive provider of a broad range of social and medical services in the home. Its services include personal care and assistance with activities of daily living, skilled nursing and rehabilitative therapies, and adult day care. The company's consumers are individuals with special needs who are at risk of hospitalization or institutionalization, such as the elderly, chronically ill, and disabled, with payment being provided by federal, state, and local governmental agencies, commercial insurers, and private individuals. The company provides services through over 129 locations across 16 states to more than 27,000 consumers. Addus operates in two business segments: home & community services and home health services. Predecessor company founded in 1979; incorporated in Delaware in 2006.

Directors (In addition to indicated officers)

R. DIrk Allison	Steven I. Geringer
Simon A. Bachleda	Wayne B. Lowell
Mark L. First	W. Andrew Wright, III

Officers (Directors*)

*Mark S. Heaney, Chm., Pres. & C.E.O.
Dennis Meulemans, C.F.O. & Secy.
Daniel Schwartz, C.O.O.
Darby Anderson, V.P.—Home & Community
    Svcs., Addus HealthCare

Gregory Breemes, V.P.—Home Health Svcs.,
    Addus Health Care
Paul Diamond, V.P.—Hum. Res.,
    Addus HealthCare

Consolidated Balance Sheet As of December 31, 2010 (000 omitted)

Assets		Liabilities & Stockholders' Equity	
Current assets	$ 85,798	Current liabilities	$ 37,132
Net property & equipment	2,923	Long-term debt	40,027
Goodwill	63,930	Other liabilities	1,674
Other assets	14,273	*Stockholders' equity	88,091
Total	$166,924	Total	$166,924

*10,751,000 shares common stock outstanding.

Consolidated Income Statement

Years Ended Dec. 31	Thousands — — — —		Per Share — — — —		Common Stock Price Range [a] Calendar Year
	Net Revenue	Net Income [b]	Diluted Earnings [b]	Cash Dividends	
2010	$271,732	$6,028	$ 0.57	$0.00	$9.72—2.80
2009	259,305	(1,785) [c]	(0.66)	0.00	9.50—7.52
2008	236,306	(247)	(0.24)	0.00	
2007	194,567	(3,685)	(3.62)	0.00	
2006 [d]	52,256	(673)	(0.66)	0.00	
2006 [e]	125,927	4,811	4,455.06	0.00	

[a] Initial public offering October 27, 2009 at $10.00 per share.
[b] Applicable to common shareholders.
[c] Includes one-time charges relating to initial public offering, including $1.2 million of separation costs; a charge to interest expense pursuant to the contingent payment agreement in which an amount equal to $12.7 million was paid upon the completion of initial public offering, of which $1.8 million was deemed interest expense; and the write-off of $0.8 million in unamortized debt issuance costs relating to former credit facility that was charged to interest expense.
[d] Successor company, from September 19, 2006 through December 31, 2006.
[e] Predecessor company, from January 1, 2006 through September 18, 2006.

Transfer Agent & Registrar: Computershare Investor Services

Corporate Counsel:	Winston & Strawn LLP	Traded (Symbol):	NASDAQ GM (ADUS)
Investor Relations:	Amy Glynn, The Ruth Group	Stockholders:	20 (R)
Human Resources:	Paul Diamond, V.P.	Employees	13,284
Info. Tech.:	Michael Siegel, V.P.—IS	Annual Meeting:	In June
Auditors:	BDO USA, LLP		

Akorn, Inc.

1925 West Field Court, Suite 300, Lake Forest, Illinois 60045

Telephone: (800) 932-5676   www.akorn.com

Akorn, Inc. develops, manufactures, and markets multisource and branded pharmaceuticals in the areas of ophthalmology, antidotes, anti-infectives, and controlled substances for pain management and anesthesia in the United States and overseas. Customers include physicians, optometrists, hospitals, surgery centers, clinics, long-term care facilities, wholesalers, group purchasing organizations, retail pharmacies, and other pharmaceutical companies. The company has manufacturing operations in Illinois and New Jersey. In May 2011, the company announced that it had entered into an agreement to acquire Advanced Vision Research, Inc., a Woburn, Massachusetts-based company that develops and markets eye care products. The company also announced plans to launch a new Consumer Health Division and to further expand by licensing new products and developing private-labeled eye care products for major retailers. Incorporated in Louisiana in 1971.

Directors (In addition to indicated officers)

John N. Kapoor, Ph.D., Chm.
Kenneth S. Abramowitz
Ronald M. Johnson

Steven J. Meyer
Brian Tambi
Alan Weinstein

Officers (Directors*)

Raj Rai, C.E.O.
Timothy A. Dick, Sr. V.P. & C.F.O.
Bruce Kutinsky, Pres.—Consumer Health Div.
Mark M. Silverberg, Exec. V.P.—Oper., Gbl.
  Qual. Assurance & Tech. Svcs.

Joseph Bonaccorsi, Sr. V.P., Gen. Coun. & Secy.
John R. Sabat, Sr. V.P.—Natl. Accounts &
  Trade Rel.

Consolidated Balance Sheet As of December 31, 2010 (000 omitted)

Assets		Liabilities & Stockholders' Equity	
Current assets	$ 73,613	Current liabilities	$ 21,940
Net property, plant & equipment	32,731	Other liabilities	2,424
Other assets	4,772	*Stockholders' equity	86,752
Total	$111,116	Total	$111,116

*90,389,597 shares common stock outstanding.

Consolidated Income Statement

Years Ended Dec. 31	Thousands — — — — —		Per Share — — — — —		Common Stock Price Range Calendar Year
	Revenues	Net Income a	Diluted Earnings	Cash Dividends	
2010	$86,409	$21,824	$0.22	$0.00	$6.50—1.27
2009	75,891	(25,306)	(0.28)	0.00	2.69—0.73
2008	93,598	(7,939)	(0.09)	0.00	8.19—1.11
2007	52,895	(19,168)	(0.22)	0.00	8.00—5.00
2006	71,250	(6,806)	(0.09)	0.00	6.61—3.01

a Available to common shareholders.

Transfer Agent & Registrar: Computershare Investor Services

Corporate Counsel: Luce, Forward, Hamilton &
            Scripps LLP
Investor Relations: Tim Dick, C.F.O.
Human Resources: Karen Logan, Mgr.
Info. Tech.:   Vin Das

Auditors: Ernst & Young LLP
Traded (Symbol): NASDAQ GM (AKRX)
Stockholders: 448 (R)
Employees: 410
Annual Meeting: In April

Allscripts Healthcare Solutions, Inc.

222 Merchandise Mart Plaza, Suite 2024, Chicago, Illinois 60654
Telephone: (312) 506-1200   www.allscripts.com

Allscripts Healthcare Solutions, Inc. provides clinical, financial, connectivity, information solutions, and related professional services to hospitals, physicians, and post-acute organizations. More than 180,000 physicians, 1,500 hospitals and nearly 10,000 post-acute and homecare organizations use Allscripts. The company operates 44 locations in 24 states, Canada, India, the Middle East, and Asia. Clinical software applications include electronic health records, physician practice management, revenue cycle management for hospitals and physicians, claims clearinghouse services, electronic prescribing, integrated hospital care management and discharge management solutions, document imaging solutions, and a variety of applications for home care and other post-acute organizations. The August 2010 merger of Allscripts and Eclipsys combined the former's physician-office and post-acute applications with the latter's enterprise solutions for hospitals and health systems. Incorporated in Illinois in 1986; reincorporated in Delaware in 1999.

Directors (In addition to indicated officers)

Dennis H. Chookaszian
Eugene Fife
Marcel L. "Gus" Gamache

Philip D. Green
Edward Kangas
Michael J. Kluger

Officers (Directors*)

*Philip M. Pead, Chm.
*Glen E. Tullman, C.E.O.
Lee A. Shapiro, Pres.
William J. Davis, C.F.O.
Eileen McPartland, C.O.O.
Diane Adams, Exec. V.P.—Culture & Talent
John P. Gomez, Exec. V.P. & Chf. Tech. Off.

Stephen Lalonde, Exec. V.P.—Sales & Oper.
Stephen Shute, Exec. V.P.—Sales
Laurie McGraw, Chief Client Off.
Daniel S. Michelson, Chf. Mktg. & Strategy Off.
Jacqueline Studer, Sr. V.P. & Gen. Coun.
Joe Carey, V.P.—Strategic Accounts

Consolidated Balance Sheet As of December 31, 2010 (000 omitted)

Assets		Liabilities & Stockholders' Equity	
Current assets	$ 575,456	Current liabilities	$ 431,071
Intangible assets, net	554,669	Long-term debt	459,750
Goodwill, net	1,037,004	Other liabilities	143,998
Other assets	251,458	*Stockholders' equity	1,383,768
Total	$2,418,587	Total	$2,418,587

*188,288,000 shares common stock outstanding.

Consolidated Income Statement [a]

Years Ended Dec 31	Thousands — — — —		Per Share — — — —		Common Stock Price Range For Periods Shown
	Total Revenue	Net Income	Diluted Earnings	Cash Dividends	
2010 [b]	$613,309	$ (5,565)	$(0.03)	$0.00	$19.97—15.65
2010 [c]	704,502	62,870	0.42	0.00	22.55—12.69
2009 [c]	548,439	26,022	0.21	0.00	13.23— 4.87
2008 [d]	383,771	25,399	0.31	0.00	18.81— 8.76
2007 [e]	379,693	3,854	0.05	0.00	30.99—17.13

[a] In 2010, Allscripts Healthcare Solutions, Inc. changed its fiscal year end from May 31 to December 31. Refer to the company's 10K for detailed footnote information.
[b] Seven months ended December 31, 2010.
[c] Fiscal year ended May 31.
[d] January 1 through October 10.
e Fiscal year ended December 31.

Transfer Agent & Registrar: BNY Mellon Shareowner Services

General Counsel:	Jacqueline Studer, Sr. V.P.	Traded (Symbol):	NASDAQ (MDRX)
Investor Relations:	Seth Frank, V.P.	Stockholders:	4732 (R)
Human Resources:	Diane Adams, Exec. V.P.	Employees:	5,580
Auditors:	PricewaterhouseCoopers LLP	Annual Meeting:	In May

The Allstate Corporation

2775 Sanders Road, Northbrook, Illinois 60062-6127

Telephone: (847) 402-5000   www.allstate.com

The Allstate Corporation is a holding company which conducts its business primarily through Allstate Insurance Company (AIC) and Allstate Life Insurance Company. Allstate is primarily engaged in the personal property and casualty insurance business and the life insurance, retirement, and investment products business. It is the largest publicly held personal lines insurance company in the United States. Allstate provides insurance to more than 16 million households and has approximately 14,000 exclusive agencies and financial specialists in the United States and Canada. Allstate's two main business units are Allstate Protection and Allstate Financial. Allstate Protection sells private passenger auto and homeowners insurance, as well as commercial lines, condominium, renters, and involuntary auto insurance. Allstate Financial provides life insurance, retirement, investment, and voluntary accident and health insurance products to individual and institutional customers. Products include fixed annuities, variable annuities, life insurance, and voluntary accident and health insurance. Life insurance and savings products are distributed through Allstate agents and a variety of other distribution channels including broker-dealers, financial institutions, and thousands of independent agents and brokers. Incorporated in Delaware in 1992.

Directors (In addition to indicated officers)

F. Duane Ackerman
Robert D. Beyer
W. James Farrell
Jack M. Greenberg

Ronald T. LeMay
Andrea Redmond
H. John Riley, Jr.

Joshua I. Smith
Judith A. Sprieser
Mary Alice Taylor

Officers (Directors*)

*Thomas J. Wilson, Chm., Pres. & C.E.O.
Don Civgin, Exec. V.P. & C.F.O.
Michele Coleman Mayes, Exec. V.P. & Gen. Coun.
Catherine S. Brune, Pres.—Allstate Protection, So. Reg., AIC
Anurag Chandra, C.O.O.—Allstate Fin.
James D. Devries, Exec. V.P. & Chf. Admin. Off., AIC
Judith P. Greffin, Exec. V.P. & Chf. Invest. Off., AIC

Suren Gupta, Exec. V.P.—Allstate Tech. & Oper.
Guy Hill, Pres.—Allstate Protection, CA/East Reg., AIC
Mark R. LaNeve, Exec. V.P. & Chf. Mktg. Off., AIC
Michael J. Roche, Exec. V.P.—Claims, AIC
Steven P. Sorenson, Exec. V.P.—Prod. Oper., AIC
Joan H. Walker, Exec. V.P.—Corp. Rel., AIC
Matthew E. Winter, Pres. & C.E.O.—Allstate Fin.

Consolidated Balance Sheet As of December 31, 2010 (000 omitted)

Assets		Liabilities & Stockholders' Equity	
Investments	$100,483,000	Insurance reserves	$ 32,950,000
Premium installment receivables	4,839,000	Contractholder funds	48,195,000
Deferred policy acquisition costs	4,769,000	Unearned premiums	9,800,000
Reinsurance recoverables, net	6,552,000	Long-term debt	5,908,000
Other assets	5,555,000	Other liabilities	6,301,000
Separate accounts	8,676,000	Separate accounts	8,676,000
		*Stockholders' equity	19,044,000
Total	$130,874,000		$130,874,000

*533,000,000 shares common stock outstanding.

Consolidated Income Statement

Years Ended Dec. 31	Thousands — — — —		Per Share — — — —		Common Stock Price Range Calendar Year
	Total Revenues	Net Income	Diluted Earnings	Cash Dividends	
2010	$31,400,000	$ 928,000	$1.71	$0.80	$35.51—26.86
2009	32,013,000	854,000	1.58	0.80	33.50—13.77
2008	29,394,000	(1,679,000)	(3.06)	1.64	52.90—17.72
2007	36,769,000	4,636,000	7.76	1.52	65.85—48.90
2006	35,796,000	4,993,000	7.83	1.40	66.14—50.22

Transfer Agent & Registrar: Wells Fargo Shareowner Services

General Counsel:	Michele C. Mayes, Sr. V.P.	Traded (Symbol):	NYSE, CSE (ALL)
Investor Relations:	Robert Block, Sr. V.P.	Stockholders:	108,052 (R)
Human Resources:	James D. DeVries, Exec. V.P.	Employees:	36,000
Info. Tech.:	Suren Gupta, Exec. V.P.	Annual Meeting:	In May
Auditors:	Deloitte & Touche LLP		

THE PRIVATEBANK GUIDE   9

AMCOL International Corporation
2870 Forbs Avenue, Hoffman Estates, Illinois 60192
Telephone: (847) 851-1500
www.amcol.com

AMCOL International Corporation is a leading international producer and marketer of specialty minerals and related products. Established in 1927 as American Colloid Company, AMCOL is a leading supplier of bentonite, a non-metallic clay primarily composed of the mineral montmorillonite, to markets that include metalcasting, well drilling, building materials, pet products, detergents, and personal care products. The company operates in five segments: minerals and materials, environmental, oilfield services, transportation, and corporate. The minerals and materials segment mines, processes, and distributes clays and similar products to industrial and consumer markets. The environmental segment processes and distributes minerals and similar products for use as a moisture barrier in commercial construction, landfill liners, and other industrial and commercial applications. The oilfield services segment provides both onshore and offshore water treatment filtration, pipeline separation, waste fluid treatment, and other services for the oil and gas industry. The transportation segment includes long-haul trucking and freight brokerage businesses that serve its plants and outside customers. The corporate segment includes the elimination of intersegment shipping revenues as well as certain expenses associated with research and development, management, benefits, and information technology activities. Incorporated in South Dakota in 1924 as Bentonite Mining & Manufacturing Co.; reincorporated in Delaware in 1959; present name adopted in 1995.

Directors (In addition to indicated officers)

John Hughes, Chm.	Clarence O. Redman
Arthur Brown	Dale E. Stahl
Daniel P. Casey	Audrey L. Weaver
Jay D. Proops	Paul C. Weaver

Officers (Directors*)

*Ryan F. McKendrick, Pres. & C.E.O.
Gary L. Castagna, Sr. V.P. & Pres.—Gbl.
  Minerals & Materials
Robert J. Trauger, V.P. & Pres.—Environmental

Michael R. Johnson, V.P. & Pres.—CETCO Oilfield
  Svcs.
Donald W. Pearson, V.P., C.F.O. & Treas.
James W. Ashley, Jr., Secy.

Consolidated Balance Sheet As of December 31, 2010 (000 omitted)

Assets

Current assets	$361,564
Net property, plant & equipment	260,488
Other assets	177,041
Total	$799,093

*31,246,825 shares common stock outstanding.

Liabilities & Stockholders' Equity

Current liabilities	$ 112,475
Long-term debt	236171
Other liabilities	50,011
*Stockholders' equity & non-controlling interest	400,436
Total	$799,093

Consolidated Income Statement

Years Ended Dec. 31	Thousands — — — — Net Sales	Net Income	Per Share — — — — Diluted Earnings	Cash Dividends	Common Stock Price Range Calendar Year
2010	$852,538	$29,924	$0.96	$0.72	$32.60—22.12
2009	703,237	34,799	1.12	0.72	30.00—10.84
2008	883,552	25,331	0.82	0.68	38.33—13.50
2007	744,334	56,735[a]	1.83[a]	0.60	42.70—23.76
2006	611,556	50,248[b]	1.62[b]	0.49	33.49—18.71

[a] Includes loss from discontinued operations of $286,000 ($0.01 per diluted share).
[b] Includes gain from discontinued operations of $585,000 ($0.02 per diluted share).

Transfer Agent & Registrar: American Stock Transfer & Trust Co.	
Corporate Counsel: Locke, Lord, Bissell & Liddell LLP	**Traded (Symbol):** NYSE (ACO)
Investor Relations: Donald W. Pearson, V.P. & C.F.O.	**Stockholders:** 6,907 (R)
Human Resources: Ed McCann, Dir.	**Employees:** 2,383
Auditors: Ernst & Young LLP	**Annual Meeting:** In May

Anixter International Inc.

2301 Patriot Boulevard, Glenview, Illinois 60026
Telephone: (224) 521-8000   **www.anixter.com**

Anixter International Inc. (formerly Itel Corporation) is engaged in the distribution of communications and electrical wire and cable products as well as fasteners and small parts, known as "C" class inventory components, through Anixter Inc. and its subsidiaries. The company distributes these products from top suppliers to contractors, installers, integrators, and to end users, such as manufacturers, natural resources companies, utilities, and original equipment manufacturers (OEMs). It is also a leading global distributor of data, voice, video, and security network communication products that companies use to support their operations. The company maintains a logistics network of approximately 228 warehouses in 50 countries. In 2010, the company derived 59.6% of sales from the United States, 18.7% from Europe, 11.5% from Canada, and 10.2% from emerging markets (Asia Pacific and Latin America). Incorporated in Delaware in 1967; present name adopted in 1995.

Directors (In addition to indicated officers)

Samuel Zell, Chm.
Lord James Blyth
Frederic F. Brace
Linda Walker Bynoe
Robert W. Grubbs, Jr.

F. Philip Handy
Melvyn N. Klein
George Muñoz
Stuart M. Sloan
Matthew Zell

Officers (Directors*)

*Robert J. Eck, Pres. & C.E.O.
Ted A. Dosch, Exec. V.P.—Fin. & C.F.O.
Terrance A. Faber, V.P.—Cont.
Philip F. Meno, V.P.—Taxes

Rodney A. Shoemaker, V.P.—Treas.
Rodney A. Smith, V.P.—Hum. Res.
John A. Dul, V.P., Gen. Coun. & Secy.

Consolidated Balance Sheet As of December 31, 2010 (000 omitted)

Assets		Liabilities & Stockholders' Equity	
Current assets	$2,281,200	Current liabilities	$ 1,071,200
Net property & equipment	84,600	Long-term debt	688,800
Goodwill	374,300	Other liabilities	162,500
Other assets	193,200	*Stockholders' equity	1,010,800
Total	$2,933,300	Total	$2,933,300

*34,323,061 shares common stock outstanding.

Consolidated Income Statement

Years Ended Abt. Dec. 31	Thousands — — — —		Per Share — — — —		Common Stock Price Range Calendar Year
	Net Sales	Net Income	Diluted Earnings	Cash Dividends	
2010	$5,472,100	$108,500	$ 3.05	$3.25 [a]	$61.17—38.42
2009	4,982,400	(29,300) [b]	(0.83) [b]	0.00	48.55—24.46
2008	6,136,600	187,900	4.87	0.00	75.07—20.97
2007	5,852,900	245,500	5.81	0.00	88.40—49.28
2006	4,938,600	206,300	4.79	0.00	61.45—38.67

[a] Special dividend paid October 28, 2010

[b] Includes reduction of $115 million ($3.16 per diluted share) relating to goodwill impairment charge; severance costs; market adjustments and foreign exchange losses related to Venezuela operations; and losses related to early retirement of debt and cancellation of interest rate hedging contracts.

Transfer Agent & Registrar: Wells Fargo Shareowner Services

General Counsel:	John A. Dul, V.P.	Traded (Symbol):	NYSE (AXE)
Investor Relations:	Ted A. Dosch, C.F.O.	Stockholders:	2,340 (R)
Human Resources:	Rodney A. Smith, V.P.	Employees:	7,989
Info. Tech.:	David Lemme	Annual Meeting:	In May
Auditors:	Ernst & Young LLP		

Aon Corporation

200 East Randolph Street, Chicago, Illinois 60601

Telephone: (312) 381-1000   **www.aon.com**

Aon Corporation is a leading global provider of risk management services, insurance and reinsurance bro-kerage, and human capital consulting. The company has more than 500 offices in more than 120 countries. Clients include corporations and businesses, insurance companies, professional organizations, independent agents and brokers, governments, and other entities. The company also serves individuals through personal lines, affinity groups, and certain specialty operations. Aon's resources are delivered through three primary businesses: Aon Hewitt, which provides human resources solutions; Aon Benfield, which provides reinsur-ance solutions; and Aon Risk Solutions, which offers a range of insurance and risk management products. In October 2010 Aon completed the acquisition of Hewitt Associates, Inc. Incorporated in Delaware in 1979.

Directors (In addition to indicated officers)

Lester B. Knight, Chm.	Jan Kalff	Richard B. Myers
Fulvio Conti	J. Michael Losh	Richard C. Notebaert
Cheryl A. Francis	R. Eden Martin	John W. Rogers, Jr.
Judson C. Green	Andrew J. McKenna	Gloria Santona
Edgar D. Jannotta	Robert S. Morrison	Dr. Carolyn Y. Woo

Officers (Directors*)

*Gregory C. Case, Pres. & C.E.O.
Gregory J. Besio, Exec. V.P., Chf. Hum. Res. Off.
Christa Davies, Exec. V.P. & C.F.O.
Peter Lieb, Exec. V.P. & Gen. Coun.
Matthew Levin, Exec. V.P. Gbl. Strat.
Stephen P. McGill, Chm. & C.E.O.—Aon Risk Solutions

Michael J. O'Connor, C.O.O.—Aon Risk Solutions
Kristi Savacool, Co-C.E.O.—Aon Hewitt
Baljit Dail, Co-C.E.O.—Aon Hewitt
Laurel G. Meissner, Sr. V.P. & Gbl. Cont.
Philip B. Clement, Gbl. Chf. Mktg. & Commun. Off.

Consolidated Balance Sheet As of December 31, 2010 (000 omitted)

Assets		Liabilities & Stockholders' Equity	
Current assets	$14,519,000	Current liabilities	$12,949,000
Goodwill	8,647,000	Long-term debt	4,014,000
Intangible assets, net	3,611,000	Other liabilities	3,713,000
Net fixed assets	781,000	*Stockholders' equity	8,251,000
Other assets	1,424,000	Noncontrolling interest	55,000
Total	$28,982,000	Total	$28,982,000

*332,300,000 shares common stock outstanding.

Consolidated Income Statement

Years Ended Dec. 31	Thousands — — — — Total Revenues	Net Income [a]	Per Share — — — — Diluted Earnings [a]	Cash Dividends	Common Stock Price Range Calendar Year
2010	$8,512,000	$ 706,000	$2.37	$0.60	$46.24—35.10
2009	7,595,000	747,000	2.57	0.60	46.19—34.81
2008	7,528,000	1,462,000	4.80	0.60	50.00—32.83
2007	7,234,000	864,000	2.66	0.60	51.32—34.30
2006	6,688,000	720,000	2.10	0.60	42.76—31.01

[a] Includes a loss of $27.0 million ($0.09 per diluted share) in 2010; and income from discontinued operations of $111.0 million ($0.38 per diluted share) in 2009; $841.0 million ($2.76 per diluted share) in 2008; $202.0 million ($0.62 per diluted share) in 2007; and $230.0 million ($0.67 per diluted share) in 2006.

Transfer Agent & Registrar: Computershare Investor Services

General Counsel:	Peter Lieb, Exec. V.P.	Traded (Symbol):	NYSE (AON)
Investor Relations:	Scott L. Malchow, V.P.	Stockholders:	9,300 (R)
Human Resources:	Gregory J. Besio, Exec. V.P.	Employees:	59,000
Info Tech:	Adam Stanley, Global C.T.O.	Annual Meeting:	In May
Auditors:	Ernst & Young LLP		

APAC Customer Services, Inc.

2201 Waukegan Road, Suite 300, Bannockburn, Illinois 60015

Telephone: (847) 374-4980   www.apaccustomerservices.com

APAC Customer Services, Inc. is a leading provider of customer care services and solutions to market leaders in healthcare, business services, communications, media and publishing, travel and entertainment, and financial services. APAC partners with its clients to deliver custom solutions that enhance bottom line performance. As of January 3, 2010, the company operated 15 customer care centers: eight domestic, two domestic client-owned facilities, four off-shore centers located in the Philippines and one near-shore center located in the Dominican Republic. Domestic operations involved approximately 6,300 workstations and international operations consisted of approximately 4,600 workstations. These are managed centrally through the application of telecommunications and computer technology to promote the consistent delivery of quality service. In July 2011, the company agreed to be acquired by One Equity Partners, subject to shareholder and regulatory approvals. The transaction is expected to close in the fourth quarter of 2011. Incorporated in Illinois in 1973.

Directors (In addition to indicated officers)

Katherine Andreasen	Samuel K. Skinner
John J. Park	John L. Workman

Officers (Directors*)

*Theodore G. Schwartz, Chm.	Andrew B. Szafran, Sr. V.P. & C.F.O.
*Kevin T. Keleghan, Pres. & C.E.O.	Joseph R. Doolan, V.P. & Cont.
Greg Carr, Sr. V.P. & Chf. Mktg. & Sales Off.	Michael V. Hoehne, V.P.—Chf. Hum. Res. Off.
Christopher H. Crowley, Sr. V.P.—Sales	Mark E. McDermott, V.P. & C.I.O.
Arthur D. DiBari, Sr. V.P.—Oper.	
Robert B. Nachwalter, Sr. V.P. & Gen. Coun.	

Consolidated Balance Sheet As of January 2, 2011 (000 omitted)

Assets		Liabilities & Stockholders' Equity	
Current assets	$113,137	Current liabilities	$ 37,158
Net property & equipment	28,030	Other liabilities	4,536
Goodwill	13,338	*Stockholders' equity	121,471
Other assets	8,660		
Total	$163,165	Total	$163,165

*52,488,457 shares common stock outstanding.

Consolidated Income Statement

Years Ended Abt. Dec. 31	Thousands — — — —		Per Share — — — —		Common Stock Price Range Calendar Year
	Net Revenue	Net Income	Diluted Earnings	Cash Dividends	
2010	$325,958	$22,854	$0.42	$0.00	$6.64—4.61
2009 [a]	293,177	58,053	1.09	0.00	7.02—0.94
2008	248,799	3,019	0.06	0.00	2.39—0.68
2007	224,683	5,089	0.10	0.00	5.18—1.00
2006	224,297	(30,539)	(0.62)	0.00	3.84—1.42

[a] 53 weeks.

Transfer Agent & Registrar: Mellon Investor Services LLC

General Counsel:	Robert Nachwalter, Sr. V.P.	Traded (Symbol):	NASDAQ (APAC)
Investor Relations:	Andrew B. Szafran, Sr. V.P.	Stockholders:	760 (R)
Human Resources:	Michael V. Hoehne, V.P.	Employees:	13,400
Info. Tech.:	Mark E. McDermott, V.P.	Annual Meeting:	In June
Auditors:	Ernst & Young LLP		

Aptargroup, Inc.

475 West Terra Cotta Avenue, Suite E, Crystal Lake, Illinois 60014

Telephone: (815) 477-0424   **www.aptar.com**

Aptargroup, Inc. is a leading global supplier of innovative dispensing systems for the personal care, fragrance/cosmetic, pharmaceutical, household, and food/beverage markets. The company develops, manufactures, and sells products including spray and lotion pumps, dispensing closures, and aerosol valves. Aptargroup has more than 5,000 customers in the global consumer product marketing industry. Manufacturing facilities are located in North America, Europe, Asia, and South America. In 2010, Aptargroup announced the strategic realignment of its businesses under three market-focused business segments: Aptar Beauty + Home, Aptar Food + Beverage, and Aptar Pharma. Incorporated in Delaware in 1992.

Directors (In addition to indicated officers)

King W. Harris, Chm.
Stefan A. Baustert
Alain Chevassus
George L. Fotiades
Rodney L. Goldstein

Leo A. Guthart
Giovanna Kampouri Monnas
Dr. Joanne C. Smith
Ralph K. Wunderlich

Officers (Directors*)

*Peter H. Pfeiffer, Pres. & C.E.O.
*Stephen J. Hagge, Exec. V.P., C.O.O.
Robert Kuhn, Exec. V.P. & C.F.O. & Secy.
Ursla Saint-Leger, V.P.—Hum. Res.

Patrick Doherty, Pres.—Aptar Beauty + Home
Olivier Fourment, Pres.—Aptar Pharma
Eric S. Ruskoski, Pres.—Aptar Food + Beverage

Consolidated Balance Sheet As of December 31, 2010 (000 omitted)

Assets		Liabilities & Stockholders' Equity	
Current assets	$ 1,063,983	Current liabilities	$ 423,322
Net property, plant & equipment	724,984	Long-term debt	258,773
Goodwill	227,029	Deferred items & other	70,849
Other assets	16,722	*Stockholders' equity	1,279,774
Total	$2,032,718	Total	$2,032,718

*66,800,000 shares common stock outstanding.

Consolidated Income Statement

Years Ended Dec. 31	Thousands — — — —		Per Share a — — — —		Common Stock Price Range a Calendar Year
	Net Sales	Net Income	Diluted Earnings	Cash Dividends	
2010	$2,076,719	$173,481	$2.48	$0.66	$48.45—34.46
2009	1,841,616	124,623[b]	1.79[b]	0.60	38.96—24.95
2008	2,071,685	153,495[b]	2.18[b]	0.56	46.19—23.74
2007	1,892,167	141,739[b]	1.98[b]	0.50	44.75—28.73
2006	1,601,385	102,896[b]	1.44[b]	0.42	31.15—23.43

[a] Restated to reflect 2-for-1 stock split effected May 2007.
[b] Includes charge for the expensing of stock options of $7.3 million ($0.11 per diluted share) in 2009; $8 million ($0.12 per diluted share) in 2008; $10.5 million ($0.15 per diluted share) in 2007; and $8.7 million ($0.12 per diluted share) in 2006.

Transfer Agent & Registrar: Wells Fargo Shareowner Services
Corporate Counsel: Sidley Austin LLP
Investor Relations: Matthew DellaMaria, V.P.
Human Resources: Ursla Saint-Leger, V.P.
Auditors: PricewaterhouseCoopers LLP

Traded (Symbol): NYSE (ATR)
Stockholders: 400 (R)
Employees: 8,600
Annual Meeting: In May

Archer-Daniels-Midland Company

4666 Faries Parkway, Decatur, Illinois 62525

Telephone: (217) 424-5200
www.adm.com

Archer-Daniels-Midland Company (ADM) is one of the world's largest processors of oilseeds, corn, wheat, and cocoa. The company's operations are classified into four business segments: oilseeds processing, corn processing, agricultural services, and other operations. The oilseeds processing segment is engaged in processing oilseeds such as soybeans, cottonseed, sunflower seeds, canola, peanuts, and flaxseed into vegetable oils and protein meals principally for the food and feed industries. Partially refined oils are used in chemicals, paints, and biodiesel. The corn processing segment is engaged in dry milling and wet milling corn operations. Products produced for use in the food and beverage industry include syrup, starch, glucose, dextrose, and sweeteners. The agricultural services segment utilizes the company's vast grain elevator and transportation network to buy, store, clean, and transport agricultural commodities such as oilseeds, corn, wheat, milo, oats, rice, and barley, and resells these commodities primarily as food or animal feed ingredients and as raw materials for the agricultural processing industry. In other operations, the company mills wheat, corn, and milo into flour; processes cocoa beans; and produces a variety of soy protein products. ADM conducts operations on six continents and in more than 60 countries. Incorporated in Delaware in 1923.

Directors (In addition to indicated officers)

George W. Buckley	Pierre DuFour	Antonio Maciel Neto	Kelvin R. Westbrook
Mollie Hale Carter	Donald E. Felsinger	Patrick J. Moore	
Terrell K. Crews	Victoria F. Haynes	Thomas F. O'Neill	

Officers (Directors*)

*Patricia A. Woertz, Chm., Pres. & C.E.O.
John D. Rice, V. Chm—Off. of Chm.
Steven R. Mills, Sr. Exec. V.P.—Performance & Growth
Juan R. Luciano, Exec. V.P. & C.O.O.
David J. Smith, Exec. V.P., Secy. & Gen. Coun.
Ray G. Young, Sr. V.P. & C.F.O.
Michael D'Ambrose, Sr. V.P.—Hum. Res.
Mark Bemis, Sr. V.P. & Pres.—Corn
Craig Huss, Sr. V.P. & Pres.—Ag. Svcs.
Matthew Jansen, Sr. V.P. & Pres.—Oilseeds

Michael Baroni, V.P.—Econ. Policy
Mark J. Cheviron, V.P.—Corp. Security
Shannon Herzfeld, V.P.—Govt. Rel.
Kevin L. Hess, V.P.—Oilseeds Processing Oper.
Randall R. Kampfe, V.P.—Corn Processing Oper.
Mark L. Kolkhorst, V.P. & Pres.—Milling & Cocoa
Domingo A. Lastra, V.P. & Pres S. Amer.
Michael Lusk, V.P.—Ins. & Risk Mgt.
Vikram Luthar, V.P.—Fin. & Treas.
Victoria Podesta, V.P.—Corp. Commun.

Dennis Riddle, Sr. Advisor, Corn
Ismael Roig, V.P. & Exec. Dir., Asia-Pacific
Scott A. Roney, V.P.—Compliance & Ethics
Marc Sanner, V.P. & Gen. Auditor
John Stott, V.P. & Cont.
Joseph Taets, V.P. & Pres.—Grain
Ronald S. Bandler, Asst. Treas.
Stuart E. Funderburg, Asst. Secy. & Asst. Gen. Coun.
Scott A. Roberts, Asst. Secy. & Asst. Gen. Coun.

Consolidated Balance Sheet
As of June 30, 2011 (000 omitted, Unaudited)

Assets		Liabilities & Stockholders' Equity	
Current assets	$27,504,000	Current liabilities	$13,218,000
Net property, plant & equipment	9,500,000	Long-term liabilities	10,137,000
Inv. in & advances to affiliates	3,240,000	*Stockholders' equity	18,838,000
Other assets	1,949,000		
Total	$42,193,000	Total	$42,193,000

*675,787,233 shares common stock outstanding.

Consolidated Income Statement

Years Ended June 30	Thousands — — — — Net Sales	Net Earnings	Per Share — — — — Diluted Earnings	Cash Dividends	Common Stock Price Range Fiscal Year
2011	$80,676,000	$2,036,000	$3.13	$0.62	$38.02—25.02
2010	61,682,000	1,930,000	3.00	0.58	33.00—24.22
2009	69,207,000	1,684,000 [ab]	2.62 [ab]	0.54	33.91—13.53
2008	69,816,000	1,780,000 [a]	2.76 [a]	0.49	48.95—31.28
2007	44,018,000	2,154,000 [ac]	3.31 [ac]	0.43	45.05—30.20

[a] Restated to reflect change in accounting standard.
[b] Includes a non-cash charge of $275 million ($175 million or $0.27 per share after tax) related to currency derivative losses, and a $158 million income tax charge ($0.24 per share) related to the reorganization of a holding company structure for an equity investment.
[c] Includes gains of $643 million after tax ($0.98 per share) related to exchange of company interests, securities gains, and the sale of businesses.

Transfer Agent & Registrar: Hickory Point Bank & Trust, fsb

General Counsel:	David J. Smith, Exec. V.P.	**Traded (Symbol):**	NYSE, Frankfurt (ADM)
Investor Relations:	Dwight Grimestad, V.P.	**Stockholders:**	12,740 (R)
Human Resources:	Michael D'Ambrose, Sr. V.P.	**Employees:**	30,000
Info. Tech.:	Gary Mruz, Sr. Oper. Off.	**Annual Meeting:**	In November
Auditors:	Ernst & Young LLP		

BAB, Inc.

500 Lake Cook Road, Suite 475, Deerfield, Illinois 60015
Telephone: (847) 948-7520   **www.babcorp.com**

BAB, Inc. operates, franchises, and licenses bagel and muffin retail units under the Big Apple Bagels and My Favorite Muffin trade names. At November 30, 2010, the company had 106 units in operation in 26 states. Of these, 98 are franchised locations, 7 are licensees, and 1 is a company-owned store. The company additionally derives income from the sale of its trademark bagels, muffins, and coffee through nontraditional channels of distribution, under licensing agreements with Mrs. Fields Famous Brands and Kohr Bros. Frozen Custard, Braeda Cafe, Kaleidoscoops, and through direct home delivery of specialty muffin gift baskets and coffee. Big Apple Bagels units are concentrated in the Midwest and Western United States; My Favorite Muffin units are clustered in the Middle Atlantic states; and Brewster's Coffee products are currently featured in most franchised units and in the company-owned store. Incorporated in Delaware in 2000.

Directors (In addition to indicated officers)

Steven G. Feldman   James A. Lentz

Officers (Directors*)

*Michael W. Evans, Pres. & C.E.O.   Jeffrey M. Gorden, C.F.O. & Treas.
*Michael K. Murtaugh, V.P. &
  Gen. Coun.

Consolidated Balance Sheet   As of November 30, 2010 (000 omitted)

Assets		Liabilities & Stockholders' Equity	
Current assets	$1,774	Current liabilities	$ 711
Net property & equipment	32	Long-term debt	153
Trademarks	442	*Stockholders' equity	3,207
Goodwill	1,494		
Other assets	329		
Total	$4,071	Total	$4,071

*7,263,508 shares common stock outstanding.

Consolidated Income Statement

Years Ended Nov. 30	Thousands — — — —		Per Share — — — —		Common Stock Price Range Calendar Year
	Revenues	Net Income	Diluted Earnings	Cash Dividends	
2010	$2,914	$ 410	$0.06	$0.04	$0.64—0.25
2009	3,173	(2,318)	(0.32)	0.05	0.92—0.35
2008	3,778	623	0.09	0.06	1.10—0.62
2007	3,995	1,244	0.17	0.10	1.15—0.85
2006	3,917	717	0.10	0.10	1.22—0.73

Transfer Agent & Registrar: Illinois Stock Transfer Company
General Counsel: Michael K. Murtaugh, V.P.   Traded (Symbol):   OTC BB (BABB)
Investor Relations: Michael K. Murtaugh, V.P.   Stockholders: 180 (R); 1,100 (B)
Human Resources: Jeffrey M. Gorden, C.F.O.   Employees: 24
Info. Tech.:   Jeffrey M. Gorden, C.F.O.   Annual Meeting: In May
Auditors: Sassetti LLC

BankFinancial Corporation

15W060 North Frontage Road, Burr Ridge, Illinois 60527

Telephone: (800) 894-6900   **www.bankfinancial.com**

BankFinancial Corporation is the holding company for BankFinancial, F.S.B. BankFinancial, F.S.B. is a full-service, community-oriented federal savings bank principally engaged in the business of commercial, family, and personal banking, and offers its customers a broad range of loan, deposit, and other financial products and services through 18 full-service banking offices and three express branch facilities, which are located in Cook, DuPage, Lake, and Will counties in Illinois, as well as through its Internet branch, www.bankfinancial.com. The bank's business consists primarily of accepting deposits from the general public and investing those deposits, together with funds generated from operations and borrowings, in multi-family mortgage loans, non-residential real estate loans, commercial and construction loans, and commercial leases, as well as one- to four-family residential mortgage loans and agency and mortgage-backed securities. It also provides investment, financial planning, and other wealth management services through its Wealth Management Group. Through its Financial Assurance Services, Inc. subsidiary, the bank sells life insurance, fixed annuities, property and casualty insurance, and other insurance services on an agency basis. BankFinancial, F.S.B. was originally organized in 1924. Incorporated in Maryland in 2005.

Directors (In addition to indicated officers)

John M. Hausmann	Joseph A. Schudt
Cassandra J. Francis	Terry R. Wells
Sherwin R. Koopmans	Glen R. Wherfel

Officers (Directors*)

*F. Morgan Gasior, Chm., Pres. & C.E.O.	Patricia Smith-Lawler, Exec. V.P.—Hum. Res. Div.
James J. Brennan, Exec. V.P., Gen. Coun. & Corp. Secy.	Christa Calabrese, Regl. Pres.—Northern Region
Paul A. Cloutier, Exec. V.P. & C.F.O.	William J. Deutsch, Jr., Pres.—Nat'l. Commer. Leasing
Gregg T. Adams, Exec. V.P.—Mktg. & Sales	John G. Manos, Regl. Pres.—Southern Region
	Elizabeth A. Doolan, Sr. V.P.—Cont.

Consolidated Balance Sheet As of December 31, 2010 (000 omitted)

Assets		Liabilities & Stockholders' Equity	
Cash & cash equivalents	$ 220,810	Deposits	$1,235,377
Securities, at fair value	120,747	Borrowings	23,749
Loans, net	1,050,766	Other liabilities	18,244
Stock in FHLB	15,598	*Stockholders' equity	253,285
Net property & equipment	32,495		
Goodwill, net	22,566		
Other assets	67,673		
Total	$1,530,655	Total	$1,530,655

*21,072,966 shares common stock outstanding.

Consolidated Income Statement

Years Ended Dec. 31	Thousands — — — — Total Income	Net Income	Per Share — — — — Diluted Earnings	Cash Dividends	Common Stock Price Range Calendar Year
2010	$ 72,064	$ (4,307)	$(0.22)	$0.28	$10.16— 8.12
2009	81,348	(738)	(0.04)	0.28	11.10— 7.19
2008	88,378	(19,389)	(0.98)	0.28	16.44— 9.07
2007	101,618	7,155	0.35	0.28	17.98—13.01
2006	104,640	10,046	0.45	0.18	18.50—14.55

Transfer Agent & Registrar: Computershare Investor Services

General Counsel:	James J. Brennan, Exec. V.P.	Traded (Symbol):	NASDAQ (BFIN)
Investor Relations:	Elizabeth A. Doolan, Sr. V.P.	Stockholders:	1,820 (R)
Human Resources:	Patricia Smith-Lawler, Exec. V.P.	Employees:	337
Info. Tech.:	Mark W. Collins, Exec. V.P.	Annual Meeting:	In June
Auditors:	Crowe Horwath LLP		

Baxter International Inc.

One Baxter Parkway, Deerfield, Illinois 60015-4633

Telephone: (847) 948-2000

www.baxter.com

Baxter International Inc. is a global diversified medical products and services company. With expertise in medical devices, pharmaceuticals, and biotechnology, Baxter assists health-care professionals and their patients with the treatment of complex medical conditions including hemophilia, immune disorders, infectious diseases, kidney disease, trauma, and other conditions. The company operates in three segments: Medication Delivery and Renal (collectively Medical Products), and BioScience. The Medication Delivery segment manufactures intravenous (IV) solutions and administration sets, premixed drugs and drug-reconstitution systems, pre-filled vials and syringes for injectable drugs, IV nutrition products, infusion pumps, and inhalation anesthetics, as well as products and services related to pharmacy compounding, drug formulation, and packaging technologies. The BioScience segment processes recombinant and plasma-based proteins, plasma-based therapies, products for regenerative medicine, and vaccines. The Renal segment provides products to treat end-stage kidney disease. Baxter's products and services are used in more than 100 countries by hospitals, kidney dialysis centers, clinical and medical research laboratories, rehabilitation centers, nursing homes, and doctors' offices, as well as by at-home patients under a physician's care. Baxter operates over 50 manufacturing facilities in 27 countries. Incorporated in Delaware in 1931.

Directors (In addition to indicated officers)

Walter E. Boomer	James R. Gavin III, M.D., Ph.D.	Thomas T. Stallkamp
Blake E. Devitt	Peter S. Hellman	K. J. Storm
John D. Forsyth	Wayne T. Hockmeyer, Ph.D.	Albert P. L. Stroucken
Gail D. Fosler	Carole J. Shapazian	

Officers (Directors*)

*Robert L. Parkinson, Jr., Chm. & C.E.O.
Carlos Alonso, Corp. V.P. & Pres.—Renal
Phillip L. Batchelor, Corp. V.P.—Qual.
Michael J. Baughman, Corp. V.P. & Cont.
Robert M. Davis, Corp. V.P. & Pres.—Med. Prods.
Ludwig N. Hantson, Ph.D., Corp. V.P. & Pres.—BioScience
Robert J. Hombach, Corp. V.P. & C.F.O.
Wolf F. Kupatt, Corp. V.P. & Pres.—Latin Amer. & Canada

Mary Kay Ladone, Corp. V.P.—Inv. Rel.
Gerald Lema, Corp. V.P. & Pres.—Asia Pacific
Paul E. Martin, Corp. V.P. & C.I.O.
Jeanne K. Mason, Ph.D., Corp. V.P.—Hum. Res.
Peter Nicklin, Corp. V.P. & Pres.—Eur.
Norbert G. Riedel, Ph.D., Corp. V.P. & Chf. Scientific Off.
James K. Saccaro, Corp. V.P. & Treas.
David P. Scharf, Corp. V.P. & Gen. Coun.
Stephanie A. Shinn, Corp. V.P., Assoc. Gen. Coun. & Corp. Secy.

Consolidated Balance Sheet As of December 31, 2010 (000 omitted)

Assets		Liabilities & Stockholders' Equity	
Current assets	$ 7,989,000	Current liabilities	$ 4,041,000
Net property, plant & equipment	5,260,000	Long-term debt & leases	4,363,000
Goodwill	2,015,000	Other liabilities	2,289,000
Other assets	2,225,000	*Stockholders' equity	6,796,000
Total	$17,489,000	Total	$17,489,000

*580,733,356 shares common stock outstanding.

Consolidated Income Statement

Years Ended Dec. 31	Thousands — — — — —		Per Share — — — — —		Common Stock Price Range Calendar Year
	Net Sales	Net Income [a]	Basic Earnings	Cash Dividends	
2010	$12,843,000	$1,420,000 [b]	$2.41 [b]	$1.18	$61.71—40.47
2009	12,562,000	2,205,000 [c]	3.63 [c]	1.07	60.50—46.41
2008	12,348,000	2,014,000 [d]	3.22 [d]	0.91	71.15—48.50
2007	11,263,000	1,707,000 [e]	2.65 [e]	0.72	61.09—46.33
2006	10,378,000	1,398,000 [f]	2.15 [f]	0.58	47.21—35.45

[a] From continuing operations.
[b] Includes a $588 million charge related to U.S. infusion pump recall, a $257 million business optimization charge, a $112 million impairment charge associated with divesting U.S. generic injectables business, and $163 million in other charges.
[c] Includes cost optimization charge of $79 million, impairment charge of $54 million, and charge of $27 million relating to infusion pumps.
[d] Includes charges of $125 million relating to infusion pumps, an impairment charge of $31 million, and charges totaling $19 million relating to acquired in-process and collaboration research and development (IPR&D).
[e] Includes a restructuring charge of $70 million, a charge of $56 million relating to litigation, and IPR&D charges of $61 million.
[f] Includes a charge of $76 million relating to infusion pumps.

Transfer Agent & Registrar: Computershare Trust Company, N.A.

General Counsel:	David P. Scharf, Corp. V.P.	Traded (Symbol):	NYSE, CSE, SWISS (BAX)
Investor Relations:	Mary Kay Ladone, Corp. V.P.		
Human Resources:	Jeanne K. Mason, Corp. V.P.	Stockholders:	43,715 (R)
Info. Tech.:	Paul E. Martin, C.I.O.	Employees:	47,600
Auditors:	PricewaterhouseCoopers LLP	Annual Meeting:	In May

THE PRIVATEBANK GUIDE

Beam Inc.

510 Lake Cook Road, Deerfield, Illinois 60015-5611

Telephone: (847) 484-4400   www.beamglobal.com

Beam Inc., formerly part of Fortune Brands Inc., became an independently traded company following the sale of Fortune Brands' Acushnet Company golf business in June 2011 and the spin off of Fortune Brands Home and Security, Inc. on October 3, 2011. The company is the fourth largest premium spirits company in the world with 10 of the top 100 premium brands. The major brands of Beam Inc. include Jim Beam, Maker's Mark, and Knob Creek bourbon, Sauza tequila, Canadian Club whisky, Courvoisier cognac, Cruzan rum, Teacher's and Laphroaig scotch, EFFEN vodka, Skinnygirl margarita, and DeKuyper cordials. The company's brands enjoy broad international distribution with some 59 facilities located worldwide. Incorporated in Delaware in 1985.

Directors (In addition to indicated officers)

David Mackay, Chm.	Ann Fritz Hackett	Anne Tatlock
Richard Goldstein	Pierre E. Leroy	Peter Wilson

Officers (Directors*)

*Matt Shattock, Pres. & C.E.O.
Bob Probst, Sr. V.P. & C.F.O.
Bill Newlands, Pres.—North America
Albert Baladi, Pres.—Europe/Middle East/Africa
Phil Baldock, Pres.—Asia Pacific/South America
Donald Gaynor, Sr. V.P.—Corp. Dev.

Kevin George, Sr. V.P. & Gbl. Chf. Mktg. Off.
Ian Gourlay, Sr. V.P.—Gbl. Oper. & Supply Chain
C. Clarkson Hine, Sr. V.P.—Corp. Commun. & Pub. Affs.
Mindy Mackenzie, Sr. V.P.—Hum. Res.
Kent Rose, Sr. V.P., CAO & Gen. Coun.

Consolidated Balance Sheet As of June 30, 2011 (Unaudited, pro forma, 000 omitted)

Assets		Liabilities & Stockholders' Equity	
Current assets	$2,798,100	Current liabilities	$1,185,000
Net property, plant & equipment	721,300	Long-term debt	1,862,300
Goodwill	2,221,700	Deferred income taxes	451,200
Other intangible assets, net	2,315,400	Other liabilities	291,100
Other assets	118,900	*Stockholders' equity	4,385,800
Total	$8,175,400	Total	$8,175,400

*156,900,000 shares common stock outstanding.

Consolidated Income Statement

Years Ended Dec. 31	Thousands — — — — —		Per Share — — — — —		Common Stock Price Range Calendar Year [b]
	Net Sales [a]	Net Income [a]	Diluted Earnings [a]	Cash Dividends	
2010	$2,665,900	$308,400	$2.00	$0.76	$63.51—37.05
2009	2,469,600	234,700	1.55	1.01	46.77—17.68

[a] Unaudited, pro forma financial information.
[b] Fortune Brands Inc. common stock.

Transfer Agent & Registrar: Wells Fargo Shareowner Services
General Counsel: Kent Rose, Sr. V.P.
Human Resources: Mindy Mackenzie, Sr. V.P.
Auditors: PricewaterhouseCoopers LLP

Traded (Symbol): NYSE (BEAM)
Stockholders: 17,109 (R)
Employees: 3,100
Annual Meeting: In April

John Bean Technologies Corporation

70 West Madison Street, Suite 4400, Chicago, Illinois 60602

Telephone: (312) 861-5900   **www.jbtcorporation.com**

John Bean Technologies Corporation is a leading global technology solutions provider to the food processing and air transportation industries. It designs, manufactures, tests, and services technologically sophisticated systems and products for regional and multi-national industrial food processing customers through its JBT FoodTech segment and for domestic and international air transportation customers through its JBT AeroTech segment. The product offerings of its JBT FoodTech businesses include freezer, protein processing, in-container processing, and fruit processing solutions. The product offerings of the company's JBT AeroTech businesses include ground support equipment for cargo loading, aircraft deicing, and aircraft towing; gate equipment for passenger boarding, on the ground aircraft power, and cooling; airport services for maintenance of airport equipment, systems, and facilities; military equipment for cargo loading, aircraft towing, and on the ground aircraft cooling; and automatic guided vehicles for material handling in the automotive, printing, food and beverage, manufacturing, warehouse, and hospital industries. Incorporated in Delaware in 1994.

Directors (In addition to indicated officers)

C. Maury Devine	Polly B. Kawalek
Alan D. Feldman	James M. Ringler
James E. Goodwin	James R. Thompson

Officers (Directors*)

*Charles H. Cannon, Jr., Chm., Pres. & C.E.O.	Ronald D. Mambu, V.P., C.F.O. & Cont.
Torbjörn Arvidsson, V.P. & Div. Mgr.—Food Solutions and Svcs. Div.	Mark K. Montague, V.P.—Hum. Res.
Kenneth Dunn, V.P., Gen. Coun. & Asst. Secy.	Juan C. Podestá, V.P. & Div. Mgr.—Food Processing Sys. Div.
John Lee, V.P. & Div. Mgr.—AeroTech Div.	Megan Donnelly, Chf. Acct. Off

Consolidated Balance Sheet As of December 31, 2010 (000 omitted)

Assets		Liabilities & Stockholders' Equity	
Current assets	$356.400	Current liabilities	$242,000
Net property & equipment	128,700	Long-term debt	145,400
Goodwill	28,400	Other liabilities	101,800
Other assets	68,700	*Stockholders' equity	93,000
Total	$582,200	Total	$582,200

*28,185,834 shares common stock outstanding.

Consolidated Income Statement

Years Ended Dec. 31	Thousands — — — — —		Per Share — — — — —		Common Stock
	Total Revenue	Net Income	Diluted Earnings	Cash Dividends	Price Range [a] Calendar Year
2010	$ 880,400	$37,300	$1.28	$0.28	$20.78—14.35
2009	841,600	32,800	1.15	0.28	19.00— 8.67
2008	1,028,100	44,200	1.59	0.07	14.50— 5.86
2007	978,000	36,400	1.32		
2006	844,300	34,600	1.26		

[a] Stock began trading August 1, 2008 on New York Stock Exchange, following spin-off from FMC Technologies, Inc.

Transfer Agent & Registrar: Computershare Investor Services

General Counsel:	Kenneth Dunn, V.P.	Traded (Symbol):	NYSE (JBT)
Investor Relations:	Cindy Shiao, Dir.	Stockholders:	3,330 (R)
Human Resources:	Mark K. Montague, V.P.	Employees:	3,300
Auditors:	KPMG LLP	Annual Meeting:	In May

BioSante Pharmaceuticals, Inc.

111 Barclay Boulevard, Lincolnshire, Illinois 60069

Telephone: (847) 478-0500   **www.biosantepharma.com**

BioSante Pharmaceuticals, Inc. is a specialty pharmaceutical company that licenses and develops products for female sexual health, menopause, contraception, and male hypogonadism, as well as oncology. Symptoms addressed by these therapies include testosterone and sexual activity deficiency in men and menopausal symptoms in women including hot flashes and decreased libido. BioSante also is developing a portfolio of cancer vaccines that are designed to stimulate the patient's immune system to effectively fight cancer. The company is developing its calcium phosphate technology (CaP) for aesthetic medicine (BioLook), as a vaccine adjuvant, and drug delivery. In October 2009, BioSante Pharmaceuticals completed a transaction with Cell Genesys, Inc., resulting in the acquisition of the assets and liabilities of Cell Genesys. The company is evaluating and seeking opportunities for its 2A/Furin and other technologies it acquired in its merger with Cell Genesys. Incorporated in Delaware in 2001.

Directors (In addition to indicated officers)

Fred Holubow
Ross Mangano
John T. Potts, Jr., M.D.

Edward C. Rosenow III, M.D.
Stephen A. Sherwin, M.D.
Louis W. Sullivan, M.D.

Officers (Directors*)

*Stephen M. Simes, V. Chm., Pres. & C.E.O.
Michael C. Snabes, M.D., Ph.D., Sr. V.P.—
   Med. Affs.
Phillip B. Donenberg, V.P.—Fin., C.F.O. & Secy.

Bill Milling, V.P.—Oper.
Jeffrey W. Winkelman, Ph.D., J.D., V.P.—Oncology
   Programs
Joanne Zborowski, V.P.—Clinical Dev.

Consolidated Balance Sheet   As of December 31, 2010 (000 omitted)

Assets		Liabilities & Stockholders' Equity	
Current assets	$40,625	Current liabilities	$ 8,184
Net property, plant & equipment	636	Convertible senior notes	17,436
Other assets	3,506	*Stockholders' equity	19,147
Total	$44,767	Total	$44,767

*81,391,130 shares common stock and 391,286 shares Class C special stock outstanding.

Consolidated Income Statement

Years Ended Dec. 31	Thousands — — — —		Per Share — — — —		Common Stock Price Range [a] Calendar Year
	Revenue	Net Income	Diluted Earnings	Cash Dividends	
2010	$ 2,474	$(46,196)	$(0.70)	$0.00	$2.50—1.29
2009	1,258	(47,528) [b]	(1.40) [b]	0.00	2.70—1.03
2008	3,781	(17,425)	(0.64)	0.00	5.85—0.81
2007	493	(7,584)	(0.30)	0.00	8.00—2.55
2006	14,438	2,791	0.13	0.00	4.69—1.55

[a] Stock traded on the American Stock Exchange from October 1, 2003 to November 2, 2007 and on the Nasdaq Global Market since November 5, 2007.
[b] Reflects the purchase price allocation and charges related to the merger, which included adjustments to carrying values of the acquired net assets based on their estimated fair values as of that date.

Transfer Agent & Registrar: Computershare Investor Services
Corporate Counsel: Oppenheimer Wolff &
                   Donnelly LLP
Investor Relations: Phillip B. Donenberg, C.F.O.
Auditors: Deloitte & Touche LLP

Traded (Symbol): NASDAQ (BPAX)
Stockholders: 783 (R), common;
                  6 (R), Class C
Employees: 45
Annual Meeting: In May

The Boeing Company

100 North Riverside Plaza, Chicago, Illinois 60606-1596

Telephone: (312) 544-2000   www.boeing.com

The Boeing Company is one of the world's major aerospace firms. The company operates in five principal segments: Commercial Airplanes; Boeing Military Aircraft, Network and Space Systems, and Global Services and Support (collectively, Boeing Defense, Space & Security (BDS)); Boeing Capital Corporation; and Other. The Commercial Airplanes segment develops, produces, and markets commercial jet aircraft and support services to airlines worldwide. The BDS segments provide research, development, production, modification, and support of global strike systems, global mobility systems, airborne surveillance and reconnaissance aircraft, network and tactical systems, intelligence and security systems, missile defense systems, space and intelligence systems, and space exploration. Boeing Capital Corporation supports Boeing's major business units by facilitating, arranging, structuring, and providing financing solutions. Principal subsidiaries include Boeing Satellite Systems (BSS); McDonnell Douglas Corporation; Jeppesen Sanderson, Inc.; and Continental Graphics Corp. Incorporated in Delaware in 1916; present name adopted in 1973.

Directors (In addition to indicated officers)

John E. Bryson	Kenneth M. Duberstein	Susan C. Schwab
David L. Calhoun	Edmund P. Giambastiani, Jr.	Ronald A. Williams
Arthur D. Collins, Jr.	Edward M. Liddy	Mike S. Zafirovski
Linda Z. Cook	John F. McDonnell	

Officers (Directors*)

*W. James McNerney, Jr., Chm., Pres. & C.E.O.
James F. Albaugh, Exec. V.P.; Pres. & C.E.O.— Boeing Commer. Airplanes
James A. Bell, Exec. V.P., Corp. Pres. & C.F.O.
J. Michael Luttig, Exec. V.P. & Gen. Coun.
Dennis A. Muilenburg, Exec. V.P.; Pres. & C.E.O.—Boeing Defense, Space & Security
Michael J. Cave, Sr. V.P.; Pres.—Boeing Capital Corp.
Wanda K. Denson-Low, Sr. V.P.—Office of Internal Governance
Thomas J. Downey, Sr. V.P.—Commun.

Shephard W. Hill, Sr. V.P.—Bus. Dev. & Strat.; Pres.—Boeing Intl.
Timothy J. Keating, Sr. V.P.—Govt. Oper.
Richard D. Stephens, Sr. V.P.—Hum. Res. & Admin.
John J. Tracy, Sr. V.P.—Eng., Oper. & Tech. & Chf. Tech. Off.
David A. Dohnalek, V.P.—Fin. & Treas.
Michael F. Lohr, V.P., Corp. Secy. & Asst. Gen. Coun.
Diana Sands, V.P.—Inv. Rel., Fin. Plan. & Analysis
Gregory D. Smith, V.P.—Fin. & Corp. Cont.
Robert J. Pasterick, Pres.—Shared Svcs. Grp.

Consolidated Balance Sheet As of December 31, 2010 (000 omitted)

Assets		Liabilities & Stockholders' Equity	
Current assets	$40,572,000	Current liabilities	$35,395,000
Net property, plant & equipment	8,931,000	Long-term debt	11,473,000
Customer financing, net	4,395,000	Other liabilities	18,835,000
Other assets	14,667,000	Noncontrollinig interest	96,000
		*Stockholders' equity	2,766,000
Total	$68,565,000	Total	$68,565,000

*735,300,000 shares common stock outstanding.

Consolidated Income Statement

Years Ended Dec. 31	Thousands — — — — —		Per Share — — — — —		Common Stock Price Range Calendar Year
	Operating Revenues	Net Income [a]	Basic Earnings	Cash Dividends	
2010	$64,306,000	$3,307,000	$4.50	$1.68	$ 76.00—54.80
2009	68,281,000	1,312,000	1.89	1.68	56.56—29.05
2008	60,909,000	2,672,000	3.68	1.62	88.29—36.17
2007	66,387,000	4,074,000	5.36	1.45	107.83—84.60
2006	61,530,000	2,215,000	2.88	1.25	92.05—65.90

[a] Includes gains on disposal of discontinued operations, net of tax, of $18 million in 2008; $16 million in 2007; and $9 million in 2006; and losses of $4 million in 2010 and $23 million in 2009.

Transfer Agent & Registrar: Computershare Investor Services
General Counsel: J. Michael Luttig, Exec. V.P.
Investor Relations: David A. Dohnalek, V.P.
Human Resources: Richard D. Stephens, Sr. V.P.
Info. Tech.: Kim Hammonds, C.I.O.
Auditors: Deloitte & Touche LLP

Traded (Symbol): NYSE, CSE, BSE, CIN, PHSE, AMST, BELG, LON, SWISS (BA)
Stockholders: 212,290 (B)
Employees: 160,500
Annual Meeting: In May

Broadwind Energy, Inc.

47 East Chicago Avenue, Suite 332, Naperville, Illinois 60540
Telephone: (630) 637-0315   **www.bwen.com**

Broadwind Energy, Inc. provides technologically advanced high-value products and services to energy, mining, and infrastructure sector customers. The company manufactures wind towers and gearboxes and provides technical and precision repair and engineering services to manufacturers of wind turbines and developers and operators of wind farms. Broadwind Energy also provides precision gearing and specialty weldments to industrial customers. In March 2011, the company completed the sale of its Badger Transport, Inc. subsidiary to BTI Logistics, LLC. Incorporated in Nevada in 1996; reincorporated in Delaware in 2008; present name adopted in 2008.

Directors (In addition to indicated officers)

David P. Reiland, Chm.
Charles H. Beynon
William T. Fejes, Jr.

Terence P. Fox
Thomas A. Wagner

Officers (Directors*)

*Peter C. Duprey, Pres. & C.E.O.
Jesse E. Collins, Jr., Exec. V.P. & C.O.O.
Stephanie K. Kushner, Exec. V.P., C.F.O.
  & Treas.

J.D. Rubin, V.P., Gen. Coun. & Secy.

Consolidated Balance Sheet As of December 31, 2010 (000 omitted)

Assets		Liabilities & Stockholders' Equity	
Current assets	$ 64,990	Current liabilities	$ 44,502
Net property & equipment	106,317	Other liabilities	12,808
Other assets	12,199	*Stockholders' equity	126,196
Total	$183,506	Total	$183,506

*107,112,817 shares common stock outstanding.

Consolidated Income Statement

Years Ended Dec. 31	Thousands — — — — —		Per Share — — — —		Common Stock Price Range [a] Calendar Year
	Revenue	Net Income	Diluted Earnings	Cash Dividends	
2010	$136,896	$ (69,753)[b]	$(0.66)[b]	$0.00	$ 8.47—1.42
2009	184,798	(107,026)[b]	(1.11)[b]	0.00	12.49—2.60
2008	207,349	(25,278)[b]	(0.28)[b]	0.00	29.00—4.25
2007	29,804	(3,362)	(0.07)	0.00	14.50—1.76
2006	4,023	(2,735)	(0.08)	0.00	3.20—1.10

[a] Common stock transferred trading from the OTC Bulletin Board (symbol "BWEN.OB") to the NASDAQ on April 9, 2009.
[b] Includes impairment charges of $40.8 million in 2010; $82.2 million in 2009; and $2.4 million in 2008.

Transfer Agent & Registrar: Wells Fargo Shareowner Services
General Counsel: J.D. Rubin, V.P.
Investor Relations: John Segvich
Auditors: Grant Thornton LLP

Traded (Symbol):	NASDAQ (BWEN)
Stockholders:	82 (R)
Employees:	850
Annual Meeting:	In May

Brunswick Corporation

1 North Field Court, Lake Forest, Illinois 60045-4811

Telephone: (847) 735-4700 **www.brunswick.com**

Brunswick Corporation is a designer, manufacturer, and marketer of leading consumer brands, including: Mercury and Mariner outboard engines; Mercury MerCruiser sterndrives and inboard engines; MotorGuide trolling motors; Attwood marine parts and accessories; Land 'N' Sea, Kellogg Marine, and Diversified Marine parts and accessories distributors; Arvor, Bayliner, Boston Whaler, Cabo Yachts, Crestliner, Cypress Cay, Harris FloteBote, Hatteras, Lowe, Lund, Meridian, Princecraft, Quicksilver, Rayglass, Sea Ray, Sealine, Suncruiser, Trophy, Uttern, and Valiant boats; Life Fitness and Hammer Strength fitness equipment; Brunswick bowling centers, equipment, and consumer products; and Brunswick billiards tables and foosball tables. Incorporated in Delaware in 1907.

Directors (In addition to indicated officers)

Nolan D. Archibald
Anne E. Bélec
Jeffrey L. Bleustein
Cambria W. Dunaway
Manuel A. Fernandez

Graham H. Phillips
Ralph C. Stayer
J. Steven Whisler
Lawrence A. Zimmerman

Officers (Directors*)

*Dustan E. McCoy, Chm. & C.E.O.
Peter B. Hamilton, Sr. V.P. & C.F.O.
Bruce J. Byots, V.P.—Corp. & Inv. Rel.
Christopher E. Clawson, V.P. & Pres.—Life Fitness
Kristin M. Coleman, V.P., Gen. Coun. & Secy.
Andrew E. Graves, V.P. & Pres.—Boat Grp.
William J. Gress, V.P. & Pres.—Brunswick Latin Amer.
Kevin S. Grodzki, V.P. & Pres.—Mercury Marine
   Sales, Mktg. & Commer. Oper.

Tina A. Hotop, V.P.—Audit
B. Russell Lockridge, V.P. & Chf. Hum. Res. Off.
Alan L. Lowe, V.P. & Cont.
William L. Metzger, V.P. & Treas.
John C. Pfeifer, V.P. & Pres.—Brunswick Marine
   in EMEA and Pres.—Brunswick Gbl. Structure
Mark Schwabero, V.P. & Pres.—Mercury Marine
Stephen M. Wolpert, V.P. & Pres.—Gbl. Boat Oper.
Judith P. Zelisko, V.P.—Tax

Consolidated Balance Sheet As of December 31, 2010 (000 omitted)

Assets		Liabilities & Stockholders' Equity	
Current assets	$1,535,800	Current liabilities	$ 951,600
Net property & equipment	630,200	Long-term liabilities	1,656,000
Goodwill	290,900	*Stockholders' equity	70,400
Other assets	221,100		
Total	$2,678,000	Total	$2,678,000

*88,661,000 shares common stock outstanding.

Consolidated Income Statement

Years Ended Dec. 31	Thousands — — — — — Net Sales	Net Income	Per Share — — — — — Diluted Earnings	Cash Dividends	Common Stock Price Range Calendar Year
2010	$3,403,300	$(110,600)a	$(1.25)a	$0.05	$22.62—10.34
2009	2,776,100	(586,200)b	(6.63)b	0.05	13.11— 2.18
2008	4,708,700	(788,100)c	(8.93)c	0.05	19.28— 2.01
2007	5,671,200	111,600 d	1.24 d	0.60	34.80—17.05
2006	5,665,000	133,900 e	1.41 e	0.60	42.30—27.56

a Includes $62.3 million of pretax trade name impairment charges and restructuring, exit, and impairment charges.
b Includes $172.5 million of pretax restructuring, exit, and impairment charges.
c Includes $688.4 million of pretax goodwill impairment charges, trade name impairment charges, and restructuring, exit, and other impairment charges.
d Includes $88.6 million of pretax trade name impairment charges and restructuring, exit, and other charges. Also includes net gain of $29.8 million related to sales of discontinued businesses.
e Includes $17.1 million of pretax restructuring, exit, and other charges. Also includes an $85.6 million impairment charge, after tax, from discontinued operations.

Transfer Agent & Registrar: Computershare Investor Services

General Counsel:	Kristin M. Coleman, V.P.	Traded (Symbol):	NYSE, CSE (BC)
Investor Relations:	Bruce J. Byots, V.P.	Stockholders:	12,031 (R)
Human Resources:	B. Russell Lockridge, V.P.	Employees:	15,290
Info. Tech.:	Mike Schulz	Annual Meeting:	In May
Auditors:	Ernst & Young LLP		

Cabot Microelectronics Corporation

870 North Commons Drive, Aurora, Illinois 60504
Telephone: (630) 375-6631   www.cabotcmp.com

Cabot Microelectronics is the leading supplier of sophisticated polishing compounds and a provider of polishing pads used in the manufacture of advanced semiconductors (chips) and rigid disks. The company's slurry (liquid that contains abrasives and chemicals) and pad products are the critical materials required for a highly accurate and critical polishing process—chemical mechanical planarization (CMP), which enables multiple layers of intricate circuitry to be built upon the wafer surface and results in high-performance chips. The CMP process used for rigid disks media results in a high-quality, mirror-like finish that enables high-density storage of data on the rigid disk. The company's products enable the manufacture of smaller, faster, and more complex devices by its customers. In August 2010, the company completed the second part of its two-step acquisition of Epoch Material Co., Ltd., a manufacturer of copper CMP slurries and CMP cleaning solutions for the semiconductor industry. Incorporated in Delaware in 1999.

Directors (In addition to indicated officers)

Robert J. Birgeneau   Edward J. Mooney
John P. Frazee, Jr.   Steven V. Wilkinson
H. Laurance Fuller   Bailing Xia
Barbara A. Klein

Officers (Directors*)

*William P. Noglows, Chm., Pres. & C.E.O.   Daniel J. Pike, V.P.—Corp. Dev.
H. Carol Bernstein, V.P., Secy. & Gen. Coun. Stephen R. Smith, V.P.—Mktg.
Yumiko Damashek, V.P.—Japan & Oper. Asia   Adam F. Weisman, V.P.—Bus. Oper.
William S. Johnson, V.P. & C.F.O.   Daniel S. Wobby, V.P.—Gbl. Sales
David H. Li, V.P.—Asia Pacific Region   Thomas S. Roman, Prin. Acct. Off. & Corp. Cont.
Ananth Naman, Ph.D., V.P.—Res. & Dev.

Consolidated Balance Sheet of September 30, 2010 (000 omitted)

Assets		Liabilities & Stockholders' Equity	
Current assets	$381,029	Current liabilities	$ 53,330
Net property, plant & equipment	115,811	Other liabilities	4,083
Other assets	74,916	*Stockholders' equity	514,343
Total	$571,756	Total	$571,756

*22,938,646 shares common stock outstanding.

Consolidated Income Statement

Years Ended Sept. 30	Thousands — — — — —		Per Share — — — — —		Common Stock Price Range Fiscal Year
	Revenue	Net Income	Diluted Earnings	Cash Dividends	
2010	$408,201	$49,458	$2.13	$0.00	$42.69—29.81
2009	291,372	11,187	0.48	0.00	36.04—19.01
2008	375,069	38,338	1.64	0.00	46.44—30.48
2007	338,205	33,836	1.42	0.00	44.56—28.24
2006	320,795	32,948	1.36	0.00	38.25—25.84

Transfer Agent & Registrar: Computershare Trust Company, N.A.

General Counsel: H. Carol Bernstein, V.P.   Traded (Symbol): NASDAQ (CCMP)
Investor Relations: Amy L. Ford, Dir.   Stockholders: 988 (R)
Human Resources: Lisa A. Polezoes   Employees: 933
Info. Tech.   Tim Roessler   Annual Meeting: In March
Auditors: PricewaterhouseCoopers LLP

Calamos Asset Management, Inc.
2020 Calamos Court, Naperville, Illinois 60563

Telephone: (630) 245-7200   **www.calamos.com**

Calamos Asset Management, Inc. is a diversified investment firm offering equity, low-volatility equity, convertible, alternative, enhanced fixed income, total return, and fixed income strategies, among others. The firm serves institutions and individuals via separately managed accounts, and a family of open-end and closed-end funds, offering a risk-managed approach to capital appreciation and income-producing strategies. As of March 31, 2011, the company had $38 billion of client assets under management. Original firm founded in 1977; incorporated in Delaware in 2004.

Directors (In addition to indicated officers)

G. Bradford Bulkley
Mitchell S. Feiger

Richard W. Gilbert
Arthur L. Knight

Officers (Directors*)

*John P. Calamos, Sr., Chm., C.E.O. & Co-Chf. Invest. Off.
*Nick P. Calamos, Pres.—Invests. & Co-Chf. Invest. Off.
James J. Boyne, Pres.—Distr. & Oper.
James F. Baka, Exec. V.P.—Wealth Mgt.

Nimish S. Bhatt, Sr. V.P. & Dir.—Oper.
Gary J. Felsten, Sr. V.P. & Dir.—Hum. Res.
J. Christopher Jackson, Sr V.P., Gen. Coun. & Secy.
Randall T. Zipfel, Sr. V.P. & C.O.O.—Invests. & Info. Technology

Consolidated Balance Sheet As of December 31, 2010 (000 omitted)

Assets		Liabilities & Stockholders' Equity	
Current assets	$485,785	Current liabilities	$ 83,706
Net property & equipment	26,745	Long-term debt	92,115
Deferred tax assets, net	66,960	Other long-term liabilities	10,033
Deferred sales commissions	8,515	Minority interest in partnership invest.	1,697
Other non-current assets	1,241	Minority interest in Calamos Holdings	218,679
		*Stockholders' equity	183,016
Total	$589,246	Total	$589,246

*19,942,317 shares common stock outstanding.

Consolidated Income Statement

Years Ended Dec. 31	Thousands — — — —		Per Share — — — —		Common Stock Price Range Calendar Year
	Total Revenue	Net Income	Diluted Earnings	Cash Dividends	
2010	$326,039	$ 19,928	$ 0.99	$0.30	$15.33— 8.45
2009	281,738	12,424	0.62	0.22	15.47— 2.74
2008	391,589	(24,521)	(1.24)	0.39	29.67— 2.55
2007	473,477	27,745	1.22	0.44	34.61—20.08
2006	485,172	34,008	1.45	0.36	44.10—24.23

Transfer Agent & Registrar: BNY Mellon Shareowner Services
General Counsel: J. Christopher Jackson, Sr. V.P.
Investor Relations: Jennifer McGuffin
Human Resources: Gary J. Felsten, Sr. V.P.
Info. Tech.: Randall T. Zipfel, Sr. V.P.
Auditors: McGladrey & Pullen LLP

Traded (Symbol): NASDAQ (CLMS)
Stockholders: 61 (R)
Employees: 318
Annual Meeting: In June

Career Education Corporation

231 N. Martingale Road, Schaumburg, Illinois 60173
Telephone: (847) 781-3600   www.careered.com

Career Education Corporation owns and operates private, for-profit, post-secondary educational institutions with approximately 116,000 students across the world. The approximately 90 campuses that serve these students are located throughout the U.S. and in France, Italy, the United Kingdom, and Monaco, and offer doctoral, master's, bachelor's, and associate degrees and diploma and certificate programs in career-oriented disciplines through online, on-ground, and hybrid learning program offerings. During 2010, Career Education Corporation organized its businesses across four reporting segments: University, Health Education, Culinary Arts, and International. The company's schools are: American InterContinental University, Colorado Technical University, International Academy of Design & Technology, Briarcliffe College, Brooks Institute, Brown College, Collins College, Harrington College of Design, California Culinary Academy, Le Cordon Bleu College (or Institute) of Culinary Arts, Texas Culinary Academy, Missouri College, Gibbs College of Boston, Inc., Gibbs College, Sanford-Brown College, Sanford-Brown Institute, The INSEEC Group, International University of Monaco, and Istituto Marangoni. The company closed AIU-Los Angeles in December 2010. Incorporated in Delaware in 1994.

Directors (In addition to indicated officers)

Dennis H. Chookaszian	Gregory L. Jackson
David W. Devonshire	Thomas B. Lally
Patrick W. Gross	Leslie T. Thornton

Officers (Directors*)

*Steven H. Lesnik, Chm., Pres. & C.E.O.
Michael J. Graham, Exec. V.P. & C.F.O.
Jeffrey D. Ayers, Sr. V.P., Gen. Coun.,
   Corp. Secy. & Chf. Compliance Off.
Thomas G. Budlong, Sr. V.P., Chf. Admin. Off.
   & Chf. of Staff
Veronica Campbell, Sr. V.P.—Reg. Compliance &
   Academic Integrity

Robert DeYoung, Sr. V.P.—Corp. Mktg. & Chf. Mktg. Off.
Jason T. Friesen, Sr. V.P.—Fin., Inv. Rel. & Treas.
Thomas A. McNamara, Sr. V.P.—Art & Design
Colleen M. O'Sullivan, Sr. V.P. & Chf. Acct. Off.
Brian R. Williams, Sr. V.P.—Culinary Arts
Stephen J. Tober, C.E.O.—American InterContinental
   Univ.
Jeremy J. Wheaton, C.E.O.—Colorado Tech. Univ.

Consolidated Balance Sheet As of December 31, 2010 (000 omitted)

Assets		Liabilities & Stockholders' Equity	
Current assets	$ 619,357	Current liabilities	$ 464,073
Net property & equipment	366,775	Deferred rent obligations	103,996
Goodwill	381,476	Other liabilities	58,403
Other assets	193,248	*Stockholders' equity	934,384
Total	$1,560,856	Total	$1,560,856

*81,209,410 shares common stock outstanding.

Consolidated Income Statement

Years Ended Dec. 31	Thousands — — — —		Per Share — — — —		Common Stock Price Range Calendar Year
	Total Revenue [a]	Net Income [b]	Diluted Earnings [b]	Cash Dividends	
2010	$2,124,236	$157,773 [c]	$1.95 [c]	$0.00	$35.88—16.36
2009	1,833,796	81,219 [d]	0.94 [d]	0.00	28.87—17.06
2008	1,651,114	60,142 [d]	0.67 [d]	0.00	25.15—11.57
2007	1,652,209	59,553 [d]	0.63 [d]	0.00	36.68—24.36
2006	1,766,338	46,569 [e]	0.47 [e]	0.00	42.59—17.60

[a] Prior period financial results have been recast to reflect schools that have ceased operations as discontinued operations.
[b] Includes losses, net of tax, from discontinued operations of $8,817,000 ($0.11 per diluted share) in 2010; $68,288,000 ($0.79 per diluted share) in 2009; $33,688,000 ($0.37 per diluted share) in 2008; $54,685,000 ($0.58 per diluted share) in 2007; and $47,297,000 ($0.50 per diluted share) in 2006.
[c] Includes goodwill and asset impairment charges of $71,800,000.
[d] Includes asset impairment charges of $2,500,000 in 2009; $8,900,000 in 2008; and $5,600,000 in 2007.
[e] Includes $86,300,000 in goodwill and other intangible asset impairment charges.

Transfer Agent & Registrar: Computershare Trust Company, N.A.

General Counsel:	Jeffrey D. Ayers, Sr. V.P.	Traded (Symbol):	NASDAQ (CECO)
Investor Relations:	Jason T. Friesen, Sr. V.P.	Stockholders:	459 (R)
Info. Tech.:	Manoj Kulkarni, C.I.O.	Employees:	15,598
Auditors:	Ernst & Young LLP	Annual Meeting:	In May

A.M. Castle & Co.

1420 Kensington Road, Oak Brook, Illinois 60523

Telephone: (847) 455-7111

www.amcastle.com

A.M. Castle & Co. is a global distributor of specialty metal (89% of net sales) and plastic products (11% of net sales) and supply chain services, principally serving the producer durable equipment, oil and gas, aerospace, heavy industrial equipment, industrial goods, construction equipment, retail, marine, and automotive sectors of the economy. Its customer base includes many Fortune 500 companies as well as thousands of medium and smaller-sized firms spread across a variety of industries. Within its core metals business, it specializes in the distribution of alloy, aluminum, stainless steel, nickel, titanium, and carbon. Through its subsidiary, Total Plastics, Inc., the company also distributes a broad range of value-added industrial plastics. The company operates 60 service centers located throughout North America, Europe, and Asia. Incorporated in Illinois in 1904; reincorporated in Delaware in 1966; reincorporated in Maryland in 2001.

Directors (In addition to indicated officers)

Brian P. Anderson, Chm.
Thomas A. Donahoe
Ann M. Drake
Patrick J. Herbert, III
Terrence J. Keating

James D. Kelly
Pamela Forbes Lieberman
John McCartney
Michael Simpson

Officers (Directors*)

*Michael H. Goldberg, Pres. & C.E.O.
Stephen V. Hooks, Exec. V.P.; Pres.—
    Castle Metals
Patrick R. Anderson, V.P., Corp. Cont.
    & Chf. Acct. Off.
Albert J. Biemer, V.P.—Corp. Supply Chain
Kevin Coughlin, V.P.—Oper.
Kevin P. Fitzpatrick, V.P.—Hum. Res.

Thomas L. Garrett, V.P. & Pres.—Total Plastics, Inc.
Kevin H. Glynn, V.P. & C.I.O.
G. Nicholas Jones, V.P. & Pres.—Castle Metals
    Oil & Gas
Robert J. Perna, V.P., Gen. Coun. & Secy.
Scott F. Stephens, V.P., C.F.O. & Treas.
Blain A. Tiffany, V.P. & Pres.—Castle
    Metals Aerospace

Consolidated Balance Sheet As of December 31, 2010 (000 omitted)

Assets		Liabilities & Stockholders' Equity	
Current assets	$311,022	Current liabilities	$115,914
Net property, plant & equipment	76,715	Long-term debt	61,127
Goodwill	50,110	Deferred income taxes	26,754
Other assets	91,505	Other liabilities	12,098
		*Stockholders' equity	313,459
Total	$529,352	Total	$529,352

*22,986,000 shares common stock outstanding.

Consolidated Income Statement [a]

Years Ended Dec. 31	Thousands — — — — —		Per Share — — — — —		Common Stock Price Range Calendar Year
	Net Sales	Net Income [b]	Diluted Earnings [b]	Cash Dividends	
2010 [c]	$ 943,706	$ (5,640)	$(0.25)	$0.00	$19.29— 9.55
2009 [d]	812,638	(26,903)	(1.18)	0.06	14.41— 5.29
2008 [d]	1,501,036	(17,082)	(0.76)	0.24	34.20— 6.12
2007	1,420,353	51,806	2.41	0.24	38.10—22.72
2006	1,177,600	55,119	2.89	0.24	44.25—22.16

[a] Includes the results of the September 2006 and January 2008 acquisitions of Transtar and Metals U.K., respectively, and the October 2007 divestiture of Metal Express.
[b] From continuing operations.
[c] Includes facility consolidation charges of $2.4 million.
[d] Includes goodwill impairment charge of $1.4 million in 2009 and $58.9 million in 2008.

Transfer Agent & Registrar: American Stock Transfer & Trust Co.

General Counsel:	Robert J. Perna, V.P.	Traded (Symbol):	NYSE (CAS)
Investor Relations:	Scott F. Stephens, C.F.O.	Stockholders:	1,081 (R)
Human Resources:	Kevin P. Fitzpatrick, V.P.	Employees:	1,619
Info. Tech.:	Kevin H. Glynn, V.P.	Annual Meeting:	Fourth Thursday in April
Auditors:	Deloitte & Touche LLP		

Caterpillar Inc.

100 Northeast Adams Street, Peoria, Illinois 61629
Telephone: (309) 675-1000   **www.CAT.com**

Caterpillar Inc. and its consolidated subsidiaries operate in three principal categories: the design, manufacture, marketing, and sales of construction, mining, and forestry machinery and equipment; the design, manufacture, marketing, and sales of engines; and the offering of a wide range of financial services. Machinery manufactured includes track and wheel tractors, track and wheel loaders, pipelayers, motor graders, wheel tractor-scrapers, track and wheel excavators, log skidders, backhoe loaders, log loaders, off-highway trucks, articulated trucks, paving products, skid steer loaders, underground mining equipment, tunnel boring equipment, and related parts. The company designs engines for Caterpillar machinery; electric power generation systems; and marine, petroleum, agricultural, construction, and industrial applications. Caterpillar Financial Services Corporation assists customers in acquiring Caterpillar machinery and engines, solar gas turbines, as well as other equipment and marine vessels. Caterpillar maintains manufacturing facilities in the U.S., Australia, Belgium, Brazil, Canada, China, France, Germany, Hungary, India, Indonesia, Italy, Japan, Malaysia, Mexico, the Netherlands, Nigeria, Poland, Russia, South Korea, Switzerland, Tunisia, and the United Kingdom. In August 2010, Caterpillar's wholly owned subsidiary, Progress Rail Services, acquired Electro-Motive Diesel (EMD), headquartered in LaGrange, Illinois. EMD has the largest installed base of diesel-electric locomotives in the world. Incorporated in California in 1925; reincorporated in Delaware in 1986.

Directors (In addition to indicated officers)

David L. Calhoun	Jesse J. Greene, Jr.	Edward B. Rust, Jr.
Daniel M. Dickinson	Peter A. Magowan	Susan C. Schwab
Eugene V. Fife	Dennis A. Muilenburg	Joshua I. Smith
Juan Gallardo	William A. Osborn	Miles D. White
David R. Goode	Charles D. Powell	

Officers (Directors*)

*Douglas R. Oberhelman, Chm. & C.E.O.
Richard P. Lavin, Grp. Pres.
Stuart L. Levenick, Grp. Pres
Edward J. Rapp, Grp. Pres. & C.F.O.
Gérard R. Vittecoq, Grp. Pres.

Steven H. Wunning, Grp. Pres.
James B. Buda, Sr. V.P. & Chf.
  Legal Off.
Jananne A. Copeland, Chf. Acct. Off. &
  Corp. Cont.

Consolidated Balance Sheet As of December 31, 2010 (000 omitted)

Assets		Liabilities & Stockholders' Equity	
Current assets	$31,810,000	Current liabilities	$22,020,000
Net property, plant & equipment	12,539,000	Long-term debt	20,437,000
Finance receivables	11,264,000	Other liabilities	10,238,000
Other assets	8,407,000	Minority interest	461,000
		*Stockholders' equity	10,864,000
Total	$64,020,000	Total	$64,020,000

*638,822,714 shares common stock outstanding.

Consolidated Income Statement

Years Ended Dec. 31	Thousands — — — — —		Per Share — — — — —		Common Stock Price Range Calendar Year
	Sales & Revenues	Net Income	Diluted Earnings	Cash Dividends	
2010	$42,588,000	$2,700,000	$4.15	$1.74	$94.89—50.50
2009	32,396,000	895,000	1.43	1.68	61.28—21.71
2008	51,324,000	3,557,000	5.66	1.62	85.96—31.95
2007	44,958,000	3,541,000	5.37	1.38	87.00—57.98
2006	41,517,000	3,537,000	5.17	1.15	82.03—57.05

Transfer Agent & Registrar: BNY Mellon Shareowner Services
General Counsel: James B. Buda, Sr. V.P.
Investor Relations: Mike DeWalt, Dir.
Human Resources: Kimberly S. Hauer, V.P.
Info. Tech.: John S. Heller, V.P.
Auditors: PricewaterhouseCoopers LLP

Traded (Symbol): NYSE, BELG, GER, LON, PAR, SWISS (CAT)
Stockholders: 39,353 (R)
Employees: 104,490
Annual Meeting: In June

CBOE Holdings, Inc.

400 South LaSalle Street, Chicago, Illinois 60605

Telephone: (312) 786-5600   www.cboe.com

CBOE Holdings, Inc. is the holding company for the Chicago Board Options Exchange, Incorporated (CBOE) and other subsidiaries. CBOE is the largest U.S. options exchange and creator of listed options. It offers equity, index, and exchange-traded fund (ETF) options, including proprietary products, such as S&P 500 options (SPX), and options on the CBOE Volatility Index (VIX), the world's barometer for market volatility. Other CBOE Holdings subsidiaries include: CBOE Futures Exchange, LLC; C2 Options Exchange; and Market Data Express, LLC. In conjunction with its initial public offering, the CBOE converted from a non-stock corporation owned by its members into a stock corporation that is a wholly owned subsidiary of CBOE Holdings, Inc. CBOE Holdings initiated its initial public offering in June 2010. Incorporated in Delaware in 2006.

Directors (In addition to indicated officers)

James R. Boris
Mark F. Duffy
David A. Fisher
Janet P. Froetscher
Paul Kepes
Stuart J. Kipnes
Duane R. Kullberg
Benjamin R. Londergen

R. Eden Martin
Roderick A. Palmore
Susan M. Phillips
William R. Power
Samuel K. Skinner
Carole E. Stone
Eugene E. Sunshine

Officers (Directors*)

*William J. Brodsky, Chm. & C.E.O.
Edward T. Tilly, Exec. V. Chm.
Edward J. Joyce, Pres. & C.O.O.
Alan J. Dean, Exec. V.P., C.F.O. & Treas.
Richard G. DuFour, Exec. V.P.—Corp. Planning
   & Dev.

Joanne Moffic-Silver, Exec. V.P., Gen.
   Coun. & Secy.
Gerald T. O'Connell, Exec. V.P. & C.I.O.
Edward L. Provost, Exec. V.P.—Bus. Dev.
David S. Reynolds, Chf. Acct. Off.

Consolidated Balance Sheet   As of December 31, 2010 (000 omitted)

Assets		Liabilities & Stockholders' Equity	
Current assets	$109,934	Current liabilities	$ 48,816
Net property & equipment	82,084	Long-term liabilities	29,422
Other assets	62,094	*Stockholders' equity	175,874
Total	$254,112	Total	$254,112

* 51,782,717 shares unrestricted common stock outstanding.

Consolidated Income Statement

Years Ended Dec. 31	Thousands — — — —		Per Share — — — —		Common Stock
	Operating Revenues	Net Income	Diluted Earnings	Cash Dividends	Price Range [a] Calendar Year
2010	$437,104	$ 98,166	$1.03	$0.20	$34.18—19.60
2009 [b]	426,082	106,451	1.17		
2008 [c]	416,783	115,288	1.27		
2007 [c]	344,270	83,168	0.92		
2006 [cd]	253,243	42,108	0.46		

[a] Initial public offering was effective on June 14, 2010 at $29.00 per share.
[b] Includes $24.1 million of deferred revenue from 2007 and 2008.
[c] Certain amounts have been reclassified to conform to current year presentation.
[d] On January 1, 2006, the company began operating its business on a for-profit basis.

Transfer Agent & Registrar: BNY Mellon Shareowner Services
General Counsel: Joanne Moffic-Silver, Exec. V.P. Traded (Symbol): NASDAQ (CBOE)
Investor Relations: Deborah L. Koopman, Dir.   Stockholders: 592
Human Resources: Deborah Woods, V.P.   Employees: 581
Info. Tech: Gerald T. O'Connell, C.I.O.   Annual Meeting: In May
Auditors: Deloitte & Touche LLP

CF Industries Holdings, Inc.

4 Parkway North, Suite 400, Deerfield, Illinois 60015
Telephone: (847) 405-2400   **www.cfindustries.com**

CF Industries Holdings, Inc. is the holding company for CF Industries, Inc., a global leader in fertilizer manufacturing and distribution, the second largest nitrogen fertilizer producer in the world and the third largest phosphate fertilizer among public companies. In April, 2010, the company acquired Terra Industries Inc. to establish its position as the premier nitrogen and phosphate fertilizer manufacturer in North America and a leader in nitrogen fertilizer globally. CF Industries operates seven nitrogen fertilizer manufacturing complexes in the central U.S. region and Canada; phosphate mining and productin operations in central Florida; and a network of fertilizer distribution terminals and warehouses, located primarily in major grain producing states in the U.S. Midwest. The company also owns 50% interests in KEYTRADE AG, a global fertilizer trading organization headquartered near Zurich, Switzerland; GrowHow UK Limited, a fertilizer manufacturer in the United Kingdom; and an ammonia facility in The Republic of Trinidad and Tobago. Incorporated in Delaware in 2005 as the successor to a business founded in 1946.

Directors (In addition to indicated officers)

Robert C. Arzbaecher	David R. Harvey
Wallace W. Creek	John D. Johnson
William Davisson	Robert G. Kuhbach
Stephen A. Furbacher	Edward A. Schmitt
Stephen J. Hagge	

Officers (Directors*)

*Stephen R. Wilson, Chm., Pres. & C.E.O.	Philipp P. Koch, V.P.—Supply Chain
Douglas C. Barnard, V.P., Gen. Coun. & Secy.	Wendy S. Jablow Spertus, V.P.—Hum. Res.
Bert A. Frost, V.P.—Sales & Market Dev.	Lynn F. White, V.P.—Corp. Dev.
Richard A. Hoker, V.P. & Corp. Cont.	W. Anthony Will, V.P.—Mfg. & Distr.

Consolidated Balance Sheet As of December 31, 2010 (000 omitted)

Assets		Liabilities & Stockholders' Equity	
Current assets	$1,341,400	Current liabilities	$ 946,600
Net property, plant & equipment	3,925,600	Long-term debt	1,954,100
Goodwill, net	2,085,700	Other liabilities	1,424,400
Other assets	1,405,800	*Stockholders' equity	4,433,400
Total	$8,758,500	Total	$8,758,500

*71,267,185 shares common stock outstanding.

Consolidated Income Statement

Years Ended Dec. 31	Thousands — — — — —		Per Share — — — — —		Common Stock Price Range Calendar Year
	Net Sales	Net Income [a]	Diluted Earnings	Cash Dividends	
2010	$3,965,000	$349,200	$ 5.34	$0.40	$110.00—57.56
2009	2,608,400	365,600	7.42	0.40	95.13—42.30
2008	3,921,100	684,600	12.13	0.40	172.99—37.71
2007	2,756,700	372,700	6.56	0.08	118.88—25.70
2006	2,032,900	33,300	0.60	0.08	26.60—12.91

[a] Attributable to common stockholders.

Transfer Agent & Registrar: BNY Mellon Shareowner Services
General Counsel: Douglas C. Barnard, V.P.
Investor Relations: Terry Huch, Sr. Dir.
Human Resources: Wendy Jablow Spertus, V.P.
Info. Tech.: Dan Zaremba, Dir.
Auditors: KPMG LLP

Traded (Symbol): NYSE (CF)
Stockholders: 16,800 (B)
Employees: 2,400
Annual Meeting: In May

Chicago Rivet & Machine Co.

901 Frontenac Road, P.O. Box 3061, Naperville, Illinois 60566

Telephone: (630) 357-8500   www.chicagorivet.com

Chicago Rivet & Machine Co. operates in two segments of the fastener industry: fasteners and assembly equipment. The fastener segment consists of the manufacture and sale of rivets, cold-formed fasteners, and parts and screw machine products. The assembly equipment segment consists primarily of the manufacture of automatic rivet setting machines, automatic assembly equipment, and parts and tools for these machines. The company also leases automatic rivet setting machines. The principal market for the company's products is the North American automotive industry. The company's administrative and sales offices are located in Naperville, Illinois, and Norwell, Massachusetts. Manufacturing divisions are located in Tyrone, Pennsylvania and Albia, Iowa. The company's H & L Tool Company, Inc. subsidiary is located in Madison Heights, Michigan. Incorporated in Illinois in 1927.

Directors (In addition to indicated officers)

Edward L. Chott
Kent H. Cooney
William T. Divane, Jr.

George P. Lynch
Walter W. Morrissey

Officers (Directors*)

*John A. Morrissey, Chm. & C.E.O.
*Michael J. Bourg, Pres., C.O.O. & Treas.

Kimberly A. Kirhofer, Secy.

Consolidated Balance Sheet   As of December 31, 2010 (000 omitted)

Assets		Liabilities & Stockholders' Equity	
Current assets	$16,180	Current liabilities	$ 1,552
Net property, plant & equipment	7,479	Deferred items	745
		*Stockholders' equity	21,362
Total	$23,659	Total	$23,659

*966,132 shares common stock outstanding.

Consolidated Income Statement

Years Ended Dec. 31	Thousands — — — — —		Per Share — — — —		Common Stock Price Range Calendar Year
	Net Sales	Net Income	Basic Earnings	Cash Dividends	
2010	$28,521	$ 606	$ 0.63	$0.42	$19.93—12.40
2009	21,391	(1,283)	(1.33)	0.48	16.81—10.15
2008	28,519	(825)	(0.85)	0.87[a]	25.75— 9.81
2007	37,776	1,267	1.31	0.72	26.10—19.40
2006	40,370[b]	1,121	1.16	0.72	24.89—17.50

a Includes an extra dividend of $0.15 per share.
b Total revenues.

Transfer Agent & Registrar: Continental Stock Transfer & Trust Company

Investor Relations:	Kimberly A. Kirhofer, Secy.	Traded (Symbol):	NYSE Amex (CVR)
Info. Tech.:	Susan Dundon	Stockholders:	210 (R)
Auditors:	Grant Thornton LLP	Employees:	219
		Annual Meeting:	In May

CME Group Inc.

20 South Wacker Drive, Chicago, Illinois 60606

Telephone: (312) 930-1000   **www.cme.com**

CME Group, building on the heritage of its futures exchanges (CME, CBOT, NYMEX, and COMEX), serves the risk management needs of customers around the globe. As an international marketplace, CME Group brings buyers and sellers together on the CME Globex electronic trading platform and on trading floors in Chicago and New York. CME Group offers the widest range of benchmark products available across all major asset classes, including futures and options based on interest rates, equity indexes, foreign exchange, energy, agricultural commodities, metals, and alternative investment products such as weather and real estate. CME Clearing matches and settles all trades and guarantees the creditworthyness of every transaction that takes place in these markets. Predecessor company founded in 1898; incorporated in Delaware in 2001.

Directors (In addition to indicated officers)

Jeffrey Bernacchi	Daniel R. Glickman	John L. Pietrzak
Timothy S. Bitsberger	J. Dennis Hastert	Edemir Pinto
Charles P. Carey	Bruce F. Johnson	Alex J. Pollock
Mark E. Cermak	Gary M. Katler	John F. Sandner
Dennis H. Chookaszian	Leo Melamed	Terry L. Savage
Jackie M. Clegg	William P. Miller, II	William R. Shepard
Robert F. Corvino	Joseph Niciforo	Howard J. Siegel
James A. Donaldson	C. C. Odom, II	Christopher Stewart
Martin J. Gepsman	James E. Oliff	Dennis A. Suskind
Larry G. Gerdes	Ronald E. Pankau	David J. Wescott

Officers (Directors*)

*Terrence A. Duffy, Chm.
*Craig S. Donohue, C.E.O.
Phupinder S. Gill, Pres.
Kathleen M. Cronin, Managing Dir., Gen. Coun. & Secy.
Bryan T. Durkin, C.O.O. & Managing Dir.—Prods. & Svcs.
Julie Holzrichter, Managing Dir.—Gbl. Oper.
Kevin Kometer, Managing Dir. & C.I.O.
James E. Parisi, Managing Dir.—Fin. & Corp. Dev. & C.F.O.
Laurent Paulhac, Managing Dir.—OTC Prods. & Svcs.

Hilda Harris Piell, Managing Dir. & Chf. Hum. Res. Off.
John Pietrowicz, Managing Dir.—Bus. Dev. & Corp. Fin.
Derek Sammann, Managing Dir.—FX & Interest Rate Prods.
Sean Tully, Managing Dir.—Interest Rate Prod.
Kimberly S. Taylor, Managing Dir. & Pres.—CME Clearing House Div.
Kendal Vroman, Managing Dir.—Commodity Prods., OTC Svcs. & Info. Prods.
Scott E. Warren, Managing Dir.—Equity Index Prods. & Index Svcs.
Michael Kilgallen, Managing Dir.—Equity Prod.

Consolidated Balance Sheet As of December 31, 2010 (000 omitted)

Assets		Liabilities & Stockholders' Equity	
Current assets	$ 5,387,500	Current liabilities	$ 4,781,200
Intangible assets—trading prod.	17,040,500	Other liabilities	10,136,700
Net property	786,800	Redeemable non-control. interest	68,100
Goodwill	7,983,600	*Stockholders' equity	20,060,100
Other assets	3,847,700		
Total	$35,046,100	Total	$35,046,100

*66,847,000 shares Class A common stock outstanding.

Consolidated Income Statement [a]

Years Ended Dec. 31	Thousands — — — —		Per Share — — — —		Common Stock Price Range Calendar Year
	Total Revenues	Net Income	Basic Earnings	Cash Dividends	
2010	$3,003,700	$951,400	$14.35	$4.60	$353.03—234.50
2009	2,612,800	825,800	12.44	4.60	346.24—155.06
2008	2,561,019	715,486	12.18	9.60 [b]	686.43—155.49
2007	1,756,101	658,533	15.05	3.44	714.48—593.58
2006	1,089,947	407,348	11.74	2.52	557.97—354.51

[a] Includes financial results of CBOT Holdings beginning July 13, 2007, Credit Market Analysis beginning March 24, 2008, and NYMEX Holdings beginning August 23, 2008.
[b] Includes September 25, 2008 special dividend of $5.00.

Transfer Agent & Registrar: Computershare Investor Services

General Counsel:	Kathleen M. Cronin, Managing Dir.	**Traded (Symbol):**	NASDAQ (CME)
Investor Relations:	John Peschier, Dir.	**Stockholders:**	3,319 (R), Class A;
Human Resources:	Hilda Harris Piell, Managing Dir.		1,751 (R), Class B
Info. Tech.:	Kevin Kometer, C.I.O.	**Employees:**	2,570
Auditors:	Ernst & Young LLP	**Annual Meeting:**	In June

CNA Financial Corporation

CNA Center, 333 South Wabash Avenue, Chicago, Illinois 60604

Telephone: (312) 822-5000   www.cna.com

CNA Financial Corporation is a holding company whose primary subsidiaries consist of property and casualty insurance companies. Property and casualty insurance operations are conducted by Continental Casualty Company, The Continental Insurance Company, and their affiliates. The company's insurance products include standard commercial lines, specialty lines, surety, marine, and other property and casualty coverages. CNA's services include risk management, information services, and warranty and claims administration for customers such as small, medium, and large businesses; associations; professionals; and groups and individuals. CNA is the 7th largest commercial insurer and the 13th largest property and casualty insurer in the United States. On June 9, 2011, CNA Financial announced the successful completion of its acquisition of CNA Surety Corporation. Loews Corporation holds approximately a 90 percent ownership position in CNA Financial Corp. Incorporated in Delaware in 1967.

Directors (In addition to indicated officers)

Paul J. Liska
Jose O. Montemayor
Don M. Randel
Joseph Rosenberg

Andrew H. Tisch
James S. Tisch
Marvin Zonis

Officers (Directors*)

*Thomas F. Motamed, Chm. & C.E.O.
Jonathan D. Kantor, Exec. V.P., Gen. Coun. & Secy.
D. Craig Mense, Exec. V.P. & C.F.O.
George R. Fay, Exec. V.P.—WW Prop. & Cas. Claim

Larry A. Haefner, Exec. V.P. & Chf. Actuary
Thomas Pontarelli, Exec. V.P. & Chf. Admin. Off.
Timothy J. Szerlong, Pres.—WW Field Oper.
Robert A. Lindemann, Pres. & C.O.O.—CNA Commercial

Consolidated Balance Sheet   As of December 31, 2010 (000 omitted)

Assets		Liabilities & Stockholders' Equity	
Investments	$42,655,000	Insurance reserves	$37,590,000
Insurance & reinsurance	8,636,000	Long-term debt	2,251,000
receivables	333,000	Other liabilities	3,966,000
Property & equipment	3,707,000	Minority interest	570,000
Other assets		*Stockholders' equity	10,954,000
Total	$55,331,000	Total	$55,331,000

*269,139,138 shares common stock outstanding.

Consolidated Income Statement

Years Ended Dec. 31	Thousands — — — —		Per Share — — — —		Common Stock
	Revenues	Net Income	Basic Earnings	Cash Dividends	Price Range Calendar Year
2010	$ 9,209,000	$ 690,000	$ 2.28	$0.00	$29.50—21.71
2009	8,472,000	419,000	1.10	0.00	26.51— 6.41
2008	7,799,000	(299,000)	(1.18)	0.45	35.04— 8.50
2007	9,885,000	851,000	3.13	0.35	51.96—32.26
2006	10,376,000	1,108,000	4.06	0.00	40.32—29.88

Transfer Agent & Registrar: Wells Fargo Shareowner Services
General Counsel: Jonathan D. Kantor, Exec. V.P. Traded (Symbol): NYSE, CSE (CNA)
Investor Relations: Nancy Bufalino, Sr. V.P.   Stockholders: 1,519 (R)
Human Resources: Thomas Pontarelli, Exec. V.P.   Employees: 8,000
Info. Tech.:   Ray Oral, Sr. V.P.   Annual Meeting: In April
Auditors: Deloitte & Touche LLP

Cobra Electronics Corporation

6500 West Cortland Street, Chicago, Illinois 60707

Telephone: (773) 889-8870 **www.cobra.com**

Cobra Electronics Corporation is a leading designer and marketer of two-way mobile communications and mobile navigation products that ranks in the top two positions in each of its longstanding product lines, and is targeting a similar position for businesses recently entered into: marine VHF radios, photo-enforcement detection, and mobile navigation for professional drivers. Cobra® is a leading brand in Citizens Band radios, radar detectors, speed camera detection, truck navigation, and two-way radios. Cobra markets its products in the U.S., Canada, and Europe. Substantially all of the company's products are manufactured to its specifications and engineering designs by a number of suppliers, primarily in China, Hong Kong, and South Korea. In October 2006, the company completed the acquisition of Performance Products Limited (PPL), a U.K.-based designer and marketer of mobile navigation and photo-enforcement detection products, primarily marketed under the Snooper® brand, as well as the AURA™ database of photo-enforcement locations in the U.K. and elsewhere in Europe. Incorporated in Delaware in 1961; present name adopted in 1993.

Directors (In addition to indicated officers)

William P. Carmichael
John S. Lupo
Ian R. Miller

S. Sam Park
Robert P. Rohleder

Officers (Directors*)

*James R. Bazet, Chm., Pres. & C.E.O.
 Robert J. Ben, Sr. V.P. & C.F.O.

Sally A. Washlow, Sr. V.P.—Mktg. & Sales
Gerald M. Laures, V.P.—Fin. & Corp. Secy.

Consolidated Balance Sheet As of December 31, 2010 (000 omitted)

Assets		Liabilities & Stockholders' Equity	
Current assets	$54,057	Current liabilities	$30,492
Net property, plant & equipment	5,492	Deferred compensation	7,145
Intangible assets	9,315	Other liabilities	2,103
Other assets	5,490	Minority interest	28
		*Stockholders' equity	34,586
Total	$74,354	Total	$74,354

*6,471,280 shares common stock outstanding.

Consolidated Income Statement

Years Ended Dec. 31	Thousands — — — —		Per Share — — — —		Common Stock Price Range Calendar Year
	Net Sales	Net Income	Diluted Earnings	Cash Dividends	
2010	$110,520	$ 1,577	$ 0.24	$0.00	$ 3.30—1.51
2009	105,229	(10,272)	(1.59)	0.00	1.90—0.81
2008	124,745	(18,839)	(2.91)	0.16	5.42—0.75
2007	155,935	(4,422)	(0.68)	0.16	10.95—4.11
2006 [a]	153,695	(1,630)	(0.25)	0.16	14.00—8.02

[a] Reflects the acquisition of Performance Products Limited on October 20, 2006.

Transfer Agent & Registrar: American Stock Transfer & Trust Co.
Corporate Counsel: Sidley Austin LLP
Investor Relations: Cindy Frederick
Human Resources: Lucy Erikson, V.P.
Info. Tech.: Jamie Byrd
Auditors: Grant Thornton LLP

Traded (Symbol): NASDAQ (COBR)
Stockholders: 461 (R)
Employees: 152
Annual Meeting: In May

Coleman Cable Inc.

1530 Shields Drive, Waukegan, Illinois 60085

Telephone: (847) 672-2300   **www.colemancable.com**

Coleman Cable, Inc. is a leading designer, developer, manufacturer, and supplier of electrical wire and cable products for consumer, commercial, and industrial applications, with operations primarily in the U.S. and, to a lesser degree, Canada. The company supplies a broad line of wire and cable products, offering its customers a single source for many of their wire and cable product requirements. The company sells its products to more than 8,500 active customers in diverse end markets, including a wide range of specialty distributors, retailers, and original equipment manufacturers. In April 2007, Coleman acquired Copperfield, LLC, one of the largest privately owned manufacturers and suppliers of electrical wire and cable products in the U.S. In November 2007, the company acquired the Woods Industries electrical products business of Katy Industries, Inc. The principal business of Woods was the design and distribution of consumer electrical cord products. In March 2011, Coleman announced a definitive merger agreement with Technology Research Corporation, a recognized leader in providing cost-effective engineered solutions for applications involving power management and control, intelligent battery systems technology, and electrical safety products. In May 2011, the company completed the acquisition of the assets of First Capitol Wire & Cable, as well as the assets of Continental Wire & Cable, leading manufacturers of industrial wire and cable products. Incorporated in Delaware in 1999.

Directors (In addition to indicated officers)

David Bistricer, Co-Chm.
Nachum Stein, Co-Chm.
Shmuel D. Levinson
Dennis J. Martin

Isaac M. Neuberger
Harmon S. Spolan
Denis E. Springer

Officers (Directors*)

*G. Gary Yetman, Pres. & C.E.O.
Richard N. Burger, Exec. V.P., C.F.O., Secy. & Treas.
Richard Carr, Exec. V.P.—Oper.

Michael Frigo, Exec. V.P.—OEM Grp.
J. Kurt Hennelly, Exec. V.P.—Oper.
Kenneth A. McAllister, Exec. V.P.—Distr. Grp.
Kathy Jo Van, Exec. V.P.—Retail Grp.

Consolidated Balance Sheet   As of December 31, 2010 (000 omitted)

Assets		Liabilities & Stockholders' Equity	
Current assets	$232,836	Current liabilities	$ 52,216
Net property & equipment	45,731	Long-term debt	271,820
Goodwill	29,134	Other liabilities	5,853
Other assets	33,410	*Stockholders' equity	11,222
Total	$341,111	Total	$341,111

*16,939,000 shares common stock outstanding.

Consolidated Income Statement

Years Ended Dec. 31	Thousands — — — — —		Per Share — — — —		Common Stock Price Range [b] Calendar Year
	Net Sales	Net Income	Diluted Earnings [a]	Cash Dividends	
2010	$703,763	$ 3,727	$ 0.21	$0.00	$ 7.83—3.35
2009	504,152	(67,019)	(3.99)	0.00	5.94—1.35
2008	972,968	(28,261)	(1.68)	0.00	13.46—2.85
2007 [c]	864,144	14,890	0.88	0.00	29.99—9.27
2006	423,358	29,359	2.15	0.00	

[a] Reflects 312.6079-for-1 stock split that occurred on October 10, 2006.
[b] Stock began trading March 1, 2007.
[c] Includes the results of operations of acquisitions beginning with their respective acquisition dates.

Transfer Agent & Registrar: American Stock Transfer & Trust Co.
Corporate Counsel: Winston & Strawn LLP   Traded (Symbol): NASDAQ (CCIX)
Investor Relations: Philip Kranz, Dresner Corp. Svcs. Stockholders: 45 (R)
Auditors: Deloitte & Touche LLP   Employees: 1,052
                                   Annual Meeting: In April

Consolidated Communications Holdings, Inc.

121 South 17th Street, Matoon, Illinois 61938-3987

Telephone: (217) 235-3311   www.consolidated.com

Consolidated Communications Holdings, Inc. is an established rural local exchange company (RLEC) providing voice, data, and video services to residential and business customers in Illinois, Texas, and Pennsylvania. Consolidated Communications offers a wide range of telecommunications services, including local and long-distance service; high-speed broadband Internet access ("DSL"); standard and high-definition digital television ("IPTV"); digital telephone service ("VOIP"); custom calling features; private line services; carrier access services; network capacity services over its regional fiber optic network; directory publishing; and Competitive Local Exchange Carrier (CLEC) services. With 237,141 local access lines, 106,387 DSL lines, 29,236 IPTV subscribers, and an estimated 81,090 CLEC access line equivalents, Consolidated Communications is the 13th largest independent local telephone company in the United States. In February 2010, the company sold its Consolidated Market Response (CMR) division to Solix, Inc. Incorporated in Delaware in 2002 as the successor to businesses dating back to 1894.

Directors (In addition to indicated officers)

Richard A. Lumpkin, Chm.
Jack W. Blumenstein

Roger H. Moore
Maribeth S. Rahe

Officers (Directors*)

*Robert J. Currey, Pres. & C.E.O.
Steven L. Childers, Sr. V.P. & C.F.O.
Steven J. Shirar, Sr. V.P. & Corp. Secy.

C. Robert Udell, Jr., Sr. V.P. & C.O.O.
Christopher A. Young, C.I.O.

Consolidated Balance Sheet As of December 31, 2010 (000 omitted)

Assets		Liabilities & Stockholders' Equity	
Current assets	$ 136,250	Current liabilities	$ 75,592
Net property, plant & equipment	356,057	Long-term debt	880,000
Goodwill, net	520,562	Deferred taxes	73,628
Other assets	196,677	Other liabilities	108,451
		Minority interests	4,922
		Stockholders' equity	66,953
Total	$1,209,546	Total	$1,209,546

*29,763,122 shares common stock outstanding.

Consolidated Income Statement

Years Ended Dec. 31	Thousands — — — —		Per Share [a] — — — —		Common Stock Price Range [a] Calendar Year
	Total Oper. Revenues	Net Income [b]	Diluted Earnings [b]	Cash Dividends	
2010	$383,400	$32,600	$1.09	$1.55	$19.50—16.27
2009	406,200	24,900	0.84	1.55	17.48— 7.90
2008 [c]	418,400	12,500 [d]	0.42 [d]	1.55	19.19— 7.82
2007 [c]	329,200	11,400	0.43	1.55	23.71—15.50
2006	320,800	13,300	0.48	1.55	20.94—12.46

[a] Stock began trading on July 25, 2005.
[b] Attributable to common stockholders.
[c] North Pittsburgh acquired on December 31, 2007. Includes North Pittsburgh operations beginning January 1, 2008.
[d] Includes non-cash extraordinary gain of $7.2 million, net of tax ($0.24 per diluted share), relating to discontinuance of SFAS No. 71.

Transfer Agent & Registrar: Computershare Investor Services

Investor Relations:	Matthew Smith, Dir.	**Traded (Symbol):**	NASDAQ (CNSL)
Human Resources:	Steven J. Shirar, Sr. V.P.	**Stockholders:**	1,510 (R)
Info. Tech.:	Christopher A. Young, C.I.O.	**Employees:**	970
Auditors:	Ernst & Young LLP	**Annual Meeting:**	In May

Continental Materials Corporation

200 South Wacker Drive, Suite 4000, Chicago, Illinois 60606

Telephone: (312) 541-7200

Continental Materials Corporation operates as a holding company primarily within two industry groups: Heating, Ventilation, and Air Conditioning (HVAC) and Construction Products. The company reports two segments in each of the two groups: the Heating and Cooling segment and the Evaporative Cooling segment in the HVAC industry group, and the Concrete, Aggregates, and Construction Supplies segment and the Door segment in Construction Products. In the Heating and Cooling segment, Williams Furnace Company of Colton, California produces and sells gas-fired wall furnaces, console heaters, and fan coils. In the Evaporative Cooling segment, Phoenix Manufacturing, Inc. of Phoenix, Arizona produces and sells evaporative coolers. Concrete, Aggregates, and Construction Supplies are offered from numerous locations along the southern portion of the Front Range of Colorado by Castle Concrete Company and Transit Mix Concrete Co., of Colorado Springs, and Transit Mix of Pueblo, Inc. of Pueblo. Doors are fabricated and sold along with the related hardware by McKinney Door and Hardware, Inc. of Pueblo and Colorado Springs, Colorado. In July 2009, the company sold Rocky Mountain Ready Mix Concrete, Inc., a ready mix concrete business in the Denver metropolitan area. Incorporated in Delaware in 1954.

Directors (In addition to indicated officers)

William D. Andrews
Thomas H. Carmody
Betsy R. Gidwitz
Ralph W. Gidwitz

Ronald J. Gidwitz
Theodore R. Tetzlaff
Peter E. Thieriot
Darrell M. Trent

Officers (Directors*)

*James G. Gidwitz, Chm. & C.E.O.
Joseph J. Sum, V.P., C.F.O. & Treas.

Mark S. Nichter, Secy. & Cont.

Consolidated Balance Sheet As of January 1, 2011 (000 omitted)

Assets		Liabilities & Stockholders' Equity	
Current assets	$41,288	Current liabilities	$15,324
Net property, plant & equipment	23,693	Long-term debt	4,410
Other assets	14,580	Deferred income taxes	1,324
		Other liabilities	7,698
		*Stockholders' equity	50,805
Total	$79,561	Total	$79,561

*1,598,000 shares common stock outstanding.

Consolidated Income Statement [a]

Years Ended Abt. Dec. 31	Thousands — — — — —		Per Share — — — — —		Common Stock Price Range Calendar Year
	Sales	Net Income	Diluted Earnings		
2010	$114,284	$ (381)[b]	$(0.24)[b]	$0.00	$22.35—10.75
2009	113,461	(1,442)[b]	(0.90)[b]	0.00	16.86— 7.72
2008	145,714	(40)[bc]	(0.03)[b]	0.00	26.62—16.00
2007	168,429	(563)	(0.35)	0.00	30.99—24.77
2006	158,767	2,042	1.27	0.00	29.40—26.10

a Includes the activity of CSSL in the Door segment since January 1, 2006 and the activity of ASCI in the Concrete, Aggregates, and Construction Supplies segment since June 30, 2006, the respective dates each was acquired.
b Includes losses from discontinued operations, net of income tax benefits, of $97,000 ($0.06 per diluted share) in 2010; $640,000 ($0.40 per diluted share) in 2009; and $1,797,000 ($1.12 per diluted share) in 2008.
c Includes a pre-tax gain on the sale of land of $1,947,000 and a pre-tax impairment charge for long-lived assets of $784,000.

Transfer Agent & Registrar: Registrar and Transfer Company
Corporate Counsel: Ungaretti & Harris LLP
Investor Relations: Mark S. Nichter, Secy.
Human Resources: Annemarie Bruckner, Office Mgr.
Info. Tech.: Stephen R. Shay, Dir.
Auditors: BKD LLP

Traded (Symbol): NYSE Amex (CUO)
Stockholders: 327 (R)
Employees: 623
Annual Meeting: Fourth Wednesday in May

Corn Products International, Inc.

5 Westbrook Corporate Center, Westchester, Illinois 60154

Telephone: (708) 551-2600   www.cornproducts.com

Corn Products International, Inc. is a leading corn refiner and major supplier of high-quality food ingredients and industrial products derived from the wet milling and processing of corn and other starch-based materials, such as tapioca, potatoes, and rice. Founded in 1906, the company is a leading producer of dextrose and a leading regional producer of starch, high fructose corn syrup, and glucose. The company supplies a broad range of customers, most of whom are in the food and beverage, pharmaceutical, paper and corrugated products, textile, brewing, and personal care industries, as well as in animal nutrition and corn oil markets worldwide. Approximately 56 percent of the company's 2010 net sales were from its operations in North America, with the remainder coming from its South America, Asia/Africa, and Europe operations. On October 1, 2010, the company acquired National Starch, a global provider of specialty starches from Akzo Nobel N.V., headquartered in the Netherlands. Incorporated in Delaware in 1997.

Directors (In addition to indicated officers)

Richard J. Almeida
Luis Aranguren–Trellez
Paul Hanrahan
Karen L. Hendricks
Wayne M. Hewett

Gregory B. Kenny
Barbara A. Klein
James M. Ringler
Dwayne A. Wilson

Officers (Directors*)

*Ilene S. Gordon, Chm., Pres. & C.E.O.
Cheryl K. Beebe, Exec. V.P. & C.F.O.
Jack C. Fortnum, Exec. V.P. & Pres.—Gbl. Beverage, Industrial & North Amer. Sweetener Solutions
James P. Zallie, Exec. V.P. & Pres.—Gbl. Ingredient Solutions
Julio dos Reis, Sr. V.P. & Pres.—South Amer. Ingredient Solutions

Diane J. Frisch, Sr. V.P.—Hum. Res.
Mary Ann Hynes, Sr. V.P., Gen. Coun., Corp. Secy. & Chf. Compliance Off.
John F. Saucier, Sr. V.P.—Corp. Strat. & Gbl. Bus. Dev.
Robin A. Kornmeyer, V.P. & Cont.
Kimberly A. Hunter, Corp. Treas.

Consolidated Balance Sheet   As of December 31, 2010 (000 omitted)

Assets		Liabilities & Stockholders' Equity	
Current assets	$1,753,000	Current liabilities	$ 891,000
Net property, plant & equipment	2,123,000	Long-term debt	1,681,000
Other assets	1,195,000	Other liabilities	497,000
		Minority interests	26,000
		*Stockholders' equity	1,976,000
Total	$5,071,000	Total	$5,071,000

*76,023,251 shares common stock outstanding.

Consolidated Income Statement

Years Ended Dec. 31	Thousands — — — — —		Per Share — — — — —		Common Stock Price Range Calendar Year
	Net Sales	Net Income	Diluted Earnings	Cash Dividends	
2010 [a]	$4,367,000	$169,000 [b]	$2.20 [b]	$0.56	$48.00—26.23
2009	3,672,000	41,000 [c]	0.54 [c]	0.56	32.37—17.80
2008	3,944,000	267,000	3.52	0.54	54.96—17.51
2007	3,391,000	198,000	2.59	0.40	49.30—25.48
2006	2,621,000	124,000	1.63	0.33	37.49—22.92

[a] Includes results of National Starch from October 1, 2010 forward.
[b] Includes after-tax charges of $14 million ($0.18 per diluted share) for bridge loan and other financing costs, $22 million ($0.29 per diluted share) associated with Chile operations, and $18 million ($0.23 per diluted share) relating to the sale of National Starch inventory. Also includes after-tax acquisition-related costs of $26 million ($0.34 per diluted share).
[c] Includes after-tax charge of $110 million ($1.47 per diluted share) for impaired assets and restructuring costs.

Transfer Agent & Registrar: BNY Mellon Shareowner Services

General Counsel:	Mary Ann Hynes, Sr. V.P.	Traded (Symbol):	NYSE (CPO)
Investor Relations:	Aaron Hoffman, V.P.	Stockholders:	6,600 (R)
Human Resources:	Diane J. Frisch, Sr. V.P.	Employees:	10,700
Auditors:	KPMG LLP	Annual Meeting:	In May

Cosi, Inc.

1751 Lake Cook Road, Suite 600, Deerfield, Illinois 60015

Telephone: (847) 597-8800   **www.getcosi.com**

Cosi, Inc. owns, operates, and franchises premium convenience restaurants that offer breakfast, lunch, afternoon coffee, dinner, and dessert menus full of fresh, flavorful foods and beverages. Cosi has developed featured foods that are built around a secret, generations-old recipe for crackly-crust flatbread, which is freshly baked in front of customers throughout the day in open-flame stone-hearth ovens prominently located in each of the restaurants. The Cosi menu features Cosi sandwiches, freshly tossed salads, breakfast wraps, melts, soups, Cosi bagels, flatbread pizzas, S'mores, snacks, and other desserts, and a wide range of coffee and coffee-based drinks and other specialty beverages, with beer and wine in some locations. Cosi has 83 company-owned and 59 franchise restaurants in 18 states, the District of Columbia, and the United Arab Emirates. Incorporated in Delaware in 1998.

Directors (In addition to indicated officers)

Creed L. Ford, III   Michael O'Donnell
Robert Merritt   Karl Okamoto

Officers (Directors*)

*Mark Demilio, Chm., & Interim Pres. & C.E.O.   Pat Enright, V.P.—Info. Tech.
 William Koziel, C.F.O., Treas. & Secy.   Becky Iliff, V.P.—People
 Vicki J. Baue, V.P., Gen. Coun., Chf.   Steve Scrima, V.P.—Purchasing & Distr.
   Compliance & Legal Off. & Asst. Secy.

Consolidated Balance Sheet   As of December 27, 2010 (000 omitted)

Assets		Liabilities & Stockholders' Equity	
Current assets	$13,893	Current liabilities	$12,835
Net property & equipment	15,009	Long-term liabilities	4,592
Other assets	2,449	Other liabilities	2,238
		*Stockholders' equity	11,686
Total	$31,351	Total	$31,351

*51,443,348 shares common stock outstanding.

Consolidated Income Statement

Years Ended Abt. Dec. 31	Thousands — — — —		Per Share — — — —		Common Stock Price Range Calendar Year
	Total Revenues	Net Income	Diluted Earnings	Cash Dividends	
2010	$109,699	$ (3,141)	$(0.06)	$0.00	$ 1.34—0.57
2009	118,573	(11,104)	(0.27)	0.00	1.00—0.19
2008	135,579	(16,222)a	(0.40)a	0.00	3.15—0.18
2007	134,556	(20,783)a	(0.53)a	0.00	6.67—2.10
2006	123,698	(12,328)a	(0.32)a	0.00	10.99—4.27

a Includes losses from discontinued operations of $312,000 in 2008; $4,253,000 ($0.11 per diluted share) in 2007; and $1,439,000 ($0.04 per diluted share) in 2006.

Transfer Agent & Registrar: American Stock Transfer & Trust Co.

General Counsel: Vicki J. Baue, V.P.   Traded (Symbol):   NASDAQ (COSI)
Investor Relations: William Koziel, C.F.O.   Stockholders: 82 (R)
Human Resources: Becky Iliff, V.P.   Employees: 2,038
Info. Tech.:   Pat Enright, V.P.   Annual Meeting: In May
Auditors: BDO USA, LLP

CTI Industries Corporation

22160 North Pepper Road, Barrington, Illinois 60010
Telephone: (847) 382-1000   www.ctiindustries.com

CTI Industries Corporation develops, produces, markets, and sells four principal lines of products: novelty products (balloons and other inflatable toy items); flexible films (for food and other packaging and commercial applications); flexible containers (home and consumer use for the storage and preservation of food and personal items); and specialty film products (for various applications including medical uses). CTI Industries manufactures over 500 balloon designs with different shapes and sizes marketed under such names as Superloons®, Ultraloons®, Miniloons®, Card-B-Loons®, Shape-A-Loons®, Minishapes, and Balloon Jamz™. The company's balloons and related products are sold through a wide variety of retail outlets that include discount chains; florists; balloon decorators; card and gift shops; party goods stores; and grocery, merchandise, and drugstore chains. The company's wholly owned subsidiary, CTI Balloons Ltd., markets products throughout Europe from its headquarters in Rugby, England. In January 2010, CTI commenced the sales of balloon products through a facility in Frankfurt, Germany. The company also conducts operations in Mexico and Latin America through majority-owned subsidiaries CTI Mexico and Flexo Universal. Incorporated in Delaware in 1983; present name adopted in 1985. Reincorporated in Illinois in 2001.

Directors (In addition to indicated officers)

Stanley M. Brown, III	Phil Roos
John I. Collins	Bret Tayne

Officers (Directors*)

*John H. Schwan, Chm. & Exec. V.P.	Samuel Komar, V.P.—Sales & Mktg.
*Howard W. Schwan, Pres.	Timothy Patterson, V.P.—Fin. & Admin.
*Stephen M. Merrick, Exec. V.P., C.F.O. & Secy.	Richard Sherman, V.P.

Consolidated Balance Sheet As of December 31, 2010 (000 omitted)

Assets		Liabilities & Stockholders' Equity	
Current assets	$21,426	Current liabilities	$17,952
Net property, plant & equipment	9,660	Long-term liabilities	3,130
Other assets	1,775	Minority interest	(5)
		*Stockholders' equity	11,784
Total	$32,861	Total	$32,861

*3,137,348 shares common stock outstanding.

Consolidated Income Statement

Years Ended Dec. 31	Thousands — — — —		Per Share — — — —		Common Stock Price Range Calendar Year
	Net Sales	Net Income	Diluted Earnings[a]	Cash Dividends	
2010	$47,748	$1,828	$0.60	$0.05	$ 9.75—2.26
2009	41,295	1,003	0.36	0.00	2.84—1.20
2008	44,981	1,154	0.40	0.00	7.30—1.60
2007	36,510	82	0.03	0.00	10.39—2.76
2006	35,428	1,895	0.85	0.00	8.23—2.20

[a] Applicable to common stockholders.

Transfer Agent & Registrar: American Stock Transfer & Trust Co.

General Counsel:	Vanasco Genelly & Miller	Traded (Symbol):	NASDAQ CAPITAL (CTIB)
Investor Relations:	Stephen M. Merrick, C.F.O.	Stockholders:	54 (R)
Human Resources:	Mary Ellen Dammyer	Employees:	370
Auditors:	Blackman Kallick, LLP	Annual Meeting:	In June

Deere & Company

One John Deere Place, Moline, Illinois 61265-8098

Telephone: (309) 765-8000   **www.johndeere.com**

Deere & Company and its subsidiaries manufacture, distribute, and finance a full line of agricultural, commercial, consumer, construction, and forestry equipment, as well as other technological products and services. Deere & Company has operations which are categorized into three major business segments: agricultural and turf equipment (A&T), construction and forestry (C&F), and credit. Agricultural equipment includes tractors; combines, cotton and sugarcane harvesters; tillage, seeding, nutrient management, and soil preparation machinery; sprayers; hay and forage equipment; integrated agricultural management systems technology; and precision agricultural irrigation equipment and supplies. Turf equipment includes small tractors for lawn, garden, commercial, and utility purposes; riding and walk-behind mowers; golf course equipment; utility vehicles; landscape and irrigation equipment; and other outdoor power products. The construction and forestry segment consists of: backhoe loaders; crawler dozers and loaders; four-wheel-drive loaders; excavators; motor graders; articulated dump trucks; landscape loaders; skid-steer loaders; and log skidders, feller bunchers, loaders, forwarders, harvesters, and related attachments. The credit segment primarily finances sales and leases by John Deere dealers of new and used equipment. It also provides wholesale financing to these dealers, provides operating loans, finances retail revolving charge accounts, and offers certain crop risk mitigation products. Factories and sales branches are located worldwide. In December 2010, the company completed the sale of John Deere Renewables LLC, its wind energy business, to Exelon Generation Company, LLC, a wholly-owned subsidiary of Exelon Corporation. Incorporated in Delaware in 1958.

Directors (In addition to indicated officers)

Crandall C. Bowles	Dipak C. Jain	Richard B. Myers	Aulana L. Peters
Dr. Vance D. Coffman	Clayton M. Jones	Thomas H. Patrick	David B. Speer
Charles O. Holliday, Jr.	Joachim Milberg		

Officers (Directors*)

*Samuel R. Allen, Chm. & C.E.O.
James M. Field, Sr. V.P. & C.F.O.
Jean Gilles, Sr. V.P.—Power Sys., WW
  Parts Svcs., Advan. Technology &
  Eng. & Gbl. Supply Mgt. & Logistics
James R. Jenkins, Sr. V.P. & Gen. Coun.
David C. Everitt, Pres.—A&T Div.–North
  Amer., Asia & Australia,Sub-Saharan
  & So. Africa & Gbl. Tractor & Turf Prods.

James A. Israel, Pres.—WW Fin. Svcs.
Michael J. Mack, Jr., Pres.—WW C&F Div.
Markwart von Pentz, Pres.—A&T Div.–Eur., CIS, No.
  Africa, Mid. East, Latin Amer. & Gbl. Harvesting,
  Crop Care, Hay & Forage Prods.

Consolidated Balance Sheet As of October 31, 2010 (000 omitted)

Assets		Liabilities & Stockholders' Equity	
Cash & cash equivalents	$ 3,790,600	Short-term borrowings	$ 7,534,500
Net trade accounts & notes receivable	3,464,200	Accounts payable & accrued expenses	6,481,700
Net financing receivables	17,682,200	Long-term borrowings	16,814,500
Net property & equipment	3,790,700	Other liabilities	6,132,700
Inventories	3,063,000	*Stockholders' equity	6,303,400
Other assets	11,476,100		
Total	$43,266,800	Total	$43,266,800

*422,180,389 actual shares common stock outstanding.

Consolidated Income Statement

Years Ended Oct. 31	Thousands — — — —		Per Share [a] — — — —		Common Stock Price Range Fiscal Year
	Total Revenues	Net Income	Diluted Earnings	Cash Dividends [b]	
2010	$26,004,600	$1,865,000	$4.35	$1.16	$77.25—46.30
2009	23,112,400	873,500 [c]	2.06 [c]	1.12	48.38—24.83
2008	28,437,600	2,052,800 [d]	4.70 [d]	1.06	94.69—29.89
2007	24,082,200	1,821,700	4.00	0.91	78.65—41.63
2006	22,147,800	1,693,800 [e]	3.59 [e]	0.78	90.47—56.99

[a] Adjusted to reflect the 2-for-1 stock split effective November 26, 2007.
[b] Dividends declared.
[c] Includes goodwill impairment charge of $274 million after-tax ($0.65 per share), voluntary employee separation expenses of $58 million after-tax ($0.13 per share), and special charges related to Welland, Ontario, Canada of $30 million after-tax ($0.07 per share).
[d] Includes special charges of $31 million after tax ($0.07 per share) related to closing a facility in Welland, Ontario, Canada.
[e] Includes a gain from the sale of discontinued health care operations of $223 million, net of tax ($0.47 per diluted share). Also includes special charges of $44 million, net of tax ($0.09 per diluted share) for a tender offer and repurchase of outstanding notes and $28 million, net of tax, ($0.06 per diluted share) related to the closing and restructuring of certain facilities.

Transfer Agent & Registrar: BNY Mellon Shareowner Services

General Counsel:	James R. Jenkins, Sr. V.P.	Traded (Symbol):	NYSE (DE)
Investor Relations:	Marie Z. Ziegler, V.P.	Stockholders:	27,458 (R)
Human Resources:	Mary K. W. Jones, V.P.	Employees:	55,700
Info. Tech.:	Barry W. Schaffter, V.P.	Annual Meeting:	In February
Auditors:	Deloitte & Touche LLP		

DeVry Inc.

3005 Highland Parkway, Downers Grove, Illinois 60515
Telephone: (630) 515-7700   www.devryinc.com

DeVry Inc.'s purpose is to empower its students to achieve their educational and career goals. DeVry is a global provider of educational services and the parent organization of Advanced Academics, Becker Professional Education, Carrington College, Carrington College California, Chamberlain College of Nursing, DeVry Brasil, DeVry University, and Ross University Schools of Medicine and Veterinary Medicine. These institutions offer a wide array of programs in business, healthcare, and technology, and serve students in secondary through postsecondary education, as well as accounting and finance professionals. Incorporated in Delaware in 1987.

Directors (In addition to indicated officers)

Harold T. Shapiro, Ph.D., Chm.
David S. Brown, Esq.
Gary Butler
Connie R. Curran, Ed.D.
Darren R. Huston
William T. Keevan

Lyle Logan
Julia A. McGee
Lisa W. Pickrum
Fernando Ruiz
Ronald L. Taylor

Officers (Directors*)

*Daniel M. Hamburger, Pres. & C.E.O.
Christopher Caywood, Pres.—Online Services
Gregory S. Davis, Sr. V.P., Gen. Coun. & Secy.
Eric Dirst, C.I.O.
Jeffrey Elliott, Pres.—Advanced Academics
Carlos Filgueiras, Pres., DeVry Brasil
Susan Groenwald, Pres.—Chamberlain College of Nursing
Richard M. Gunst, C.F.O. & Treas.
William Hughson, Pres.—Med. & Healthcare Grp.

Donna N. Jennings, Sr. V.P.—Hum. Res.
Robert Paul, Pres.—Carrington Colleges Group, Inc.
David J. Pauldine, Pres.—DeVry Univ.
Steven Riehs, Pres.—K through 12, Prof. & Int'l. Ed.
John P. Roselli, Pres.—Becker Prof. Educ.
Thomas C. Shepherd, DHA, FACHE, Pres.—Ross Univ.
Sharon Thomas-Parrott, Sr. V.P.—External Affs. & Chf. Compliance Off.

Consolidated Balance Sheet As of June 30, 2011 (000 omitted, preliminary, unaudited)

Assets		Liabilities & Stockholders' Equity	
Current assets	$ 624,650	Current liabilities	$ 316,431
Net property, plant & equipment	468,244	Other liabilities	137,801
Goodwill	523,620	Minority interest	6,755
Other assets	233,989	*Stockholders' equity	1,389,516
Total	$1,850,503	Total	$1,850,503

*63,487,000 shares common stock outstanding.

Consolidated Income Statement

Years Ended June 30	Thousands — — — —		Per Share — — — —		Common Stock Price Range Fiscal Year
	Total Revenues	Net Income	Diluted Earnings	Cash Dividends	
2011	$2,182,371	$330,403	$4.68	$0.24	$61.86—37.50
2010	1,915,181	279.909	3.87	0.20	74.36—44.07
2009	1,461,453	165,613	2.28	0.16	64.69—38.19
2008	1,091,833	125,532	1.73	0.12	61.57—31.70
2007	933,473	76,188	1.07	0.10	36.09—19.75

Transfer Agent & Registrar: Computershare Investor Services
General Counsel: Gregory S. Davis, Sr. V.P.   Traded (Symbol): NYSE, CSE (DV)
Investor Relations: Joan Bates, Sr. Dir.   Stockholders: 466 (R)
Human Resources: Donna Jennings, Sr. V.P.   Employees: 8,777
Info. Tech.: Eric Dirst, C.I.O.   Annual Meeting: In November
Auditors: PricewaterhouseCoopers LLP

Discover Financial Services

2500 Lake Cook Road, Riverwoods, Illinois 60015

Telephone: (224) 405-0900   **www.discoverfinancial.com**

Discover Financial Services is a leading credit card issuer and electronic payment services company. Business segments include U.S. card and third-party payments. The direct banking segment includes Discover branded credit cards issued to individuals and small businesses on the signature card network (the "Discover Network") and other consumer products and services, including personal loans, private student loans, prepaid cards, and deposit products offered through the company's subsidiary, Discover Bank. In 2010, Discover decided to sell its remaining federal student loans. The payment services segment includes: the PULSE Network, an ATM, debit, and electronic funds transfer network; Diners Club International, a global payments network; and a third-party issuing business, which includes credit, debit, and prepaid cards issued by third parties on the Discover Network. The company is now one of the largest issuers in the United States. In March 2008, the company sold Goldfish, its U.K. credit card business, to Barclays Bank PLC. In December 2010, Discover expanded its private student loan business by acquiring The Student Loan Corporation. In May 2011, the company reached an agreement to acquire Home Loan Center, a subsidiary of Tree.com, Inc., adding a residential mortgage component to its direct-to-consumer banking business. Incorporated in Delaware in 1986.

Directors (In addition to indicated officers)

Jeffrey S. Aronin
Mary K. Bush
Gregory C. Case
Robert M. Devlin
Cynthia A. Glassman, Ph.D.

Richard H. Lenny
Thomas G. Maheras
Michael H. Moskow
E. Follin Smith
Lawrence A. Weinbach

Officers (Directors*)

*David W. Nelms, Chm. & C.E.O.
Roger C. Hochschild, Pres. & C.O.O.
R. Mark Graf, Exec. V.P., C.F.O. & Chf. Acct. Off.
Kathryn McNamara Corley, Exec. V.P., Gen. Coun. & Secy.
Carlos Minetti, Exec. V.P. & Pres.—Cons. Banking & Oper.

Diane E. Offereins, Exec. V.P. & Pres.— Payment Svcs.
James V. Panzarino, Exec. V.P. & Chf. Credit Risk Off.
Harit Talwar, Exec. V.P. & Pres.—U.S. Cards
Glenn Schneider, Sr. V.P. & C.I.O.

Consolidated Balance Sheet   As of November 30, 2010 (000 omitted)

Assets		Liabilities & Stockholders' Equity	
Cash & equivalents	$ 5,098,733	Deposits	$34,413,383
Investment securities	5,075,395	Long-term borrowings	17,705,728
Net loan receivables	45,532,295	Other liabilities	2,209,011
Net premises & equipment	460,732	*Stockholders' equity	6,456,846
Other assets	4,617,813		
Total	$60,784,968	Total	$60,784,968

*544,681,764 shares common stock outstanding.

Consolidated Income Statement

Years Ended Nov. 30	Thousands — — — —		Per Share [a] — — — —		Common Stock Price Range Fiscal Year
	Total Income	Net Income [b]	Diluted Earnings	Cash Dividends	
2010	$8,241,217	$ 667,938	$1.22	$0.08	$19.16—12.11
2009	7,985,675 [c]	1,206,965	2.38	0.12	17.36— 4.73
2008	6,957,021 [c]	910,510	2.18	0.24	19.87— 6.59
2007	5,961,084	572,480 [d]	1.98	0.06	29.15—15.72
2006	5,577,856	1,076,616			

a Spinoff from Morgan Stanley occurred June 30, 2007. On July 2, 2007, Discover began trading as an independent public company.
b Allocated to common stockholders.
c Includes income related to the Visa and MasterCard antitrust litigation settlement of $1.9 billion pre-tax ($1.2 billion after-tax) in 2009 and $0.9 billion pre-tax ($0.5 billion after-tax) in 2008.
d Includes a $279 million after-tax non-cash impairment charge relating to the sale of the Goldfish business on March 31, 2008.

Transfer Agent & Registrar: BNY Mellon Shareowner Services

General Counsel:	Kathryn McNamara Corley	Traded (Symbol):	NYSE (DFS)
Investor Relations:	Craig Streem	Stockholders:	86,021 (R)
Human Resources:	Marcelo Modica	Employees:	10,300
Info.Tech.:	Glenn Schneider, Sr. V.P.	Annual Meeting:	In April
Auditors:	Deloitte & Touche LLP		

R.R. Donnelley & Sons Company

111 South Wacker Drive, Chicago, Illinois 60606-4301

Telephone: (312) 326-8000   www.rrdonnelley.com

R.R. Donnelley & Sons Company is a global provider of integrated communications. Founded more than 146 years ago, the company works collaboratively with more than 60,000 customers worldwide to develop custom communications solutions that reduce costs, enhance return on investment, and ensure compliance. Drawing on a range of proprietary and commercially available digital and conventional technologies deployed across four continents, R.R. Donnelley employs a suite of leading Internet-based capabilities and other resources to provide premedia, printing, logistics, and business process outsourcing products and services to leading clients in virtually every private and public sector. In January 2009, the company acquired PROSA, a Web printing company located in Santiago, Chile. In June 2009, R.R. Donnelley acquired Prospectus Central, LLC, an e-delivery company located in Fitzgerald, Georgia. In November 2010, the company completed its acquisition of Bowne & Co., Inc., a provider of shareholder and marketing communications services headquartered in New York. In December 2010, R.R. Donnelley acquired the assets of 8touches, an online provider of easy-to-use real estate marketing tools, and Nimblefish Technologies, a provider of multi-channel marketing services to retail, technology, telecommunications, hospitality, and other customers. Incorporated in Delaware in 1956.

Directors (In addition to indicated officers)

Stephen M. Wolf, Chm.   Susan M. Ivey   Michael T. Riordan
Lee A. Chaden   Thomas S. Johnson   Oliver R. Sockwell
Judith H. Hamilton   John C. Pope

Officers (Directors*)

*Thomas J. Quinlan, III, Pres. & C.E.O.   Daniel N. Leib, Exec. V.P. & C.F.O.
 Suzanne S. Bettman, Exec. V.P., Gen. Coun., Corp.   Andrew B. Coxhead, Sr. V.P., Chf. Acct. Off. & Cont.
   Secy. & Chf. Compliance Off.   John R. Paloian, C.O.O.
 Daniel L. Knotts, Exec. V.P. & Grp. Pres.

Consolidated Balance Sheet   As of December 31, 2010 (000 omitted)

Assets		Liabilities & Stockholders' Equity	
Current assets	$3,167,300	Current liabilities	$1,973,400
Net property, plant & equipment	2,138,700	Long-term debt	3,398,600
Goodwill	2,526,800	Deferred income taxes	174,500
Other assets	1,250,400	Other liabilities	1,291,300
		*Stockholders' equity	2,245,400
Total	$9,083,200	Total	$9,083,200

*206,600,000 shares common stock outstanding.

Consolidated Income Statement [a]

Years Ended Dec. 31	Thousands — — — — — Net Sales	Net Income	Per Share — — — — — Diluted Earnings	Cash Dividends	Common Stock Price Range Calendar Year
2010	$10,018,900	$ 221,700 [b]	$ 1.06	$1.04	$23.19—14.96
2009	9,857,400	(27,300) [c]	(0.13)	1.04	22.71— 5.58
2008	11,581,600	(189,900) [d]	(0.90)	1.04	38.19— 9.53
2007	11,587,100	(48,900) [e]	(0.22)	1.04	45.25—32.59
2006	9,316,600	400,600 [f]	1.83	1.04	36.00—28.50

[a] Reflects results of acquired businesses from the relevant acquisition dates.
[b] Includes pre-tax restructuring and impairment charges of $157,900,000, $13,500,000 of acquisition-related expenses, $8,900,000 pre-tax loss on the currency devaluation in Venezuela, including an increase in loss attributable to noncontrolling interests of $3,600,000, and a pre-tax $1,100,000 write-down of affordable housing investments.
[c] Includes pre-tax restructuring and impairment charges of $382,700,000, $15,600,000 of income tax expense, a $10,300,000 pre-tax loss on senior note repurchases, reclassification of a pre-tax loss of $2,700,000, a $2,400,000 write-down of affordable housing investments, and $1,600,000 of acquisition-related expenses.
[d] Includes pre-tax restructuring and impairment charges of $1,184,700, a $9,900,000 pre-tax loss associated with termination of cross-currency swaps, and tax benefits of $266,800,000.
[e] Includes pre-tax restructuring and impairment charges of $839,000,000 and a tax benefit of $9,300,000 from the reduction in net deferred tax liabilities due to a decrease in the statutory tax rate in the United Kingdom.
[f] Includes net restructuring and impairment charges of $206,100,000, a write-down of investments in affordable housing of $16,900,000, a gain on sale of investments of $7,000,000, and a tax benefit from the realization of a deferred tax asset of $23,500,000.

Transfer Agent & Registrar: Computershare Investor Services
General Counsel: Suzanne Bettman, Exec. V.P.   Traded (Symbol):   NYSE, CSE (RRD)
Investor Relations: Dave Gardella, V.P.   Stockholders: 8,613 (R)
Info. Tech.:   Kenneth E. O'Brien, C.I.O.   Employees: 58,700
Auditors: Deloitte & Touche LLP   Annual Meeting: In May

Dover Corporation

3005 Highland Parkway, Suite 200, Downers Grove, Illinois 60515
Telephone: (630) 541-1540   **www.dovercorporation.com**

Dover Corporation is a global manufacturer comprised of over 40 individual business providing innovative components and equipment, specialty systems, and support services for a variety of applications. The company operates in four business segments: Industrial Products, Engineered Systems, Fluid Management, and Electronic Technologies. In July 2011, the company completed its acquisition of the Sound Solutions business of NXP Semiconductors N.V. Incorporated in Delaware in 1947.

Directors (In addition to indicated officers)

Robert W. Cremin, Chm.
David H. Benson
Jean-Pierre M. Ergas
Peter T. Francis
Kristiane C. Graham
Richard K. Lochridge

Bernard G. Rethore
Michael B. Stubbs
Stephen M. Todd
Stephen K. Wagner
Mary A. Winston

Officers (Directors*)

*Robert A. Livingston, Pres. & C.E.O.
Brad M. Cerepak, Sr. V.P. & C.F.O.
Joseph W. Schmidt, Sr. V.P., Gen. Coun. & Secy.
Jay L. Kloosterboer, Sr. V.P.—Hum. Res.
James H. Moyle, Sr. V.P.—Supply Chain & Global Sourcing
Stephen R. Sellhausen, Sr. V.P.—Corp. Dev.
Thomas W. Giacomini, V.P.; Pres. & C.E.O.— Dover Indus. Prods.

Raymond C. Hoglund, V.P.; Pres. & C.E.O.— Dover Engineered Sys.
Raymond T. McKay, Jr., V.P. & Cont.
William W. Spurgeon, Jr., V.P.; Pres. & C.E.O.— Dover Fluid Mgt.
David R. Van Loan, V.P.; Pres. & C.E.O.—Dover Electronic Technologies
Michael Y. Zhang, V.P.; Pres.—Asia
Paul E. Goldberg, Treas. & Dir.—Inv. Rel.

Consolidated Balance Sheet As of December 31, 2010 (000 omitted)

Assets		Liabilities & Stockholders' Equity	
Current assets	$3,261,871	Current liabilities	$1,194,386
Net property, plant & equipment	847,189	Long-term debt	1,790,886
Goodwill	3,368,033	Other liabilities	1,051,060
Other assets	1,085,801	*Stockholders' equity	4,526,562
Total	$8,562,894	Total	$8,562,894

*186,545,088 shares common stock outstanding as of February 2, 2011.

Consolidated Income Statement [a]

Years Ended Dec. 31	Thousands — — — — —		Per Share — — — — —		Common Stock Price Range Calendar Year
	Revenues	Net Income [b]	Diluted Earnings [b]	Cash Dividends	
2010	$7,132,648	$700,104	$3.70	$1.07	$59.20—40.50
2009	5,775,689	356,438	1.91	1.02	43.10—21.79
2008	7,568,888	590,831	3.12	0.90	54.57—40.50
2007	7,317,270	661,080	3.26	0.77	54.59—44.34
2006	6,419,528	561,782	2.73	0.71	51.92—40.30

[a] Reflects continuing operations, unless otherwise noted. All periods reflect the impact of certain operations that were discontinued. As a result, the data will not necessarily agree to previously issued financial statements.
[b] Includes losses from discontinued operations of $7,804,000 ($0.04 per diluted share) in 2010; $15,456,000 ($0.08 per diluted share) in 2009; $103,927,000 ($0.55 per diluted share) in 2008; $8,670,000 ($0.04 per diluted share) in 2007; and $33,898,000 ($0.16 per diluted share) in 2006.

Transfer Agent & Registrar: BNY Mellon Shareowner Services
General Counsel: Joseph W. Schmidt, Sr. V.P.
Investor Relations: Paul Goldberg, Treas.
Human Resources: Jay L. Kloosterboer, V.P.
Auditors: PricewaterhouseCoopers LLP

Traded (Symbol): NYSE (DOV)
Stockholders: 17,211 (R)
Employees: 32,000
Annual Meeting: In May

Echo Global Logistics, Inc.

600 West Chicago Avenue, Suite 725, Chicago, Illinois 60654
Telephone: (800) 354-7993   **www.echo.com**

Echo Global Logistics, Inc. is a leading provider of technology-enabled transportation and supply chain management services, delivered on a proprietary technology platform, serving the transportation and logistics needs of its clients. The company's web-based technology platform compiles and analyzes data from its network of over 24,000 transportation providers to serve its clients' shipping and freight management needs in industries such as manufacturing, construction, consumer products, and retail. In July 2011, the company acquired substantially all of the assets of Advantage Transport, Inc., a truckload transportation brokerage firm based in Phoenix, Arizona. In October 2009, Echo Global Logistics completed the initial public offering of its common stock. Incorporated in Delaware in 2006.

Directors (In addition to indicated officers)

Samuel K. Skinner, Chm.	Bradley A. Keywell
Peter J. Barris	Eric P. Lefkofsky
Anthony R. Bobulinski	John F. Sandner
Matthew Ferguson	John R. Walter

Officers (Directors*)

*Douglas R. Waggoner, C.E.O.	Scott Boyer, Sr. V.P.—Sales
David B. Menzel, C.F.O.	Michael Mobley, Sr. V.P.—Oper.
David C. Rowe, Chf. Technology Off.	Marty Sinicrope, Sr. V.P.—Station Sales

Consolidated Balance Sheet   As of December 31, 2010 (000 omitted)

Assets		Liabilities & Stockholders' Equity	
Current assets	$111,995	Current liabilities	$ 48,404
Net property & equipment	9,639	Deferred income taxes	946
Goodwill	32,597	Other liabilities	7,220
Other assets	7,317	*Stockholders' equity	104,978
Total	$161,548	Total	$161,548

*22,043,850 shares common stock outstanding.

Consolidated Income Statement

Years Ended Dec. 31	Thousands — — — — —		Per Share — — — — —		Common Stock Price Range [b] Calendar Year
	Revenues	Net Income [a]	Diluted Earnings [a]	Cash Dividends	
2010	$426,374	$8,405	$ 0.38	$0.00	$15.18—12.05
2009	259,561	4,389	0.29	0.00	16.09— 9.85
2008	202,807	1,821	0.14		
2007	95,461	(1)	0.00		
2006	33,195	(995) [c]	(0.09)		

[a] Applicable to common stockholders.
[b] Began trading on October 2, 2009.
[c] Includes loss from discontinued operations of $214,000.

Transfer Agent & Registrar: American Stock Transfer & Trust Co.			
General Counsel: Winston & Strawn, LLP		**Traded (Symbol):**	NASDAQ (ECHO)
Investor Relations: Heather Mills		**Stockholders:**	19 (R)
Auditors:	Ernst & Young LLP	**Employees:**	709
		Annual Meeting:	In June

Envestnet, Inc.

35 East Wacker Drive, Suite 2400, Chicago, Illinois 60601

Telephone: (312) 827-2800   www.envestnet.com

Envestnet, Inc. is a leading independent provider of technology-enabled, Web-based investment solutions and services to financial advisors. By integrating a wide range of investment solutions and services, its technology platform provides financial advisors with the flexibility to address their clients' needs. The company works with independent financial advisors, as well as those who are associated with small or mid-sized financial advisory firms and larger financial institutions. Envestnet focuses its technology development efforts and its sales and marketing approach on addressing financial advisors' front-, middle-, and back-office needs. The company's portfolio consulting group, Portfolio Management Consultants (PMC) offers a comprehensive suite of integrated investment solutions. Envestnet maintains offices in Boston, Charlotte, Chicago, Denver, New York, Silicon Valley, and Trivandrum, India. Founded in 1999; incorporated in Delaware in 2004.

Directors (In addition to indicated officers)

Ross Chapin   Paul Koontz
Gates Hawn   Yves Sisteron
James Johnson

Officers (Directors*)

*Judson Bergman, Chm. & C.E.O.   Babu Sivadasan, Exec. V.P.—Eng.
William Crager, Pres.   Michael Apker, Managing Dir.—Strat. Dev.
Peter D'Arrigo, C.F.O.   Michael Henkel, Managing Dir.—Portfolio
Scott Grinis, Chf. Technology Off.   Mgt. Consultants
Shelly O'Brien, Gen. Coun. & Secy.   James Patrick, Managing Dir.—Advisor
Charles Tennant, C.O.O.   Managed Programs
Brandon Thomas, Chf. Invest. Off.   Christopher Curtis, Sr. V.P. & Treas.
Lori Hardwick, Exec. V.P.—Advisory Svcs. Eric Fowler, Sr. VP. & Dir.—Prod. Dev.
James Lumberg, Exec. V.P.—Bus. Dev.   Dale Seier, Sr. V.P.—Fin.
Karen McCue, Exec. V.P.—Family Office Svcs. William Rubino, Jr., Chf. Admin. Off.—PMC
Viggy Mokkarala, Exec. V.P.—
   Client Implementations

Consolidated Balance Sheet As of December 31, 2010 (000 omitted)

Assets		Liabilities & Stockholders' Equity	
Current assets	$ 78,936	Current liabilities	$ 15,957
Net property, plant & equipment	9,713	Customer Inducements Payable	18,806
Other assets	53,219	Other liabilities	4,786
		*Stockholders' equity	102,319
Total	$141,868	Total	$ 141,868

*31,368,822 shares common stock outstanding.

Consolidated Income Statement

Years Ended Dec. 31	Thousands — — — — —		Per Share — — — — —		Common Stock Price Range [a] Calendar Year
	Total Revenues	Net Income	Diluted Earnings	Cash Dividends	
2010	$98,052	$(1,048)	$(0.05)	$0.00	$17.09—9.90
2009	77,924	(1,592)[b]	(0.12)[c]		
2008	91,842	2,646	0.19		
2007	81,469	12,058	0.91		
2006	59,051	1,760	0.16		

[a] Initial public offering July 28, 2010 at $9.00 per share.
[b] Includes $986,000 of bad debt and legal expenses.
[c] Pro forma, unaudited.

Transfer Agent & Registrar: American Stock Transfer & Trust Co.

General Counsel: Shelly O'Brien   Traded (Symbol): NYSE (ENV)
Investor Relations: Peter D'Arrigo   Stockholders: 140 (R)
Human Resources: Charles Tennant, C.O.O.   Employees: 457
Info. Tech.: Scott Grinis   Annual Meeting: In Mayf
Auditors: McGladrey & Pullen, LLP

Equity Lifestyle Properties, Inc.

Two North Riverside Plaza, Suite 800, Chicago, Illinois 60606
Telephone: (312) 279-1400   www.equitylifestyle.com

Equity Lifestyle Properties, Inc.s a real estate investment trust (REIT) that owns and operates high-quality manufactured housing communities and recreational vehicle resorts throughout the United States and British Columbia, Canada. As of December 31, 2010, the REIT owned or had an ownership interest in 307 properties containing 111,002 residential sites in 27 states and British Columbia. Properties are designed for and marketed to retirees, empty-nesters, vacationers, and second-home owners; or families and first-time homeowners. The company leases individual developed areas with access to utilities for placement of factory built homes, cottages, cabins, or recreational vehicles. Customers may lease individual sites or enter into right-to-use contracts providing the customer access to specific properties for limited stays. The resorts' residents are those seeking a second home or vacation home, as well as those looking for a long-term or full-season recreational vehicle site. Incorporated in Maryland in 1992; present name adopted in 2004.

Directors (In addition to indicated officers)

Philip C. Calian
David J. Contis
Thomas E. Dobrowski

Sheli Z. Rosenberg
Gary L. Waterman

Officers (Directors*)

*Samuel Zell, Chm.
*Howard Walker, V. Chm.
*Thomas P. Heneghan, Pres. & C.E.O.
 Michael B. Berman, Exec. V.P. & C.F.O.

Ellen Kelleher, Exec. V.P.—Property Mgt.
Roger A. Maynard, Exec. V.P.—Asset Mgt.
Marguerite Nader, Exec. V.P.—Sales & Mktg.

Consolidated Balance Sheet   As of December 31, 2010 (000 omitted)

Assets		Liabilities & Stockholders' Equity	
Net real estate investment	$1,884,322	Total liabilities	$1,588,237
Inventory	3,177	Minority interests	233,128
Other assets	160,896	*Stockholders' equity	227,030
Total	$2,048,395	Total	$2,048,395

*30,972353 shares common stock outstanding.

Consolidated Income Statement

Years Ended Dec. 31	Thousands — — — — —		Per Share — — — —		Common Stock Price Range Calendar Year
	Total Revenues	Net Income [a]	Diluted Earnings	Cash Dividends	
2010	$511,361	$38,354	$1.25	$1.20	$59.51—46.01
2009	503,221	34,005	1.22	1.10	51.18—28.34
2008	463,586	18,303	0.75	0.80	56.00—22.64
2007	437,659	32,102	1.31	0.60	59.67—43.72
2006	434,863	16,632	0.69	0.30	56.00—40.91

[a] Funds from operations (FFO), in thousands: 2010: $123,162; 2009: $118,082; 2008: $97,615; 2007: $92,752; and 2006: $82,367.

Transfer Agent & Registrar: American Stock Transfer & Trust Co.
Investor Relations: Michael Berman, Exec. V.P.   Traded (Symbol):   NYSE (ELS)
Auditors: Ernst & Young LLP   Stockholders: 9.116 (B)
                                Employees: 3,744
                                Annual Meeting: In May

Equity Residential

Two North Riverside Plaza, Suite 400, Chicago, Illinois 60606

Telephone: (312) 474-1300   **www.equityresidential.com**

Equity Residential is a real estate investment trust (REIT) which is engaged in the acquisition, development, and management of multifamily properties. It is the nation's largest publicly traded REIT owner and operator of multifamily properties. As of December 31, 2010, Equity Residential had a portfolio consisting of 451 multifamily properties containing 129,604 apartment units in 17 states and the District of Columbia. Incorporated in Maryland in 1993.

Trustees (In addition to indicated officers)

Gerald A. Spector, V. Chm.
Charles L. Atwood, Lead Director
John W. Alexander
Linda Walker Bynoe

Bradley A. Keywell
John E. Neal
Mark S. Shapiro
B. Joseph White

Officers (Trustees*)

*Samuel Zell, Chm.
*David J. Neithercut, Pres. & C.E.O.
Alan W. George, Exec. V.P. & Chf. Invest. Off.
Mark J. Parrell, Exec. V.P. & C.F.O.
John Powers, Exec. V.P.—Hum. Res.
David Santee, Exec. V.P.—Oper.

Bruce C. Strohm, Exec. V.P., Gen. Coun., &
  Corp. Secy.
Mark N. Tennison, Exec. V.P.—Dev.
Frederick C. Tuomi, Exec. V.P. & Pres.—Property
  Mgt.
Ian S. Kaufman, Sr. V.P. & Chf. Acct. Off.

Consolidated Balance Sheet As of December 31, 2010 (000 omitted)

Assets		Liabilities & Stockholders' Equity	
Net real estate investment	$15,365,014	Total liabilities	$10,592,078
Other assets	822,180	Minority interests	383,540
		*Stockholders' equity	5,090,186
		Noncontrolling interests	118,390
Total	$16,184,194	Total	$16,184.194

*290,197,242 shares common stock outstanding.

Consolidated Income Statement

Years Ended Dec. 31	Thousands — — — —		Per Share — — — —		Common Stock Price Range Calendar Year
	Total Revenues[a]	Net Income[b]	Diluted Earnings[bc]	Cash Dividends	
2010	$1,966,849	$ 269,242	$0.95	$1.47	$52.64—31.40
2009	1,828,199	374,794	1.27	1.64	36.38—15.68
2008	1,858,118	393,115	1.46	1.93	49.00—21.27
2007	1,711,929	951,242	3.40	1.87	56.46—33.79
2006	1,477,054	1,028,381	3.55	1.79	61.50—38.84

[a] From continuing operations.
[b] Funds from operations (FFO), available to common shares, in thousands: 2010: $622,786; 2009: $615,505; 2008: $618,372; 2007: $713,412; 2006: and $712,524s. Effective January 1, 2009, companies are required to retrospectively expense certain implied costs of the option value related to convertible debt. As a result, net income, net income available to common shares, and FFO have all been reduced by approximately $10.6 million, $13.3 million, $10.1 million, and $3.6 million for the years ended December 31, 2009, 2008, 2007, and 2006 respectively.
[c] Available to common shares.

Transfer Agent & Registrar: Computershare Investor Services

General Counsel:	Bruce C. Strohm, Exec. V.P.	**Traded (Symbol):**	NYSE (EQR)
Investor Relations:	Marty McKenna	**Stockholders:**	3,000 (R)
Human Resources:	John Powers, Exec. V.P.	**Employees:**	4,000
Info. Tech.:	Jay Kurtzman, Sr. V.P.	**Annual Meeting:**	In June
Auditors:	Ernst & Young LLP		

Exelon Corporation

10 South Dearborn Street, Chicago, Illinois 60603

Telephone: (312) 394-7398   **www.exeloncorp.com**

Exelon Corporation is a public utility holding company. It is one of the nation's largest electric utilities with approximately 5.4 million customers. The company has one of the industry's largest portfolios of electricity generation capacity, as well as a nationwide reach and strong positions in the Midwest and Mid-Atlantic. Exelon distributes electricity to approximately 5.4 million customers in Illinois and Pennsylvania and natural gas to 490,000 customers in the Philadelphia area. Subsidiaries include Exelon Generation Co., Commonwealth Edison Co., and PECO Energy Co. In December 2010, the company acquired John Deere Renewables, a leading operator and developer of wind power. In April 2011, Exelon announced a merger agreement with Baltimore-based Constellation Energy, a leading competitive supplier of power, natural gas, and energy products and services for homes and businesses across the continental United States. The resulting company will retain the Exelon name and be headquartered in Chicago. Exelon's power marketing business (Power Team) and Constellation's retail and wholesale business will be consolidated under the Constellation brand and be headquartered in Baltimore, along with the renewable energy business. The merger is expected to close in the first quarter of 2012, pending shareholder and regulatory approval. Incorporated in Pennsylvania in 1999.

Directors (In addition to indicated officers)

John A. Canning, Jr.	Rosemarie B. Greco	Thomas J. Ridge
M. Walter D'Alessio	Paul L. Joskow, Ph.D.	John W. Rogers, Jr.
Nicholas DeBenedictis	Ret. Admiral Richard W. Mies	Stephen D. Steinour
Judge Nelson A. Diaz	John M. Palms, Ph.D.	Donald Thompson
Sue L. Gin	William C. Richardson, Ph.D.	

Officers (Directors*)

*John W. Rowe, Chm. & C.E.O.
Christopher M. Crane, Pres. & C.O.O.; Pres.—Exelon Generation
Ruth Ann M. Gillis, Exec. V.P. & Chf. Admin. & Diversity Off.; Pres.—Bus. Svcs. Co.
Denis P. O'Brien, Exec. V.P.; Pres. & C.E.O.—PECO
William A. Von Hoene, Jr., Exec. V.P.—Fin. & Legal
Darryl M. Bradford, Sr. V.P. & Gen. Coun.
Kenneth W. Cornew, Sr. V.P. & Pres.—Power Team

Joseph Dominguez, Sr. V.P.—Federal Reg. Affs. & Pub. Policy
Matthew F. Hilzinger, Sr. V.P., C.F.O. & Treas.
Bruce G. Wilson, Sr. V.P.—Corp. Governance, Corp. Secy. & Dep. Gen. Coun.
Duane M. DesParte, V.P. & Corp. Cont.
Charles Pardee, C.O.O.—Exelon Generation
Frank M. Clark, Chm. & C.E.O.—ComEd
Anne R. Pramaggiore, Pres. & C.O.O.—ComEd

Consolidated Balance Sheet As of December 31, 2010 (000 omitted)

Assets		Liabilities & Stockholders' Equity	
Current assets	$ 6,398,000	Current liabilities	$ 4,240,000
Net utility, plant & equipment	29,941,000	Long-term debt	12,004,000
Other assets	15,901,000	Other liabilities	22,346,000
		Preferred securities of subsids.	87,000
		Noncontrolling interest	3,000
		*Stockholders' equity	13,560,000
Total	$52,240,000	Total	$52,240,000

*662,845,411 shares common stock outstanding.

Consolidated Income Statement

Years Ended Dec. 31	Thousands — — — — —		Per Share a — — — — —		Common Stock Price Range Calendar Year
	Operating Revenues	Net Income a	Diluted Earnings	Cash Dividends b	
2010	$18,644,000	$2,563,000	$3.87	$2.10	$49.88—37.24
2009	17,318,000	2,707,000	4.09	2.10	58.98—38.41
2008	18,859,000	2,737,000	4.13	2.03	92.13—41.23
2007	18,916,000	2,736,000	4.05	1.76	86.83—58.74
2006	15,655,000	1,592,000 c	2.35 c	1.60	63.62—51.13

a Available for common stock, as reported.
b Declared.
c Includes a goodwill impairment charge of $776.0 million ($1.15 per diluted share).

Transfer Agent & Registrar: Wells Fargo Shareowner Services

General Counsel:	Darryl M. Bradford, Sr. V.P.	Traded (Symbol):	NYSE, CSE, PHSE (EXC)
Investor Relations:	Stacie M. Frank, V.P.	Stockholders:	130,726 (R)
Human Resources:	John R. Samolis, Sr. V.P.	Employees:	19,214
Info. Tech.:	Daniel C. Hill, Sr. V.P. & C.I.O.	Annual Meeting:	In May
Auditors:	PricewaterhouseCoopers LLP		

Federal Signal Corporation

1415 West 22nd Street, Oak Brook, Illinois 60523-2004

Telephone: (630) 954-2000   www.federalsignal.com

Federal Signal Corporation manufactures and supplies products in the following groups: Safety and Security Systems, Fire Rescue, Federal Signal Technologies, and Environmental Solutions. The Safety and Security Systems Group designs, manufactures, and deploys comprehensive safety and security systems and products that help law enforcement, fire/rescue, and EMS, emergency operations, campuses, and industrial plant/facility first responders protect people and property. Products include lightbars and sirens, public warning sirens, and public safety software. The Fire Rescue Group designs and manufactures sophisticated, vehicle-mounted, aerial platforms for fire fighting, rescue, electric utility, and industrial uses. The Federal Signal Technologies Group provides technologies and solutions to the intelligent transportation systems (ITS) and public safety markets, including tools needed to automate data collection and analysis, transaction processing, and asset tracking. The Environmental Solutions Group manufactures and markets worldwide a full range of street cleaning and vacuum loader vehicles and high-performance water blasting equipment. Major subsidiaries include: Bronto Skylift; Elgin Sweeper Company; Federal APD; Jetstream of Houston; and Vactor Manufacturing, Inc. Federal Signal has 20 manufacturing facilities in 6 countries, serving customers in 100 countries. Federal Signal's China Wholly Owned Foreign Entity business was reclassified as discontinued operations in 2010, and its Pauluhn and Ravo businesses were reclassified as discontinued operations and sold in 2009. Incorporated in Illinois in 1901; reincorporated in Delaware in 1969.

Directors (In addition to indicated officers)

Charles R. Campbell
James E. Goodwin
Paul W. Jones
Richard R. Mudge

William F. Owens
Brenda L. Reichelderfer
Dominic A. Romeo
Joseph R. Wright, Jr.

Officers (Directors*)

*Dennis J. Martin, Pres. & C.E.O.
William G. Barker, III, Sr. V.P. & C.F.O.
Jennifer L. Sherman, Sr. V.P., Chf. Admin. Off.,
  Gen. Coun. & Secy.
Charles F. Avery, Jr., V.P.—Info. Tech. & Cont.
John A. DeLeonardis, V.P.—Taxes

Esa Peltola, Pres.—Bronto Skylift
Manfred A. Rietsch, Pres.—Federal Signal
  Technologies Grp.
Mark D. Weber, Pres.—Envir. Solutions Grp.
Bryan L. Boettger, Pres.—Pub. Safety Sys. Div.
Joseph W. Wilson, Pres.—Industrial Sys. Div.

Consolidated Balance Sheet As of December 31, 2010 (000 omitted)

Assets		Liabilities & Stockholders' Equity	
Current assets	$300,000	Current liabilities	$214,600
Intangible assets, net	84,400	Long-term pension liabilities	41,300
Net property, plant & equipment	63,200	Long-term borrowings	184,400
Goodwill	310,400	Liabilities of discontinued operations	18,200
Assets of discontinued operations	3,100	Other liabilities	85,100
Other assets & intangibles	3,400	*Stockholders' equity	220,900
Total	$764,500	Total	$764,500

*62,100,000 shares common stock outstanding.

Consolidated Income Statement

Years Ended Dec. 31	Thousands — — — — —		Per Share — — — — —		Common Stock Price Range Calendar Year
	Net Sales[a]	Net Income[a]	Diluted Earnings[a]	Cash Dividends	
2010	$726,500	$(160,700)	$(2.79)	$0.24	$10.30— 4.91
2009	750,400	19,800	0.41	0.24	9.30— 3.73
2008	878,000	28,700	0.61	0.24	17.50— 5.10
2007	854,500	35,300	0.74	0.24	17.00—10.82
2006	720,800	26,800	0.56	0.24	19.75—12.69

[a] Continuing operations only; prior year amounts have been reclassified for discontinued operations.

Transfer Agent & Registrar: Computershare Investor Services

General Counsel:	Jennifer L. Sherman, Sr. V.P.	Traded (Symbol):	NYSE (FSS)
Investor Relations:	William G. Barker, III, Sr. V.P.	Stockholders:	2,431 (R)
Info. Tech.:	Charles F. Avery, Jr., V.P.	Employees:	2,800
Auditors:	Ernst & Young LLP	Annual Meeting:	In April

The Female Health Company

515 North State Street, Suite 2225, Chicago, Illinois 60654

Telephone: (312) 595-9123   **www.femalehealth.com**

The Female Health Company manufactures, markets, and sells the FC2 female condom, the only currently available FDA-approved product under a woman's control that can prevent unintended pregnancy and sexually transmitted diseases. The product is sold through private and public sector agencies in approximately 105 countries and commercially marketed directly to consumers in 12 countries including the United States, Brazil, France, India, and Spain. In October 2009, the company completed the transition from its first generation product, FC1, to its second generation product, FC2. As of September 30, 2010, more than 80 million FC2 female condoms have been distributed in 114 countries. Incorporated in Wisconsin in 1971.

Directors (In addition to indicated officers)

David R. Bethune
Stephen M. Dearholt
Mary Margaret Frank, Ph.D.

Michael R. Walton
Richard E. Wenninger

Officers (Directors*)

*O.B. Parrish, Chm., Acting Pres. & C.E.O.
*Mary Ann Leeper, Ph.D., Sr. Strat. Adviser
*William R. Gargiulo, Jr., Secy.
 Donna Felch, V.P. & C.F.O.

Michael Pope, V.P. & Gen. Mgr.—The Female
  Health Co. (U.K.) Plc
Janet Lee, Cont.

Consolidated Balance Sheet As of September 30, 2010 (000 omitted)

Assets		Liabilities & Stockholders' Equity	
Current assets	$11,791	Current liabilities	$ 1,938
Net property & equipment	2,398	Other liabilities	298
Other assets	4,179	*Stockholders' equity	16,132
Total	$18,368	Total	$18,368

*27,458,424 shares common stock outstanding.

Consolidated Income Statement

Years Ended Sept. 30	Thousands — — — —		Per Share — — — —		Common Stock Price Range [a] Fiscal Year
	Net Revenues	Net Income	Diluted Earnings	Cash Dividends	
2010	$22,222	$6,737	$0.24	$0.15	$7.38—4.42
2009	27,543	6,535	0.24	0.00	7.65—1.95
2008	25,634	4,967	0.18	0.00	3.60—2.15
2007	19,320	1,694	0.06	0.00	2.95—1.20
2006	14,824	282	0.01	0.00	1.80—1.19

[a] In June 2009, the company transferred the listing of its common stock from the NYSE Amex to the NASDAQ Capital Market, and the company's common stock began trading on the NASDAQ Capital Market on June 9, 2009.

Transfer Agent & Registrar: Computershare Investor Services

General Counsel:	Reinhart Boerner Van Deuren s.c.	Traded (Symbol):	NASDAQ (FHCO)
		Stockholders:	337 (R)
Investor Relations:	Donna Felch, V.P.	Employees:	48
Auditors:	McGladrey & Pullen, LLP	Annual Meeting:	In March

First Bankers Trustshares, Inc.

1201 Broadway, P.O. Box 3566, Quincy, Illinois 62305-3566

Telephone: (217) 228-8000   **www.firstbankers.com**

First Bankers Trustshares, Inc. is the holding company for First Bankers Trust Company, N.A., and First Bankers Trust Services, Inc. and traces its origins back to 1946. First Bankers Trustshares, Inc. is a community-oriented financial institution providing comprehensive financial products and banking services to retail, institutional, and corporate customers. It operates 11 banking facilities in west central Illinois, serving the communities of Carthage, Macomb, Mendon, Paloma, Quincy, Rushville, and Springfield. First Bankers Trust Services, Inc. offers personal wealth management services, IRAs, HSAs, and employee benefit trust administration services. It operates facilities in Quincy, Macomb, Springfield, and Chicago, Illinois, as well as in Philadelphia, Pennsylvania, and Phoenix, Arizona. Incorporated in Delaware in 1988.

Directors (In addition to indicated officers)

Donald K. Gnuse, Chm.
Carl Adams, Jr.
William D. Daniels

Mark E. Freiburg
Phyllis J. Hofmeister
Dennis R. Williams

Officers (Directors*)

*Arthur E. Greenbank, Pres. & C.E.O.
Brian E. Ippensen, Treas.

*Steven E. Siebers, Secy.

Consolidated Balance Sheet   As of December 31, 2010 (000 omitted)

Assets		Liabilities & Stockholders' Equity	
Cash & due from banks	$ 35,044	Total deposits	$570,436
Investment securities	278,729	Short-term borrowings	37,604
Net loans	332,538	FHLB advances	5,500
Other assets	44,333	Other liabilities	20,522
		*Stockholders' equity	56,582
Total	$690,644	Total	$690,644

*2,051,476 shares common stock outstanding.

Consolidated Income Statement

Years Ended Dec. 31	Thousands — — — —		Per Share — — — —		Common Stock Price Range Calendar Year
	Total Income	Net Income	Basic Earnings	Cash Dividends [a]	
2010	$37,094	$6,440	$2.83	$0.46	$22.01—16.10
2009	35,246	5,885	2.57	0.46	18.25—12.00
2008	33,546	4,729	2.31	0.46	21.75—15.60
2007	34,327	4,243	2.07	0.42	20.00—18.00
2006	31,595	3,763	1.84	0.38	23.25—18.05

[a] Dividends paid.

Transfer Agent & Registrar: Illinois Stock Transfer Company

General Counsel:	Hunton & Williams, LLP	Traded (Symbol):	OTC PS (FBTT)
Investor Relations:	Brian Ippensen, Treas.	Stockholders:	350 (R)
Human Resources:	Kathleen McNay	Employees:	165
Info. Tech.:	David Young	Annual Meeting:	In May
Auditors:	McGladrey & Pullen, LLP		

First Busey Corporation

100 West University Avenue, Champaign, Illinois 61820

Telephone: (217) 365-4500   **www.busey.com**

First Busey Corporation is a financial holding company headquartered in Champaign, Illinois. The company has one wholly-owned bank subsidiary, Busey Bank, which has locations in three states. Busey Bank is headquartered in Champaign, Illinois and has 30 full service banking centers and 4 teller service branches serving downstate Illinois, providing a wide variety of services to individual, business, institutional, and governmental customers. Busey Bank also has a commercial service branch in Indianapolis and 7 banking centers serving southwest Florida. Busey Wealth Management, a wholly owned subsidiary of First Busey Corporation, provides a full range of trust, investment management, brokerage, and insurance services. At December 31, 2010, Busey Wealth Management had approximately $3.5 billion of assets under management. FirsTech, Inc., a wholly owned non-banking subsidiary, with offices in Decatur, Illinois and Clayton, Missouri, offers retail payment processing services. FirsTech processes more than 28 million transactions per year through online bill payments, lockbox processing, and walk-in payments through its 3,100 agent locations in 38 states. Incorporated in Delaware in 1978; reincorporated in Nevada in 1993.

Directors (In addition to indicated officers)

Gregory B. Lykins, Chm.
Joseph M. Ambrose
David J. Downey
E. Phillips Knox

V.B. Leister, Jr.
August C. Meyer, Jr.
George T. Shapland
Thomas G. Sloan

Officers (Directors*)

*Van A. Dukeman, Pres. & C.E.O.
Barbara J. Harrington, Exec. V.P. & Chf. Risk Off.
Leanne C. Kopischke, Exec. V.P. & C.I.O.
Robert F. Plecki, Jr., Exec. V.P. & Chf. Credit Off.
David B. White, Exec. V.P. & C.F.O.

Christopher M. Shroyer, Exec. V.P.—Pres. & C.E.O., Busey Bank
Howard F. Mooney, II, Pres. & C.E.O.—FirsTech, Inc.
Donna R. Greene, Pres. & C.E.O.—Busey Wealth Mgt. & Busey Trust

Consolidated Balance Sheet As of December 31, 2010 (000 omitted)

Assets		Liabilities & Stockholders' Equity	
Cash & due from banks	$ 418,965	Deposits	$2,916,366
Securities available for sale	599,459	Securities sold under repurchase	
Loans, net	2,243,055	agreements	138,982
Premises & equipment	73,218	Long-term debt	43,159
Value of bank-owned life ins.	37,425	Other liabilities	85,991
Deferred tax asset, net	64,240	*Stockholders' equity	420,505
Other assets	168,641		
Total	$3,605,003	Total	$3,605,003

*66,420,892 shares common stock outstanding.

Consolidated Income Statement

Years Ended Dec. 31	Thousands — — — — —		Per Share — — — — —		Common Stock Price Range Calendar Year
	Total Income	Net Income	Diluted Earnings	Cash Dividends	
2010	$218,936	$ 23,230	$0.27	$0.16	$ 5.56— 3.38
2009	250,524	(323,113)[a]	(7.85)[a]	0.40	18.29— 3.00
2008	276,904	(37,947)[a]	(1.06)[a]	0.80	22.49—11.07
2007	243,595	31,477	1.13	0.77	23.97—18.70
2006	174,827	28,888	1.35	0.64	23.87—19.78

[a] Includes goodwill impairment charge of $208,200,000 ($4.98 per diluted share) in 2009 and $22,600,000 ($0.63 per diluted share) in 2008.

Transfer Agent & Registrar: First Busey Corporation
Corporate Counsel: Chapman & Cutler
Investor Relations: David B. White, C.F.O.
Human Resources: Carol Slough
Info. Tech.: Leanne C. Kopischke, C.I.O.
Auditors: McGladrey & Pullen, LLP

Traded (Symbol): NASDAQ (BUSE)
Stockholders: 1,414 (R)
Employees: 866
Annual Meeting: In May

THE PRIVATEBANK GUIDE

First Clover Leaf Financial Corp.

6814 Goshen Road, Edwardsville, Illinois 62025

Telephone: (618) 656-6122   **www.firstcloverleafbank.com**

First Clover Leaf Financial Corp. is the result of a merger in 2006 between First Federal Savings and Loan Association of Edwardsville and The Cloverleaf Family Bank. The company is a full-service commercial bank that conducts business through its four branch offices located in Edwardsville and Wood River, Illinois. Principal business consists of attracting retail deposits and investing those in mortgage loans, commercial real estate loans, multifamily loans, construction and land loans, and investment securities. In October 2008, the company completed its acquisition of Partners Financial Holdings Inc., the holding company of Partners Bank. Federally incorporated in 2001.

Directors (In addition to indicated officers)

Joseph Helms, D.V.M., Chm.	Gerry Schuetzenhofer
Joseph J. Gugger	Joseph G. Stevens
Kenneth Highlander	Dennis E. Ulrich
Garry Niebur	Mary Westerhold

Officers (Directors*)

*Dennis M. Terry, Pres. & C.E.O.	Darlene F. McDonald, Sr. V.P. & C.F.O.
Brad. S. Rench, Exec. V.P. & C.O.O.	Lisa R. Fowler, Sr. V.P. & Chf. Lending Off.
Donald Engelke, Sr. V.P.	Donna Brandmeyer, Secy.
Chad Abernathy, Sr. V.P.—Retail Banking	

Consolidated Balance Sheet As of December 31, 2010 (000 omitted)

Assets		Liabilities & Stockholders' Equity	
Cash & cash equivalents	$ 66,253	Total deposits	$447,483
Securities	78,475	FHLB advances	21,924
Net property & equipment	10,562	Other liabilities	28,230
Net loans	387,568	*Stockholders' equity	77,333
Other assets	32,112		
Total	$574,970	Total	$574,970

*7,887,702 shares common stock outstanding.

Consolidated Income Statement

Years Ended Dec. 31	Thousands — — — —		Per Share [a] — — — —		Common Stock Price Range Calendar Year
	Total Income	Net Income	Diluted Earnings	Cash Dividends	
2010	$27,687	$ 3,806	$ 0.49	$0.24	$ 7.35— 5.20
2009	29,426	(8,823)	(1.08)	0.24	8.79— 6.48
2008 [b]	25,495	2,702	0.33	0.24	10.50— 6.40
2007	23,027	2,406	0.27	0.24	11.91—10.00
2006 [c]	14,167	1,837	0.23	0.24	20.60—10.26

[a] Per share amounts for periods prior to 2006 have been adjusted to reflect the 1.936-to-1 exchange ratio in connection with the company's second-step conversion completed in July 2006.
[b] Includes results of operations from Partners Financial Holdings, Inc. and its subsidiary, Partners Bank, after October 10, 2008.
[c] Includes results of operations from Clover Leaf Financial Corp. after July 10, 2006.

Transfer Agent & Registrar: Registrar and Transfer Company			
Corporate Counsel: Luse Gorman Pomerenk & Schick, P.C.		**Traded (Symbol):**	NASDAQ (FCLF)
		Stockholders:	750 (R)
Investor Relations: Dennis M. Terry, C.E.O.		**Employees:**	71
Auditors: McGladrey & Pullen, LLP		**Annual Meeting:**	In May

First Industrial Realty Trust, Inc.

311 South Wacker Drive, Suite 3900, Chicago, Illinois 60606

Telephone: (312) 344-4300   **www.firstindustrial.com**

First Industrial Realty Trust, Inc. is a real estate investment trust (REIT) that owns, manages, acquires, sells, develops, and redevelops diversified industrial real estate in 28 states and one Canadian province. With approximately 68.6 million square feet of industrial space as of December 31, 2010, its portfolio consists of 365 light industrial properties, 173 bulk warehouse properties, 129 R&D/flex properties, 88 regional warehouse properties, and 19 manufacturing properties. Incorporated in Maryland in 1993.

Directors (In addition to indicated officers)

W. Ed Tyler, Chm.
Matthew S. Dominski
H. Patrick Hackett, Jr.
Kevin W. Lynch

John Rau
L. Peter Sharpe
Robert J. Slater

Officers (Directors*)

*Bruce W. Duncan, Pres. & C.E.O.
David G. Harker, Exec. V.P.—Central Region
Peter O. Schultz, Exec. V.P.—East Region
Johannson L. Yap, Exec. V.P.—West Region
   & Chf. Invest. Off.
Scott A. Musil, Sr. V.P. & C.F.O.
Christopher M. Schneider, Sr. V.P.—Oper.
   & C.I.O.

Robert Walter, Sr. V.P.—Capital Markets
John H. Clayton, V.P.—Corp. Legal & Secy.
Donald Stoffle, Exec. Dir.—Dispositions
Arthur J. Harmon, Dir.—Inv. Rel. & Corp.
   Commun.

Consolidated Balance Sheet   As of December 31, 2010 (000 omitted)

Assets		Liabilities & Stockholders' Equity	
Current assets	$ 421,435	Total liabilities	$1,857,910
Net investment in real estate	2,109,133	Minority interest	45,266
Deferred leasing intangibles	39,718	*Stockholders' equity	846,878
Other assets	179,768		
Total	$2,750,054	Total	$2,750,054

*68,841,296 shares common stock outstanding.

Consolidated Income Statement [a]

Years Ended Dec. 31	Thousands — — — — —		Per Share — — — —		Common Stock Price Range Calendar Year
	Total Revenues	Net Income [b]	Diluted Earnings [b]	Cash Dividends	
2010	$288,541	$(222,498)	$(3.53)	$0.00	$ 9.01— 3.76
2009	351,838	(13,783)	(0.28)	0.00	7.42— 1.91
2008	443,751	20,169	0.41	2.41	36.54— 5.10
2007	303,588	130,368	2.90	2.85	49.51—34.60
2006	238,635	89,651	1.99	2.81	50.52—36.50

[a] Includes results of operations of the company as derived from its audited financial statements, adjusted for discontinued operations.
[b] Available to common stockholders and participating securities.

Transfer Agent & Registrar: Computershare Investor Services
General Counsel: John Clayton, V.P.   Traded (Symbol):   NYSE (FR)
Investor Relations: Art Harmon, Dir.   Stockholders: 611 (R)
Human Resources: John Potempa   Employees: 183
Info. Tech.:   Christopher M. Schneider, C.I.O.   Annual Meeting: In May
Auditors: PricewaterhouseCoopers LLP

First Midwest Bancorp, Inc.

One Pierce Place, Suite 1500, Itasca, Illinois 60143

Telephone: (630) 875-7450   www.firstmidwest.com

First Midwest is the premier relationship-based banking franchise in the growing Chicagoland banking market. As one of the Chicago metropolitan area's largest independent bank holding companies, First Midwest provides the full range of both business and retail banking and trust and investment management services through some 100 offices located primarily in metropolitan Chicago and northwest Indiana. Its other service areas consist of a central Illinois market, including the cities of Champaign, Danville, and Galesburg, and an Iowa market that includes the cities of Davenport, Bettendorf, Moline, and East Moline. In October 2009, First Midwest acquired substantially all the assets of First DuPage Bank; in April 2010, the company acquired certain deposits and loans of Peotone Bank and Trust Company; and in August 2010, the company acquired the deposits and loans of Palos Bank and Trust Company. All three transactions were facilitated by the FDIC. Incorporated in Delaware in 1982.

Directors (In addition to indicated officers)

Robert P. O'Meara, Chm.
Barbara A. Boigegrain
Bruce S. Chelberg
John F. Chlebowski, Jr.
Joseph W. England

Brother James Gaffney, FSC
Phupinder S. Gill
Peter J. Henseler
Patrick J. McDonnell

Ellen A. Rudnick
Michael J. Small
John L. Sterling
J. Stephen Vanderwoude

Officers (Directors*)

*Michael L. Scudder, Pres. & C.E.O.;
  C.E.O., First Midwest Bank
Mark G. Sander, Sr. Exec. V.P. & C.O.O.; Pres. &
  C.O.O., First Midwest Bank
Kent S. Belasco, Exec. V.P. & C.I.O., First
  Midwest Bank
Victor P. Carapella, Exec. V.P. & Grp.
  Mgr.—Commer. Banking, First Midwest Bank
Paul F. Clemens, Exec. V.P. & C.F.O.
Robert P. Diedrich, Exec. V.P.—Trust Div. Mgr.,
  First Midwest Bank

James P. Hotchkiss, Exec. V.P. & Treas.,
  First Midwest Bank
Michael J. Kozak, Exec. V.P. & Chf. Credit Off.,
  First Midwest Bank
David D. Kullander, Exec. V.P.—Bank Oper. Dir.
Cynthia A. Lance, Exec. V.P. & Corp. Secy.
Kevin L. Moffitt, Exec. V.P. & Chf. Risk Off.
Janet M. Viano, Grp. Pres.—Retail Banking, First
  Midwest Bank
Stephanie R. Wise, Exec. V.P.—Bus. &
  Institutional Svcs., First Midwest Bank

Consolidated Statement of Condition As of December 31, 2010 (000 omitted)

Assets		Liabilities & Stockholders' Equity	
Cash & due from banks	$ 102,495	Total deposits	$6,511,476
Securities available for sale	1,057,802	Borrowed funds	303,974
Securities held to maturity	81,320	Other liabilities	219,478
Net loans	5,332,628	*Stockholders' equity	1,112,045
Net property & equipment	140,907		
Other assets	1,431,821		
Total	$8,146,973	Total	$8,146,973

*74,096,000 shares common stock outstanding.

Consolidated Income Statement

Years Ended Dec. 31	Thousands — — — —		Per Share — — — —		Common Stock Price Range Calendar Year
	Total Income	Net Income [a]	Diluted Earnings	Cash Dividends	
2010	$420,899	$ (19,717)	$(0.27)	$0.04	$17.95— 9.26
2009	434,314	(35,551)	(0.71)	0.04	20.25— 5.94
2008	498,825	48,482	1.00	1.16	40.09—13.56
2007	588,015	80,094	1.62	1.20	39.31—29.67
2006	575,423	117,189	2.37	1.12	39.52—32.62

[a] Applicable to common shares.

Transfer Agent & Registrar: BNY Mellon Shareowner Services

General Counsel: Cynthia A. Lance, Exec. V.P.   Traded (Symbol): NASDAQ Gbl. Select (FMBI)

Investor Relations: Greg Gorbatenko   Stockholders: 2,233 (R)

Human Resources: Caryn Guinta, Exec. V.P.   Employees: 1,820

Info. Tech.: Kent S. Belasco, Exec. V.P.   Annual Meeting: In May

Auditors: Ernst & Young LLP

First Robinson Financial Corporation

501 East Main Street, Robinson, Illinois 62454

Telephone: (618) 544-8621   **www.frsb.net**

First Robinson Financial Corporation is the holding company for First Robinson Savings Bank, National Association. Originally chartered in 1883, the bank converted from a federally chartered mutual savings bank to a national bank in 1997. The company operates three full service offices and one driveup facility in Crawford County, Illinois and one full service office in Vincennes, Indiana. The branch in Vincennes goes by the popular name of First Vincennes Savings Bank. The bank's principal business is attracting deposits from the general public and investing those funds primarily in one- to four-family residential real estate loans, as well as in consumer, commercial, and agricultural real estate, and commercial business and agricultural finance loans. The bank offers a variety of deposit accounts including pass-book savings, NOW accounts, certificate accounts, IRA accounts, health savings accounts, limited accounts, and non-interest-bearing accounts. Incorporated in Delaware in 1997.

Directors (In addition to indicated officer)

Scott F. Pulliam, Chm.	Steven E. Neeley
J. Douglas Goodwine	William K. Thomas
Robin E. Guyer	

Officers (Director*)

*Rick L. Catt, Pres. & C.E.O.	Mark W. Hill, V.P.
W.E. Holt, V.P. & Sr. Loan Off.	Stacie D. Ogle, V.P.
Jamie E. McReynolds, V.P., C.F.O.,	William D. Sandiford, V.P.
Secy. & Treas.	Leslie Trotter, III, V.P.

Consolidated Balance Sheet As of March 31, 2011 (000 omitted)

Assets		Liabilities & Stockholders' Equity	
Cash & cash equivalents	$ 27,359	Total deposits	$176,352
Loans, net	120,164	Other borrowings	15,620
Securities	51,677	Other liabilities	4,094
Net property & equipment	3,848	*Stockholders' equity	12,765
Other assets	5,783		
Total	$208,831	Total	$208,831

*427,149 shares common stock outstanding.

Consolidated Income Statement

Years Ended Mar. 31	Thousands — — — — —		Per Share — — — —		Common Stock Price Range Fiscal Year
	Total Income	Net Income	Diluted Earnings	Cash Dividends	
2011	$10,878	$1,395	$ 3.25	$0.85	$35.50—28.10
2010	10,035	(30)	(0.07)	0.80	36.00—29.00
2009	9,313	791	1.77	0.75	36.75—33.25
2008	8,881	971	2.06	0.65	41.05—31.00
2007	8,094	1,013	2.04	0.55	34.50—24.90

Transfer Agent & Registrar:	Registrar and Transfer Company			
Corporate Counsel:	Katten Muchin Rosenman LLP	Traded (Symbol):	OTC BB (FRFC)	
Investor Relations:	Rick L. Catt, Pres.	Stockholders:	444 (R)	
Auditors:	BKD, LLP	Employees:	54	
		Annual Meeting:	In July	

Fortune Brands Home & Security, Inc.

520 Lake Cook Road, Deerfield, Illinois 60015
Telephone: (847) 484-4400   www.fbhs.com

Fortune Brands Home & Security, Inc. was spun off from Fortune Brands Inc. on October 3, 2011. The principal brands of Fortune Brands Home & Security, Inc. include Moen faucets, Aristokraft, Omega, Diamond, and Kitchen Craft cabinetry, Therma-Tru door systems, Simonton windows, Master Lock security products, and Waterloo storage and organization products. The company holds market leading positions in all of its market segments. Incorporated in Delaware in 1985.

Directors (In addition to indicated officers)

David M. Thomas, Chm.	A.D. David Mackay	Ronald V. Waters III
Richard A Goldstein	John G. Morikis	Norman H. Wesley
Ann Fritz Hackett		

Officers (Directors*)

Christopher Klein, C.E.O.
Greg Stoner, Pres.—MasterBrand Cabinets, Inc.
John Heppner, Pres. & C.E.O.—FOSS
David Lingafelter, Pres.—Moen Inc.
David Randich, Pres. —Therma-Tru Doors
Mark Savan, Pres.—Simonton Inc.

E. Lee Wyatt, Sr. V.P. & C.F.O.
Elizabeth R. Lane, Sr. V.P.—Hum. Res.
Lauren S. Tashma, Sr. V.P., Gen. Coun. & Secy.
Miriam Van de Sype, Sr. V.P.—Strategy
Edward Wiertel, Sr. V.P.— Finance

Consolidated Balance Sheet   As of March 31, 2011 (000 omitted, unaudited, pro forma)

Assets		Liabilities & Stockholders' Equity	
Current assets	$ 860,700	Current liabilities	$ 470,400
Net property, plant & equipment	554,100	Long-term debt	516,800
Goodwill	1,366,200	Deferred income taxes	265,000
Other assets	899,600	Other liabilities	237,100
		Minority interest	2,900
		*Stockholders' equity	2,188,400
Total	$3,680,600	Total	$3,680,600

*153,212,023 shares common stock outstanding.

Consolidated Income Statement [a]

Years Ended Dec. 31	Thousands — — — —		Per Share — — — —		Common Stock Price Range
	Net Sales	Net Income	Diluted Earnings	Cash Dividends	
2010	$3,233,500	$57,200			$14.34—11.00[b]
2009	3,006,800	(41,900)			
2008	3,759,100	(641,900)			
2007	4,550,900	153,100			
2006	4,694,200	328,200			

[a] Unaudited; based on Fortune Brands Inc operating results.

[b] Price range from the start of trading on October 4, to October 17, 2011.

Transfer Agent & Registrar: Wells Fargo Shareowner Services
General Counsel: Lauren S. Tashma, Sr. V.P.   Traded (Symbol): NYSE (FBHS)
Investor Relations: Brian Lantz, V.P.   Employees: 16,000
Human Resources: Elizabeth R. Lane, V.P.   Annual Meeting: In April
Auditors: PricewaterhouseCoopers LLP

FreightCar America, Inc.

Two North Riverside Plaza, Suite 1250, Chicago, Illinois 60606
Telephone: (800) 458-2235 **www.freightcaramerica.com**

FreightCar America, Inc. manufactures aluminum-bodied and steel-bodied railroad freight cars, specializing in coal-carrying railcars. In addition, the company refurbishes and rebuilds railcars, and sells forged, cast, and fabricated parts. Manufacturing facilities are maintained in two locations: Danville, Illinois and Roanoke, Virginia. Primary customers for the company are railroads; shippers; and financial institutions, who in turn lease the railcars to others. In May 2008, the company closed its manufacturing facility located in Johnstown, Pennsylvania. In November 2010, Freightcar America acquired the business assets of DTE Rail Services, Inc., a non-regulated subsidiary of DTE Energy Company. The acquired business is now known as FreightCar Rail Services, LLC (FCRS). FCRS provides general railcar repair and maintenance, inspections, and railcar fleet management services for all types of freight railcars from its facilities in Clinton, Indiana, and Grand Island and Hastings, Nebraska. Incorporated in Delaware in 2005 as the successor to a company founded in 1901.

Directors (In addition to indicated officers)

Thomas M Fitzpatrick, Chm.
James D. Cirar
William D. Gehl

Thomas A. Madden
S. Carl Soderstrom, Jr.
Robert N. Tidball

Officers (Directors*)

*Edward J. Whalen, Pres. & C.E.O.
Theodore W. Baun, Sr. V.P.—Mktg. & Sales
Thomas McCarthy, Sr. V.P.
Gary S. Boast, V.P.—Info. Tech.

Michael MacMahon, V.P.—Bus. Dev. & Strat.
Joseph E. McNeely, V.P.—Fin., C.F.O. & Treas.
Laurence M. Trusdell, Gen. Coun. & Corp. Secy.

Consolidated Balance Sheet As of December 31, 2010 (000 omitted)

Assets		Liabilities & Stockholders' Equity	
Current assets	$150,476	Current liabilities	$ 38,681
Net property, plant & equipment	40,503	Accrued post-retirement benefits	59,909
Goodwill, net	22,052	Other liabilities	19,473
Other assets	97,612	Minority interest	(4)
		*Stockholders' equity	192,584
Total	$310,643		$310,643

*11,941,192 shares common stock outstanding.

Consolidated Income Statement

Years Ended Dec. 31	Thousands — — — —		Per Share — — — —		Common Stock Price Range Calendar Year
	Revenues	Net Income	Diluted Earnings	Cash Dividends	
2010 [a]	$ 142,889	$ (12,771)	$ (1.07)	$0.06	$29.94—18.60
2009	248,462	4,940 [b]	0.42	0.24	26.91—14.52
2008	746,390	11,420 [bc]	0.97 [c]	0.24	44.63—17.01
2007	817,025	27,459 [bc]	2.25 [c]	0.24	58.87—32.29
2006	1,444,800	128,733	10.07	0.15	76.57—45.10

[a] Includes results of DTE Rail Services, Inc., since acquisition date of November 1, 2010.
[b] Includes plant closure charges of $20,037,000 in 2008 and $30,836,000 in 2007 and income of $495,000 in 2009 related to closure of Johnstown, Pennsylvania facility.
[c] Restated to correct historical accounting errors relating to accounts payable.

Transfer Agent & Registrar: Computershare Investor Services

General Counsel: Laurence M. Trusdell
Investor Relations: Joseph E. McNeely, V.P.
Human Resources: Thomas McCarthy, Sr. V.P.
Auditors: Deloitte & Touche LLP

Traded (Symbol): NASDAQ (RAIL)
Stockholders: 57 (R)
Employees: 464
Annual Meeting: In May

Fuel Tech, Inc.

27601 Bella Vista Parkway, Warrenville, Illinois 60555
Telephone: (630) 845-4500   www.ftek.com

Fuel Tech, Inc. uses a suite of advanced technologies to provide boiler optimization, efficiency improvement, and air pollution reduction and control solutions to utility and industrial customers worldwide. Fuel Tech focuses on the worldwide marketing of its nitrogen oxide reduction and FUEL CHEM® processes. The Air Pollution Control segment includes Low NOx and Ultra Low NOx Burners; NOxOUT® and HERT™ High Energy Reagent Technology™ SNCR systems; systems that incorporate ASCR Advanced SCR, CASCADE™, ULTRA™ and NOxOUT-SCR® processes; and Ammonia Injection Grid (AIG) and the Graduated Straightening Grid (GSG™), which reduce NOx emissions in flue gas from boilers, incinerators, furnaces, and other stationary combustion sources. The FUEL CHEM® technology segment revolves around the unique application of specialty chemicals to improve the efficiency, reliability, and environmental status of plants operating in the electric utility, industrial, pulp and paper, waste-to-energy, university, and district heating markets. In January 2009, the company acquired Advanced Combustion Technology, Inc., a leading provider of nitrogen control systems located in Hooksett, New Hampshire. Incorporated in Delaware in 2006.

Directors (In addition to indicated officers)

Ralph E. Bailey	John D. Morrow
Miguel Espinosa	Thomas S. Shaw, Jr.
Charles W. Grinnell	Delbert L. Williamson
Thomas L. Jones	

Officers (Directors*)

*Douglas G. Bailey, Chm., Pres. & C.E.O.	M. Linda Lin, Sr. V.P.—China/Pacific Rim
Vincent J. Arnone, Exec. V.P.—WW Oper.	Ellen T. Albrecht, V.P. & Cont.
Robert E. Puissant, Exec. V.P.—Sales & Mktg.	Paul G. Carmignani, V.P.—New Prod. Dev.
Vincent M. Albanese, Sr. V.P.—Reg. Affs.	Kevin R. Dougherty, V.P.—Bus. Dev. & Mktg.
Stephen P. Brady, Sr. V.P.—FUEL CHEM Sales	Tracy Krumme, V.P.—Inv. Rel. & Corp. Commun.
David S. Collins, Sr. V.P., C.F.O. & Treas.	Volker Rummenhohl, V.P.—Catalyst Technologies
William E. Cummings, Jr., Sr. V.P.—APC Sales	Christopher R. Smyrniotis, V.P.—FUEL CHEM
Timothy J. Eibes, Sr. V.P.—Proj. Execution	Technologies
Albert G. Grigonis, Sr. V.P., Gen. Coun. & Secy.	William H. Sun, V.P.—Intl. Bus. & Technologies

Consolidated Balance Sheet As of December 31, 2010 (000 omitted)

Assets		Liabilities & Stockholders' Equity	
Current assets	$ 54,456	Current liabilities	$ 17,811
Net property, plant & equipment	14,384	Other liabilities	1,482
Goodwill, net	21,051	*Stockholders' equity	83,910
Other assets	13,312		
Total	$103,203	Total	$103,203

*24,213,467 shares common stock outstanding.

Consolidated Income Statement

Years Ended Dec. 31	Thousands — — — — — Revenues	Net Income	Per Share — — — — — Diluted Earnings	Cash Dividends	Common Stock Price Range Calendar Year
2010	$81,795	$ 1,753	$ 0.07	$0.00	$10.04— 5.15
2009	71,397	(2,306)	(0.10)	0.00	14.15— 7.01
2008	81,074	3,360 a	0.14 a	0.00	27.16— 6.05
2007	80,297	7,243	0.29	0.00	38.20—16.89
2006	75,115	6,826	0.28	0.00	27.44— 8.11

a Restated to reflect change in accounting principle.

Transfer Agent & Registrar: BNY Mellon Shareowner Services

General Counsel:	Albert G. Grigonis, Sr. V.P.	Traded (Symbol):	NASDAQ (FTEK)
Investor Relations:	Tracy Krumme, V.P.	Stockholders:	17,500 (B)
Auditors:	McGladrey & Pullen LLP	Employees:	161
		Annual Meeting:	In May

Arthur J. Gallagher & Co.

The Gallagher Centre, Two Pierce Place, Itasca, Illinois 60143-3141

Telephone: (630) 773-3800   www.ajg.com

Arthur J. Gallagher & Co. and its subsidiaries are engaged in providing insurance brokerage, risk management, and related services to clients in the United States and abroad through its three operating segments: brokerage, risk management, and corporate. The brokerage segment's principal activity is the negotiation and placement of insurance for its clients. The company services and places insurance for commercial, industrial, public entity, religious, and not-for-profit organizations. Arthur J. Gallagher & Co. also specializes in furnishing risk management services. Risk management involves assisting clients in analyzing risks and in determining whether proper protection is best obtained through the purchase of insurance or through retention of all or a portion of those risks and the adoption of corporate risk management policies and cost-effective loss control and prevention programs. The risk management segment is dedicated to serving the needs of corporations and institutions worldwide. Services include claims management, loss control consulting, information management, property appraisals, and other specialized services. The corporate segment includes the company's debt, investment in clean-energy ventures, external acquisition-related costs, and other corporate costs. Arthur J. Gallagher & Co. has operations in 16 countries and does business in more than 110 countries around the world through a network of correspondent brokers and consultants. Founded in 1927; reincorporated in Delaware in 1972.

Directors (In addition to indicated officers)

William L. Bax	Elbert O. Hand	Norman L. Rosenthal, Ph.D.
Frank E. English, Jr.	David S. Johnson	James R. Wimmer
Ilene S. Gordon	Kay W. McCurdy	

Officers (Directors*)

*J. Patrick Gallagher, Jr., Chm., Pres. & C.E.O.
Walter D. Bay, Corp. V.P., Gen. Coun. & Secy.
John Caraher, Corp. V.P.
Richard C. Cary, Cont. & Chf. Acct. Off.
Norbert Chung, Corp. V.P.
James W. Durkin, Jr., Corp. V.P.
James S. Gault, Corp. V.P.
Douglas K. Howell, Corp. V.P. & C.F.O.
Scott R. Hudson, Corp. V.P.
Susan E. McGrath, Corp. V.P. & Chf. Hum. Res. Off.

David E. McGurn, Jr., Corp. V.P.
John Neumaier, Corp. V.P.
William Ziebell, Corp. V.P.
Mitchel L. Brashier, V.P.
Emil J. Bravo, V.P.
Joel D. Cavaness, V.P.
Norman P. Darling, V.P.
Thomas J. Gallagher, V.P.
Michael A. Goggio, V.P.
Joel C. Kornreich, V.P.
Jack H. Lazzaro, V.P. & Treas.
David L. Marcus, V.P.
James G. McFarlane, V.P.
David M. Melchers, V.P. & C.I.O.

Angelo M. Nardi, V.P.
Steven A. Ring, V.P.
David C. Ross, V.P.
Theodore A. Skirvin, II, V.P.
Mark P. Strauch, V.P.
Craig M. Van der Voort, V.P.
Gary M. Van der Voort, V.P.
Paul F. Wasikowski, V.P.
Sally Wasikowski, V.P.
David M. Ziegler, V.P.
Kerry Abbott, Asst. Secy.
April T. Hanes-Dowd, Asst. Secy.

Consolidated Balance Sheet As of December 31, 2010 (000 omitted)

Assets		Liabilities & Stockholders' Equity	
Current assets	$1,726,000	Current liabilities	$1,577,300
Fixed assets, net	75,800	Long-term borrowings	550,000
Deferred income taxes	245,200	Other liabilities	362,000
Goodwill	883,700	*Stockholders' equity	1,106,700
Other assets	665,300		
Total	$3,596,000	Total	$3,596,000

*108,400,000 shares common stock outstanding.

Consolidated Income Statement

Years Ended Dec. 31	Thousands — — — — —		Per Share — — — — —		Common Stock Price Range Calendar Year
	Total Revenues	Net Income [a]	Diluted Earnings [a]	Cash Dividends	
2010	$1,864,200	$174,100	$1.66	$1.28	$29.80—21.90
2009	1,729,300	128,600	1.28	1.28	26.02—14.82
2008	1,645,000	77,300	0.82	1.28	30.00—21.38
2007	1,623,300	138,800	1.43	1.24	31.83—24.01
2006	1,470,100	128,500	1.31	1.20	31.77—24.42

[a] Includes earnings from discontinued operations of $10.8 million ($0.10 per diluted share) in 2011; and loss from discontinued operations of $4.5 million ($0.04 per diluted share) in 2009; $34.1 million ($0.36 per diluted share) in 2008; and $15.8 million ($0.16 per diluted share) in 2007.

Transfer Agent & Registrar: Computershare Investor Services

General Counsel:	Walter D. Bay, Corp. V.P.	Auditors:	Ernst & Young LLP
Investor Relations:	Marsha J. Akin, Dir.	Traded (Symbol):	NYSE (AJG)
Human Resources:	Susan E. McGrath, Chf. Hum. Res. Off. & Corp. V.P.	Stockholders:	1,000 (R)
		Employees:	10,700
Info. Tech.:	David M. Melchers, C.I.O.	Annual Meeting:	In May

GATX Corporation

222 West Adams Street, Chicago, Illinois 60606-5314

Telephone: (312) 621-6200　　　　　　　　**www.gatx.com**

GATX Corporation leases, operates, and manages long-lived, widely used assets in the rail, marine, and industrial equipment markets. GATX has three financial reporting segments: Rail, Specialty, and American Steamship Company. Rail is principally engaged in leasing railcar equipment, including tank and freight railcars and locomotives, to railroads and shippers of chemical, petroleum, and food products in North America and Europe. Rail owns, manages, or has an interest in approximately 167,000 railcars and 650 locomotives. Specialty provides financing, asset remarketing, and asset management services to the marine and industrial equipment markets, seeking to invest in long-lived, widely used assets that are critical to the operations of its customers. ASC owns and operates a fleet of self-unloading marine vessels on the Great Lakes and is engaged in the waterborne transportation of dry-bulk commodities. GATX also invests in companies and joint ventures that complement its existing business activities. Incorporated in New York in 1916.

Directors (In addition to indicated officers)

Anne L. Arvia
Deborah M. Fretz
Ernest A. Häberli
Mark G. McGrath

James B. Ream
Robert J. Ritchie
David S. Sutherland
Casey J. Sylla

Officers (Directors*)

*Brian A. Kenney, Chm., Pres. & C.E.O.
Robert C. Lyons, Sr. V.P. & C.F.O.
James F. Earl, Exec. V.P. & C.O.O.
Michael T. Brooks, Sr. V.P. & C.I.O.
Mary K. Lawler, Sr. V.P.—Hum. Res.
Curt F. Glenn, Sr. V.P.—Portfolio Mgt.

Deborah A. Golden, Sr. V.P., Gen. Coun.
　& Secy.
William J. Hasek, Sr. V.P. & Treas.
William M. Muckian, Sr. V.P., Cont. & Chf. Acct. Off.
Clifford J. Porzenheim, Sr. V.P.—Strat. Growth

Consolidated Balance Sheet　As of December 31, 2010 (000 omitted)

Assets		Liabilities & Stockholders' Equity	
Cash & receivables	$ 542,300	Accounts payable & accrued exp.	$ 114,600
Net operating lease assets		Total debt	3,176,500
& facilities	4,133,800	Deferred items	750,600
Other assets	766,300	Other liabilities	287,000
		*Stockholders' equity	1,113,700
Total	$5,442,400	Total	$5,442,400

*46,360,430 shares common stock outstanding.

Consolidated Income Statement

Years Ended Dec. 31	Thousands — — — —		Per Share — — — —		Common Stock Price Range Calendar Year
	Gross Income	Net Income [a]	Diluted Earnings [a]	Cash Dividends	
2010	$1,204,900	$ 80,800	$1.72	$1.12	$36.93—25.40
2009	1,153,900	81,400	1.70	1.12	33.25—13.63
2008	1,443,100	194,800	3.88	1.08	51.53—21.05
2007	1,346,000	183,800	3.43	0.96	52.53—34.59
2006	1,229,100	147,300	2.64	0.84	48.58—35.69

[a] From continuing operations.

Transfer Agent & Registrar: BNY Mellon Shareowner Services

General Counsel:	Deborah A. Golden, Sr. V.P.	Traded (Symbol):	NYSE, CSE (GMT)
Investor Relations:	Jennifer Van Aken, Dir.	Stockholders:	2,581 (R)
Human Resources:	Mary K. Lawler, Sr. V.P.	Employees:	1,947
Info. Tech.:	Michael T. Brooks, Sr. V.P.	Annual Meeting:	In April
Auditors:	Ernst & Young LLP		

General Employment Enterprises, Inc.

One Tower Lane, Suite 2200, Oakbrook Terrace, Illinois 60181

Telephone: (630) 954-0400   www.generalemployment.com

General Employment Enterprises, Inc., and its wholly owned subsidiary Triad Personnel Services, Inc., provide contract and placement staffing services for business and industry, primarily specializing in the placement of information technology, engineering, and accounting professionals. Placement services include placing candidates into regular, full-time jobs with client-employers. Contract services include placing its professional employees on temporary assignments, under contracts with client companies. Contract workers are employees of the company, typically working at the client location and at the direction of client personnel for periods of three months to one year. The company's offices operate under the trade names General Employment Enterprises, Omni One, Triad Personnel, and Generation Technologies. In June 2010, the company acquired certain assets of On-Site Services, Inc. of Florida which provides contract staffing services for the agricultural industry. In the spring of 2011, the company completed the purchase of certain assets of DMCC Staffing, LLC and RFFG of Cleveland, LLC in Ohio. Both provide labor and human resource solutions to customers in Ohio. Incorporated in Illinois in 1962.

Directors (In addition to indicated officers)

Dennis W. Baker

Charles W. B. Wardell, III

Thomas C. Williams

Officers (Directors*)

*Salvatore J. Zizza, Chm. & C.E.O.

*Herbert F. Imhoff, Jr., Pres. & C.O.O.

James R. Harlan, C.F.O. & Treas.

Marilyn L. White, V.P.

Nancy C. Frohnmaier, Secy.

Jan V. Prieto-McCarthy, Asst. Treas.

Marlene E. Justus, Asst. Secy.

Consolidated Balance Sheet As of March 31, 2010 (000 omitted)[a]

Assets		Liabilities & Stockholders' Equity	
Current assets	$4,822	Current liabilities	$3,943
Net property & equipment	292	Long-term obligations	2,035
Goodwill	1,256	*Stockholders' equity	3,911
Intangible assets, net	3,519		
Total	$9,889	Total	$9,889

*17,652,000 average shares common stock outstanding.

[a] Unaudited

Consolidated Income Statement

Years Ended Sept. 30	Thousands — — — — —		Per Share — — — —		Common Stock Price Range Fiscal Year
	Net Revenues	Net Income	Diluted Earnings	Cash Dividends	
2010	$11,917	$(1,556)	$(0.11)	$0.00	$0.84—0.22
2009	10,394	(4,228)	(0.58)	0.00	1.47—0.19
2008	15,235	(1,806)	(0.35)	0.10	1.79—0.38
2007	19,690	914	0.17	0.10	3.47—1.52
2006	20,068	1,002	0.19	0.00	2.75—1.41

Transfer Agent & Registrar: Continental Stock Transfer & Trust Co.

General Counsel: Matthew T. Zicarrelli

Investor Relations: Salvatore J. Zizza, C.E.O.

Human Resources: Sherry L. Hubacek, Dir.

Info. Tech.: Ignacio Pruneda, Mgr.

Auditors: BDO USA, LLP

Traded (Symbol): NYSE Amex (JOB)

Stockholders: 661 (R)

Employees: 171

Annual Meeting: In February

General Growth Properties, Inc.
110 North Wacker Drive, Chicago, Illinois 60606
Telephone: (312) 960-5000   **www.ggp.com**

General Growth Properties, Inc. (GGP) is a real estate investment trust (REIT) that is one of the nation's largest shopping center owners. GGP has ownership and management interest in 166 regional and super regional shopping malls in 43 states. The company's portfolio totals 169 million square feet of space. The company and certain of its subsidiaries filed voluntary petitions for relief under Chapter 11 of the U.S. Bankruptcy Code on April 16 and April 22, 2009. GGP emerged from bankruptcy on November 9, 2010. Also on November 9, GGP spun-off a new publicly traded company, The Howard Hughes Corporation, that included master planned communities and strategic development properties that were previously in the GGP portfolio. In August 2011, the company's board of directors approved a plan to spin-off a 30-mall portfolio to holders of GGP common stock in the form of a taxable special dividend comprised of common stock in Rouse Properties, Inc., a recently formed company to which GGP plans to transfer the portfolio. Incorporated in Delaware in 1993; successor company incorporated in Delaware in 2010.

Directors (In addition to indicated officers)

Bruce J. Flatt, Chm.
Richard B. Clark
Mary Lou Fiala
John Haley

Cyrus Madon
David J. Neithercut
Mark R. Patterson
John G. Schreiber

Officers (Directors*)

*Sandeep Mathrani, C.E.O.
Shobi Khan, C.O.O.
Steven J. Douglas, Exec. V.P. & C.F.O.
Michael H. McNaughton, Exec. V.P.—Asset Mgt.
Marvin Levine, Chf. Legal Off.
Richard Pesin, Exec. V.P.—Anchors, Dev.
   & Const.

Alan Barocas, Sr. Exec. V.P.—Mall Leasing
Cathie Hollowell, Sr. V.P.—Hum. Res.
James A. Thurston, Sr. V.P. & Chf. Acct. Off.
Scott Morey, C.I.O. & Chf. Technology Off.

Consolidated Balance Sheet   As of December 31, 2010 (000 omitted)

Assets		Liabilities & Stockholders' Equity	
Current assets	$ 1,135,410	Total liabilities	$21,953,266
Net real estate investment	28,164,070	Minority interests	335,011
Other assets	3,067,899	*Stockholders' equity	10,079,102
Total	$32,367,379	Total	$32,367,379

*941,880,014 shares common stock outstanding.

Consolidated Income Statement

Years Ended Dec. 31	Thousands — — — — — Revenue	Net Income [a]	Per Share — — — — — Diluted Earnings	Cash Dividends	Common Stock Price Range Calendar Year
2010 [b]	$ 416,542	$ (254,216)	$(0.27)	$0.38 [e]	$16.50—14.31
2010 [c]	2,406,944	(1,185,758)	(3.74)	0.00	17.28— 8.58
2009 [d]	2,881,387	(1,284,689) [f]	(4.11)	0.19 [e]	13.24— 0.32
2008 [d]	3,059,098	4,719 [gh]	0.02 [gh]	1.50	44.23— 0.24
2007 [d]	2,871,170	273,642 [h]	1.12 [h]	1.85	67.43—39.31
2006 [d]	2,586,526	59,273 [f]	0.24	1.68	56.14—41.92

[a] Funds from operations (FFO), in thousands: 2010 (successor company): $(82,668); 2010 (predecessor company): $683,151; 2009: $(421,384); 2008: $833,086; 2007: $1,083,439; 2006: $902,361.
[b] Successor company, represents period from November 10, 2010 through December 31, 2010.
[c] Predecessor company, represents period from January 1, 2010 through November 9, 2010.
[d] Predecessor company.
[e] The 2009 and 2010 dividends were paid 90% in common stock and 10% in cash in January 2010 and January 2011, respectively.
[f] Includes losses from discontinued operations of $966,000 in 2009 and $823,000 in 2006.
[g] Includes income from discontinued operations of $55,044,000 ($0.18 per diluted share).
[h] Restated to reflect adoption of new generally accepted accounting principles.

Transfer Agent & Registrar: BNY Mellon Shareowner Services			
General Counsel: Marvin Levine, Chf. Legal Off.	**Traded (Symbol):**	NYSE (GGP)	
Investor Relations: Andrew Joa, V.P.	**Stockholders:**	3,334 (R)	
Human Resources: Cathie Hollowell, Sr. V.P.	**Employees:**	2,800	
Info. Tech.: Scott Morey, C.I.O.	**Annual Meeting:**	In April	
Auditors: Deloitte & Touche LLP			

W.W. Grainger, Inc.

100 Grainger Parkway, Lake Forest, Illinois 60045-5201

Telephone: (847) 535-1000   www.grainger.com

W.W. Grainger, Inc. is North America's leading broad line supplier of maintenance, repair, and operating products. The company also has an expanding presence in Asia and Latin America. Grainger provides access to more than one million products and replacement parts in a variety of product categories, including: material handling and storage, safety and security, cleaning and maintenance, pumps, lighting, electrical, hand and power tools, HVAC, motors, and plumbing. Grainger serves approximately 2.0 million customers through a network of 607 branches, 24 distribution centers, and multiple Web sites. During 2010, the company acquired one business in the United States, three in Canada, and an 80 percent ownership of a joint venture in Colombia. Founded in 1927 and incorporated in Illinois in 1928.

Directors (In addition to indicated officers)

Brian P. Anderson	Neil S. Novich
Wilbur H. Gantz	Michael J. Roberts
V. Ann Hailey	Gary L. Rogers
William K. Hall	E. Scott Santi
Stuart L. Levenick	James D. Slavik
John W. McCarter, Jr.	

Officers (Directors*)

*James T. Ryan, Chm., Pres. & C.E.O.	Donald G. Macpherson, Sr. V.P.—Gbl. Supply Chain
Laura D. Brown, Sr. V.P.—Commun. & Inv. Rel.	Joseph High, Sr. V.P.—Hum. Res.
Court Carruthers, Sr. V.P.; Pres.—Grainger Intl.	Michael A. Pulick, Sr. V.P.; Pres.—Grainger U.S.
Timothy M. Ferrarell, Sr. V.P. & C.I.O.	Gregory S. Irving, V.P. & Cont.
John L. Howard, Sr. V.P. & Gen. Coun.	
Ronald L. Jadin, Sr. V.P. & C.F.O.	

Consolidated Balance Sheet As of December 31, 2010 (000 omitted)

Assets		Liabilities & Stockholders' Equity	
Current assets	$2,238,071	Current liabilities	$ 869,303
Net property, plant & equipment	963,672	Long-term debt	420,446
Other assets	702,634	Other liabilities	326,958
		Minority interest	82,454
		*Stockholders' equity	2,205,216
Total	$3,904,377	Total	$3,904,377

*69,377,802 shares common stock outstanding.

Consolidated Income Statement

| Years Ended Dec. 31 | Thousands — — — — | | Per Share — — — — | | Common Stock |
	Net Sales	Net Income	Diluted Earnings	Cash Dividends	Price Range Calendar Year
2010	$7,182,158	$510,885	$6.93	$2.08	$139.09—96.13
2009	6,221,991	430,666	5.62	1.78	102.54—59.95
2008	6,850,032	475,355	5.97 [a]	1.55	93.99—58.86
2007	6,418,014	420,120	4.91 [a]	1.34	98.60—68.77
2006	5,883,654	383,399	4.24	1.11	79.95—60.60

[a] Restated to reflect change in accounting guidance.

Transfer Agent & Registrar:	Computershare Investor Services		
General Counsel:	John L. Howard, Sr. V.P.	Traded (Symbol):	NYSE, CSE (GWW)
Investor Relations:	Laura D. Brown, Sr. V.P.	Stockholders:	930 (R)
Human Resources:	Joseph High, Sr. V.P.	Employees:	18,500
Info. Tech.:	Timothy M. Ferrarell, Sr. V.P.	Annual Meeting:	Last Wednesday in April
Auditors:	Ernst & Young LLP		

Great American Bancorp, Inc.

1311 South Neil Street, P.O. Box 1010, Champaign, Illinois 61824-1010
Telephone: (217) 356-2265   **www.greatamericanbancorp.com**

Great American Bancorp, Inc. is the holding company for First Federal Savings Bank of Champaign-Urbana, which conducts business from its administrative and branch office located in Champaign, Illinois. It also has another branch office in Champaign and one in Urbana. The bank is a community-oriented savings institution whose business consists primarily of accepting deposits from customers within its market area, and investing those funds in mortgage loans secured by one- to four-family residences. The bank also invests in the following types of loans: multi-family mortgage, commercial real estate, construction, land development, and commercial and consumer. In addition to its lending activities, the bank also invests in US Government sponsored agency residential mortgage-backed securities. The bank's subsidiary, Park Avenue Service Corporation, sells insurance products through the GTPS Insurance Agency. Incorporated in Delaware in 1995.

Directors (In addition to indicated officers)

Ronald E. Guenther, Chm.   Jack B. Troxell
Ronald L. Kiddoo

Officers (Directors*)

*George R. Rouse, Pres. & C.E.O.   Jane F. Adams, C.F.O., Secy. & Treas.

Consolidated Balance Sheet As of December 31, 2010 (000 omitted)

Assets		Liabilities & Stockholders' Equity	
Cash & equivalents	$ 43,628	Deposits	$134,071
Securities	716	FHLB advances	6,000
Net loans	103,487	Other liabilities	2,679
Net premises & equipment	5,114	*Stockholders' equity	15,310
Other assets	5,115		
Total	$158,060	Total	$158,060

*486,945 shares common stock outstanding.

Consolidated Income Statement

Years Ended Dec. 31	Thousands — — — —		Per Share — — — —		Common Stock Price Range Calendar Year
	Total Income	Net Income	Diluted Earnings	Cash Dividends	
2010	$10,464	$1,340	$2.69	$0.56	$35.50—33.00
2009	11,073	1,321	2.53	0.56	32.00—27.00
2008	11,236	1,110	1.91	0.54	33.50—26.50
2007	11,880	1,158	1.78	0.46	34.50—30.00
2006	11,749	1,523	2.21	0.44	34.50—30.15

Transfer Agent & Registrar: Computershare Investor Services
Corporate Counsel: Locke Lord Bissell &   Traded (Symbol):   OTC BB (GTPS.OB)
                   Liddell LLP   Stockholders: 202 (R)
Investor Relations: Jane F. Adams, C.F.O.   Employees: 71
Auditors: McGladrey & Pullen, LLP   Annual Meeting: In April

Great Lakes Dredge & Dock Corporation

2122 York Road, Oak Brook, Illinois 60523

Telephone: (630) 574-3000   **www.gldd.com**

Great Lakes Dredge & Dock Corporation is the largest provider of dredging services in the United States and the only U.S. dredging company with significant international operations. Dredging enhances or preserves the navigability of waterways or the protection of shorelines through removing or replenishing soil, sand, or rock. The company also provides commercial and industrial demolition services, primarily in the Northeast. The company owns a majority interest in NASDI, a demolition services provider in the Boston area, and also has a 50% interest in a marine sand mining operation in New Jersey, which supplies sand and aggregate used for road and building construction. In December 2010, Great Lakes Dredge & Dock acquired substantially all of the assets of L.W. Matteson, Inc., a maintenance and environmental dredging and levee construction company located in Burlington, Iowa. The acquisition expands the company's service into inland, river, lakes, and environmental dredging and to levee construction using dredged material. Incorporated in Delaware in 2006.

Directors (In addition to indicated officers)

Carl A. Albert
Stephen H. Bittel
Peter R. Deutsch

Nathan D. Leight
Douglas B. Mackie
Jason G. Weiss

Officers (Directors*)

*Johathan W. Berger, C.E.O.
*Bruce J. Biemeck, Pres. & C.F.O.
David E. Simonelli, Pres.—Dredging Oper.
Kyle D. Johnson, Sr. V.P.—Oper.
John F. Karas, Sr. V.P.—Estimating
Stephen E. Pegg, Sr. V.P.—Corp. Dev.
Steven W. Becker, V.P.
J. Christopher Gillespie, V.P.
Bradley T.J. Hansen, V.P.
William H. Hanson, V.P.

John T. O'Brien, V.P.
Steven F. O'Hara, V.P.
William F. Pagendarm, V.P.
Christopher Roberts, V.P.
Edward B. Smith, V.P. & Cont.
Russell Zimmerman, V.P.
Kathleen M. LaVoy, Chf. Legal Off., Chf. Compliance
    Off. & Secy.
Katherine M. Hayes, Treas. & Asst. Secy.
Ellen Parker Burke, Asst. Treas.

Consolidated Balance Sheet   As of December 31, 2010 (000 omitted)

Assets		Liabilities & Stockholders' Equity	
Current assets	$222,969	Current liabilities	$132,817
Net property, plant & equipment	323,231	Senior subordinated notes	175,000
Goodwill, net	98,049	Other liabilities	109,183
Other assets	49,576	Minority interest	(2,128)
		*Stockholders' equity	278,953
Total	$693,825	Total	$693,825

*58,770,369 shares common stock outstanding.

Consolidated Income Statement

Years Ended Dec. 31	Thousands — — — —		Per Share — — — —		Common Stock Price Range [a] Calendar Year
	Total Revenues	Net Income [b]	Diluted Earnings	Cash Dividends	
2010	$686,900	$34,600	$ 0.59	$0.07	$ 8.08—4.04
2009	622,244	17,468	0.30	0.07	7.46—1.78
2008	586,879	4,979	0.09	0.07	8.78—2.64
2007	515,761	7,056	0.14	0.02	10.18—6.42
2006	425,980	(8,803)	(0.90)	0.00	6.45—6.35

[a] Stock began trading on the NASDAQ Global Market on December 27, 2006.
[b] Available to common stockholders.

Transfer Agent & Registrar: Continental Stock Transfer & Trust Co.

General Counsel:	Kathleen M. LaVoy, Chf. Legal Off.	Auditors:	Deloitte & Touche LLP
		Traded (Symbol):	NASDAQ GM (GLDD)
Investor Relations:	Katherine Hayes	Stockholders:	37 (R)
Human Resources:	Maureen Kinn	Employees:	1,440
Info. Tech.:	John Masczyk	Annual Meeting:	In May

Heidrick & Struggles International, Inc.
233 South Wacker Drive, Suite 4200, Chicago, Illinois 60606-6303
Telephone: (312) 496-1200 **www.heidrick.com**

Heidrick & Struggles International, Inc. is a leading provider of senior-level executive search and leadership consulting services, including succession planning, talent retention management, transition consulting for newly appointed executives, executive assessment, executive development, and M&A human capital integration consulting. The company facilitates the recruitment, development, and retention of personnel for its clients' executive management and board director positions. As of December 31, 2010, the company had 347 consultants in 36 countries to provide services to its clients, who include Fortune 1,000 companies, major international companies, middle-market and emerging-growth companies, government, higher education, and not-for-profit organizations, as well as other public and private concerns. Incorporated in Delaware in 1968.

Directors (In addition to indicated officers)

Richard I. Beattie, Chm.
John A. Fazio
Mark Foster
Jane D. Hartley

Jill Kanin-Lovers
Gary E. Knell
Robert E. Knowling, Jr.
V. Paul Unruh

Officers (Directors*)

*L. Kevin Kelly, Pres. & C.E.O.
Richard Pehlke, Exec. V.P. & C.F.O.
Stephen W. Beard, Exec. V.P., Gen. Coun.
& Secy.

Richard J. Caldera, Exec. V.P. & Chf.
 Hum. Res. Off.
S. John Kim, Managing Partner—Gbl. Practices

Consolidated Balance Sheet As of December 31, 2010 (000 omitted)

Assets		Liabilities & Stockholders' Equity	
Current assets	$312,466	Current liabilities	$172,456
Net property & equipment	34,406	Other liabilities	78,029
Other assets	198,155	*Stockholders' equity	294,452
Total	$545,027	Total	$545,027

*17,558,098 shares common stock outstanding.

Consolidated Income Statement

Years Ended Dec. 31	Thousands — — — —		Per Share — — — —		Common Stock Price Range Calendar Year
	Total Revenue	Net Income	Diluted Earnings	Cash Dividends	
2010	$513,236	$7,493 [a]	$ 0.42 [a]	$0.52	$32.15—16.29
2009	414,718	(20,908) [b]	(1.24) [b]	0.52	31.65—13.52
2008	644,860	39,074	2.20	0.52	37.98—17.86
2007	648,266	56,463	2.97	0.26	55.22—30.96
2006	501,994	34,243 [c]	1.81 [c]	0.00	43.49—29.87

[a] Includes restructuring charges of $1.6 million and other charges of $4.2 million.
[b] Includes restructuring charges of $22 million, adjustment of $300,000 in Europe related to a previously restructured office, and impairment charges totalling $4 million.
[c] Includes restructuring charges of $408,000.

Transfer Agent & Registrar: BNY Mellon Shareowner Services
General Counsel: Stephen W. Beard, Exec. V.P. Traded (Symbol): NASDAQ (HSII)
Investor Relations: Julie Creed, V.P. Stockholders: 107 (R)
Human Resources: Richard J. Caldera, Exec. V.P. Employees: 1,516
Info. Tech.: Alwin Brunner, Sr. V.P. & C.I.O. Annual Meeting: In May
Auditors: KPMG LLP

Heritage-Crystal Clean, Inc.

2175 Point Boulevard, Suite 375, Elgin, Illinois 60123

Telephone: (847) 836-5670   www.crystal-clean.com

Heritage-Crystal Clean, Inc. is the second largest provider of parts cleaning services in the U.S. and a leading provider of containerized waste services. The company provides parts cleaning, hazardous, and non-hazardous waste services to small and mid-sized customers in both the manufacturing and automotive service sectors. Its service programs include parts cleaning, containerized waste management, used oil collection, and vacuum truck services, which help customers manage their used chemicals and liquid and solid wastes, while also helping to minimize their regulatory burdens. Customers include businesses involved in vehicle maintenance operations (car dealerships, automotive repair shops, and trucking firms), as well as small manufacturers, such as metal product fabricators and printers. The company operates through 67 branches serving over 44,000 customer locations. Incorporated in Delaware in 2007.

Directors (In addition to indicated officers)

Fred Fehsenfeld, Jr., Chm.	Carmine Falcone
Donald Brinckman	Charles E. Schalliol
Bruce Bruckmann	Robert W. Willmschen, Jr.

Officers (Directors*)

*Joseph Chalhoub, Pres. & C.E.O.	John Lucks, V.P.—Sales & Mktg.
Gregory Ray, C.F.O., V.P.—Bus. Mgt. & Secy.	Ellie Chaves, Chf. Acct. Off.
Tom Hillstrom, V.P.—Oper.	

Consolidated Balance Sheet As of January 1, 2011 (000 omitted)

Assets		Liabilities & Stockholders' Equity	
Current assets	$49,794	Current liabilities	$ 14,352
Net property, plant & equipment	37,051	Other liabilities	1,676
Software & intangible assets, net	2,727	*Stockholders' equity	73,544
Total	$89,572	Total	$89,572

*14,220,321 shares common stock outstanding.

Consolidated Income Statement

Years Ended Abt. Dec. 31	Thousands — — — —		Per Share — — — —		Common Stock Price Range [b] Calendar Year
	Sales	Net Income [a]	Diluted Earnings [a]	Cash Dividends	
2010	$112,118	$ 3,271	$ 0.26	$0.00	$12.39—7.51
2009	98,398	1,793	0.17	0.00	13.57—6.90
2008 [c]	108,143	(1,147) [d]	(0.11)	0.00	18.69—8.40
2007	89,734	5,377 [e]	0.74		
2006	73,717	2,596	0.36		

[a] Available to common stockholders.
[b] Initial public offering completed March 12, 2008.
[c] 53 weeks.
[d] Includes $2.8 million non-cash inventory impairment charge.
[e] Includes impairment charge of $2.2 million to reduce solvent inventories to net realizable value in connection with a settlement.

Transfer Agent & Registrar: Registrar and Transfer Company			
General Counsel:	Brent Amato	Traded (Symbol):	NASDAQ GS (HCCI)
Investor Relations:	Gregory Ray, C.F.O.	Stockholders:	202 (R)
Human Resources:	Ellie Chaves, Mgr.	Employees:	583
Info. Tech.:	Craig Rose, C.I.O.	Annual Meeting:	In May
Auditors:	Grant Thornton LLP		

Horace Mann Educators Corporation

1 Horace Mann Plaza, Springfield, Illinois 62715-0001
Telephone: (217) 789-2500   www.horacemann.com

Horace Mann Educators Corporation is an insurance holding company which, through its subsidiaries, markets and underwrites personal lines of property/casualty (primarily private passenger automobile and homeowners) insurance, retirement annuities, and life insurance. Horace Mann markets its products primarily to K-12 teachers, administrators, and other employees of public schools and their families. The company markets and services its products principally through its own sales force, and annuity products are supplementally sold through an independent agent distribution channel. Subsidiaries are Horace Mann Insurance Company, Teachers Insurance Company, Horace Mann Property & Casualty Insurance Company, Horace Mann Life Insurance Company, and Horace Mann Lloyds. Founded in 1945 in Springfield, Illinois; incorporated in Delaware in 1968.

Directors (In addition to indicated officers)

Gabriel L. Shaheen, Chm.
Mary H. Futrell
Stephen J. Hasenmiller
Ronald J. Helow

Roger J. Steinbecker
Robert Stricker
Charles R. Wright

Officers (Directors*)

*Peter H. Heckman, Pres. & C.E.O.
Dwayne D. Hallman, Exec. V. P. & C.F.O.
Stephen P. Cardinal, Exec. V.P. & Chf. Mktg. Off.
Thomas C. Wilkinson, Exec. V.P.—Prop. & Cas.
Paul D. Andrews, Sr. V.P.—Hum. Res. & Admin. Ops.

Dennis E. Bianchi, Sr. V.P.—Prop. & Cas. Claims
Bret A. Conklin, Sr. V. P. & Cont.
Ann M. Caparrós, Gen. Coun., Chf. Compliance
Off. & Corp. Secy.
Angela S. Christian, V.P. & Treas.

Consolidated Balance Sheet As of December 31, 2010 (000 omitted)

Assets		Liabilities & Stockholders' Equity	
Investments	$5,073,623	Policy liabilities	$4,068,733
Variable annuity assets	1,375,656	Long-term debt	199,679
Deferred policy acquisition costs	272,825	Variable annuity liabilities	1,375,656
Other assets	283,437	Other liabilities	481,466
		*Stockholders' equity	880,007
Total	$7,005,541	Total	$7,005,541

*39,655,952 shares common stock outstanding.

Consolidated Income Statement

Years Ended Dec. 31	Thousands — — — —		Per Share — — — —		Common Stock Price Range Calendar Year
	Total Revenues	Net Income	Diluted Earnings	Cash Dividends	
2010	$974,711	$80,862	$1.97	$0.35	$19.50—11.16
2009	937,427	73,486	1.81	0.24	14.81— 6.09
2008	834,818	10,917	0.27	0.37	19.12— 4.00
2007	887,005	82,788	1.86	0.42	23.23—16.08
2006	885,842	98,708	2.19	0.42	21.01—16.05

Transfer Agent & Registrar: American Stock Transfer & Trust Co.

General Counsel: Ann M. Caparrós

Investor Relations: Todd Nelson, V.P.

Human Resources: Paul Andrews, Sr. V.P.

Info. Tech.: Paul Andrews, Sr. V.P.

Auditors: KPMG LLP

Traded (Symbol): NYSE (HMN)

Stockholders: 8,200 (R)

Employees: 1,684

Annual Meeting: In May

Horizon Pharma, Inc.

1033 Skokie Boulevard, Suite 355, Northbrook, Illinois 60062

Telephone: (224) 383-3000   www.horizonpharma.com

Horizon Pharma, Inc. is a biopharmaceutical company that is developing and commercializing innovative medicines to target unmet therapeutic needs in arthritis, pain, and inflammatory diseases. The company has two principal products: FDA-approved DUEXIS® (formerly HZT-501), a novel tablet formulation containing a fixed-dose combination of ibuprofen and famotidine in a single pill; and LODOTRA (NP-01), a proprietary programmed release formulation of low-dose prednisone that is currently marketed in Europe by Horizon Pharma's distribution partner, Mundipharma International Corporation Limited. Horizon Pharma plans to launch DUEXIS in the U.S. in the fourth quarter of 2011. The company also has a pipeline of earlier stage product candidates to treat pain-related diseases and chronic inflammation. On April 1, 2010, the company effected a recapitalization and acquisition pursuant to which it became a holding company that operates through its two wholly-owned subsidiaries, Horizon Pharma USA, Inc. (formerly known as Horizon Therapeutics, Inc.) and Horizon Pharma AG (formerly known as Nitec Pharma AG). The company completed its initial public offering on July 28, 2011. Incorporated in Delaware in 2010.

Directors (In addition to indicated officers)

Jeffrey W. Bird, M.D., Ph.D.
Hubert Birner, Ph.D.
Louis C. Bock

Jean-François Formela, M.D.
Jeff Himawan, Ph.D.
Peter Johann, Ph.D.

Officers (Directors*)

*Timothy P. Walbert, Chm., Pres. & C.E.O.
Robert J. De Vaere, Exec. V.P. & C.F.O.
Achim Schäffler, Ph.D., Exec. V.P.—Mfg. &
  Managing Dir.—Horizon Pharma GmbH
Jeffrey W. Sherman, M.D., FACP, Exec.
  V.P.—Dev., Reg. Affs. & Chf. Med. Off.

Michael Adatto, Sr. V.P.—Sales & Managed Care
Iain Duncan, Sr. V.P.—Mfg. Oper.
Amy Grahn, Sr. V.P.—Clinical Dev. & Oper.
Robert W. Metz, Sr. V.P.—Global Bus. Oper.
  & Gen. Mgr.—Eur.
Todd N. Smith, Sr. V.P.—Mktg. & Alliance Mgt.

Consolidated Balance Sheet   As of December 31, 2010 (000 omitted)

Assets		Liabilities & Stockholders' Equity	
Current assets	$ 7,368	Current liabilities	$ 25,312
Net property & equipment	2,107	Long-term liabilities	14,519
In-process research & development	108,746	Deferred tax liabilities	24,798
Other assets	43,464	*Stockholders' equity	97,056
Total	$161,685	Total	$161,685

Consolidated Income Statement

Years Ended Dec. 31	Thousands — — — —		Per Share — — — —		Common Stock Price Range [b] Calendar Year
	Total Revenues	Net Income [a]	Diluted Earnings	Cash Dividends	
2010	$2,376	$(27,065)	$(21.16)	$0.00	
2009	0	(17,011)	(40.65)	0.00	
2008	0	(27,899)	(68.01)	0.00	

[a] Attributable to common stockholders.
[b] Stock began trading on July 28, 2011.

Transfer Agent & Registrar: BNY Mellon Shareowner Services
Corporate Counsel: Cooley LLP
Investor Relations: Robert J. De Vaere, Exec. V.P.
Auditors: PricewaterhouseCoopers LLP

Traded (Symbol): NASDAQ (HZNP)
Employees: 39
Annual Meeting: To be determned

Hospira, Inc.
275 North Field Drive, Lake Forest, Illinois 60045
Telephone: (224) 212-2000   www.hospira.com

Hospira, Inc. is a global specialty pharmaceutical and medication delivery company that develops, manufactures, and markets products that help improve the safety, cost, and productivity of patient care. Hospira is the world leader in specialty generic injectable pharmaceuticals. Its portfolio includes a broad line of generic acute-care and oncology injectables, as well as integrated infusion therapy and medication management systems. Hospira's portfolio of products is used by hospitals and alternate site providers, such as clinics, home healthcare providers, and long-term care facilities. The company has 13 manufacturing and research and development facilities worldwide. In March 2010, the company completed its acquisition of the generic injectable pharmaceuticals business of Orchid Chemicals & Pharmaceuticals Ltd., a leading Indian pharmaceutical company. In July 2010, Hospira successfully completed its tender offer to acquire Javelin Pharmaceuticals, Inc. Incorporated in Delaware in 2003.

Directors (In addition to indicated officers)

Irving W. Bailey, II
Barbara L. Bowles, C.F.A.
Connie R. Curran, R.N., Ed.D.
William G. Dempsey
Roger W. Hale

Jacque J. Sokolov, M.D.
John C. Staley
Heino von Prondzynski
Mark F. Wheeler, M.D., M.P.H.

Officers (Directors*)

*Christopher B. Begley, Chm.
*F. Michael Ball, C.E.O.
Anil G. D'Souza, Corp. V.P.—Gbl. Mktg. & Corp. Dev.
Francois Dubois, Sr. V.P.—Quality
James H. Hardy, Sr. V.P.—Oper.
Thomas E. Werner, Sr. V.P.—Fin. & C.F.O.

Daphne E. Jones, Sr. V.P. & C.I.O.
Kenneth F. Meyers, Sr. V.P.—Organizational Transformation & People Dev.
Sumant Ramachandra, M.D., Ph.D., Sr. V.P.—Res. & Dev. and Medical Affs. & Chf. Scientific Off.
Brian J. Smith, Sr. V.P., Gen. Coun. & Secy.
Ron Squarer, Sr. V.P. & Chf. Commer. Off.

Consolidated Balance Sheet   As of December 31, 2010 (000 omitted)

Assets		Liabilities & Stockholders' Equity	
Current assets	$2,477,500	Current liabilities	$ 931,600
Net property & equipment	1,279,200	Long-term debt	1,714,400
Intangible assets, net	527,700	Other liabilities	216,800
Goodwill	1,471,200	*Stockholders' equity	3,183,500
Other assets	290,700		
Total	$6,046,300	Total	$6,046,300

*1673,000,000 shares common stock outstanding.

Consolidated Income Statement

Years Ended Dec. 31	Thousands — — — —		Per Share — — — —		Common Stock Price Range Calendar Year
	Net Sales	Net Earnings	Diluted Earnings	Cash Dividends	
2010	$3,917,200	$357,200	$2.11	$0.00	$59.75—48.56
2009	3,879,300	403,900	2.47	0.00	51.11—21.38
2008	3,629,500	320,900 a	1.99	0.00	43.80—25.36
2007	3,436,200	136,800 a	0.85	0.00	44.51—33.85
2006	2,688,505	237,679 a	1.48	0.00	47.63—31.17

a Includes acquired in-process research and development charges of $0.5 million, $88.0 million, and $10.0 million in 2008, 2007, and 2006, respectively.

Transfer Agent & Registrar: Computershare Investor Services

General Counsel:	Brian J. Smith, Sr. V.P.	Traded (Symbol):	NYSE (HSP)
Investor Relations:	Karen M. King, V.P.	Stockholders:	35,678 (R)
Human Resources:	Kenneth F. Meyers, Sr. V.P.	Employees:	14,000
Info. Tech.:	Daphne E. Jones, C.I.O.	Annual Meeting:	In May
Auditors:	Deloitte & Touche LLP		

Hub Group, Inc.

3050 Highland Parkway, Suite 100, Downers Grove, Illinois 60515
Telephone: (630) 271-3600   www.hubgroup.com

Hub Group, Inc. is one of North America's leading freight transportation management companies, offering comprehensive intermodal, truck brokerage, and logistics services. The company is the largest intermodal marketing company in the United States and one of the largest truck brokers. Hub Group operates through a network of operating centers throughout the United States, Canada, and Mexico. Each operating center is strategically located in a market with a significant concentration of shipping customers and one or more railroads. Through its network, the company serves customers in diverse industries, including consumer products, retail, and durable goods. The company arranges comprehensive intermodal, truckload, less-than-truckload, air freight, and logistics services through transportation carriers and equipment providers. In April 2011, Hub Group purchased Exel Tranportation Services. The wholly-owned subsidiary, headquartered in Dallas, Texas, operates under the name Mode Transportation. Incorporated in Delaware in 1995, as the successor to a business founded in 1971.

Directors (In addition to indicated officers)

Gary D. Eppen   Martin P. Slark
Charles R. Reaves

Officers (Directors*)

*David P. Yeager, Chm. & C.E.O.   Terri A. Pizzuto, Exec. V.P., C.F.O. & Treas.
*Mark A. Yeager, V. Chm., Pres. & C.O.O.   Dennis R. Polsen, Exec. V.P.—Info. Svcs.
Christopher R. Kravas, Chf. Intermodal Off   David C. Porter, Exec. V.P.—Supply Chain Solutions
David L. Marsh, Chf. Mktg. Off.   James J. Damman, Pres.—Mode Transportation
James B. Gaw, Exec. V.P.—Sales   David C. Zeilstra, V.P., Secy. & Gen. Coun.
Donald G. Maltby, Chf. Supply Chain Officer

Consolidated Balance Sheet   As of December 31, 2010 (000 omitted)

Assets		Liabilities & Stockholders' Equity	
Current assets	$329,160	Current liabilities	$167,418
Net property & equipment	47,806	Deferred items	71,739
Goodwill, net	233,029	Other liabilities	13,950
Other assets	19,412	*Stockholders' equity	376,300
Total	$629,407	Total	$629,407

*36,638,359 shares Class A common stock and 662,296 shares Class B common stock outstanding.

Consolidated Income Statement [a]

Years Ended Dec. 31	Thousands — — — — —		Per Share — — — — —		Common Stock Price Range [b] Calendar Year
	Total Revenues	Net Income	Diluted Earnings [b]	Cash Dividends	
2010	$1,833,737	$43,458	$1.16	$0.00	$37.13—21.53
2009	1,510,970	34,265	0.91	0.00	28.27—15.83
2008	1,860,608	59,245	1.58	0.00	41.75—21.82
2007	1,658,168	59,799	1.53	0.00	38.96—23.69
2006	1,609,529	48,686	1.19	0.00	29.63—17.42

[a] Includes results of Comtrak since its acquisition on March 1, 2006.
[b] Restated to reflect a 2-for-1 stock split paid June 6, 2006.

Transfer Agent & Registrar: American Stock Transfer and Trust Company

General Counsel: David C. Zeilstra, V.P.   Traded (Symbol):   NASDAQ GS (HUBG)
Investor Relations: Terri A. Pizzuto, C.F.O.   Stockholders: 318 (R)
Info. Tech.:   Dennis R. Polsen, Exec. V.P.   Employees: 1,392
Auditors: Ernst & Young LLP   Annual Meeting: In May

Huron Consulting Group Inc.

550 West Van Buren Street, Chicago, Illinois 60607

Telephone: (312) 583-8700   www.huronconsultinggroup.com

Huron Consulting Group Inc. helps clients in diverse industries improve performance, comply with complex regulations, reduce costs, recover from distress, leverage technology, and stimulate growth. The company provides services through three operating segments: Health and Education Consulting, Legal Consulting, and Financial Consulting. Huron provides services to a wide variety of both financially sound and distressed organizations, including Fortune 500 companies, medium-sized businesses, leading academic institutions, healthcare organizations, and the law firms that represent these various organizations. Incorporated in Delaware in 2002.

Directors (In addition to indicated officers)

John McCartney, Chm.
George E. Massaro, V. Chm.
DuBose Ausley

James D. Edwards
H. Eugene Lockhart
John S. Moody

Officers (Directors*)

*James H. Roth, Pres. & C.E.O.
Natalia Delgado, Senior Couns. to the
   Board of Directors & Corp. Secy.
James K. Rojas, Exec. V.P. & C.O.O.
C. Mark Hussey, C.F.O. & Treas.
Shahzad Bashir, Exec. V.P.—Huron Legal

Gordon Mountford, Exec. V.P.—Huron Healthcare
Diane Ratekin, Exec. V. P. & Gen. Couns.
Laura Yaeger, Exec. V.P.—Huron Educ. &
   Life Sciences
Patty Olsen, V.P.—Hum. Res.
Thomas W. Burns, V.P. & Cont.

Consolidated Balance Sheet As of December 31, 2010 (000 omitted)

Assets		Liabilities & Stockholders' Equity	
Current assets	$200,614	Current liabilities	$166,159
Net property & equipment	32,935	Other liabilities	274,452
Other assets	555,434	*Stockholders' equity	348,372
Total	$788,983	Total	$788,983

*21,878,086 shares common stock outstanding.

Consolidated Income Statement

Years Ended Dec. 31	Thousands — — — —		Per Share — — — —		Common Stock Price Range Calendar Year
	Total Revenues[a]	Net Income	Diluted Earnings	Cash Dividends	
2010	$604,600	$8,525	$0.41	$0.00	$26.63—17.86
2009	607,090	(32,873)[b]	(1.63)[b]	0.00	59.95—11.99
2008	528,618	10,081	0.53	0.00	78.75—40.63
2007	383,288	24,280	1.43	0.00	83.25—44.26
2006	195,294	22,859	1.40	0.00	45.98—23.90

a Includes reimbursable expenses
b Includes loss from discontinued operations of $18.4 million ($0.91 per diluted share).

Transfer Agent & Registrar: Computershare Investor Services

General Counsel:	Diane Ratekin, Exec. V.P.	Traded (Symbol):	NASDAQ GS (HURN)
Investor Relations:	Ellen Wong	Stockholders:	21 (R)
Human Resources:	Patty Olsen, V.P.	Employees:	1,558
Auditors:	PricewaterhouseCoopers LLP	Annual Meeting:	In May

Hyatt Hotels Corporation

71 South Wacker Drive, 12th Floor, Chicago, Illinois 60606
Telephone: (312) 750-1234   www.hyatt.com

Hyatt Hotels Corporation is a global hospitality company that manages, franchises, owns, and develops hotels, resorts, and residential and vacation ownership properties. As of December 31, 2010, the company's portfolio consisted of 453 properties in 45 countries. The company's brands include Park Hyatt, Grand Hyatt, Andaz, Hyatt Regency, Hyatt, Hyatt Place, Hyatt Summerfield Suites, and Hyatt Vacation Club (in the process of changing its name to Hyatt Residence Club). On November 10, 2009, Hyatt Hotels completed its initial public offering. Incorporated in Delaware in 2004; present name adopted in 2009.

Directors (In addition to indicated officers)

Bernard W. Aronson
Richard A. Friedman
Susan D. Kronick
Mackey J. McDonald
Gregory B. Penner

Penny Pritzker
Michael A. Rocca
Byron D. Trott
Richard C. Tuttle
James H. Wooten, Jr.

Officers (Directors*)

*Thomas J. Pritzker, Chm.
*Mark S. Hoplamazian, Pres. & C.E.O.
H. Charles Floyd, Exec. V.P. &
  C.O.O.—North Amer.
Stephen G. Haggerty, Exec. V.P. & Gbl.
  Head—Real Estate & Dev.

Rena Hozore Reiss, Exec. V.P., Gen. Coun. & Secy.
Rakesh Sarna, Exec. V.P. & C.O.O.—Intl.
Harmit J. Singh, Exec. V.P. & C.F.O.
John Wallis, Sr. V.P. & Gbl. Head—Mktg. &
  Brand Strat.
Robert W.K. Webb, Sr. V.P. & Chf. Hum. Res. Off.

Consolidated Balance Sheet As of December 31, 2010 (000 omitted)

Assets		Liabilities & Stockholders' Equity	
Current assets	$2,165,000	Current liabilities	$ 596,000
Net property & equipment	3,453,000	Long-term debt	714,000
Other assets	1,625,000	Other liabilities	802,000
		Noncntrolling interests	13,000
		*Stockholders' equity	5,118,000
Total	$7,243,000	Total	$7,243,000

*44,487,197 shares Class A and 129,466,000 Class B common stock outstanding.

Consolidated Income Statement

Years Ended Dec. 31	Thousands — — — —		Per Share ab — — — —		Common Stock
	Total Revenues	Net Income	Diluted Earnings	Cash Dividends	Price Range abc Calendar Year
2010	$3,527,000	$ 66,000	$ 0.29	$0.00	$46.25—28.16
2009	3,330,000	(43,000)	(0.28)	0.00	30.70—27.75
2008	3,835,000	168,000	0.90		
2007	3,735,000	270,000	1.98		
2006	3,467,000	315,000	2.41		

a Class A common stock.
b Adjusted to reflect a one-for-two reverse split of common stock effected on October 14, 2009
c Stock began trading on the New York Stock Exchange on November 5, 2009. Initial public offering completed November 10, 2009.

Transfer Agent & Registrar: Wells Fargo Bank, N.A.

General Counsel:	Rena Hozore Reiss	Traded (Symbol):	NYSE (H)
Investor Relations:	Atish Shah, Sr. V.P.	Stockholders:	26 (R)
Human Resources:	Robert W.K. Webb	Employees:	45,000
Auditors:	Deloitte & Touche LLP	Annual Meeting:	In June

IDEX Corporation

1925 West Field Court, Lake Forest, Illinois 60045

Telephone: (847) 498-7070　　　　　　　**www.idexcorp.com**

IDEX Corporation and its subsidiaries design, manufacture, and market a broad range of proprietary pumps and metering products, dispensing equipment, and other engineered products. The company is organized into four segments: Fluid & Metering Technologies, Health & Science Technologies, Dispensing Equipment, and Fire & Safety/Diversified Products. The Fluid & Metering Technologies segment designs, produces, and distributes pumps, flow meters, and related controls for the movement of liquids and gases in a diverse range of end markets from industrial infrastructure to food and beverage. The Health & Science Technologies segment designs, produces, and distributes a wide variety of small-scale, highly accurate pumps, valves, fittings, and medical devices, as well as compressors used in medical, dental, and industrial applications. The Dispensing Equipment segment produces highly engineered equipment for dispensing, metering, and mixing colorants and paints, as well as refinishing equipment. The Fire & Safety/Diversified Products segment produces firefighting pumps and controls, rescue tools, lifting bags, and other components and systems for the fire and rescue industry, as well as engineered stainless steel banding and clamping devices. In June 2011, IDEX acquired CVI Melles Griot, a global leader in the design and manufacture of precision photonic solutions used in the life sciences, research, semiconductor, security, and defense markets. Incorporated in Delaware in 1987.

Directors (In addition to indicated officers)

Bradley J. Bell	Gregory F. Milzcik
Ruby R. Chandy	Ernest J. Mrozek
William M. Cook	Livingston Satterthwaite
Frank S. Hermance	Michael T. Tokarz

Officers (Directors*)

*Lawrence D. Kingsley, Chm., Pres. & C.E.O.
Kevin G. Hostetler, V.P.—Grp. Exec.–Fluid & Metering Technologies
Heath A. Mitts, V.P. & C.F.O.
Harold Morgan, V.P.—Hum. Res.
Frank J. Notaro, V.P., Gen. Coun. & Secy.

Daniel J. Salliotte, V.P.—Strat. & Bus. Dev.
Andrew K. Silvernail, V.P.—Grp. Exec.–Health & Science Technologies, Gbl. Dispensing & Fire & Safety/Diversified Prods.
Michael J. Yates, V.P. & Chf. Acct. Off.

Consolidated Balance Sheet As of December 31, 2010 (000 omitted)

Assets		Liabilities & Stockholders' Equity	
Current assets	$ 692,758	Current liabilities	$ 353,668
Net property, plant & equipment	188,562	Long-term debt	408,450
Goodwill	1,207,001	Other liabilities	243,917
Intangible assets	281,392	*Shareholders' equity	1,375,660
Other assets	11,982		
Total	$2,381,695	Total	$2,381,695

*82,069,683 shares common stock outstanding.

Consolidated Income Statement

Years Ended Dec. 31	Thousands — — — — —		Per Share [a] — — — —		Common Stock Price Range [b] Calendar Year
	Net Sales	Net Income	Diluted Earnings	Cash Dividends	
2010	$1,513,073	$157,100	$1.90	$0.60	$40.29—27.54
2009	1,329,661	113,391	1.40	0.48	32.85—16.67
2008	1,489,471	127,026	1.53	0.48	40.75—17.70
2007	1,358,631	153,700 [b]	1.87 [b]	0.48	44.99—30.41
2006	1,154,940	144,569 [c]	1.78 [c]	0.40	35.65—26.00

[a] Restated to reflect 3-for-2 stock split in the form of a 50% stock dividend in May 2007.
[b] Includes loss from discontinued operations, net of tax, of $719,000 ($0.01 per diluted share).
[c] Includes income from discontinued operations, net of tax, of $12,949,000 ($0.16 per diluted share).

Transfer Agent & Registrar: BNY Mellon Shareowner Services

General Counsel:	Frank J. Notaro, V.P.	Traded (Symbol):	NYSE, CSE (IEX)
Investor Relations:	Heath A. Mitts, C.F.O.	Stockholders:	7,000 (R)
Human Resources:	Harold Morgan, V.P.	Employees:	5,966
Info. Tech.:	Divakar Kamath, C.I.O.	Annual Meeting:	In April
Auditors:	Deloitte & Touche LLP		

Illinois Tool Works Inc.

3600 West Lake Avenue, Glenview, Illinois 60026-1215

Telephone: (847) 724-7500 **www.itw.com**

Illinois Tool Works Inc. manufactures and markets a variety of highly engineered products and systems that provide specific, problem-solving solutions for a diverse customer base worldwide. The company's reportable segments include: Industrial Packaging (steel, plastic, and paper products used for bundling, shipping, and protecting goods in transit); Power Systems & Electronics (equipment and consumables associated with specialty power conversion, metallurgy, and electronics); Transportation (components, fasteners, fluids, and polymers, as well as truck remanufacturing and related parts and service); Food Equipment (commercial food equipment such as warewashing, cooking, and refrigerating equipment); Construction Products (tools, fasteners, and other products); Polymers & Fluids (adhesives, sealants, lubrication, and cutting fluid, and hygiene products); Decorative Surfaces (laminate furniture, countertops, flooring, and worktops); and All Other (includes plastic bags and fasteners and other items). The company has approximately 840 operating units located in 57 countries. In April 2011, the company announced that it had entered into a definitive agreement to sell its finishing group of businesses, consisting of paint spray systems and technologies, to Graco Inc. Founded in 1912 and incorporated in Delaware in 1961.

Directors (In addition to indicated officers)

Susan Crown	David B. Smith, Jr.
Don H. Davis, Jr.	Pamela B. Strobel
Robert C. McCormack	Kevin M. Warren
Robert S. Morrison	Anré D. Williams
James A. Skinner	

Officers (Directors*)

*David B. Speer, Chm. & C.E.O.	David C. Parry, Exec. V.P.
Thomas J. Hansen, V. Chm.	Juan Valls, Exec. V.P.
E. Scott Santi, V. Chm.	Jane L. Warner, Exec. V.P.
Robert E. Brunner, Exec. V.P.	Sharon M. Brady, Sr. V.P.—Hum. Res.
Timothy J. Gardner, Exec. V.P.	Ronald D. Kropp, Sr. V.P. & C.F.O.
Philip M. Gresh, Jr., Exec. V.P.	Allan C. Sutherland, Sr. V.P.—Taxes & Invests.
Craig A. Hindman, Exec. V.P.	James H. Wooten, Jr., Sr. V.P., Gen. Coun. & Secy.
Roland M. Martel, Exec. V.P.	John L. Brooklier, V.P.—Inv. Rel.
Steven L. Martindale, Exec. V.P.	Mark Croll, V.P.—Intellectual Property
Sundaram Nagarajan, Exec. V.P.	Randall J. Scheuneman, V.P. & Chf. Acct. Off.
Christopher O'Herlihy, Exec. V.P.	

Consolidated Balance Sheet As of December 31, 2010 (000 omitted)

Assets		Liabilities & Stockholders' Equity	
Current assets	$ 5,968,401	Current liabilities	$ 3,093,592
Net property, plant & equipment	2,023,045	Long-term debt	2,511,959
Goodwill	4,879,312	Other liabilities	1,263,476
Other assets	3,379,515	*Stockholders' equity	9,381,246
Total	$16,250,273	Total	$16,250,273

*497,744,301 shares common stock outstanding.

Consolidated Income Statement [a]

Years Ended Dec. 31	Thousands — — — — — Operating Revenues	Net Income [c]	Per Share [b]— — — — — Diluted Earnings [c]	Cash Dividends	Common Stock Price Range [b] Calendar Year
2010	$15,870,376	$1,527,193	$3.03	$1.30	$53.89—40.33
2009	13,877,068	969,490	1.93	1.24	51.16—25.60
2008	17,100,341	1,691,093	3.24	1.18	55.59—28.50
2007	16,110,267	1,827,691	3.29	0.98	60.00—45.60
2006	13,788,346	1,680,551	2.95	0.75	53.54—41.54

[a] Certain reclassifications of prior years' data have been made to conform with current year reporting, including discontinued operations.
[b] Adjusted to reflect a 2-for-1 stock split distributed May 25, 2006.
[c] From continuing operations.

Transfer Agent & Registrar: Computershare Investor Services

General Counsel:	James Wooten, Jr., Sr. V.P.	**Traded (Symbol):**	NYSE (ITW)
Investor Relations:	John L. Brooklier, V.P.	**Stockholders:**	9,879 (R)
Human Resources:	Sharon M. Brady, Sr. V.P.	**Employees:**	61,000
Auditors:	Deloitte & Touche LLP	**Annual Meeting:**	In May

Inland Real Estate Corporation

2901 Butterfield Road, Oak Brook, Illinois 60523

Telephone: (630) 218-8000   **www.inlandrealestate.com**

Inland Real Estate Corporation is a real estate investment trust (REIT) that acquires, owns, operates, and develops open-air neighborhood retail centers, community centers, power and lifestyle shopping centers, and single-user retail properties in California, Idaho, Florida, Illinois, Indiana, Michigan, Minnesota, Missouri, Nebraska, Ohio, Tennessee, and Wisconsin. Inland Real Estate has ownership interests in 61 neighborhood retail centers totaling approximately 4,019,000 gross leasable square feet, 22 community centers totaling approximately 2,985,000 gross leasable square feet, 29 power centers totaling approximately 4,560,000 gross leasable square feet, one lifestyle center totaling approximately 547,000 gross leasable square feet, and 29 single-user properties totaling approximately 1,392,000 gross leasable square feet. Incorporated in Maryland in 1994.

Directors (In addition to indicated officers)

Thomas P. D'Arcy, Chm.
Daniel L. Goodwin
Joel G. Herter
Heidi N. Lawton

Thomas H. McAuley
Thomas R. McWilliams
Joel D. Simmons

Officers (Directors*)

Mark E. Zalatoris, Pres. & C.E.O.
Beth Sprecher Brooks, Sr. V.P., Gen.
    Coun. & Secy.
Brett A. Brown, Sr. V.P., C.F.O. & Treas.

William W. Anderson, V.P.—Transactions
D. Scott Carr, Pres.—Inland Commer. Prop. Mgt.
Kristi A. Rankin, Sr. V.P.—Inland Commer. Prop.
    Mgt.

Consolidated Balance Sheet As of December 31, 2010 (000 omitted)

Assets		Liabilities & Stockholders' Equity	
Net investment properties	$1,018,956	Mortgages payable	$ 483,186
Cash & cash equivalents	13,566	Unsecured credit facilities	195,000
Accounts receivable, net	37,755	Other liabilities	178,662
Other assets	184,564	Minority interest	104
		*Stockholders' equity	397,889
Total	$1,254,841	Total	$1,254,841

*87,838,000 shares common stock outstanding.

Consolidated Income Statement

Years Ended Dec. 31	Thousands — — — — —		Per Share — — — — —		Common Stock Price Range Calendar Year
	Total Revenues	Net Income [ab]	Diluted Earnings [b]	Cash Dividends	
2010	$167,029	$ (263)	$0.00	$0.57	$10.29— 7.17
2009	168,025[c]	8,212	0.10	0.69	13.03— 5.79
2008	185,885[c]	30,425[c]	0.46[c]	0.98	16.97— 8.20
2007	184,664	42,095[c]	0.64[c]	0.98	21.14—13.50
2006	175,856	45,184	0.67	0.96	19.88—12.70

[a] Funds from operations (FFO), in thousands: 2010: $51,592; 2009: $68,172; 2008: $85,154; 2007: $91,950; 2006: $89,163.
[b] Available to common stockholders.
[c] Restated to conform with current year presentation.

Transfer Agent & Registrar: Registrar and Transfer Company
General Counsel: Beth S. Brooks, Sr. V.P.
Investor Relations: Theresa Strino
Auditors: KPMG LLP

Traded (Symbol):   NYSE (IRC)
Stockholders: 4,567 (R)
Employees: 113
Annual Meeting: In June

InnerWorkings, Inc.

600 West Chicago Avenue, Suite 850, Chicago, Illinois 60654
Telephone: (312) 642-3700   www.iwprint.com

InnerWorkings, Inc. is a leading provider of managed print and promotional procurement solutions to corporate clients in the United States. Its proprietary software applications and database, PPM4™, create a fully integrated solution that stores, analyzes, and tracks the production capabilities of the supplier network, including quote and price data for each bid received and print job executed. Through a network of over 8,000 suppliers, InnerWorkings offers a full range of print, fulfillment, and logistics services. In February 2011, the company acquired CPRO Services Ltd., the primary provider of business process outsourcing solutions for the print category in Latin America. Incorporated in Delaware in 2006 as a successor company.

Directors (In addition to indicated officers)

Jack M. Greenberg, Chm.   Eric P. Lefkofsky
Sharyar Baradaran   John R. Walter
Peter J. Barris   Linda S. Wolf
Charles K. Bobrinskoy

Officers (Directors*)

*Eric D. Belcher, Pres. & C.E.O.   Richard L. Doss, Pres.—Southern Region
 Joseph M. Busky, C.F.O. & Secy.   David Freundlich, Pres.—Eastern Region
 Todd Andrews, Sr. V.P. & Gen. Coun.   Michael R. Holewinski, Pres.—Central Region
 Seth M. Kessler, Sr. V.P.—Gbl. Strat.   Richard M. Morgan, Pres.—Western Region

Consolidated Balance Sheet   As of December 31, 2010 (000 omitted)

Assets		Liabilities & Stockholders' Equity	
Current assets	$146,476	Current liabilities	$ 68,938
Net property, plant & equipment	9,887	Capital lease obligations	7
Goodwill	93,476	Other liabilities	50,796
Other assets	30,086	*Stockholders' equity	160,184
Total	$279,925	Total	$279,925

*46,092,291 shares common stock outstanding.

Consolidated Income Statement

Years Ended Dec. 31	Thousands — — — —		Per Share — — — —		Common Stock Price Range b Calendar Year
	Revenue	Net Income a	Diluted Earnings a	Cash Dividends	
2010	$482,212	$11,210	$0.24	$0.00	$ 7.73— 4.95
2009	400,447	6,309	0.13	0.00	6.86— 1.92
2008 c	419,017	15,953	0.32	0.00	16.20— 4.83
2007	288,431	22,504	0.45	0.00	18.69—11.08
2006	160,515	6,871	0.21	0.00	18.15—10.10

a Applicable to common stockholders.
b Initial public offering completed August 16, 2006.
c Includes results of acquired businesses since dates of acquisition: etrinsic (May 1), MediaLink (July 1), Marketing-Out-of-the-Box Inc. (July 1), Mikam Graphics (August 1), and Origen Partners (October 1). Also includes restructuring liabilities of $486,609.

Transfer Agent & Registrar: BNY Mellon Shareowner Services
General Counsel: Todd Andrews, Sr. V.P.   Traded (Symbol):   NASDAQ (INWK)
Investor Relations: Joseph M. Busky, C.F.O.   Stockholders: 67 (R)
Auditors: Ernst & Young LLP   Employees: 743
                                                   Annual Meeting: In June

Integrys Energy Group, Inc.

130 East Randolph Drive, Chicago, Illinois 60601-6207

Telephone: (312) 228-5400   **www.integrysgroup.com**

Integrys Energy Group, Inc. , formed in early 2007 as the result of a merger between WPS Resources Corporation and Peoples Energy Corporation, is a diversified holding company with regulated utility operations operating through six wholly owned subsidiaries: Wisconsin Public Service Corporation, The Peoples Gas Light and Coke Company, North Shore Gas Company, Upper Peninsula Power Company, Michigan Gas Utilities Corporation, and Minnesota Energy Resources Corporation. The company's nonregulated operations serve the U.S. competitive energy markets through its wholly owned nonregulated subsidiary, Integrys Energy Services. Integrys Energy Group also holds a 34% equity ownership interest in American Transmission Company LLC (an electric transmission company operating in Wisconsin, Michigan, Minnesota, and Illinois). As of December 31, 2010, Integrys Energy Group served approximately 1,673,000 regulated natural gas utility customers and approximately 491,000 regulated electric utility customers. In March 2010, the company's subsidiary Integrys Energy Services closed on the sale of its Environmental Markets business to EDF Trading North America, LLC. In April 2010, Integrys Energy Services closed on the sale of its wholesale electric marketing trading business to Macquarie Cook Power, Inc., as part of its strategy to reduce the size and scope of its operations. This transaction completes the divestiture of Integrys Energy Services' wholesale business. Incorporated in Wisconsin in 1993.

Directors (In addition to indicated officers)

Keith E. Bailey	Ellen Carnahan	James L. Kemerling
William J. Brodsky	Michelle L. Collins	Michael E. Lavin
Albert J. Budney, Jr.	Kathryn M. Hasselblad-Pascale	William F. Protz, Jr.
Pastora San Juan Cafferty	John W. Higgins	

Officers (Directors*)

*Charles A. Schrock, Chm., Pres. & C.E.O.
Phil Mikulsky, Exec. V.P.—Bus. Performance & Shared Svcs.
Mark A. Radtke, Exec. V.P. & Chf. Strat. Off.
Joseph P. O'Leary, Sr. V.P. & C.F.O.
Diane L. Ford, V.P. & Corp. Cont.
William J. Guc, V.P. & Treas.
William D. Laakso, V.P.—Hum. Res.
Barth J. Wolf, V.P., Chf. Legal Off. & Secy.

James F. Schott, V.P.—External Affs.
Lawrence T. Borgard, Pres. & C.O.O.—Utilities
Daniel J. Verbanac, Pres.—Integrys Energy Svcs.
Charles A. Cloninger, Pres—MN Energy Resources Corp. and MI Gas Utilities Corp.
Willard S. Evans, Jr., Pres.—Peoples Gas Light & Coke Co. and Pres.—North Shore Gas Co.
Barbara A. Nick, Pres.—Upper Peninsula Power Co.

Consolidated Balance Sheet   As of December 31, 2010 (000 omitted)

Assets		Liabilities & Stockholders' Equity	
Current assets	$2,050,400	Current liabilities	$1,657,800
Net property, plant & equipment	5,013,400	Long-term debt	2,161,600
Goodwill	642,500	Other liabilities	3,091,500
Other assets	2,110,500	Minority interest	100
		*Stockholders' equity	2,905,800
Total	$9,816,800	Total	$9,816,800

*77,350,079 shares common stock outstanding.

Consolidated Income Statement

Years Ended Dec. 31	Thousands — — — — — Operating Revenues	Net Income [a]	Per Share — — — — — Basic Earnings [a]	Cash Dividends [b]	Common Stock Price Range Fiscal Year
2010	$ 5,203,200	$220,900	$ 2.85	$2.72	$54.45—40.53
2009 [c]	7,499,800	(69,600)	(0.91)	2.72	45.10—19.44
2008 [c]	14,047,800	116,500	1.52	2.68	53.92—36.91
2007 [d]	10,292,400	251,300	3.51	2.56	60.63—48.10
2006 [ef]	6,890,700	155,800	3.68	2.28	57.75—47.39

[a] Attributed to common shareholders. [b] Declared.
[c] Certain amounts have been retrospectively adjusted due to change in accounting policy in 2010.
[d] Includes the impact of the PEC merger on February 21, 2007. [e] Results of successor company.
[f] Includes the impact of the acquisition of natural gas distribution operations from Aquila by MGU on 04/01/06 and MERC on 07/01/06.

Transfer Agent & Registrar: American Stock Transfer & Trust Co.

Corporate Counsel:	Foley & Lardner	Traded (Symbol):	NYSE (TEG)
Investor Relations:	Steven P. Eschbach, V.P.	Stockholders:	30,352 (R)
Human Resources:	William D. Laakso, V.P.	Employees:	4,612
Info. Tech.:	David W. Harpole, V.P.	Annual Meeting:	In May
Auditors:	Deloitte & Touche LLP		

Jones Lang LaSalle Incorporated

200 East Randolph Drive, Chicago, Illinois 60601

Telephone: (312) 782-5800   **www.joneslanglasalle.com**

Jones Lang LaSalle is a leading real estate services and money management firm, operating 185 corporate offices worldwide. The company provides comprehensive integrated real estate and investment management expertise on a local, regional, and global level to owners, occupiers, and investors. Jones Lang LaSalle is also an industry leader in property and corporate facility management services, with a portfolio of approximately 1.8 billion square feet under management worldwide. LaSalle Investment Management, the company's investment management business, is one of the world's largest and most diverse real estate money management firms, with over $41 billion of assets under management. In May 2011, Jones Lang LaSalle announced it will merge with international property consultancy King Sturge. All 43 King Sturge offices and businesses across Europe, including 24 in the UK, will become part of Jones Lang LaSalle and will operate under the Jones Lang LaSalle brand. Incorporated in Maryland in 1997.

Directors (In addition to indicated officers)

Sheila A. Penrose, Chm.	Ming Lu
Hugo Bagué	Martin H. Nesbitt
Darryl Hartley-Leonard	David B. Rickard
DeAnne Julius	Thomas C. Theobald

Officers (Directors*)

*Colin Dyer, Pres. & C.E.O.
*Lauralee E. Martin, Exec. V.P., C.O.O. & C.F.O.
*Roger T. Staubach, Chm.—Americas
Mark J. Ohringer, Exec. V.P., Gbl. Gen. Coun. & Corp. Secy.
Nazneen Razi, Exec. V.P. & Chf. Hum. Res. Off.
Alastair Hughes, C.E.O.—Asia Pacific
Jeff A. Jacobson, C.E.O.—LaSalle Invest. Mgt.
Peter C. Roberts, C.E.O.—Americas

Christian Ulbrich, C.E.O.—Eur., Middle East & Africa
Charles J. Doyle, Chf. Mktg. & Commun. Off.
Mark K. Engel, Gbl. Cont.
James S. Jasionowski, Gbl. Dir.—Tax
David A. Johnson, C.I.O.
Corey Lewis, Gbl. Dir.—Internal Audit
Joe Romenesko, Gbl. Treas.

Consolidated Balance Sheet   As of December 31, 2010 (000 omitted)

Assets		Liabilities & Stockholders' Equity	
Current assets	$1,194,841	Current liabilities	$1,296,312
Net property & equipment	198,685	Deferred items	165,469
Goodwill	1,444,708	Other liabilities	316,145
Other assets	511,627	Minority interest	3,004
		*Stockholders' equity	1,568,931
Total	$3,349,861	Total	$3,349,861

*42,659,999 shares common stock outstanding.

Consolidated Income Statement

Years Ended Dec. 31	Thousands — — — — —		Per Share — — — — —		Common Stock Price Range Calendar Year
	Total Revenue	Net Income [a]	Diluted Earnings [a]	Cash Dividends	
2010	$2,925,613	$153,524	$ 3.48	$0.20	$ 88.51—57.01
2009	2,480,736	(4,109)	(0.11)	0.20	61.57—16.94
2008	2,697,586	83,515	2.44	0.75	90.19—19.18
2007	2,652,075	256,490	7.64	0.85	123.17—70.48
2006	2,013,578	175,344 [b]	5.24 [b]	0.60	93.21—52.75

[a] Attributable to common shareholders.
[b] Includes gain of $1,180,000 ($0.03 per diluted share) due to cumulative effect of change in accounting principle (SFAS No. 123).

Transfer Agent & Registrar:	BNY Mellon Shareowner Services
General Counsel:	Mark J. Ohringer, Exec. V.P.
Investor Relations:	Joe Romenesko, Gbl. Treas.
Human Resources:	Nazneen Razi, Exec. V.P.
Info. Tech.:	David A. Johnson, C.I.O.
Auditors:	KPMG LLP

Traded (Symbol):   NYSE (JLL)
Stockholders: 48,873 (B)
Employees: 40,300
Annual Meeting: In May

KapStone Paper and Packaging Corporation

1101 Skokie Boulevard, Suite 300, Northbrook, Illinois 60062
Telephone: (847) 239-8800   www.kapstonepaper.com

KapStone Paper & Packaging Corp. is a leading North American producer and seller of a variety of unbleached kraft paper, linerboard, saturating kraft, and unbleached folding carton board. The company was formed in April 2005 to effect a business combination with a suitable operating business in the paper, packaging, forest products, and related industries. KapStone Paper and Packaging Corporation is the parent company of KapStone Kraft Paper Corporation, which includes paper mills in Roanoke Rapids, North Carolina and North Charleston, South Carolina, a lumber mill in Summerville, South Carolina, and five chipping mills in South Carolina. In January 2007, the company purchased the Kraft Papers Business from International Paper Company, and in July 2008, KapStone acquired the Charleston Kraft Division from MeadWestvaco Corporation. In March 2009, KapStone sold its Ride Rite division to Illinois Tool Works Inc. Incorporated in Delaware in 2005.

Directors (In addition to indicated officers)

John M. Chapman
Jonathan R. Furer
Brian G. Gamache
Ronald J. Gidwitz

Matthew H. Paull
S. Jay Stewart
David P. Storch

Officers (Directors*)

*Roger W. Stone, Chm. & C.E.O.
*Matthew Kaplan, Pres. & Secy.

Timothy P. Keneally, V.P. & Gen. Mgr.
Andrea K. Tarbox, V.P. & C.F.O.

Consolidated Balance Sheet As of December 31, 2010 (000 omitted)

Assets		Liabilities & Stockholders' Equity	
Current assets	$222,247	Current liabilities	$115,554
Net property, plant & equipment	466,019	Long-term debt & notes, net	92,857
Other assets	31,461	Other liabilities	92,682
		*Stockholders' equity	418,634
Total	$719,727	Total	$719,727

*46,041,712 shares common stock outstanding.

Consolidated Income Statement

Years Ended Dec. 31	Thousands — — — —		Per Share [a] — — — —		Common Stock Price Range [a] Calendar Year
	Net Sales	Net Income	Diluted Earnings	Cash Dividends	
2010	$782,676	$65,041	$1.38	$0.00	$15.56—8.08
2009	632,478	80,280	2.29	0.00	9.90—1.05
2008 [b]	524,549	19,665	0.57	0.00	7.97—2.06
2007 [b]	256,795	26,963	0.75	0.00	7.79—6.10
2006 [b]		2,196	0.07	0.00	6.49—5.32
2006 [c]	246,161	19,967			

[a] Common stock traded on NASDAQ Global Market from May 29, 2007 through January 3, 2010; began trading on NYSE effective January 4, 2010.
[b] Successor company.
[c] Predecessor company, Kraft Papers Business.

Transfer Agent & Registrar:	Continental Stock Transfer & Trust Co.		
General Counsel:	Timothy P. Davisson	Traded (Symbol):	NYSE (KS)
Investor Relations:	Andrea K. Tarbox, C.F.O.	Stockholders:	6,742 (B)
Auditors:	Ernst & Young LLP	Employees:	1,600
		Annual Meeting:	In May

Kemper Corporation

One East Wacker Drive, Chicago, Illinois 60601-1802
Telephone: (312) 661-4600   www.kempercorporation.com

Kemper Corporation, formerly Unitrin, Inc., is a diversified insurance company with subsidiaries that provide automobile, homeowners, life, health, and other insurance products for individuals and small businesses. The company offers these products through a network of 10,000 independent insurance professionals and 2,600 career agents. Kemper Corporation conducts its operations through several business lines: Kemper Preferred, Unitrin Specialty, Unitrin Direct, and Life and Health Insurance. The company completed the sale of Fireside Bank's automobile finance loan portfolio in the third quarter of 2011. Incorporated in Delaware in 1990.

Directors (In addition to indicated officers)

James E. Annable
Douglas G. Geoga
Reuben L. Hedlund
Julie M. Howard

Wayne Kauth
Fayez S. Sarofim
David M. Storch
Richard C. Vie

Officers (Directors*)

*Donald G. Southwell, Chm., Pres. & C.E.O.
Scott Renwick, Sr. V.P., Gen. Coun. & Secy.
Dennis R. Vigneau, Sr. V.P. & C.F.O.
John M. Boschelli, V.P. & Chf. Invest. Off.
Lisa M. King, V.P.—Hum. Res.

Edward J. Konar, V.P.
Christopher L. Moses, V.P. & Treas.
Richard Roeske, V.P. & Chf. Acct. Off.
Dennis J. Sandelski, V.P.—Tax
Frank J. Sodaro, V.P.—Plan. & Analysis

Consolidated Balance Sheet As of December 31, 2010 (000 omitted)

Assets		Liabilities & Stockholders' Equity	
Investments	$6,250,800	Insurance reserves	$4,182,400
Automobile loan receivables	337,600	Investment certificates	321,400
Other receivables	606,700	Unearned premiums	678,600
Other assets	1,163,400	Notes payable	609,800
		Other liabilities	452,900
		*Stockholders' equity	2.113,400
Total	$8,358,500	Total	$8,358,500

*61,066,587 shares common stock outstanding.

Consolidated Income Statement

Years Ended Dec. 31	Thousands — — — — —		Per Share — — — —		Common Stock Price Range Calendar Year
	Total Revenues	Net Income [a]	Diluted Earnings [a]	Cash Dividends	
2010	$2,743,400	$183,800	$ 2.97	$0.88	$31.12—21.63
2009	2,933,400	162,200	2.60	1.07	23.87— 7.96
2008	2,742,200	(38,000)	(0.60)	1.88	47.74—13.05
2007 [b]	2,903,000	178,100	2.70	1.82	53.00—39.65
2006 [b]	2,862,400	267,200	3.92	1.76	51.45—39.33

[a] From continuing operations.
[b] Adjusted for the retrospective application of a change in accounting principle.

Transfer Agent & Registrar: Computershare Investor Services

General Counsel:	Scott Renwick, Sr. V.P.	Traded (Symbol):	NYSE (KMPR)
Investor Relations:	Diana J. Hickert-Hill, V.P.	Stockholders:	5,200 (R)
Human Resources:	Lisa M. King, V.P.	Employees:	7,130
Info. Tech.:	Shawn Crawford	Annual Meeting:	In May
Auditors:	Deloitte & Touche LLP		

THE PRIVATEBANK GUIDE

85

Kraft Foods Inc.

Three Lakes Drive, Northfield, Illinois 60093-2753
Telephone: (847) 646-2000   www.kraftfoodscompany.com

Kraft Foods Inc. is the world's second largest food company. Its brand portfolio is sold in approximately 170 countries. Major brands include Kraft, Nabisco, Oscar Mayer, Maxwell House, Philadelphia, Jacobs, Milka, and LU. The company operates 223 manufacturing and processing facilities worldwide. In March 2007, Altria Group, Inc. spun off its remaining 89% interest in the company to its stockholders. In August 2008, Kraft completed the split-off of its Post cereals business into Ralcorp Holdings, Inc. In February 2010, Kraft acquired Cadbury plc, whose brands include Cadbury Dairy Milk and Green & Black's chocolate; Trident, Dentyne, Hollywood, and Bubbaloo gum products; and Halls, Cadbury Eclairs, Bassett's, and The Natural Confectionery Co. candy products. In March 2010, the company sold its frozen pizza products business to Nestle USA, Inc. Incorporated in Virginia in 2000.

Directors (In addition to indicated officers)

Ajaypal S. Banga	Richard A. Lerner, M.D.
Myra M. Hart	Mackey J. McDonald
Peter B. Henry, Ph.D.	John C. Pope
Lois D. Juliber	Fredric G. Reynolds
Mark D. Ketchum	Jean-François M.L. van Boxmeer

Officers (Directors*)

*Irene B. Rosenfeld, Chm. & C.E.O.
David Brearton, Exec. V.P. & C.F.O.
Timothy P. Cofer, Exec. V.P. & Pres.—Kraft Eur.
Marc S. Firestone, Exec. V.P.—Corp. & Legal Affs. & Gen. Coun.
Sanjay Khosla, Exec. V.P. & Pres.—Developing Markets
Karen J. May, Exec. V.P.—Gbl. Hum. Res.

Sam B. Rovit, Exec. V.P.—Strat.
Jean E. Spence, Exec. V.P.—Res., Dev. & Qual.
W. Anthony Vernon, Exec. V.P. & Pres.—Kraft Foods North Amer.
Mary Beth West, Exec. V.P. & Chf. Category & Mktg. Off.
Carol J. Ward, V.P. & Corp. Secy.

Consolidated Balance Sheet As of December 31, 2010 (000 omitted)

Assets		Liabilities & Stockholders' Equity	
Current assets	$16,221,000	Current liabilities	$15,660,000
Net property, plant & equipment	13,792,000	Long-term debt	26,859,000
Goodwill	37,856,000	Other liabilities	16,828,000
Other assets	27,420,000	Minority interest	108,000
		*Stockholders' equity	35,834,000
Total	$95,289,000	Total	$95,289,000

*1,748,000,000 shares common stock outstanding.

Consolidated Income Statement

Years Ended Dec. 31	Thousands — — — — — Net Revenues [a]	Net Income [bc]	Per Share — — — — — Basic Earnings [bc]	Cash Dividends	Common Stock Price Range Calendar Year
2010	$49,207,000	$4,114,000	$2.39	$1.16	$32.67—27.09
2009	38,754,000	3,021,000	2.03	1.16	29.84—20.81
2008	40,492,000	2,884,000	1.90	1.12	34.97—24.75
2007	34,580,000	2,721,000	1.70	1.04	37.20—29.95
2006	31,849,000	3,060,000	1.84	0.96	36.67—27.44

[a] Restated.
[b] Attributable to Kraft Foods.
[c] Includes earnings from discontinued operations of $1,644,000,000 ($0.95 per diluted share) in 2010; $218,000,000 ($0.14 per diluted share) in 2009; $1,215,000,000 ($0.80 per diluted share) in 2008; $381,000,000 ($0.24 per diluted share) in 2007; and $372,000,000 ($0.22 per diluted share) in 2006.

Transfer Agent & Registrar: Wells Fargo Shareowner Services

General Counsel:	Marc S. Firestone, Exec. V.P.	Traded (Symbol):	NYSE (KFT)
Investor Relations:	Chris Jakubik, V.P.	Stockholders:	80,245 (R)
Human Resources:	Karen J. May, Exec. V.P.	Employees:	127,000
Auditors:	PricewaterhouseCoopers LLP	Annual Meeting:	In May

Landauer, Inc.

2 Science Road, Glenwood, Illinois 60425-1586

Telephone: (708) 755-7000   **www.landauerinc.com**

Landauer, Inc. is a leading provider of technical and analytical services to determine occupational and environmental radiation exposure and is the leading domestic provider of outsourced medical physics services. The company provides complete radiation dosimetry services to hospitals, medical and dental offices, universities, national laboratories, nuclear facilities, and other industries in which radiation poses a potential threat to employees. Landauer's services include the manufacture of various types of radiation detection monitors, the distribution and collection of the monitors to and from clients, and the analysis and reporting of exposure findings. Luxel®, the company's proprietary, optically stimulated luminescent (OSL) technology, was introduced in 1998 and provides enhanced radiation measurement performance and service benefits. The company also produces InLight™, an automated dosimetry system using its OSL technology. Medical physics services are provided through the company's Global Physics Solutions, Inc. subsidiary. Landauer is the market leader in the U.S. by a substantial margin and has operations in Europe. It owns 50 percent of a Japanese joint venture, Nagase-Landauer; a 75 percent interest in the leading dosimetry service provider in Brazil named SAPRA-Landauer; and a 70 percent ownership of Beijing-Landauer Ltd., a joint venture in China. The company also owns 56.25% of ALSA Dosimetria, S. de R.L. de C.V. in Mexico City. Landauer's operations also include services for the measurement and monitoring of radon gas. Incorporated in Delaware in 1987.

Directors (In addition to indicated officers)

Robert J. Cronin, Chm.
William G. Dempsey
Michael T. Leatherman

David E. Meador
Stephen C. Mitchell
Thomas M. White

Officers (Directors*)

*William E. Saxelby, Pres. & C.E.O.
Richard E. Bailey, Sr. V.P.—Oper.; Pres. &
  C.E.O.—Gbl. Physics Solutions, Inc.
Douglas R. Gipson, Chf. Nuclear Exec.

Jonathon M. Singer, Sr. V.P.—Fin., C.F.O.,
  Treas. & Secy.
R. Craig Yoder, Ph.D., Sr. V.P.—Mktg. & Tech.

Consolidated Balance Sheet As of September 30, 2010 (000 omitted)

Assets		Liabilities & Stockholders' Equity	
Current assets	$ 46,157	Current liabilities	$ 49,552
Net property, plant & equipment	39,815	Non-current liabilities	21,441
Goodwill & other intangible assets	49,270	Minority interest in subsidiary	913
Other assets	15,454	*Stockholders' equity	78,790
Total	$150,696	Total	$150,696

*9,452,765 shares common stock outstanding.

Consolidated Income Statement

Years Ended Sept. 30	Thousands — — — —		Per Share — — — —		Common Stock Price Range Fiscal Year
	Net Revenues	Net Income	Diluted Earnings	Cash Dividends	
2010	$114,367	$23,674 [a]	$2.52 [a]	$2.15	$71.71—50.26
2009	93,827	23,366 [b]	2.49 [b]	2.10	74.51—46.08
2008	89,954	22,983 [c]	2.47 [c]	2.00	73.52—47.00
2007	83,716	19,316 [d]	2.10 [d]	1.90	57.29—45.50
2006	79,043	19,046 [e]	2.09 [e]	1.80	53.00—43.11

[a] Includes acquisition and reorganization costs of $2,028,000 ($0.17 per diluted share).
[b] Includes pension curtailment and transition costs of $2,236,000 ($0.16 per diluted share) and reorganization charges of $416,000 ($0.03 per diluted share).
[c] Includes accelerated depreciation charges of $376,000 ($0.02 per diluted share).
[d] Includes accelerated depreciation and impairment charges of $2,875,000 ($0.19 per diluted share).
[e] Includes reorganization charges and management transition charges of $1,650,000 ($0.11 per diluted share).

Transfer Agent & Registrar: American Stock Transfer & Trust Co.

Corporate Counsel:	Sidley Austin LLP	Traded (Symbol):	NYSE (LDR)
Investor Relations:	Jonathon M. Singer, Sr. V.P.	Stockholders:	301 (R)
Human Resources:	Katherine Bober, Dir.	Employees:	540
Info. Tech.:	Doug King, C.I.O.	Annual Meeting:	In February
Auditors:	PricewaterhouseCoopers LLP		

Lawson Products, Inc.

1666 East Touhy Avenue, Des Plaines, Illinois 60018
Telephone: (847) 827-9666   www.lawsonproducts.com

Lawson Products, Inc. is sells and distributes specialty products to the industrial. commercial, institutional, and government maintenance, repair, and operations market (MRO). The company also manufactures, sells, and distributes specialized component parts, with services to original equipment manufacturers through Automatic Screw Machine Products Company. This market includes the aerospace, off-road equiipment, military, and oil and gas exploration industries. Lawson Products, Inc. sells MRO products in all 50 states, Canada, Mexico, and the Caribbean. In addition, the company exports products that support U.S. military efforts in the Middle East and Europe. Incorporated in Illinois in 1952; reincorporated in Delaware in 1982.

Directors (In addition to indicated officers)

Ronald B. Port, M.D., Chm.
Andrew B. Albert
I. Steven Edelson
James S. Errant

Lee S. Hillman
Thomas S. Postek
Robert G. Rettig
Wilma J. Smelcer

Officers (Directors*)

*Thomas J. Neri, Pres. & C.E.O.
Harry A. Dochelli, Exec. V.P. & C.O.O.
Neil E. Jenkins, Exec. V.P., Gen. Coun. & Secy.
Robert O. Border, Sr. V.P & C.I.O.
Stewart Howley, Sr. V.P.—Strat. Bus. Dev.
Ronald J. Knutson, Sr. V.P. & C.F.O.

Larry Krema, Sr. V.P.—Hum. Res.
Michelle Russell, Sr. V.P.—ERP Exec. Spon.
Victor Galvez, V.P. & Cont.
William Holmes, V.P. & Treas.
Mike Truvell, V.P.—Finance
Frank Ziegler, V.P., Chf. Compliance Off. & Asst Secy.

Consolidated Balance Sheet As of December 31, 2010 (000 omitted)

Assets		Liabilities & Stockholders' Equity	
Current assets	$134,906	Current liabilities	$ 55,551
Net property, plant & equipment	44,442	Other liabilities	37,968
Other assets	57,036	*Stockholders' equity	142,865
Total	$236,384	Total	$236,384

*8,5534,028 shares common stock outstanding.

Consolidated Income Statement

| Years Ended Dec. 31 | Thousands — — — — | | Per Share — — — — | | Common Stock Price Range Calendar Year |
	Net Sales[a]	Net Income	Basic Earnings	Cash Dividends	
2010 [a]	$316,780	$ 6,937	$ 0.81	$0.32	$27.11—12.64
2009	301,769	(2,736)[c]	(0.32)	0.18	26.68— 9.96
2008 [b]	376,572	(27,631)[c]	(3.24)	0.80	38.49—11.81
2007	390,307	10,629 [c]	1.25	0.80	47.00—29.96
2006	386,780	12,612 [c]	1.42	0.80	44.02—32.21

[a] Includes a $4.1 million benefit from legal settlements and a $1.7 million gain on sale of assets.
[b] Includes a $4.0 million charge related to unclaimed property liabilities.
[c] Settlement and related charges of $0.2 million, $31.7 million, $5.8 million, and $3.2 million related to the investigation and Deferred Prosecution Agreement were recorded in 2009, 2008, 2007, and 2006 respectively.

Transfer Agent & Registrar: Computershare Investor Services

General Counsel:	Neil E. Jenkins, Exec. V.P.	Traded (Symbol):	NASDAQ GS (LAWS)
Investor Relations:	Ronald J. Knutson, Sr. V.P.	Stockholders:	570 (R)
Human Resources:	Larry Krema, Sr. V.P.	Employees:	930
Info. Tech.:	Robert O. Border, Sr. V.P.	Annual Meeting:	In May
Auditors:	Ernst & Young LLP		

Lifeway Foods, Inc.
6431 West Oakton Street, Morton Grove, Illinois 60053
Telephone: (847) 967-1010   **www.lifeway.net**

Lifeway Foods, Inc. produces and distributes probiotic, cultured, functional dairy and non-dairy health food products. The company's primary products are kefir, a drinkable dairy beverage similar to but distinct from yogurt, in several flavors sold under the name Lifeway Kefir and Helios Nutrition Organic Kefir; a line of various drinkable yogurts sold under the Tuscan and Lassi brands; and BasicsPlus, a dairy-based immune-supporting dietary supplement beverage. Lifeway also manufactures Lifeway Farmer Cheese, a line of variousfarmer cheeses, a line of gourmet cream cheeses, and Sweet Kiss, a fruit sugar-flavored spreadable cheese. The company also manufactures and markets a vegetable-based seasoning under the Golden Zesta brand. Products are all manufactured at company-owned facilities and distributed primarikly throughout the United States. In October 2010, Lifeway purchased certain assets of First Juice, Inc., a producer of organic fruit and vegetable juice beverages designed for children. Incorporated in Illinois in 1986.

Directors (In addition to indicated officers)

Ludmila Smolyansky, Chm.   Pol Sikar
Renzo Bernardi   Gustavo Carlos Valle
Eugene G. Katz

Officers (Directors*)

*Julie Smolyansky, Pres. & C.E.O.   Valeriy Nikolenko, V.P.—Oper. & Secy.
 Edward P. Smolyansky, C.F.O., Chf. Acct. Off.,
   Treas. & Cont.; Pres. & C.E.O.—Fresh Made
   Dairy, Inc.

Consolidated Balance Sheet As of December 31, 2010 (000 omitted)

Assets		Liabilities & Stockholders' Equity	
Current assets	$16,836	Current liabilities	$ 8,886
Net property & equipment	15,153	Deferred income taxes	3,402
Other assets	20,070	Notes payable	6,122
		*Stockholders' equity	33,649
Total	$52,029	Total	$52,059

*16,536,657 shares common stock outstanding.

Consolidated Income Statement

Years Ended Dec. 31	Thousands — — — — — Sales	Net Income	Per Share — — — — Basic Earnings[a]	Cash Dividends	Common Stock Price Range[a] Calendar Year
2010	$63,543	$3,622	$0.22	$0.00	$12.70—8.07
2009	58,116	5,570	0.33	0.00	14.94—6.07
2008	44,461	1,912	0.11	0.00	15.48—5.43
2007	38,729	3,153	0.19	0.00	20.75—8.51
2006	27,261	2,896	0.17	0.00	10.85—5.06

[a] Restated to reflect 2-for-1 stock split in August 2006.

Transfer Agent & Registrar: Computershare Investor Services

Corporate Counsel:	Futro & Associates	Traded (Symbol):	NASDAQ GM (LWAY)
Investor Relations:	Edward P. Smolyansky, C.F.O.	Stockholders:	82 (R)
Info. Tech.:	Julie Smolyansky, Pres.	Employees:	315
Auditors:	Plante & Moran, PLLC	Annual Meeting:	In June

Lime Energy Co.

1280 Landmeier Road, Elk Grove Village, Illinois 60007-2410
Telephone: (847) 437-1666   **www.lime-energy.com**

Lime Energy Co. is a leading provider of energy efficiency and renewable energy services. The company evaluates, designs, and installs projects that save energy at client facilities, reduce operations and maintenance costs, and improve building infrastructure and value. Lime Energy also assists clients in mananging their carbon footprints to limit the environmental impact of their operations. Clients include commercial and industrial building owners, utilities, energy service companies, federal, state, and local governments. The company has worked in high-rise office complexes, large government sites, schools, and hospitals. Work is performed by a staff of engineers, certified energy managers, technicians, and construction and installation professionals. The company plans to complete the relocation of its headquarters to Huntersville, NC in the third quarter of 2011. Incorporated in Delaware in 1998; present name adopted in 2006.

Directors (In addition to indicated officers)

Richard P. Kiphart, Lead Director
Gregory T. Barnum
Christopher W. Capps
William R. (Max) Carey, Jr.

Joseph F. Desmond
Stephen Glick
Pradeep Kapadia
Daniel W. Parke

Officers (Directors*)

*David R. Asplund, Exec. Chm.
*John E. O'Rourke, Pres. & C.E.O.
Jeffrey R. Mistarz, Exec. V.P., C.F.O., Treas. & Corp. Secy.
Eric Dupont, Group Pres.—Lime Energy Asset Dev.

Adam Procell, Group Pres.—Energy Consult & Tech. Svcs.
James G. Smith, Group Pres.—Energy Efficiency Svcs.

Consolidated Balance Sheet As of December 31, 2010 (000 omitted)

Assets		Liabilities & Stockholders' Equity	
Current assets	$58,722	Current liabilities	$31,417
Net property & equipment	2,940	Long-term debt	418
Long-term receivables	543	*Stockholders' equity	54,441
Other assets	24,071		
Total	$86,276	Total	$86,276

*23,804,776 shares common stock outstanding as of March 8, 2011.

Consolidated Income Statement

Years Ended Dec. 31	Thousands — — — — —		Per Share [a] — — — —		Common Stock Price Range [a] Calendar Year
	Revenue	Net Income [b]	Diluted Earnings [b]	Cash Dividends	
2010	$95,718	$(5,235)	$ (0.22)	$0.00	$ 5.76— 2.77
2009	70,802	(19,527)[c]	(1.23)[c]	0.00	8.94— 3.01
2008	54,975[d]	(13,323)[c]	(1.59)[c]	0.00	12.00— 3.26
2007	16,384[d]	(15,553)[c]	(2.06)[c]	0.00	15.75— 5.60
2006 [e]	8,144	(40,795)[c]	(10.61)[c]	0.00	117.60— 4.90

[a] Restated to reflect 1-for-15 reverse stock splits effected June 15, 2006 and January 25, 2007; and a 1-for-7 reverse stock split effected January 28, 2008.
[b] Applicable to common stockholders.
[c] Includes loss from discontinued operations of $1.79 million ($0.11 per diluted share) in 2009; $2.48 million ($0.30 per diluted share) in 2008; $7.77 million ($1.03 per diluted share) in 2007; and $0.21 million ($0.01 per diluted share) in 2006.
[d] Restated to exclude results of discontinued operations.
[e] Includes $4.83 million of stock compensation expense related to adoption of SFAS 123(R).

Transfer Agent & Registrar: Wells Fargo Shareholder Services

General Counsel:	Anne Berg	Traded (Symbol):	NASDAQ (LIME)
Investor Relations:	Jeffrey R. Mistarz, C.F.O.	Stockholders:	4,400 (B)
Auditors:	BDO USA, LLP	Employees:	364
		Annual Meeting:	In June

Littelfuse, Inc.

8755 West Higgins Road, Suite 500, Chicago, Illinois 60631

Telephone: (773) 628-1000   **www.littelfuse.com**

Littelfuse is the worldwide leader in circuit protection, offering the industry's broadest and deepest port-folio of circuit protection products and solutions. The company's products are components in virtually every product that uses electrical energy, including portable and consumer electronics, automobiles, industrial equipment, and telecom/datacom circuits. In addition to its Chicago headquarters, Littelfuse has more than 20 sales, distribution, manufacturing, and engineering facilities in the Americas, Europe, and Asia. In December 2010, Littelfuse purchased all the outstanding stock of Cole Hersee Co., a Boston, Massachusetts-based company that operates in the off-road truck and bus market. Founded in 1927; Incorporated in Delaware in 1991.

Directors (In addition to indicated officers)

T.J. Chung
John P. Driscoll
Anthony Grillo

John E. Major
William P. Noglows
Ronald L. Schubel

Officers (Directors*)

*Gordon Hunter, Chm., Pres. & C.E.O.
Paul M. Dickinson, V.P. & Gen. Mgr.—
Semiconductor Prods.
Dal Ferbert, V.P. & Gen. Mgr.—Electrical
Bus. Unit
Philip G. Franklin, V.P.—Oper. Support,
C.F.O. & Treas.

David W. Heinzmann, V.P.—Global Oper.
Dieter Roeder, V.P. & Gen. Mgr.—Automotive Bus.
Unit
Chen-Ming Wang, V.P. & Gen. Mgr.—Electronics
Bus. Unit
Ryan K. Stafford, V.P.—Hum. Res. & Gen. Coun.
Mary S. Muchoney, Corp. Secy.

Consolidated Balance Sheet As of January 1, 2011 (000 omitted)

Assets		Liabilities & Stockholders' Equity	
Current assets	$318,956	Current liabilities	$ 109.848
Net property, plant & equipment	130,147	Long-term debt	41,000
Intangible assets, net	154,515	Other liabilities	17,621
Other assets	17,511	Minority interest	143
		*Stockholders' equity	452,517
Total	$621,129	Total	$621,129

*21,752,536 shares common stock outstanding.

Consolidated Income Statement

Years Ended Abt Dec. 31	Thousands — — — —		Per Share — — — —		Common Stock Price Range Calendar Year
	Net Sales	Net Income	Diluted Earnings	Cash Dividends	
2010	$608,021	$78,663	$3.52	$0.15	$49.09— 28.30
2009 a	430,147	9,411	0.43	0.00	33.19— 8.82
2008	530,869	8,016	0.37	0.00	39.21— 11.48
2007	536,144	36,835	1.64	0.00	44.99— 30.16
2006	534,859	23,824	1.03	0.00	38.00— 26.42

a 53 weeks.

Transfer Agent & Registrar: Wells Fargo Shareowner Services

General Counsel:	Ryan K. Stafford, V.P.	Traded (Symbol):	NASDAQ GS (LFUS)
Investor Relations:	Philip G. Franklin, V.P.	Stockholders:	116 (R)
Human Resources:	Ryan K. Stafford, V.P.	Employees:	6,000
Auditors:	Ernst & Young LLP	Annual Meeting:	In April

LKQ Corporation

120 North LaSalle Street, Suite 3300, Chicago, Illinois 60602
Telephone: (312) 621-1950   www.lkqcorp.com

LKQ Corporation is the largest nationwide provider of aftermarket and recycled collision replacement parts and refurbished collision replacement products, including wheels, bumper covers, and lights. The company is also a leading provider of mechanical replacement parts, including remanufactured engines. All of the company's products are used in the repair of automobiles and other vehicles. LKQ operates more than 325 facilities in the U.S., Canada, Mexico, and Central America. Customers include collision and mechanical repair shops, new and used car dealerships, and, indirectly, insurance companies and extended warranty companies. In 2011, the company acquired the paint distribution business, consisting of 40 locations across the U.S., of AkzoNobel Coatings, Inc. Incorporated in Delaware in 1998.

Directors (In addition to indicated officers)

A. Clinton Allen
Robert M. Devlin
Kevin F. Flynn
Ronald G. Foster

Paul M. Meister
John F. O'Brien
William M. Webster, IV

Officers (Directors*)

*Joseph M. Holsten, Acting Chm. & Co-C.E.O.
Robert L. Wagman, Pres. & Co-C.E.O.
John S. Quinn, Exec. V.P. & C.F.O.
*Victor M. Casini, Sr. V.P., Gen. Coun. & Secy.

Walter P. Hanley, Sr. V.P.—Dev. & Assoc. Gen.
   Coun. & Asst. Secy.
Michael Clark, V.P.—Fin. & Cont.

Consolidated Balance Sheet   As of December 31, 2010 (000 omitted)

Assets		Liabilities & Stockholders' Equity	
Current assets	$ 836,876	Current liabilities	$ 225,321
Net property & equipment	331,312	Long-term obligations	548,066
Intangibles	1,102,275	Other noncurrent liabilities	45,902
Other assets	29,046	Deferred income tax liability	66,059
		*Stockholders' equity	1,414,161
Total	$2,299,509	Total	$2,299,509

*145,466,575 shares common stock outstanding.

Consolidated Income Statement [a]

Years Ended Dec. 31	Thousands — — — — —		Per Share — — — — —		Common Stock Price Range Calendar Year
	Revenue	Net Income[b]	Diluted Earnings[b]	Cash Dividends	
2009	$2,469,881	$167,118	$1.15	$0.00	$23.26—17.29
2009	2,047,942	127,137	0.88	0.00	20.07—10.75
2008	1,908,532	97,092	0.69	0.00	25.00— 8.70
2007	1,112,351	63,622	0.53	0.00	23.66— 9.93
2006	784,023	43,891	0.39	0.00	25.49—17.44

[a] Includes results of operations of acquired businesses from dates of acquisition.
[b] From continuing operations.

Transfer Agent & Registrar: IST Shareholder Services

General Counsel:	Victor M. Casini, Sr. V.P.	Traded (Symbol):	NASDAQ GS (LKQX)
Investor Relations:	Joseph P. Boutross, Dir.	Stockholders:	30 (R)
Human Resources:	Victor M. Casini, Sr. V.P.	Employees:	12,000
Auditors:	Deloitte & Touche LLP	Annual Meeting:	In May

Manitex International, Inc.

9725 Industrial Drive, Bridgeview, Illinois 60455

Telephone: (708) 430-7500   **www.manitexinternational.com**

Manitex International, Inc. is a leading provider of engineered lifting solutions, including cranes, rough terrain forklifts, indoor electric forklifts, and special mission oriented vehicles. Through its Manitex subsidiary it manufactures and markets a comprehensive line of boom trucks and sign cranes, which are primarily used for industrial projects, energy exploration, and infrastructure development, including roads, bridges, and commercial construction. Through its Manitex Liftking subsidiary, the company also manufactures a complete line of rough terrain forklifts, stand-up electric forklifts, cushioned tired forklifts, as well as other specialized carriers, heavy material handling transporters, and steel mill equipment. The Badger Equipment Company subsidiary is a Winona, Minnesota-based manufacturer of specialized rough terrain cranes and material handling products. The Manitex Load King, Inc. subsidiary is an Elk Point, South Dakota-based manufacturer of specialized trailer and hauling systems. In June 2011, the company's Italian subsidiary, CVS Ferrari srl, received Italian court approval to acquire certain assets of CVS SpA under Italian bankruptcy law. The acquisition is expected to close in the third quarter of 2011. Successor to a company founded in 1993; incorporated in Michigan in 2003; present name adopted in 2008.

Directors (In addition to indicated officers)

Robert M. Clark	Marvin P. Rosenberg
Robert S. Gigliotti	Stephen J. Tober

Officers (Directors*)

*David J. Langevin, Chm. & C.E.O.	Robert Litchev, Pres.—Mfg. Operations
Andrew M. Rooke, Pres. & C.O.O.	Scott Rolston, Sr. V.P.—Sales & Mktg., Manitex Intl.
David H. Gransee, C.F.O., V.P., Secy. & Treas.	

Consolidated Balance Sheet As of December 31, 2010 (000 omitted)

Assets		Liabilities & Stockholders' Equity	
Current assets	$ 54,703	Current liabilities	$ 23,011
Intangible assets, net	20,403	Notes payable	6,119
Goodwill, net	14,452	Revolving term credit facilities	20,007
Other assets	15,959	Other liabilities	14,577
		*Stockholders' equity	43,274
Total	$105,517	Total	$105,517

*11,160,455 shares common stock outstanding.

Consolidated Income Statement [a]

Years Ended Dec. 31	Thousands — — — —		Per Share — — — —		Common Stock Price Range Calendar Year
	Revenue [a]	Net Income [a]	Diluted Earnings [a]	Cash Dividends	
2009	$ 95,875	$2,109	$ 0.19	$0.00	$3.98—1.61
2009	55,887	3,639	0.33	0.00	2.99—0.39
2008	106,341	1,799	0.17	0.00	6.05—0.63
2007	106,946	2,126	0.23	0.00	8.31—5.37
2006	40,676	(547)	(0.10)	0.00	5.80—2.61

[a] From continuing operations.

Transfer Agent & Registrar: Broadridge Corporate Issuer Solutions, Inc.

Corporate Counsel: Foley & Lardner LLP		Traded (Symbol):	NASDAQ CM (MNTX)
Investor Relations: David Langevin, C.E.O.		Stockholders:	66 (R)
Auditors: UHY LLP		Employees:	229
		Annual Meeting:	In May

Material Sciences Corporation

2200 East Pratt Boulevard, Elk Grove Village, Illinois 60007
Telephone: (847) 439-2210   **www.matsci.com**

Material Sciences Corporation designs, manufactures, and markets material-based solutions for acoustical and coating applications. The company's technologies are used to solve noise, vibration, and harshness (NVH) and temperature problems for customers in the automotive, home appliance, telecommunications, HVAC, electronics, lawn and power equipment, and construction industries. Material Sciences Corporation operates four manufacturing facilities in the United States and Europe, and its products are sold to manufacturers and distributors of industrial and consumer products around the world. Incorporated in Delaware in 1983.

Directors (In addition to indicated officer)

John P. Reilly, Chm.
Terry L. Bernander
Frank L. Hohmann, III

Sam Licavoli
Patrick J. McDonnell
Dominick J. Schiano

Officers (Director*)

*Clifford D. Nastas, C.E.O.
James D. Pawlak, V.P., C.F.O., Corp. Cont.,
  & Corp. Secy.

John M. Klepper, V.P.—Hum. Res.
Matthew M. Murphy, V.P.—Gen. Mgr. of Asia
Michael R. Wilson, V.P.—Oper.

Consolidated Balance Sheet As of February 28, 2011 (000 omitted)

Assets		Liabilities & Stockholders' Equity	
Current assets	$ 80,160	Current liabilities	$ 23,337
Net property, plant & equipment	30,476	Long-term liabilities	11,795
Other assets	3,294	*Stockholders' equity	78,198
Total	$113,930	Total	$113,930

*12,893,560 shares common stock outstanding.

Consolidated Income Statement

Years Ended Abt. Feb. 28	Thousands — — — —		Per Share — — — —		Common Stock Price Range Fiscal Year
	Net Sales	Net Income	Diluted Earnings	Cash Dividends	
2010	$137,624	$12,044 [a]	$0.19 [a]	$0.00	$ 7.32—1.70
2010	137,820	(11,620) [b]	(0.89) [b]	0.00	2.25—0.51
2009	187,026	(33,111) [c]	(2.41) [c]	0.00	8.67—0.90
2008	234,991	(6,464) [d]	(0.45) [d]	0.00	13.15—5.41
2007	262,627	6,287	0.43	0.00	13.33—8.72

[a] Includes a gain of $6.64 million on the sales of the Middletown facility and equipment and certain Elk Grove Village coil coating assets; a charge of $3.72 million related to asset impairment; and a charge of $1.32 million related to restruccturing expenses in connection with the sale of the Elk Grove Village coil coating assets.
[b] Includes restructuring expenses of $1.64 million.
[c] Includes a charge of $17.466 million related to the valuation allowance for deferred tax assets; a charge of $8.09 million related to long-lived asset impairment; a gain of $5.90 million on the sale of the assets and real property located in Morrisville, Pennsylvania; and a charge of $2.21 million related to forward purchase contracts for nickel and natural gas.
[d] Includes a charge of $1.32 million related to goodwill impairment.

Transfer Agent & Registrar: BNY Mellon Shareowner Services
Corporate Counsel: Neal, Gerber &
                   Eisenberg LLP
Investor Relations: James D. Pawlak, V.P.
Human Resources: John M. Klepper, V.P.
Auditors: Deloitte & Touche LLP

Traded (Symbol): NASD CM (MASC)
Stockholders: 416 (R)
Employees: 264
Annual Meeting: In June

Mattersight Corporation

200 South Wacker Drive, Suite 820, Chicago, Illinois 60606
Telephone: (877) 235-6925   www.mattersight.com

Mattersight Corporation (known prior to May 31, 2011, as eLoyalty Corporation) engages in enterprise analytics. The company's Behavioral Analytics service captures, analyzes, and creates insights from unstructured conversations, emails, employee desktop activity, and customer data. Mattersight's customers use these analytics to improve call center performance, increase customer satisfaction and retention, reduce fraud, and streamline back office operations. In May 2011, the company completed the sale of the Integrated Contact Solutions Business Unit. Incorporated in Delaware in 1999; Articles amended in 2011.

Directors (In addition to indicated officers)

Tench Coxe
Harry J. Feinberg
John T. Kohler

David B. Mullen
Michael J. Murray
John C. Staley

Officers (Directors*)

*Kelly D. Conway, Pres. & C.E.O.
William B. Noon, V.P. & C.F.O.
Christine R. Carsen, V.P., Gen. Coun., &
    Corp. Secy.

Karen Bolton, V.P.—Client Mgt.
Christopher D. Danson, V.P.—Delivery

Consolidated Balance Sheet As of January 1, 2011 (000 omitted)

Assets		Liabilities & Stockholders' Equity	
Current assets	$46,580	Current liabilities	$34,730
Net property & equipment	5,870	Other liabilities	9,210
Other assets	13,740	Series B convertible preferred stock	18,100
		*Stockholders' equity	4,150
Total	$66,190	Total	$66,190

*14,790,000 shares common stock outstanding.

Consolidated Income Statement

Years Ended Abt. Dec. 31	Thousands — — — — —		Per Share — — — —		Common Stock Price Range Calendar Year
	Total Revenue	Net Income	Diluted Earnings	Cash Dividends	
2010 [a]	$ 88,100	$(13,320)	$(1.06)	$0.00	$7.61—4.90
2009 [b]	101,613	(10,620)	(0.90)	0.00	10.46—2.45
2008 [b]	91,197	(21,653)	(2.21)	0.00	13.62—1.77
2007 [a]	102,105	(18,738)	(2.40)	0.00	25.84—9.60
2006 [a]	89,828	(11,148)	(1.86)	0.00	19.80—9.63

[a] Update.
[b] Reclassified.

Transfer Agent & Registrar: BNY Mellon Shareowner Services

General Counsel: Christine R. Carsen, V.P.
Investor Relations: William B. Noon, C.F.O.
Auditors: Grant Thornton LLP

Traded (Symbol): NASDAQ (MATR)
Stockholders: 92 (R)
Employees 369
Annual Meeting: In May

MB Financial, Inc.
800 West Madison Street, Chicago, Illinois 60607
Telephone: (888) 422-6562   **www.mbfinancial.com**

MB Financial, Inc. is the holding company for MB Financial Bank, N.A. The bank is locally operated and provides financial services to small- and middle-market businesses and individuals through 90 offices in the Chicagoland area. MB Financial Bank, N.A., also has one banking office in Philadelphia. Primary lines of business include commercial and retail banking and wealth management. Other subsidiaries include broker/dealer Vision Investment Services, Inc. and a majority-owned asset management firm, Cedar Hill Associates LLC. In 2009 and 2010, the bank assumed deposits and loans of several Illinois-based banks, facilitated by the Federal Deposit Insurance Corporation: Glenwood-based Heritage Community Bank, Oak Forest-based InBank, Chicago-based Corus Bank, Aurora-based Benchmark Bank, Chicago-based Broadway Bank, and Chicago-based New Century Bank. Incorporated in Delaware in 1993; reincorporated in Maryland in 2001.

Directors (In addition to indicated officers)

Thomas H. Harvey, Chm.
James N. Hallene, V. Chm.
David P. Bolger
Robert S. Engelman, Jr.

Charles J. Gries
Richard J. Holmstrom
Karen J. May
Ronald D. Santo

Officers (Directors*)

*Mitchell Feiger, Pres. & C.E.O.
Jill E. York, V.P. & C.F.O.
Burton J. Field, V.P.; Pres.—Lease Banking,
  MB Fin. Bank
Rosemarie Bouman, V.P.; Exec. V.P. & Chf. Admin
  Off., MB Fin. Bank

Larry J. Kallembach, Exec. V.P. & C.I.O., MB Fin. Bank
Susan Peterson, Exec. V.P. & Chf. Retail Banking Off.,
  MB Fin. Bank
Brian Wildman, Exec. V.P.—Wealth Mgmt.,
  MB Fin. Bank

Consolidated Balance Sheet   As of December 31, 2010 (000 omitted)

Assets		Liabilities & Stockholders' Equity	
Cash & cash equivalents	$ 844,159	Deposits	$ 8,152,958
Securities available for sale	1,597,743	Short-term debt	268,844
Loans, net	6,425,594	Long-term debt	285,073
Premises & equipment, net	210,886	Other liabilities	268,703
Goodwill, net	387,069	Minority interest	2,521
Other assets	854,913	*Stockholders' equity	1,342,265
Total	$10,320,364	Total	$10,320,364

*50,964,495 shares common stock outstanding.

Consolidated Income Statement

Years Ended Dec. 31	Thousands — — — —		Per Share — — — —		Common Stock Price Range Calendar Year
	Total Income	Net Income [a]	Basic Earnings [a]	Cash Dividends	
2010	$615,396	$ 20,528	$ 0.19	$0.04	$28.18— 9.25
2009	520,692	(26,126)	(0.91)	0.15	28.04— 9.25
2008	494,181	16,164	0.44	0.72	44.29—18.76
2007	540,794	93,863	2.61	0.72	37.89—29.13
2006	438,747	67,114	2.15	0.66	38.35—33.00

[a] Includes income from discontinued operations, net of tax, of $6,453,000 ($0.16 per basic share) in 2009; $439,000 ($0.01 per basic share) in 2008; $32,518,000 ($0.89 per basic share) in 2007; and $4,115,000 ($0.13 per basic share) in 2006.

Transfer Agent & Registrar: BNY Mellon Shareowner Services

Investor Relations:	Jill E. York, V.P. & C.F.O.	**Traded (Symbol):**	NASDAQ Gbl. Select (MBFI)
Human Resources:	Rosemarie Bowman, Exec. V.P.	**Stockholders:**	1,578 (R)
Info. Tech.:	Larry J. Kallembach, Exec. V.P.	**Employees:**	1,703
Auditors:	McGladrey & Pullen, LLP	**Annual Meeting:**	In June

McDonald's Corporation

One McDonald's Plaza, Oak Brook, Illinois 60523

Telephone: (630) 623-3000   www.aboutmcdonalds.com

McDonald's Corporation is the world's leading foodservice retailer, with more than 32,000 restaurants in 117 countries. All restaurants are operated either by the company or by franchisees, including conventional franchisees under franchise agreements, and foreign affiliated markets and developmental licensees under license agreements. McDonald's restaurants serve a varied, yet limited, value-priced menu. Reincorporated in Delaware in 1965 to continue a business established in 1955.

Directors (In addition to indicated officers)

Andrew J. McKenna, Chm.
Susan E. Arnold
Robert A. Eckert
Enrique Hernandez, Jr.

Jeanne P. Jackson
Richard H. Lenny
Walter E. Massey
Cary D. McMillan

Sheila A. Penrose
John W. Rogers, Jr.
Roger W. Stone
Miles D. White

Officers (Directors*)

*James A. Skinner, V. Chm. & C.E.O.
Donald Thompson, Pres. & C.O.O.
Peter J. Bensen, Exec. V.P. & C.F.O.
Mary Dillon, Exec. V.P. & Gbl. Chf. Mktg. Off.
Richard Floersch, Exec. V.P. & Chf. Hum. Res. Off.
Jose Armario, Exec. V.P.—Gbl. Supply Chn. Real Estate Dev. & Franchising
Jim Johannesen, Exec. V.P. & C.O.O.—U.S.A.
Kevin Newell, Exec. V.P. & Chf. Brand Officer
Gloria Santona, Exec. V.P., Gen. Coun. & Secy.
Jeffrey Stratton, Exec. V.P. & Chf. Restaurant Off.
Kevin M. Ozan, Sr. V.P. & Cont.
Janice L. Fields, Pres.—McDonald's U.S.A.
Mike Andres, Pres.—U.S. Central Div.

Douglas Goare, Pres.—Eur.
Timothy Fenton, Pres.—Asia/Pacific, Middle East & Africa
Khamzat Khasbulatov, Pres.—East Eur. Div.
Karen King, Pres.—U.S. East Div.
Bane Knezevic, Pres.—Eur. West Div.
Gillian McDonald, Pres.—Eur. North Div.
David Murphy, Pres.—Pacific/Africa/Singapore/ Malaysia/Korea Div.
Jean-Pierre Petit, Pres.—Eur. South Div.
Steven Plotkin, Pres.—U.S. West Div.
Peter Rodwell, Pres.—APMEA Greater Asia & Middle East Div.
Fred Turner, Hon. Chm.

Consolidated Balance Sheet As of December 31, 2010 (000 omitted)

Assets		Liabilities & Stockholders' Equity	
Current assets	$ 4,368,500	Current liabilities	$ 2,924,700
Net property & equipment	22,060,600	Long-term debt	11,497,000
Other assets	5,546,100	Deferred items	1,332,400
		Other liabilities	1,586,900
		*Stockholders' equity	14,634,200
Total	$31,975,200	Total	$31,975,200

*1,053,600,000 shares common stock outstanding.

Consolidated Income Statement

Years Ended Dec. 31	Thousands — — — — —		Per Share — — — — —		Common Stock Price Range Calendar Year
	Total Revenues	Net Income	Diluted Earnings	Cash Dividends [a]	
2010	$24,075,000	$4,946,000	$4.58	$2.26	$80.94—61.06
2009	22,744,700	4,551,000	4.11	2.05	64.75—50.44
2008	23,522,400	4,313,200	3.76	1.63	67.00—45.79
2007	22,786,600	2,395,100 [b]	1.98 [b]	1.50	63.69—42.31
2006	20,895,200	3,544,200	2.83	1.00	44.68—31.73

[a] Declared.
[b] Includes pretax operating charges of $1.7 billion ($1.32 per share) related to impairment and other charges; a tax benefit of $316.4 million ($0.26 per share) resulting from the completion of an IRS examination of the 2003-2004 U.S. federal tax returns; and income of $60.1 million ($0.05 per share) related to discontinued operations primarily from the sale of the company's investment in Boston Market.

Transfer Agent & Registrar: Computershare Investor Services

General Counsel:	Gloria Santona, Exec. V.P.	Traded (Symbol):	NYSE, (MCD)
Investor Relations:	Mary Kay Shaw, V.P.	Stockholders:	1,348,000 (B)
Human Resources:	Richard Floersch, Exec. V.P.	Employees:	400,000
Info. Tech.:	David Weick, Sr. V.P.	Annual Meeting:	In May
Auditors:	Ernst & Young LLP		

Mead Johnson Nutrition Company

2701 Patriot Boulevard, Glenview, Illinois 60026-8039
Telephone: (847) 832-2420   www.meadjohnson.com

Mead Johnson Nutrition Company is a global leader in pediatric nutrition. Its Enfa family of brands, including Enfamil® infant formula, is the world's leading brand franchise in pediatric nutrition. Mead Johnson's comprehensive product portfolio addresses a broad range of nutritional needs for infants, children, and expectant and nursing mothers. The company markets its portfolio of more than 70 products to mothers, health care professionals, and retailers in more than 50 countries in Asia, North America, Latin America, and Europe. The Mead Johnson name has been associated with science-based pediatric nutrition products for more than 100 years. Mead Johnson Nutrition Company was incorporated in Delaware in 2008.

Directors (In addition to indicated officers)

James M. Cornelius, Chm.
Steven M. Altschuler, M.D.
Howard B. Bernick
Kimberly A. Casiano

Anna C. Catalano
Celeste A. Clark, Ph.D.
Peter G. Ratcliffe
Elliott Sigal, M.D., Ph.D.
Robert S. Singer

Officers (Directors*)

*Stephen W. Golsby, Pres. & C.E.O.
Lynn H. Clark, Sr. V.P.—Hum. Res.
Dirk Hondmann, Sr. V.P.—Gbl. Res. & Dev.
James Jeffrey Jobe, Sr. V.P.—Gbl. Supply Chain
Peter G. Leemputte, Sr. V.P. & C.F.O.

William C. P'Pool, Sr. V.P., Gen. Coun. & Secy.
Stanley D. Burhans, V.P. & Cont.
Peter Kasper Jakobsen, Pres.—Americas
Charles M. Urbain, Pres.—Asia & Eur.

Consolidated Balance Sheet As of December 31, 2010 (000 omitted)

Assets		Liabilities & Stockholders' Deficit	
Current assets	$1,449,000	Current liabilities	$ 976,100
Net property, plant & equipment	550,500	Other liabilities	1,675,300
Goodwill	117,500	Minority interest	9,100
Other assets	176,100	*Stockholders' deficit	(367,400)
Total	$2,293,100	Total	$2,293,100

*204,800,000 shares common stock outstanding.

Consolidated Income Statement

Years Ended Dec. 31	Thousands — — — — Net Sales	Net Income	Per Share a — — — — Diluted Earnings	Cash Dividends	Common Stock Price Range a Calendar Year
2010	$3,141,600	$452,700	$2.20	$0.90	$63.38—43.50
2009	2,826,500	399,600	1.99	0.70	50.35—25.72
2008	2,882,400	393,900	2.32		
2007	2,576,400	422,500	2.49		
2006	2,345,100	398,200	2.34		

a Initial public offering completed on February 17, 2009.

Transfer Agent & Registrar: BNY Mellon Shareowner Services

General Counsel:	William C. P'Pool, Sr. V.P.	Traded (Symbol):	NYSE (MJN)
Investor Relations:	Kathy MacDonald, V.P.	Stockholders:	1,655 (R)
Human Resources:	Lynn H. Clark, Sr. V.P.	Employees:	6,500
Info. Tech.:	Derek L. Faughn, C.I.O.	Annual Meeting:	In April
Auditors:	Deloitte & Touche LLP		

Methode Electronics, Inc.

7401 West Wilson Avenue, Chicago, Illinois 60706-4548

Telephone: (708) 867-6777   www.methode.com

Methode Electronics, Inc. is a global designer and manufacturer of electro-mechanical devices with manufacturing, design, and testing facilities in the United States, Mexico, Malta, United Kingdom, Germany, the Philippines, India, Lebanon, Singapore, and China. The company designs, manufactures, and markets devices employing electrical, electronic, wireless, radio remote control, sensing, and optical technologies. Its business is managed on a technology product basis, with those technology segments being automotive, interconnect, power products, and other. The company's components are found in the primary end markets of the aerospace, appliance, automotive, construction, consumer and industrial equipment markets, communications (including information processing and storage, networking equipment, wireless and terrestrial voice/data systems), rail, and other transportation industries. In March 2011, Methode sold its 75 percent ownership in Optokon, its Czech Republic optical operation. Incorporated in Illinois in 1946; reincorporated in Delaware in 1966.

Directors (In addition to indicated officers)

Warren L. Batts, Chm.	Isabelle C. Goossen
Walter J. Aspatore	Christopher J. Hornung
Dr. J. Edward Colgate	Paul G. Shelton
Dr. Darren M. Dawson	Lawrence B. Skatoff
Stephen F. Gates	

Officers (Directors*)

*Donald W. Duda, Pres. & C.E.O.	Joseph E. Khoury, V.P. —Eur.
Thomas D. Reynolds, Sr. V.P.—Global Ops.	Theodore P. Kill, V.P.—WW Automotive Sales
Timothy R. Glandon, V.P. & G.M.—North Amer. Oper.	Douglas A. Koman, V.P.—Global Sales & C.F.O.
	Ronald L. G. Tsoumas, Treas. & Cont.

Consolidated Balance Sheet As of May 1, 2011 (000 omitted)

Assets		Liabilities & Stockholders' Equity	
Current assets	$195961	Current liabilities	$ 62,855
Net property, plant & equipment	61,511	Other liabilities	10,745
Goodwill	16,422	Minority interest	2,111
Other assets	60,850	*Stockholders' equity	259,033
Total	$334,744	Total	$334,744

*36,970,055 shares common stock outstanding.

Consolidated Income Statement

Years Ended Abt. Apr. 30	Thousands — — — —		Per Share — — — —		Common Stock Price Range Fiscal Year
	Net Sales	Net Income	Diluted Earnings	Cash Dividends	
2011	$428,215	$ 19,500	$ 0.52	$0.28	$13.73— 7.85
2010	373,136	13,655 a	0.37 a	0.28	14.32— 5.28
2009	425,644	(112,483) b	(3.05) b	0.26	13.65— 2.59
2008 c	551,073	39,754	1.06	0.20	18.90— 9.89
2007	448,427	26,084	0.71	0.20	16.04— 7.07

a Includes a pre-tax charge of $7.8 million relating to restructuring activities and $5.8 million of pre-tax legal expense relating to the Delphi supply agreement and patent lawsuit.
b Includes pre-tax charges of $94.4 million related to goodwill and other asset impairments and $25.3 million related to restructuring activities.
c 53 weeks.

Transfer Agent & Registrar:	Continental Stock Transfer & Trust Co.		
Corporate Counsel: Locke Lord Bissell & Liddell, LLP		Traded (Symbol):	NYSE (MEI)
Investor Relations: Kristine Walczyk, Dresner Co.		Stockholders:	574 (R)
Human Resources: Mary Haley		Employees:	3,500
Auditors:	Ernst & Young LLP	Annual Meeting:	In September

MFRI, Inc.

7720 North Lehigh Avenue, Niles, Illinois 60714

Telephone: (847) 966-1000   **www.mfri.com**

MFRI, Inc. is a holding company whose subsidiaries are engaged in the manufacture and sale of products in four distinct operating units: piping systems, filtration products, and industrial process cooling equipment, and heating, ventilating, and air conditioning (HVAC) systems. Perma-Pipe is the largest manufacturer of pre-insulated piping systems in North America, supplying a customer base that includes industrial, chemical, and petroleum producers, airports, governmental agencies, housing projects, universities, and prisons. Midwesco Filter helps industry to protect the environment through the manufacture and supply of air filtration elements. Thermal Care is a leading manufacturer of energy efficient liquid chillers and pliant circulating systems used to remove head from industrial processes. Midwesco Mechanical provides energy efficient HVAC systems for large commercial, industrial, and institutional projects. The company's products are sold throughout the U.S., Canada, and Latin America, as well as Europe and Asia Pacific. Incorporated in Delaware in 1993; present name adopted in 1994.

Directors (In addition to indicated officers)

Dennis Kessler, Lead Director
Arnold F. Brookstone
Michael J. Gade

Eugene Miller
Stephen B. Schwartz
Mark A. Zorko

Officers (Directors*)

*David Unger, Chm. & C.E.O.
*Bradley E. Mautner, Pres. & C.O.O.
Michael D. Bennett, V.P., C.F.O., Secy. & Treas.
Stephen C. Buck, Pres.—Thermal Care
Edward A. Crylen, Pres.—Midwesco
   Mechanical & Energy
Fati A. Elgendy, V.P.; Pres.—Perma-Pipe

Mark Foster, Pres.—Midwesco Filter Resources
Avin Gidwani, Pres.—Perma-Pipe Middle East FZC
Thomas A. Benson, V.P.—Thermal Care
John Carusiello, V.P.—Perma-Pipe
Billy E. Ervin, V.P.—Perma-Pipe
Robert A. Maffei, V.P.—Perma-Pipe
Timothy P. Murphy, V.P.—Hum. Res.

Consolidated Balance Sheet As of January 31, 2011 (000 omitted)

Assets		Liabilities & Stockholders' Equity	
Current assets	$ 99,068	Current liabilities	$ 40,253
Net property, plant & equipment	43,655	Long-term debt	36,192
Other assets	20,552	Other liabilities	8,409
		*Stockholders' equity	78,421
Total	$163,275	Total	$163,275

*6,851,000 shares common stock outstanding.

Consolidated Income Statement

Years Ended Jan. 31	Thousands — — — — Net Sales	Net Income	Per Share — — — — Diluted Earnings	Cash Dividends	Common Stock Price Range Fiscal Year
2011	$218,598	$4,510	$ 0.66	$0.00	$ 11.00— 5.86
2010	230,381	4,671	0.68	0.00	8.04— 4.85
2009	303,066	6,689 [a]	0.98	0.00	18.00— 4.25
2008	239,487	(298)	(0.04)	0.00	31.21—10.56
2007	213,471	4,593	0.82	0.00	24.63— 6.26

[a] Includes non-cash charge of $2.79 million for goodwill impairment.

Transfer Agent & Registrar: Continental Stock Transfer & Trust Co.

Legal Counsel:	DLA Piper	Traded (Symbol):	NASDAQ GM (MFRI)
Investor Relations:	Michael D. Bennett, V.P.	Stockholders:	73 (R)
Human Resources:	Timothy P. Murphy, V.P.	Employees:	1,123
Info. Tech.	David Mautner	Annual Meeting:	In June
Auditors:	Grant Thornton LLP		

Midas, Inc.

1300 Arlington Heights Road, Itasca, Illinois 60143
Telephone: (630) 438-3000   www.midasinc.com

Midas, Inc. is a large provider of automotive service, including brake, maintenance, tires, steering, suspension, and exhaust services. There are more than 1,600 franchsied and company-owned Midas locations in the United States and Canada. There are also more than 800 licensed and franchised stores in the following countries: Australia, Austria, Belgium, the Bahamas, Costa Rica, France, Honduras, Italy, Mexico, Morocco, New Zealand, Poland, Portugal, and Spain. In April 2008, Midas acquired the SpeeDee Oil Change & Tune-up franchise system, which it now sells separately and as Midas-SpeeDee co-branded franchises. Predecessor company incorporated in Delaware in 1959; reincorporated in Delaware in 1997; present name adopted in 1997.

Directors (In addition to indicated officers)

Robert R. Schoeberl, Lead Director
Thomas L. Bindley
Archie R. Dykes

Jarobin Gilbert, Jr.
Diane L. Routson

Officers (Directors*)

*Alan D. Feldman, Chm., Pres. & C.E.O.
William M. Guzik, Exec. V.P. & C.F.O.
Frederick W. Dow, Jr., Sr. V.P. & Chf. Mktg. Off.
Michael J. Gould, Sr. V.P.—Franchise Oper.

Alvin K. Marr, Sr. V.P., Gen. Coun. & Secy.
Audrey Gualandri, V.P. & Cont.
Ben Parma, V.P.—Hum. Res.
Bennett Cikoch, V.P.—Mgt. Info. Sys.

Consolidated Balance Sheet   As of January 1, 2011 (000 omitted)

Assets		Liabilities & Stockholders' Equity	
Current assets	$ 60,200	Current liabilities	$ 70,500
Net property, plant & equipment	81,100	Long-term debt	62,700
Other assets	88,500	Other liabilities	75,500
		Non-vested restricted stock	3,800
		*Stockholders' equity	17,200
Total	$229,700	Total	$229,700

*14,200,000 shares common stock outstanding.

Consolidated Income Statement

Years Ended Abt. Dec. 31	Thousands — — — —		Per Share — — — —		Common Stock Price Range Calendar Year
	Sales & Revenues	Net Income	Diluted Earnings	Cash Dividends	
2010	$192,400	$(13,400) a	$(0.97)	$0.00	$12.50— 6.29
2009	182,800	2,600	0.19	0.00	11.99— 6.03
2008	187,400	7,800 b	0.56	0.00	19.12— 6.57
2007	178,200	13,000 b	0.89	0.00	23.73—14.67
2006	174,900	10,300	0.66	0.00	23.95—16.85

a Includes a $25.5 million European arbitration award expense and a $2.5 million reductiion in selling, general, and administrative expense for the fee recovery and a corresponding receivable.

b Includes favorable pre-tax adjustments to estimated warranty liability of $0.6 million in 2009 $3.4 million in 2008, and $8.3 million in 2007.

Transfer Agent & Registrar: Computershare Investor Services

Investor Relations:	Bob Troyer, Dir.	Traded (Symbol):	NYSE (MDS)
Human Resources:	Ben Parma, V.P.	Stockholders:	4,063 (R)
Info. Tech.:	Bennett Cikoch, V.P.	Employees:	940
Auditors:	KPMG LLP	Annual Meeting:	In May

The Middleby Corporation

1400 Toastmaster Drive, Elgin, Illinois 60120

Telephone: (847) 741-3300   www.middleby.com

The Middleby Corporation is engaged in the manufacture and sale of commercial foodservice equipment. It designs, develops, manufactures, markets, distributes, and services a broad line of equipment used for the preparation and cooking of food in commercial and institutional kitchens and restaurants as well as food processing operations in the United States and internationally. The compay's principal brand names include: Alkar®; Anets®; Beech®; Blodgett®; Blodgett Combi®; Bloomfield®; Carter Hoffmann®; CookTek®; Cozzini®; CTX®; Danfotech®; Doyon®; FriFri®; Giga®; Holman®; Houno®; Jade®; Lang®; Lincat®; MagiKitch'n®; Mauer-Atmos®; Middleby Marshall®; MP Equipment®; NuVu®; PerfectFry®; Pitco Frialator®; RapidPak®; Southbend®; Star®; Toastmaster®; TurboChef®; and Wells®. Products manufactured by the company include conveyor oven equipment, convection ovens, cooking equipment, ranges, fryer equipment, steam cooking equipment, toasters, charbroilers, food warming equipment, griddles, coffee brewers, tea brewers, beverage dispensing equipment, food preparation equipment, and packaging and food safety equipment. The company operates 13 manufacturing facilities throughout the U.S. and facilities in Canada, China, Denmark, Italy, and the Philippines. Incorporated in Delaware in 1985.

Directors (In addition to indicated officers)

Robert B. Lamb
Ryan Levenson
John R. Miller, III

Gordon O'Brien
Philip G. Putnam
Sabin C. Streeter

Officers (Directors*)

*Selim A. Bassoul, Chm., Pres. & C.E.O.
David Brewer, C.O.O.
Timothy J. FitzGerald, V.P. & C.F.O.
Martin M. Lindsay, Corp. Treas. & Asst. Secy.

Ivo Cozzini, Group Pres.—Sales & Mktg.
Magdy Albert, Group Pres.—Ops.
Karl Doyon, Pres.—Middleby Canada
James K. Pool III, Pres—TurboChef Div.

Consolidated Balance Sheet As of January 1, 2011 (000 omitted)

Assets		Liabilities & Stockholders' Equity	
Current assets	$263,659	Current liabilities	$183,852
Net property, plant & equipment	43,656	Long-term debt	208,920
Goodwill	369,989	Other liabilities	55,487
Other assets	195,868	*Stockholders' equity	424,913
Total	$873,172	Total	$873,172

*18,458,011 shares common stock outstanding.

Consolidated Income Statement

Years Ended Abt. Dec. 31	Thousands — — — — —		Per Share a — — — —		Common Stock Price Range a Calendar Year
	Net Sales	Net Earnings	Diluted Earnings	Cash Dividends	
2010	$719,121	$72,867	$3.97	$0.00	$86.35—42.17
2009	646,629	61,156	3.29	0.00	56.51—20.76
2008	651,888	63,901	3.75	0.00	76.62—24.80
2007	500,472	52,614	3.11	0.00	77.20—50.95
2006	403,131	42,377	2.57	0.00	52.70—36.80

a Adjusted for a 2-for-1 stock split on June 15, 2007.

Transfer Agent & Registrar:	BNY Mellon Shareowner Services		
Corporate Counsel:	Skadden, Arps, Slate, Meagher & Flom LLP	Traded (Symbol):	NASDAQ (MIDD)
		Stockholders:	34,000 (R)
Investor Relations:	Darcy Bretz	Employees:	2,060
Auditors:	Deloitte & Touche LLP	Annual Meeting:	In May

Molex Incorporated

2222 Wellington Court, Lisle, Illinois 60532-1682

Telephone: (630) 969-4550   www.molex.com

Molex Incorporated is a worldwide designer, developer, manufacturer, and distributor of electronic components, including electrical and fiber optic interconnection products and systems, switches, and integrated products. Molex serves original equipment manufacturers in industries that include automotive, business equipment, computer, computer peripherals, consumer products, industrial equipment, premise wiring, and telecommunications. Molex has more than 100,000 products which are sold through direct sales offices and authorized distributors. Manufacturing facilities include 39 plants in 16 countries. Incorporated in Delaware in 1972.

Directors (In addition to indicated officers)

Michael J. Birck	David L. Landsittel
Michelle L. Collins	Joe W. Laymon
Anirudh Dhebar	Donald G. Lubin
Edgar D. Jannotta	James S. Metcalf
Fred L. Krehbiel	Robert J. Potter

Officers (Directors*)

*Frederick A. Krehbiel, Co-Chm.
*John H. Krehbiel, Jr., Co-Chm.
*Martin P. Slark, V. Chm. & C.E.O.
Liam McCarthy, Pres. & C.O.O.
David D. Johnson, Exec. V.P., C.F.O. & Treas.
Graham C. Brock, Exec. V.P. & Pres.—
  Gbl. Sales & Mktg. Div.
James E. Fleischhacker, Exec. V.P. &
  Pres.—Gbl. Comm. Prods. Div.

Katsumi Hirokawa, Exec. V.P. & Pres.—
  Gbl. Micro Prods. Div.
J. Michael Nauman, Exec. V.P. & Pres.—
  Gbl. Integrated Prods. Div.
Gary J. Matula, Sr. V.P.—Info. Sys. & C.I.O.
Ana G. Rodriguez, Sr. V.P.—Gbl. Hum. Res.

Consolidated Balance Sheet As of June 30, 2011 (000 omitted)

Assets		Liabilities & Stockholders' Equity	
Current assets	$2,055,345	Current liabilities	$ 882,047
Net property, plant & equipment	1,68,448	Long-term debt	222,794
Goodwill	149,452	Accrued pension and	
Other assets	224,607	post-retirement benefits	100,866
		Other liabilities	23,879
		*Stockholders' equity	2,368,266
Total	$3,597,852	Total	$3,597,852

*174,812,000 average shares common stock outstanding.

Consolidated Income Statement [a]

Years Ended June 30	Thousands — — — — —		Per Share — — — — —		Common Stock Price Range [b] Fiscal Year
	Net Revenue	Net Income	Diluted Earnings	Cash Dividends	
2011	$3,587,334	$298,808	$ 1.71	$0.70 25	$28.51—17.50
2010	3,007,207	76,930 [c]	0.44	0.61	23.43—14.18
2009	2,581,841	(322,036) [d]	(1.84)	0.61	25.96— 9.72
2008	3,328,347	215,720 [e]	1.19	0.45	30.66—21.82
2007	3,265,874	245,744 [f]	1.32	0.30	39.49—28.01

[a] Some prior period amounts have been restated to reflect adjustments to the historical consolidated financial statements.
[b] Common stock.
[c] Includes a charge for restructuring costs and asset impairments of $92.8 million after tax and after-tax net loss on unauthorized activities in Japan of $17.1 million.
[d] Includes a charge for restructuring costs and asset impairments of $151.5 million ($111.8 million after tax), a $264.1 pre-tax and after-tax goodwill impairment charge and after-tax net loss on unauthorized activities in Japan of $1.7 million.
[e] Includes a charge for restructuring costs and asset impairments of $31.2 million ($21.0 million after tax) and after-tax net loss on unauthorized activities in Japan of $3 million.
[f] Includes a charge for restructuring costs and asset impairments of $36.9 million ($30.3 million after tax).

Transfer Agent & Registrar: Computershare Investor Services

General Counsel:	Robert Zeitler	Traded (Symbol):	NASDAQ, LON (MOLX, com.
Investor Relations:	Steve Martens, V.P.		stock; MOLXA, Class A)
Human Resources:	Ana G. Rodriguez, Sr. V.P.	Stockholders:	2,264 com.; 7,172 Class A (R)
Info. Tech.:	Gary J. Matula, C.I.O.	Employees:	35,519
Auditors:	Ernst & Young LLP	Annual Meeting:	In October

Morningstar, Inc.

22 West Washington Street, Chicago, Illinois 60602
Telephone: (312) 696-6000   www.global.morningstar.com

Morningstar, Inc. is a leading provider of independent investment research in North America, Europe, Australia, and Asia. The company offers an extensive line of products and services for individual investors, financial advisors, and institutional clients. With operations in 26 countries, Morningstar coverage includes data on 400,000 investment offerings, including stocks, mutual funds and similar vehicles, along with real-time market data on more than 5 million equities, indexes, futures, options, commodities, and preciousmetals, in addition to foreign exchange and Treasury markets. Morningstar serves approximately 7.4 million individual investors, 270,000 financial advisors, and 4,300 institutional clients. The company offers investment consulting and retirement planning services through wholly owned subsidiaries Morningstar Associates, LLC and Ibbotson Associates and an asset management service for financial advisors through Morningstar Investment Services, Inc. Incorporated in Illinois in 1984.

Directors (In addition to indicated officers)

Cheryl Francis	Jack Noonan
Steve Kaplan	Paul Sturm
Bill Lyons	Hugh Zentmyer

Officers (Directors*)

*Joe Mansueto, Chm. & C.E.O.	Bevin Desmond, Pres.—Intl. Ops. & Gbl. Human Res.
*Don Phillips, Pres.—Fund Res.	Elizabeth Kirscher, Pres.—Data Div.
Scott Cooley, C.F.O.	Catherine Gillis Odelbo, Pres.—Equity & Credit Res.
David W. Williams, Managing Dir.—Design	
Chris Boruff, Pres.—Software Div.	
Peng Chen, Pres.—Inv. Mgmt. Div.	Richard E. Robbins, Gen. Coun. & Corp. Secy.

Consolidated Balance Sheet As of December 31, 2010 (000 omitted)

Assets		Liabilities & Stockholders' Equity	
Current assets	$ 507,280	Current liabilities	$ 252,724
Net property & equipment	62,105	Accrued compensation	4,965
Investment in unconsolidated entities	24,262	Other liabilities	47,188
Goodwill	317,661	Minority interest	1,109
Intangible assets, net	169,023	*Stockholders' equity	780,316
Other assets	5,971		
Total	$1,086,302	Total	$1,086,302

*48,874,392 shares common stock outstanding.

Consolidated Income Statement

Years Ended Dec. 31	Thousands — — — —		Per Share — — — —		Common Stock Price Range Calendar Year
	Revenue	Net Income [a]	Diluted Earnings [a]	Cash Dividends	
2010	$555,351	$86,370	$1.70	$0.05	$54.09—39.61
2009	478,996	82,129	1.65	0.00	54.75—26.70
2008	502,457	89,629	1.82	0.00	77.81—25.78
2007	435,107	73,334	1.52	0.00	85.50—44.60
2006	315,175	50,643	1.08	0.00	47.56—32.99

[a] Attributable to Morningstar, Inc.

Transfer Agent & Registrar: Computershare Investor Services

General Counsel:	Richard E. Robbins	Traded (Symbol):	NASDAQ GS (MORN)
Investor Relations:	Amy Arnott	Stockholders:	1,466 (R)
Human Resources:	Bevin Desmond	Employees:	3,300
Info. Tech.:	Greg Goff, C.T.O.	Annual Meeting:	In May
Auditors:	Ernst & Young LLP		

Morton's Restaurant Group, Inc.

325 North LaSalle Street, Suite 500, Chicago, Illinois 60654
Telephone: (312) 923-0030   **www.mortons.com**

Morton's Restaurant Group, Inc. owner and operator of upscale steakhouse restaurants. As of January 2, 2011, the company owned and operated 77 Morton's steakhouses and 1 Trevi Italian restaurant located in 64 cities across 26 states and Puerto Rico, and 6 international locations (Toronto, Hong Kong, Shanghai, Macau, Mexico City, and Singapore). The restaurants are designed to appeal to a broad spectrum of consumer tastes and target separate price points and dining experiences. Incorporated in Delaware in 1988.

Directors (In addition to indicated officers)

William C. Anton
John K. Castle
Dr. John J. Connolly
Robert A. Goldschmidt
Stephen E. Paul

David B. Pittaway
Dianne H. Russell
Zane Tankel
Alan A. Teran

Officers (Directors*)

*Christopher J. Artinian, Pres. & C.E.O.
Klaus W. Fritsch, V. Chm.
Ronald M. DiNella, Sr. V.P., C.F.O. & Treas.
Roger J. Drake, Sr. V.P.—Mktg. & Commun.

James W. Kirkpatrick, Sr. V.P.—Dev.
Scott D. Levin, Sr. V.P., Gen. Coun. & Secy.
Patsy Pleuss, V.P.—Mktg. & Sales.
Kevin E. Weinert, Sr. V.P.—Oper.

Consolidated Balance Sheet As of January 2, 2011 (000 omitted)

Assets		Liabilities & Stockholders' Equity	
Current assets	$ 24,151	Current liabilities	$ 53,011
Net property, plant & equipment	91,494	Long-term debt	63,631
Goodwill, net	6,938	Deferred items	68,377
Intangible asset	73,000	Other liabilities	3,671
Other assets	6,231	*Stockholders' equity	13,124
Total	$201,814	Total	$201,814

*16,035,571 shares common stock outstanding.

Consolidated Income Statement

Years Ended Abt. Dec. 31	Thousands — — — —		Per Share — — — —		Common Stock
	Revenues	Net Income	Diluted Earnings	Cash Dividends	Price Range [a] Calendar Year
2010	$296,100	$4,100	$0.27	$0.00	$ 8.09— 2.93
2009	281,100	(77,500) [b]	(4.87)	0.00	4.97— 1.42
2008 [c]	329,400	(61,800) [d]	(3.84)	0.00	9.41— 1.75
2007	325,800	13,800 [e]	0.81	0.00	20.82— 8.75
2006	293,600	(14,400) [f]	(0.89)	0.00	20.25—13.45

[a] Initial public offering February 9, 2006.
[b] Includes charge of $6.2 million after-tax, relating to the settlement of labor claims; non-cash asset-impairment charges of $18.3 million after-tax; charge of $0.1 million after-tax for the partial write-off of deferred financing costs related to the amendment of the company's senior revolving credit facility; a charge of $52.9 million related to the full valuation allowance against U.S. deferred tax assets; and a charge of $0.8 million after-tax, relating to the resignation of the company's former President and C.E.O.
[c] 53 weeks.
[d] Includes non-cash impairment charges of $70.2 million after-tax, associated with the impairment of goodwill and assets. Also includes a charge of $0.6 million after-tax, relating to the closing of the company's New York office and two Morton's steakhouses.
[e] Includes pre-tax non-cash impairment charge of $0.9 million for property and equipment at one Morton's steakhouse and $3 million tax benefit due to amended previous years' tax returns.
[f] Includes pre-tax charges of $37.5 million.

Transfer Agent & Registrar:	American Stock Transfer & Trust Co.		
Legal Counsel:	Schulte Roth & Zabel LLP	Traded (Symbol):	NYSE (MRT)
Investor Relations:	Ronald M. DiNella, C.F.O.	Stockholders:	359 (R)
Info. Tech.:	Loren Rapp, Dir.	Employees:	4,154
Auditors:	KPMG LLP	Annual Meeting:	In May

Motorola Mobility Holdings, Inc.
600 North U.S. Highway 45, Libertyville, Illinois 60048

Telephone: (847) 576-5000 **www.motorola.com**

Motorola Mobility Holdings, Inc. was formed on January 4, 2011, with the completed separation of Motorola, Inc. into two separate, independent corporations. Motorola Mobility fuses innovative technology with human insights to create experiences that simplify, connect, and enrich people's lives. The company offers products in two categories: Mobile Devices and Home products. The Mobile Devices portfolio includes smartphones based on the Android™ operating system and led by the DROID family of products, as well as tablets, and Bluetooth® accessories. These are supported by the company's proprietary, cloud-based services platform: MOTOBLUR™. Motorola Mobility's Home portfolio includes video, voice, and data solutions for service providers' networks to the home, in the home, and beyond the home. The company's Medios software suite enables service providers to deliver more content on more devices, anywhere, at any time.

Directors (In addition to indicated officers)

Jon E. Barfield	Thomas J. Meredith	Anthony J. Vinciquerra
Jeanne P. Jackson	Daniel A. Ninivaggi	Dr. Andrew J. Viterbi
Keith A. Meister	James R. Stengel	

Officers (Directors*)

*Sanjay K. Jha, Chm. & C.E.O.	Scott Offer, Sr. V.P. & Gen. Coun.
Dan Moloney, Pres.	Bill Ogle, Sr. V.P. & Chf Mktg. Off.
Marshall Brown, V.P. & Chf. of Staff	Walt Oswald, Corp. V.P. & Chf. Info. Off.
John Bucher, Corp. V.P. & Chf. Strat. Off.	Geoff Roman, Sr. V.P. & Chf. Tech. Off
Scott Crum, Sr. V.P. & Chf. People Off.	Marc Rothman, Sr. V.P. & C.F.O.
Mike Fleming, Sr. V.P. & Chf. Supply Chain Off.	Dale Stone, Sr. V.P.—Gov't. Rel.

Consolidated Balance Sheet As of December 31, 2010 (000 omitted)

Assets		Liabilities & Stockholders' Equity	
Current assets	$3,119,000	Current liabilities	$3,846,000
Net property, plant & equipment	806,000	Other liabilities	603,000
Goodwill	1,396,000	Minority interest	23,000
Other assets	883,000	*Stockholders' equity	1,732,000
Total	$6,204,000	Total	$6,204,000

*294,300,000 shares common stock outstanding.

Consolidated Income Statement

Years Ended Dec. 31	Thousands — — — —		Per Share — — — —		Common Stock Price Range [a] Calendar Year
	Net Sales	Net Income	Diluted Earnings	Cash Dividends	
2010	$11,460,000	$ (79,000)	$ (0.29)	$0.00	
2009	11,050,000	(1,335,000)	(1.56)	0.00	
2008	17,099,000	(2,972,000)	(10.02)	0.00	

[a] The company began trading as an independent entity in January 2011.

Transfer Agent & Registrar: BNY Mellon Shareowner Services

General Counsel:	Scott Offer, Sr. V.P.	Traded (Symbol):	NYSE (MMI)
Investor Relations:	Dean Lindroth, Corp. V.P.	Stockholders:	49,545 (R)
Human Resources:	Scott Crum, Sr. V.P.	Employees:	19,000
Info. Tech.:	Geoff Roman, C.T.O.	Annual Meeting:	In May
Auditors:	KPMG LLP		

Motorola Solutions, Inc.

1303 East Algonquin Road, Schaumburg, Illinois 60196

Telephone: (847) 576-5000   **www.motorolasolutions.com**

Motorola Solutions, Inc. was formed on January 4, 2011, with the completed separation of Motorola, Inc. into two separate, independent corporations and the name change from Motorola, Inc. to Motorola Solutions, Inc. Motorola Solutions connects people through technology and conducts its operations through two business segments: Government and Enterprise. The Government Segment focuses on providing two-way radio and other equipment for public safety systems as well as designing, installing, maintaining, and optimizing those public safety networks. The Enterprise Segment includes the sales and maintenance of enterprise mobile computing devices, scanning devices, wireless broadband systems, RFID data capture solutions, and iDEN infrastructure. The company maintains offices in 65 countries and conducts sales in 100 countries worldwide. Originally incorporated in Illinois in 1928; reincorporated in Delaware in 1973.

Directors (In addition to indicated officers)

William J. Bratton
Kenneth C. Dahlberg
David W. Dorman

General Michael V. Hayden
Samuel C. Scott, III
Vincent J. Intrieri

Judy C. Lewent
Dr. John A. White

Officers (Directors*)

*Gregory Q. Brown, Chm. & C.E.O.
Michael Annes, Sr. V.P.—Bus. Dev. & Ventures
Michele Aguilar Carlin, Sr. V.P.—Hum. Res.
Eduardo Conrado, Sr. V.P. & Chf. Mktg. Off.
Gene Delaney, Exec. V.P.—Prod. & Bus. Oper.

Edward J. Fitzpatrick, Exec. V.P. & C.F.O.
Kelly S. Mark, Corp. V.P.—Strat. & Customer
 Solutions
Mark Moon, Exec. V.P.—Sales & Field Oper.
Lewis Steverson, Sr. V.P. & Gen. Coun.

Consolidated Balance Sheet   As of December 31, 2010 (000 omitted)

Assets		Liabilities & Stockholders' Equity	
Current assets	$17,154,000	Current liabilities	$ 8,710,000
Net property, plant & equipment	922,000	Long-term debt	2,098,000
Deferred income taxes	1,920,000	Other liabilities	3,045,000
Goodwill	1,429,000	Liabilities held for disposition	737,000
Other assets	976,000	Stockholders' equity	10,987,000
Assets held for disposition	3,176,000		
Total	$25,577,000	Total	$25,577,000

*336,300,000 shares common stock outstanding.

Consolidated Income Statement

| Years Ended Dec. 31 | Thousands — — — — | | Per Share — — — — | | Common Stock |
	Net Sales	Net Income	Diluted Earnings[a]	Cash Dividends	Price Range[a] Calendar Year
2010	$7,871,000	$ 633,000	$ 1.87	$0.00	$ 64.26—42.28
2009	7,180,000	(51,000)	(0.15)	0.35	66.15—20.86
2008	8,140,000	(4,244,000)	(13.11)	1.40	

[a] Price range for Motorola, Inc. common stock; adjusted for 1 for 7 reverse stock split in Jamuary 2011.

Transfer Agent & Registrar: BNY Mellon Shareowner Services
General Counsel: Lewis Steverson, Sr. V.P.
Human Resources: Michele A. Carlin, Sr. V.P.
Auditors: KPMG LLP

Traded (Symbol): NYSE (MSI)
Stockholders: 61,903 (R)
Employees: 23,000
Annual Meeting: In May

MYR Group Inc.

1701 Golf Road, Suite 3-1012, Rolling Meadows, Illinois 60008
Telephone: (847) 290-1891   **www.myrgroup.com**

MYR Group Inc. is a leading specialty contractor serving the electrical infrastructure industry and commercial and industrial markets through a nationwide network of local offices.. Its operations are conducted through six subsidiaries: The L. E. Myers Co., Harlan Electric Company, Hawkeye Construction, Inc., Great Southwestern Construction, Inc., Sturgeon Electric Company, Inc., and MYR Transmission Services, Inc. Transmission and distribution clients include more than 125 electric utilities, cooperatives, and municipalities nationwide. MYR Group also provides commercial and industrial electrical contracting services to facility owners and general contractors in the western United States. The company's broad range of services includes design, engineering, procurement, construction, upgrade, maintenance, and repair services. Incorporated in Delaware in 1982.

Directors (In addition to indicated officers)

Jack L. Alexander
Larry F. Altenbaumer
Henry W. Fayne
Betty R. Johnson

Gary R. Johnson
Maurice E. Moore
William D. Patterson

Officers (Directors*)

*William A. Koertner, Chm., Pres. & C.E.O.
Gerald B. Engen, Jr., Sr. V.P., Chf. Legal
  Off. & Secy.
William H. Green, Sr. V.P. & C.O.O.

Richard S. Swartz, Jr., Sr. V.P.
Marco A. Martinez, V.P., C.F.O. & Treas.
John A. Fluss, Grp. V.P.

Consolidated Balance Sheet   As of December 31, 2010 (000 omitted)

Assets		Liabilities & Stockholders' Equity	
Total current assets	$223,923	Total current liabilities	$138,832
Net property & equipment	96,591	Long-term debt	30,000
Goodwill	46,599	Other liabilities	18,607
Other assets	13,035	*Stockholders' equity	192,709
Total	$380,148	Total	$380,148

*20,007,081 shares common stock outstanding.

Consolidated Income Statement

Years Ended Dec. 31	Thousands — — — — —		Per Share [a] — — — —		Common Stock Price Range [a] Calendar Year
	Net Revenues	Net Income	Diluted Earnings	Cash Dividends	
2010 [b]	$597,077	$16,122	$ 0.78	$0.00	$21.80—12.98
2009 [b]	631,168	17,235	0.83	0.00	22.88—10.00
2008 [b]	616,107	23,633	1.14	0.00	16.60— 5.90
2007 [b]	610,314	(3,202)	(0.19)		
2006 [c]	46,202	933	0.06		
2006 [d]	489,055	10,018	0.61		

[a] Stock began trading on August 12, 2008.
[b] Successor company.
[c] Successor company, represents period from December 1 through December 31, 2006.
[d] Predecessor company, represents period from January 1 through November 30, 2006.

Transfer Agent & Registrar: IST Shareholder Services

General Counsel:	Gerald B. Engen, Jr., Sr. V.P.	Traded (Symbol):	NASDAQ GM (MYRG)
Investor Relations:	Philip Kranz, Dresner	Stockholders:	25 (R)
	Corp. Svcs.	Employees:	2,800
Auditors:	Ernst & Young LLP	Annual Meeting:	In May

Nalco Holding Company

1601 West Diehl Road, Naperville, Illinois 60563

Telephone: (630) 305-1000   **www.nalco.com**

Nalco Holding Company is a global leader in water, energy, air, and process technologies and services that deliver savings for customers and improve the environment. The company's programs and services are used in water treatment applications to prevent corrosion, contamination, and the buildup of harmful deposits and in production processes to enhance process efficiency, extend asset life, improve its customers' end products, and enhance air quality for customers in aerospace, chemical, pharmaceutical, petroleum, steel, power, food and beverage, medium and light manufacturing, and pulp and papermaking industries as well as institutions such as hospitals, universities, and hotels. The company operates in two main divisions: Water and Process Services; and Energy. The Water and Process Services Division encompasses two main segments: Water Services, which focuses on customers across various industrial and institutional markets, and Paper Services, serving the pulp and paper industries. The Energy Services Division provides on-site, technology-driven solutions to the drilling, oil and gas production, refining, and petrochemical industries. Incorporated in Delaware in 2003 as the successor to a business founded in 1928.

Directors (In addition to indicated officers)

Carl M. Casale	Douglas A. Pertz
Rodney F. Chase	Daniel S. Sanders
Richard B. Marchese	Mary M. VanDeWeghe
Paul J. Norris	

Officers (Directors*)

*J. Erik Frywald, Chm., Pres. & C.E.O.
David E. Flitman, Sr. Exec. V.P.; Pres.—Water & Process Svcs.
David Johnson, Exec. V.P.; Pres.—Eur., Africa, Middle East
Eric G. Melin, Exec. V.P.; Pres.—Asia Pacific
Kathryn A. Mikells, Exec. V.P. & C.F.O.
Steve M. Taylor, Exec. V.P.; Pres.—Energy Svcs.
Mary Kay Kaufmann, Chf. Mktg. Off. & Grp. V.P.—Commer. Oper., Water & Process Svcs., Americas

Stewart H. McCutcheon, C.I.O.
Manian Ramesh, Chf. Technology Off.
Stephen N. Landsman, V.P., Gen. Coun. & Secy.
Laurie M. Marsh, V.P.—Hum. Res.
Richard A. Bendure, Grp. V.P.—Gbl. Water & Process Mktg. & Bus. Dev.
Mark R. Stoll, Grp. V.P.—Energy Svcs.
Scott Hinkle, Corp. Cont.

Consolidated Balance Sheet   As of December 31, 2010 (000 omitted)

Assets		Liabilities & Stockholders' Equity	
Current assets	$1,434,700	Current liabilities	$ 858,200
Net property, plant & equipment	729,100	Long-term debt	2,782,000
Goodwill & other intangibles, net	2,867,400	Deferred taxes	260,300
Other assets	192,500	Other liabilities	595,700
		Minority interest	30,700
		*Stockholders' equity	696,800
Total	$5,223,700	Total	$5,223.700

*138,389,129 shares common stock outstanding.

Consolidated Income Statement

Years Ended Dec. 31	Thousands — — — — Net Sales	Net Income	Per Share — — — — Diluted Earnings	Cash Dividends	Common Stock Price Range Calendar Year
2010	$4,250,500	$ 196,200 [a]	$ 1.41	$0.14	$32.62—20.15
2009	3,746,800	60,500 [b]	0.44	0.14	26.05— 9.38
2008	4,212,400	(342,600) [c]	(2.44)	0.14	26.28— 7.80
2007	3,912,500	129,000	0.88	0.14	30.98—19.94
2006	3,602,600	98,900	0.67	0.00	21.51—15.83

[a] Includes a $27.4 million charge for the early repayment of debt and $17.8 million of foreign currency transaction losses.
[b] Includes a $20.5 million charge for the early repayment of debt.
[c] Includes goodwill impairment charge of $544.2 million and $10.7 million of foreign currency transaction losses.

Transfer Agent & Registrar: Computershare Investor Services

General Counsel:	Stephen N. Landsman, V.P.	Traded (Symbol):	NYSE (NLC)
Investor Relations:	Lisa Curran, Div. V.P.	Stockholders:	53,300 (R)
Human Resources:	Laurie M. Marsh, V.P.	Employees:	12,495
Info. Tech.:	Stewart McCutcheon, C.I.O.	Annual Meeting:	In April
Auditors:	PricewaterhouseCoopers LLP		

Nanophase Technologies Corporation

1319 Marquette Drive, Romeoville, Illinois 60446
Telephone: (630) 771-6708   **www.nanophase.com**

Nanophase Technologies Corporation develops applications, and produces engineered nanomaterial products for use in a variety of diverse markets: personal care, sunscreens, architectural coatings, industrial coatings, architectural window cleaning and restoration, plastic additives, and a variety of polishing applications, including semiconductors and optics. Nanomaterials generally are made of particles (nanoparticles) that are less than 100 nanometers in diameter; a nanometer is a billionth of a meter. These nanomaterials include both singular and multi-element oxides. The company's technologies are designed to deliver an engineered nanomaterial solution for a particular target market or specific customer application and consist of two distinct nanoparticle or nanomaterial manufacturing processes (physical vapor synthesis ("PVS") and NanoArc™ synthesis), nanoparticle surface treatment(s) technologies, and dispersion technologies. Nanophase's products are available as nanoparticles, surface-treated nanoparticles, and stable nanoparticle dispersions in aqueous or organic media, providing customers with nanomaterials in readily usable forms. Recently, the company evolved from the role of strictly a materials provider to that of a solutions provider. Nanophase maintains two manufacturing facilities in the Chicago area. Incorporated in Illinois in 1989; reincorporated in Delaware in 1997.

Directors (In addition to indicated officers)

Donald S. Perkins, Chm.
George A. Vincent, III, V. Chm.
James A. Henderson
James A. McClung, Ph.D.

Jerry K. Pearlman
Richard W. Siegel, Ph.D.
W. Ed Tyler
R. Janet Whitmore

Officers (Directors*)

*Jess A. Jankowski, Pres. & C.E.O.
Frank Cesario, C.F.O.
Nancy Baldwin, V.P.—Hum. Res. & Inv. Rel.

H. Glenn Judd, V.P.—Oper.
Patrick Murray, V.P.—Res. & Dev.
David W. Nelson, V.P.—Sales & Mktg.

Consolidated Balance Sheet As of December 31, 2010 (000 omitted)

Assets		Liabilities & Stockholders' Equity	
Current assets	$ 8,726	Current liabilities	$ 2,263
Net equipment & leasehold		Long-term debt & other liabilities	777
improvements	4,722	*Stockholders' equity	10,443
Other assets	35		
Total	$13,483	Total	$13,483

*21,204,162 shares common stock outstanding.

Consolidated Income Statement

| Years Ended Dec. 31 | Thousands — — — — | | Per Share — — — — | | Common Stock |
	Total Revenue	Net Income	Diluted Earnings	Cash Dividends	Price Range [a] Calendar Year
2010	$ 9,461	$(4,078)	$(0.19)	$0.00	$2.18—0.75
2009	6,320	(4,889)	(0.23)	0.00	1.43—0.71
2008	10,214	(6,438) [b]	(0.30) [b]	0.00	4.17—0.76
2007	12,209	(3,724) [c]	(0.19) [c]	0.00	7.46—3.05
2006	8,991	(5,178)	(0.28)	0.00	8.42—5.10

[a] Stock transferred trading from NASDAQ Global Market to NASDAQ Capital Market effective May 31, 2011.
[b] Includes gain of $40,588 ($0.01 per diluted share) due to the effect of a change in accounting method.
[c] Includes loss of $133,097 ($0.01 per diluted share) due to the effect of a change in accounting method.

Transfer Agent & Registrar: Broadridge Corporate Issuer Solutions, Inc.

General Counsel:	Wildman, Harrold, Allen & Dixon LLP	Auditors:	McGladrey & Pullen, LLP
		Traded (Symbol):	NASDAQ Capital (NANX)
Investor Relations:	Nancy Baldwin, V.P.	Stockholders:	137 (R)
Human Resources:	Nancy Baldwin, V.P.	Employees:	49
Info. Tech.:	Nancy Baldwin, V.P.	Annual Meeting:	In August

National Holdings Corporation

875 North Michigan Avenue, Suite 1560, Chicago, Illinois 60611

Telephone: (312) 751-8833   **www.nationalsecurities.com**

National Holdings Corporation, formerly known as Olympic Cascade Financial Corporation, is a diversified financial services company operating through its wholly owned subsidiaries, National Securities Corporation, vFinance Investments, Inc., EquityStation, Inc. (collectively, the "broker-dealer subsidiaries"), and National Insurance, that conducts a national securities brokerage business through its main offices in Seattle, Washington, Boca Raton, Florida, and New York City, and through other domestic and international offices. There are currently 690 registered representatives affiliated with the broker-dealer subsidiaries, operating throughout the United States and Europe. The broker-dealer subsidiaries offer full service retail brokerage to approximately 46,000 retail, high net worth, and institutional clients, provide investment banking, merger, acquisition, and advisory services to companies, and engage in trading securities and provides liquidity in the U.S. Treasury marketplace. The brokers operate primarily as independent contractors. vFinance is also a mortgage lender focused primarily on the commercial sector, providing bridge loans and commercial mortgages through its nationwide network of lenders. National Insurance provides a full array of fixed insurance products to its clients. In July 2010, the company sold a 24.9% share of EquityStation, Inc. to Osage, LLC. Incorporated in Delaware in 1996. Present name adopted in 2006.

Directors (In addition to indicated officers)

Paul J. Coviello	Frank Plimpton
Marshall S. Geller	Jorge A. Ortega
Robert W. Lautz, Jr.	Michael Weiss

Officers (Directors*)

*Mark A. Goldwasser, Chm. &. C.E.O.	William L. Groeneveld, Pres.—vFinance
*Leonard J. Sokolow, V. Chm. & Pres.	Inv. & EquityStation
Alan B. Levin, C.F.O. & Secy.	Jonathan C. Rich, Exec. V.P.—vFinance
Mark D. Roth, C.O.O. & Gen. Coun.	Robert H. Daskal, V.P.—Fin.

Consolidated Balance Sheet As of September 30, 2010 (000 omitted)

Assets		Liabilities & Stockholders' Deficit	
Current assets	$12,634	Current liabilities	$16,100
Net property & equipment	1,127	Other liabilities	7,509
Other assets	3,619	Noncontrolling interest	42
		*Stockholders' deficit	(6,271)
Total	$17,380	Total	$17,380

*17,276,704 shares common stock outstanding.

Consolidated Income Statement

Years Ended Abt. Sept. 30	Thousands — — — — —		Per Share — — — — —		Common Stock Price Range Fiscal Year
	Total Revenues	Net Income	Diluted Earnings	Cash Dividends	
2010	$110,952	$ (7,021)[a]	$(0.41)[a]	$0.00	$0.76—0.22
2009	115,170	(6,794)[a]	(0.41)[a]	0.00	0.90—0.30
2008 [b]	82,143	(21,017)[c]	(2.02)	0.00	2.80—0.70
2007	72,819	1,372	0.13	0.00	3.30—1.10
2006	58,727	595	0.04	0.00	1.60—0.53

[a] Attributable to common stockholders.
[b] Includes financial information of vFinance, Inc., for fourth quarter.
[c] Includes impairment charge of $12,999,000 related to the intangible asset acquired in the merger with vFinance, Inc.

Transfer Agent & Registrar: Computershare Investor Services

Legal Counsel:	Littman Krooks LLP	Traded (Symbol):	OTC BB (NHLD)
Investor Relations:	Alan B. Levin, C.F.O.	Stockholders:	1,000 (B)
Auditors:	Sherb & Co., LLP	Employees:	170
		Annual Meeting:	In April

Navigant Consulting, Inc.

30 South Wacker Drive, Suite 3550, Chicago, Illinois 60606

Telephone: (312) 573-5600   **www.navigantconsulting.com**

Navigant Consulting, Inc. is an independent specialty consulting firm combining deep industry knowledge with technical expertise to enable companies to create and protect value in the face of complex and critical business risks and opportunities. Professional services include dispute, investigative, economic, operational, risk management, and financial and risk advisory solutions. The company operates in four segments: Dispute and Investigative Services; Business Consulting Services; International Consulting; and Economic Consulting. The company markets its services directly to corporate counsel, law firms, government entities, corporate boards, corporate executives, and special committees. Navigant Consulting maintains offices throughout the United States and has an international presence with offices in Canada, the United Kingdom, and China. In May 2010, the company acquired Daylight Forensic & Advisory LLC, an international regulatory consulting and investigative firm specializing in financial investigations, anti-money-laundering (AML) consulting, regulatory compliance, forensic technology services, and fraud risk management. In October 2010, Navigant Consulting acquired EthosPartners Healthcare Management Group, Inc., a national healthcare consulting group specializing in physician and hospital alignment, physician practice operations management, and physician revenue cycle management. Incorporated in Delaware in 1996.

Directors (In addition to indicated officers)

Thomas A. Gildehaus
Cynthia A. Glassman, Ph.D.
Stephan A. James
Peter B. Pond

Samuel K. Skinner
Gov. James R. Thompson
Michael L. Tipsord

Officers (Directors*)

*William M. Goodyear, Chm. & C.E.O.
Julie M. Howard, Pres. & C.O.O.
Thomas A. Nardi, Exec. V.P. & C.F.O.
Jeffrey H. Stoecklein, V.P.—Corp. Dev.

David E. Wartner, V.P.—Oper. & Treas.
Monica M. Weed, V.P., Gen. Coun. & Secy.
Scott S. Harper, Corp. Cont.

Consolidated Balance Sheet   As of December 31, 2010 (000 omitted)

Assets		Liabilities & Stockholders' Equity	
Current assets	$219,485	Current liabilities	$155,579
Net property & equipment	38,903	Other liabilities	252,735
Goodwill & intangible assets, net	584,196	*Stockholders' equity	460,721
Other assets	26,451		
Total	$869,035	Total	$869,035

*50,137,000 shares of common stock outstanding.

Consolidated Income Statement

Years Ended Dec. 31	Thousands — — — —		Per Share — — — —		Common Stock Price Range Calendar Year
	Total Revenues	Net Income	Diluted Earnings	Cash Dividends	
2010	$703,660	$24,057	$0.48	$0.00	$15.10— 8.32
2009	707,239	21,947	0.44	0.00	15.46—11.07
2008	810,640	40,057	0.83	0.00	21.78—11.19
2007	767,058	33,396	0.66	0.00	21.60—12.12
2006	681,745	52,974	0.97	0.00	23.28—17.45

Transfer Agent & Registrar: BNY Mellon Shareowner Services
General Counsel: Monica M. Weed, V.P.
Investor Relations: Jennifer Moreno Reddick, Exec. Dir.
Human Resources: Jennifer Schulte
Info. Tech.: Changappa Kodendera, C.I.O.
Auditors: KPMG LLP

Traded (Symbol): NYSE (NCI)
Stockholders: 303 (R)
Employees: 2,359
Annual Meeting: In April

Navistar International Corporation

4201 Winfield Road, P.O. Box 1488, Warrenville, Illinois 60555
Telephone: (630) 753-5000   **www.navistar.com**

Navistar International Corporation is s a holding company whose principal operating subsidiaries are Navistar, Inc., and Navistar Financial Corporation. Navistar, Inc., is an international manufacturer of International brand commercial and military trucks, IC Bus® brand school and commercial buses, Monaco RV brands of recreational vehicles, MaxxForce® brand diesel engines, Workhorse Custom Chassis, LLC brand chassis for motor homes and step vans, Navistar Defense, LLC military vehicles, and a provider of service parts for all makes of trucks and trailers. Additionally, the company is a private-label designer and manufacturer of diesel engines for the pickup truck, van, and SUV markets. Products, parts, and services are sold through a network of 783 dealer and retail outlets in the United States and Canada, 91 Mexican dealer locations, and 103 international dealer locations as of October 31, 2010. Navistar Financial Corporation, a wholly-owned finance subsidiary, supports the sale of Navistar products by helping finance dealer inventory and customer purchases. Incorporated in Delaware in 1902 and reincorporated in 1993.

Directors (In addition to indicated officers)

Eugenio Clariond	Michael N. Hammes	Steven J. Klinger
John D. Correnti	David D. Harrison	Gen. Stanley McChrystal
Diane H. Gulyas	James H. Keyes	Dennis D. Williams

Officers (Directors*)

*Daniel C. Ustian, Chm., Pres. & C.E.O.
Andrew J. Cederoth, Exec. V.P. & C.F.O.
Phyllis E. Cochran, Pres.—Parts Grp.
Steven K. Covey, Sr. V.P., Gen. Coun. & Chf. Ethics Off.
Gregory W. Elliott, Sr. V.P.—Hum. Res. & Admin.
John J. Allen, Pres.—North Amer. Truck Grp.
David Johanneson, Pres. & C.E.O.—Navistar Financial Corp.

Dee Kapur, Pres.—Truck Grp.
James M. Moran, V.P. & Treas.
William H. Osborne, V.P.—Custom Prods.
Richard Tarapchak, V.P. & Corp. Cont.
Curt A. Kramer, Assoc. Gen. Coun. & Corp. Secy.
Don Sharp, V.P. & C.I.O.

Consolidated Balance Sheet As of October 31, 2010 (000 omitted)

Assets		Liabilities & Stockholders' Deficit	
Current assets	$5,835,000	Current liabilities	$3,589,000
Property & equipment, net	1,442,000	Other liabilities	7,073,000
Other assets	2,453,000	Minority interest	49,000
		*Stockholders' deficit	(981,000)
Total	$9,730,000	Total	$9,730,000

*71,800,000 shares common stock outstanding.

Consolidated Income Statement

| Years Ended Oct. 31 | Thousands — — — — | | Per Share — — — — | | Common Stock |
	Sales & Revenues	Net Income [a]	Diluted Earnings [a]	Cash Dividends	Price Range [b] Fiscal Year
2010	$12,145,000	$ 223,000	$ 3.05	$0.00	$58.00—31.53
2009	11,569,000	320,000 [c]	4.46 [c]	0.00	48.94—15.24
2008	14,724,000	134,000	1.82	0.00	79.05—21.95
2007	12,295,000	(120,000)	(1.70)	0.00	74.60—26.89
2006	14,200,000	301,000	4.12	0.00	30.55—20.53

[a] Attributable to Navistar International Corporation.
[b] Traded on OTC market for part of the second quarter of 2007, the third and fourth quarters of 2007, the first and second quarters of 2008, and for part of the third quarter of 2008.
[c] Includes extraordinary gain of $23 million ($0.32 per diluted share) due to the fair value of the assets acquired from Monaco Coach Corporation exceeding the purchase price.

Transfer Agent & Registrar: BNY Mellon Shareowner Services

General Counsel:	Steven K. Covey, Sr. V.P.	Traded (Symbol):	NYSE (NAV)
Investor Relations:	Heather Kos, V.P.	Stockholders:	12,792 (R)
Human Resources:	Gregory W. Elliott, Sr. V.P.	Employees:	15,800
Info. Tech.:	Don Sharp, V.P. & C.I.O.	Annual Meeting:	In February
Auditors:	KPMG LLP		

Neutral Tandem Inc.

550 West Adams Street, Suite 900, Chicago, Illinois 60661
Telephone: (312) 384-8000   **www.neutraltandem.com**

Neutral Tandem, Inc. is a leading provider of U.S. and international voice, IP transit, and ethernet tele-communications services, primarily on a wholesale basis, to wireless, wireline, cable, and broadband telephony companies, facilitating inter-carrier communications with a cost-effective alternative to the Incumbent Local Exchange Carrier (ILEC) network. The company's solutions build redundancy, security, and operational efficiencies into the nation's telecommunications infrastructure. As of December 31, 2010, Neutral Tandem was capable of connecting approximately 526 million telephone numbers assigned to carriers. Its two largest customers, AT&T and Sprint Nextel, accounted for 22% and 18%, respectively, of its total revenues for the year ended December 31, 2010. Neutral Tandem has switch sites located in Arizona, California, Colorado, Florida, Georgia, Illinois, Indiana, Massachusetts, Michigan, Minnesota, Missouri, New Jersey, New York, North Carolina, Ohio, Oregon, Pennsylvania, Puerto Rico, Texas, Virginia, Washington, and Wisconsin. In October 2010, the company acquired Tinet S.p.A., an Italian corporation. This acquisition allowed Neutral Tandem to evolve from a primarily U.S. voice intercon-nection company into a global IP-based network services company. Incorporated in Delaware in 2001.

Directors (In addition to indicated officers)

James P. Hynes, Chm.
Peter J. Barris
Edward Greenberg
Robert C. Hawk

Lawrence M. Ingeneri
Timothy A. Samples
Rian J. Wren

Officers (Directors*)

*G. Edward Evans, C.E.O.
Surendra Saboo, Pres. & C.O.O.
Robert Junkroski, Exec. V.P. & C.F.O.
John Harrington, Sr. V.P.—Reg. & Litigation

David A. Lopez, Sr. V.P.—Sales
Richard L. Monto, Gen. Coun., Corp. Secy. &
  Sr. V.P.—External Affs.
Paolo Susnik, Managing Dir.—Tinet

Consolidated Balance Sheet   As of December 31, 2010 (000 omitted)

Assets		Liabilities & Stockholders' Equity	
Current assets	$154,786	Current liabilities	$ 32,943
Net property & equipment	77,683	Other liabilities	11,301
Other assets	83,058	*Stockholders' equity	271,283
Total	$315,527	Total	$315,527

*33,166,242 shares common stock outstanding.

Consolidated Income Statement

Years Ended Dec. 31	Thousands — — — — —		Per Share — — — — —		Common Stock Price Range [a] Calendar Year
	Revenue	Net Income	Diluted Earnings	Cash Dividends	
2010 [b]	$199,826	$32,608	$0.97	$0.00	$23.72— 9.87
2009	168,906	41,315	1.22	0.00	33.24—14.63
2008	120,902	24,020	0.72	0.00	22.90—12.86
2007	85,555	6,258	0.24	0.00	20.28—17.42
2006	52,866	4,658	0.20		

[a] Initial public offering of common stock completed on November 7, 2007.
[b] Includes Tinet from date of acquisition, October 1, 2010.

Transfer Agent & Registrar: Computershare Investor Services
General Counsel: Richard L. Monto, Sr. V.P.   Traded (Symbol):   NASDAQ (TNDM)
Investor Relations: Jim Polson   Stockholders: 7,000 (R)
Auditors: Deloitte & Touche LLP   Employees: 230
                                                   Annual Meeting: In May

Nicor Inc.

1844 Ferry Road, P.O. Box 3014, Naperville, Illinois 60563-9600
Telephone: (630) 305-9500   **www.nicor.com**

Nicor Inc. is a holding company whose principal businesses are Nicor Gas, one of the nation's largest natural gas distribution companies, and Tropical Shipping, a leading transporter of containerized freight in the Bahamas and the Caribbean. Nicor Gas delivers natural gas to 2.2 million customers in a service territory that encompasses most of the northern third of Illinois, excluding the city of Chicago. Tropical Shipping, with a fleet which includes 11 owned and 3 chartered vessels, transports containerized freight from the east coast of the United States and Canada to the Caribbean region. Nicor also owns several unregulated energy-related subsidiaries, including Nicor Services, Nicor Solutions, and Nicor Advanced Energy, which provide energy-related products and services for retail markets, Nicor Enerchange, a wholesale natural gas marketing company, and Central Valley, which is developing a natural gas storage company. In December 2010, Nicor announced plans to merge with a subsidiary of AGL Resources. Following the merger, expected to close in the second half of 2011, AGL Resources will maintain its corporate headquarters in Atlanta, Georgia and locate its newly expanded gas distribution headquarters in Naperville, Illinois. Incorporated in Illinois in 1976.

Directors (In addition to indicated officers)

Robert M. Beavers, Jr.
Bruce P. Bickner
John H. Birdsall, III
Norman R. Bobins
Brenda J. Gaines
Raymond A. Jean

Dennis J. Keller
R. Eden Martin
Georgia R. Nelson
Armando J. Olivera
John Rau
John C. Staley

Officers (Directors*)

*Russ M. Strobel, Chm., Pres. & C.E.O.
Richard L. Hawley, Exec. V.P. & C.F.O.
Rocco J. D'Alessandro, Exec. V.P.—Oper., Nicor Gas
Daniel R. Dodge, Exec. V.P.—Diversified Ventures
Claudia J. Colalillo, Sr. V.P.—Hum. Res. & Corp. Commun.

Paul C. Gracey, Jr., Sr. V.P., Gen. Coun. & Secy.
Gerald P. O'Connor, Sr. V.P.—Fin. & Strat. Plan.
Scott Lewis, V.P.—Governmental Rel.
Karen K. Pepping, V.P. & Cont.
Douglas M. Ruschau, V.P. & Treas.
Barbara A. Zeller, V.P.—Info. Tech.
Rick Murrell, Chm.—Tropical Shipping

Consolidated Balance Sheet As of December 31, 2010 (000 omitted)

Assets		Liabilities & Stockholders' Equity	
Current assets	$ 953,600	Current liabilities	$1,074,300
Net property, plant & equipment	3,022,800	Total long-term obligations	498,400
Other assets	520,100	Other liabilities	1,819,900
		*Stockholders' equity	1,103,900
Total	$4,496,500	Total	$4,496,500

*45,546,759 shares common stock outstanding.

Consolidated Income Statement

Years Ended Dec. 31	Thousands — — — — Operating Revenues	Net Income	Per Share — — — — Diluted Earnings	Cash Dividends [a]	Common Stock Price Range Calendar Year
2010	$2,709,800	$138,400	$3.02	$1.86	$50.81—37.99
2009	2,652,100	135,500	2.98	1.86	43.39—27.50
2008	3,776,600	119,500	2.63	1.86	51.99—32.35
2007	3,176,300	135,200	2.99	1.86	53.66—37.80
2006	2,960,000	128,300 [b]	2.87	1.86	49.92—38.72

[a] Declared.
[b] Includes a litigation charge of $10,000,000.

Transfer Agent & Registrar: Wells Fargo Shareowner Services

General Counsel:	Paul C. Gracey, Jr., Sr. V.P.	Traded (Symbol):	NYSE, CSE (GAS)
Investor Relations:	Kary D. Brunner, Dir.	Stockholders:	16,700 (R)
Human Resources:	Claudia J. Colalillo, Sr. V.P.	Employees:	3,800
Info. Tech.:	Barbara A. Zeller, V.P.	Annual Meeting:	In June
Auditors:	Deloitte & Touche LLP		

NiSource Inc.

801 East 86th Avenue, Merrillville, Indiana 46410

Telephone: (877) 647-5990   www.nisource.com

NiSource Inc. is an energy holding company that, through its subsidiaries, provides natural gas, electricity, and other products and services to approximately 3,800,000 customers located in the energy corridor that runs from the Gulf Coast through the Midwest to New England. The company's primary business segments are: gas distribution, electric operations, and gas transmission and storage. Natural gas distribution operations serve more than 3,300,000 customers in 7 states and operate approximately 59,000 miles of pipeline. Electric operations generate and distribute electricity to the public through its subsidiary, Northern Indiana Public Service Company, to approximately 458,000 customers in 20 counties in Indiana. Gas transmission and storage subsidiaries own and operate approximately 15,000 miles of interstate pipelines and operate one of the nation's largest underground natural gas storage systems, serving customers in 16 states and the District of Columbia. NiSource's long-term strategy focuses on its core regulated businesses. Incorporated in Indiana in 1987; present name adopted in 1999; reincorporated in Delaware in 2000.

Directors (In addition to indicated officers)

Ian M. Rolland, Chm.	Sigmund L. Cornelius	Deborah S. Parker
Richard A. Abdoo	Michael E. Jesanis	Richard L. Thompson
Steven C. Beering, M.D.	Marty R. Kittrell	Dr. Carolyn Y. Woo
	W. Lee Nutter	

Officers (Directors*)

*Robert C. Skaggs, Jr., Pres. & C.E.O.	Robert D. Campbell, Sr. V.P.—Hum. Res.
Christopher A. Helms, Exec. V.P. & Grp. C.E.O.	Glen L. Kettering, Sr. V.P.—Corp. Affs.
Carrie J. Hightman, Exec. V.P. & Chf. Legal Off.	Violet G. Sistovaris, Sr. V.P. & C.I.O.
Stephen P. Smith, Exec. V.P. & C.F.O.	Jon D. Veurink, V.P., Cont. & Chf. Acct. Off.
Jimmy D. Staton, Exec. V.P. & Grp. C.E.O.	

Consolidated Balance Sheet As of December 31, 2010 (000 omitted)

Assets		Liabilities & Stockholders' Equity	
Current assets	$ 2,448,900	Current liabilities	$ 3,649,400
Net property, plant & equipment	11,097,000	Long-term debt	5,936,100
Investments	348,500	Deferred items	2,312,300
Other assets	6,044,400	Other liabilities	3,117,800
		*Stockholders' equity	4,923,200
Total	$19,938,800	Total	$19,938,800

*278,855,291 shares common stock outstanding.

Consolidated Income Statement

Years Ended Dec. 31	Thousands — — — —		Per Share — — — —		Common Stock
	Gross Revenues	Net Income	Diluted Earnings	Cash Dividends [a]	Price Range Calendar Year
2010	$6,422,000	$292,000 [b]	$1.04 [b]	$0.92	$17.96—14.13
2009	6,650,600	217,700 [b]	0.79 [b]	0.92	15.82— 7.79
2008	8,800,200	79,000 [c]	0.29 [c]	0.92	19.82—10.35
2007	7,861,600	321,400 [d]	1.17 [d]	0.92	25.43—17.49
2006	7,418,400	282,200 [b]	1.03 [b]	0.92	24.80—19.51

[a] Dividends paid.
[b] Includes losses from discontinued operations, net of tax, of $2.6 million ($0.01 per diluted share) in 2010; $12.8 million ($0.05 per diluted share) in 2009; and $51.9 million ($0.19 per diluted share) in 2006.
[c] Includes a loss of $291.6 million ($1.06 per diluted share) from discontinued operations, net of tax, including after-tax loss on disposition related to the sales of Whiting Clean Energy, Northern Utilities, and Granite State Gas of $32.3 million, $63.3 million, and $12.5 million, respectively, and an adjustment of $188.0 million for the Tawney litigation.
[d] Includes gain from discontinued operations, net of tax, of $18.4 million ($0.07 per diluted share).

Transfer Agent & Registrar:	BNY Mellon Shareowner Services		
General Counsel:	Schiff Hardin LLP	Traded (Symbol):	NYSE (NI)
Investor Relations:	Randy Hulen, Managing Dir.	Stockholders:	32,313 (R)
Human Resources:	Robert D. Campbell, Sr. V.P.	Employees:	7,604
Info. Tech.:	Violet Sistovaris, Sr. V.P.	Annual Meeting:	In May
Auditors:	Deloitte & Touche LLP		

Northern States Financial Corporation

1601 North Lewis Avenue, Waukegan, Illinois 60085

Telephone: (847) 244-6000   **www.nsfc.net**

Northern States Financial Corporation is a holding company for NorStates Bank. The principal business of the company consists of attracting deposits from the general public, making commercial loans and loans secured by residential and commercial real estate, making consumer loans, and operating mortgage banking and trust businesses. NorStates Bank is an Illinois-chartered bank with three banking offices in Waukegan, and one in each of the following cities: Antioch, Gurnee, Round Lake, Round Lake Beach, and Winthrop Harbor, Illinois. In 2008, the company formed a new subsidiary, NorProperties, Inc., for the purpose of managing and disposing of certain nonperforming company assets. Incorporated in Delaware in 1984.

Directors (In addition to indicated officers)

Allan J. Jacobs, Chm.
Frank Furlan, V. Chm.
Fred Abdula
Theodore A. Bertrand
Jack H. Blumberg

James A. Hollensteiner
Barbara J. Martin
Raymond M. Mota
Charles W. Smith

Officers (Directors*)

*Scott Yelvington, Pres. & C.E.O.
 Kerry J. Biegay, V.P. & Corp. Secy.
 Steven Neudecker, V.P. & C.F.O.

Thomas M. Nemeth, V.P. & Treas.
Shelly Christian, Exec. V.P. & Chf. Lending
  Off.—NorStates Bank

Consolidated Balance Sheet   As of December 31, 2010 (000 omitted)

Assets		Liabilities & Stockholders' Equity	
Cash & cash equivalents	$ 30,357	Deposits	$446,551
Securities available for sale	91,830	Subordinated debentures	10,310
Loans & leases, net	366,453	Securities sold under repurch. agts.	35,517
Other assets	43,088	Other liabilities	6,065
		*Stockholders' equity	33,285
Total	$531,728	Total	$531,728

*4,072,255 shares common stock outstanding.

Consolidated Income Statement

Years Ended Dec. 31	Thousands — — — —		Per Share — — — —		Common Stock Price Range Calendar Year
	Total Income	Net Income	Diluted Earnings	Cash Dividends [a]	
2010	$29,962	$ (6,362)	$(1.81)	$0.00	$ 4.33— 0.72
2009	33,122	(35,558)	(8.94)	0.00	7.92— 1.75
2008	28,829	(9,273)	(2.26)	0.40	22.30— 3.80
2007	43,459	4,388	1.05	0.72	25.37—18.80
2006	41,979	3,092	0.72	0.65	25.42—16.00

[a] Declared.

Transfer Agent & Registrar: American Stock Transfer & Trust Co.	
Corporate Counsel: Vedder Price, P.C.	**Traded (Symbol):** NASDAQ Capital (NSFC)
Human Resources: Kerry J. Biegay, V.P.	**Stockholders:** 287 (R)
Info. Tech.: Kerry J. Biegay, V.P.	**Employees:** 129
Auditors: Plante & Moran, PLLC	**Annual Meeting:** In May

Northern Trust Corporation

50 South LaSalle Street, Chicago, Illinois 60603

Telephone: (312) 630-6000 www.northerntrust.com

Northern Trust Corporation is a leading provider of asset management, asset servicing, fund administration, banking solutions, and fiduciary services for corporations, institutions, and affluent individuals worldwide. Northern Trust, a financial holding company based in Chicago, has offices in 18 U.S. states and 16 international locations in North America, Europe, the Middle East, and the Asia-Pacific region. As of December 31, 2010, Northern Trust had assets under custody of $4.1 trillion, assets under investment management of $643.6 billion, and banking assets of $83.8 billion. Incorporated in Delaware in 1971.

Directors (In addition to indicated officers)

Linda Walker Bynoe	Robert W. Lane	Martin P. Slark
Nicholas D. Chabraja	Robert C. McCormack	David H. B. Smith, Jr.
Susan Crown	Edward J. Mooney	Enrique J. Sosa
Dipak C. Jain	John W. Rowe	Charles A. Tribbett, III

Officers (Directors*)

*Frederick H. Waddell, Chm. & C.E.O.
Sherry S. Barrat, V. Chm.
William L. Morrison, Pres. & C.O.O.
Steven L. Fradkin, Pres.—Corp. & Institutional Svcs.
Stephen N. Potter, Pres.—Northern Trust Gbl. Invest.
Jana R. Schreuder, Pres.—Personal Fin. Svcs.
Joyce M. St. Clair, Pres.—Oper. & Tech.
Michael G. O'Grady, C.F.O. (Eff. 10/1/2011)
Aileen B. Blake, Exec. V.P. & Cont.
Robert P. Browne, Exec. V.P. & Chf. Invest. Off.
Jeffrey D. Cohodes, Exec. V.P. & Head—Corp. Risk Mgt.

William R. Dodds, Jr., Exec. V.P. & Treas.
Mark Van Grinsven, Exec. V.P.—Credit Policy
Connie L. Lindsey, Exec. V.P.—Corp. Social Responsibility
Timothy P. Moen, Exec. V.P.—Hum. Res. & Admin.
Dan E. Phelps, Exec. V.P. & Gen. Auditor
Kelly R. Welsh, Exec. V.P. & Gen. Coun.
Caroline E. Devlin, Sr. V.P. & Head—Corp. Strat.
Kelly King Dibble, Sr. V.P. & Dir.—Pub. Affs.
Beverly J. Fleming, Sr. V.P. & Dir.—Inv. Rel.
Saverio Mirarchi, Sr. V.P. & Chf. Compliance & Ethics Off.
Rose A. Ellis, Corp. Secy. & Asst. Gen. Coun.

Consolidated Statement of Condition As of December 31, 2010 (000 omitted)

Assets		Liabilities & Common Equity	
Cash & due from banks	$ 2,818,000	Deposits	$64,195,700
Securities	21,281,900	Fed. funds purchased	3,691,700
Time deposits with banks	15,351,300	Securities sold under	
Net loans & lease financing	28,132,000	agreement to repurchase	954,400
Properties & equipment	504,500	Senior notes & other	
Other assets	15,756,200	borrowings	2,243,800
		Long-term debt	2,729,300
		Other liabilities	3,198,700
		*Common equity	6,830,300
Total	$83,843,900	Total	$83,843,900

*242,268,903 shares common stock outstanding.

Consolidated Income Statement

Years Ended Dec. 31	Thousands — — — —		Per Share — — — —		Common Stock Price Range Calendar Year
	Total Income	Net Income	Diluted Earnings	Cash Dividends	
2010	$4,025,700	$669,500	$2.74	$1.12	$59.36—45.30
2009	4,193,100	864,200	3.16	1.12	66.08—43.32
2008	5,677,900	794,800	3.47	1.12	88.92—33.88
2007	5,447,800	726,900	3.24	1.03	83.17—56.52
2006	4,501,100	665,400	3.00	0.94	61.40—49.12

Transfer Agent & Registrar: Wells Fargo Bank, N.A.

General Counsel:	Kelly R. Welsh, Exec. V.P.	Traded (Symbol):	NASDAQ (NTRS)
Investor Relations:	Beverly J. Fleming, Sr. V.P.	Stockholders:	2,614 (R)
Human Resources:	Timothy P. Moen, Exec. V.P.	Employees:	12,800
Auditors:	KPMG LLP	Annual Meeting:	Third Tuesday in April

Northstar Aerospace, Inc.

6006 West 73rd Street, Bedford Park, Illinois 60638

Telephone: (708) 728-2000   **www.nsaero.com**

Northstar Aerospace, Inc. is North America's leading independent manufacturer of flight critical gears and transmissions, with operating subsidiaries in the United States and Canada. Its principal products include helicopter gears and transmissions, accessory gearbox assemblies, rotorcraft drive systems, and other machined and fabricated parts. It also provides maintenance, repair, and overhaul of transmissions and drive systems. Customers include Boeing, Sikorsky Ltd., General Electric Aviation, and Rolls-Royce plc. Plants are located in Chicago, Illinois; Phoenix, Arizona; and Milton and Windsor, Ontario. In May 2010, Northstar announced plans to close its facility in Anderson, Indiana in mid-2011. Incorporated in Ontario in 1984; present named adopted in 2002.

Directors (In addition to indicated officers)

Neil W. Baker   Michael J. Tkach
Gordon Flatt   James D. Wallace

Officers (Directors*)

*David A. Rattee, Chm.   Craig A. Yuen, V.P. & Chf. Strat. Off.
*Glenn E. Hess, Pres. & C.E.O.   Peter Jackson, Pres.—Canadian Oper.
 Greg A. Schindler, V.P. & C.F.O.

Consolidated Balance Sheet As of December 31, 2010 (000 omitted)

Assets		Liabilities & Stockholders' Equity	
Total current assets	$ 95,158	Total current liabilities	$ 49,434
Net property, plant & equipment	42,146	Long-term debt	45,260
Other assets	14,742	Other liabilities	23,148
		*Stockholders' equity	34,204
Total	$152,046	Total	$152,046

*30,370,318 shares common stock outstanding.

Consolidated Income Statement

Years Ended Dec. 31	Thousands — — — —		Per Share — — — —		Common Stock Price Range Calendar Year
	Net Revenue	Net Income	Diluted Earnings	Cash Dividends	
2010	$216,985	$ 4,158 [a]	$ 0.14 [a]	$0.00	$2.99—0.89
2009	193,919	3,501 [a]	0.12 [a]	0.00	1.33—0.35
2008	171,743	(9,414) [b]	(0.32) [b]	0.00	4.73—0.25
2007	149,715	(7,339) [b]	(0.25) [b]	0.00	5.50—3.50
2006	129,062	(10,712)	(0.36)	0.00	6.49—4.05

[a] Includes losses from discontinued operations of $308,000 ($0.01 per diluted share) in 2010 and $1,117,000 ($0.03 per diluted share) in 2009.
[b] Includes income from discontinued operations of $722,000 ($0.02 per diluted share) in 2008 and $825,000 ($0.03 per diluted share) in 2007.

Transfer Agent & Registrar: Computershare Investor Services
General Counsel: David Anderson, Gen. Coun. **Traded (Symbol):** TSX (NAS)
Investor Relations: Craig A. Yuen, Chf. Strat. Off. **Employees:** 950
Auditors: PricewaterhouseCoopers LLP **Annual Meeting:** In June

OfficeMax Incorporated

263 Shuman Boulevard, Naperville, Illinois 60563
Telephone: (630) 438-7800   **www.officemax.com**

OfficeMax Incorporated is a leader in both business-to-business and retail office products distribution. The company provides office supplies and paper, print and document services through OfficeMax ImPress, technology products and solutions, and office furniture to large, medium, and small businesses, government offices, and to retail consumers. The company's customers are served through direct sales, catalogs, the Internet, and nearly 1,000 retail stores throughout the U.S. and in Puerto Rico, the U.S. Virgin Islands, and Mexico. Incorporated in Delaware in 1931. Present name adopted in 2004.

Directors (In addition to indicated officers)

Rakesh Gangwal, Chm.
Warren F. Bryant
Joseph M. DePinto

William J. Montgoris
Francesca Ruiz de Luzuriaga
David M. Szymanski

Officers (Directors*)

*Ravichandra K. Saligram, Pres. & C.E.O.
Bruce Besanko, Exec. V.P, C.F.O. &
  Chf. Admin. Off.
Matthew Broad, Exec. V.P. & Gen. Coun.
Randy G. Burdick, Exec. V.P. & C.I.O.
Michael Lewis, Exec. V.P. & Pres.—Retail
Mike MacDonald, Exec. V.P. & Pres.—Contract
Steve Parsons, Exec. V.P. & Chf. Hum. Res. Off.

Reuben E. Slone, Exec. V.P.—Supply Chain
Ryan Vero, Exec. V.P. & Chf. Merch. Off.
Deborah A. O'Connor, Sr. V.P.—Fin. & Chf. Acct.
  Off.
Susan Wagner-Fleming, Sr. V.P., Corp. Secy. &
  Assoc. Gen. Coun.
Tony Giuliano, V.P., Treas. & Inv. Rel.

Consolidated Balance Sheet   As of December 25, 2010 (000 omitted)

Assets		Liabilities & Stockholders' Equity	
Current assets	$2,014,286	Current liabilities	$1,044,474
Net property & equipment	397,289	Long-term debt	270,435
Goodwill & intangibles, net	83,231	Non-recourse debt	1,470,000
Timber notes receivable	899,250	Other liabilities	644,009
Other assets	684,873	Minority interest	49,246
		*Stockholders' equity	600,765
Total	$4,078,929	Total	$4,078,929

*85,057,710 shares common stock outstanding.

Consolidated Income Statement

Years Ended Abt. Dec. 31	Thousands — — — — Net Sales	Net Income	Per Share — — — — Diluted Earnings	Cash Dividends	Common Stock Price Range Calendar Year
2010	$7,150,007	$ 71,155 [a]	$ 0.79 [a]	$0.00	$19.79— 9.67
2009	7,212,050	$667 [b]	(0.03) [b]	0.00	14.50— 1.86
2008	8,267,008	(1,657,932) [c]	(21.90) [c]	0.45	25.64— 2.84
2007	9,081,962	207,373 [d]	2.66 [d]	0.60	55.40—20.38
2006	8,965,707	91,721 [e]	1.19 [e]	0.60	51.80—24.72

[a] Includes pre-tax charges of $11.0 million and $13.1 million, partially offset by a $0.6 million severance reserve adjustment; and a pre-tax favorable adjustment of a reserve of $9.4 million.
[b] Includes pre-tax charges of $17.6 million, $18.1 million; pre-tax gains of $2.6 million and $4.4 million; income tax benefit of $14.9 million.
[c] Includes pre-tax charges of $1,364.4 billion, $735.8 million, $27.9 million, and income of $20.5 million.
[d] Includes pre-tax gain of $32.4 million and loss of $1.1 million.
[e] Includes pre-tax charges of $89.5 million, $46.4 million, $10.3 million, and $18 million; and income of $48 million.

Transfer Agent & Registrar: Wells Fargo Shareowner Services

General Counsel:	Matthew Broad, Exec. V.P.	**Traded (Symbol):**	NYSE (OMX)
Investor Relations:	Mike Steele, Sr. Dir.	**Stockholders:**	12,389 (R)
Human Resources	Steve Parsons, Exec. V.P.	**Employees:**	Approx. 30,000
Chf. Tech. Off.:	Randy G. Burdick, Exec. V.P.	**Annual Meeting:**	In April
Auditors:	KPMG LLP		

Oil-Dri Corporation of America

410 North Michigan Avenue, Suite 400, Chicago, Illinois 60611-4213
Telephone: (312) 321-1515   www.oildri.com

Oil-Dri Corporation of America is a leading supplier of specialty sorbent products and the world's largest manufacturer of cat litter. The company's unique mineral reserves are used to produce specialty products for agricultural, horticultural, fluids purification, and industrial and automotive markets. Oil-Dri's Pure-Flo and Perform bleaching and Ultra-Clear clarification clays are used in refining edible oils and clarifying jet fuel, respectively. Agsorb and Verge carriers are sold to agricultural chemical manufacturers, and the company markets several products for animal feed production. The company also produces turf fertilizers and sports field products, including the Pro's Choice line of products. Oil-Dri floor absorbents are used to absorb oil and grease and keep work environments clean and safe. In addition to its branded Cat's Pride and Jonny Cat litter products, Oil-Dri also manufactures private label cat litter for distributors and major retailers. The company operates seven domestic manufacturing facilities and a research and development campus in the United States as well as a facility in Canada and one in the U.K. Incorporated in Delaware in 1969 as a successor to a company founded in 1941.

Directors (In addition to indicated officers)

Richard M. Jaffee, Chm.   Michael A. Nemeroff
Joseph C. Miller, V. Chm.   Allan H. Selig
J. Steven Cole   Paul E. Suckow
Arnold W. Donald

Officers (Directors*)

*Daniel S. Jaffee, Pres. & C.E.O.   Thomas F. Cofsky, V.P.—Mfg. & Logistics
 Jeffrey M. Libert, V.P. & C.F.O.   Douglas A. Graham, V.P., Gen. Coun. & Secy.
 Steven J. Adolph, V.P.—Bus. to Bus. Prods.   Daniel T. Smith, V.P., Chf. Acct. Off. & Cont.
   Grp. & Intl. Cons. Prods.

Consolidated Balance Sheet As of July 31, 2011 (000 omitted)

Assets		Liabilities & Stockholders' Equity	
Current assets	$ 91,816	Current liabilities	$ 26,480
Net property, plant & equipment	68,028	Non-current liabilities	51,615
Other assets	13,549	*Stockholders' equity	95,298
Total	$173,393	Total	$173,393

*5,107,937 shares common stock and 2,048,118 shares Class B stock outstanding.

Consolidated Income Statement

| Years Ended July 31 | Thousands — — — — | | Per Share bc — — — — | | Common Stock |
	Net Sales a	Net Income	Diluted Earnings	Cash Dividends	Price Range bc Fiscal Year
2011	$226,755	$9,015	$1.26	$0.65	$23.00—18.73
2010	219,050	9,458	1.30	0.61	23.53—14.05
2009	236,245	9,586	1.33	0.57	19.20—10.09
2008	232,359	9,039	1.25	0.53	23.60—14.95
2007	212,117	7,660	1.09	0.49	18.83—12.83

a Restated to reflect the adoption of certain EITF standards which resulted in a reclassification of expenses and a reduction in previously reported net sales.
b Common stock.
c Restated to reflect a 5-for-4 stock split effected August 4, 2006.

Transfer Agent & Registrar: Computershare Investor Services
Corporate Counsel: SNR Denton US LLP   **Traded (Symbol):**   NYSE (ODC)
Investor Relations: Ronda J. Williams, V.P. **Stockholders:**   693 Common,
Human Resources: Kevin M. Breese, V.P.   29 Class B (R)
Info. Tech.:   Allison A. Park, V.P.   **Employees:**   815
Auditors: PricewaterhouseCoopers LLP **Annual Meeting:** In December

Old Republic International Corporation

307 North Michigan Avenue, Chicago, Illinois 60601

Telephone: (312) 346-8100   **www.oldrepublic.com**

Old Republic International Corporation is an insurance holding company whose principal subsidiaries underwrite and market specialty insurance lines in the property and liability, mortgage guaranty, and title insurance fields. A small life and health insurance business is also conducted in the U.S. and Canada, principally as an adjunct to the company's general insurance operations. The major classes of insurance Old Republic underwrites through its General Insurance Group are commercial automobile (mostly trucks), workers' compensation, and general liabilities, specializing in a number of industries including transportation, construction, forest products, and energy. The Mortgage Guaranty Group provides residential mortgage guaranty insurance for first mortgage loans to mortgage bankers, brokers, commercial banks, and other financial institutions. The Title Insurance Group provides title insurance and related real estate transfer services for individuals, businesses, and government entities. Principal subsidiaries include: Old Republic Insurance Company; Bituminous Casualty Corporation; Great West Casualty Company; Old Republic General Insurance Corporation; Old Republic National Title Insurance Company; and Republic Mortgage Insurance Company. In October 2010, Old Republic acquired PMA Capital Corporation, an insurance holding company with interests in the commercial property and liability insurance field. Incorporated in Delaware in 1969.

Directors (In addition to indicated officers)

Harrington Bischof	Leo E. Knight, Jr.	Charles F. Titterton
Jimmy A. Dew	Arnold L. Steiner	Dennis P. Van Mieghem
John M. Dixon	Fredricka Taubitz	Steven R. Walker
James C. Hellauer		

Officers (Directors*)

*Aldo C. Zucaro, Chm. & C.E.O.
James A. Kellogg, V. Chm.
Christopher S. Nard, Pres. & C.O.O.
Charles S. Boone, Sr. V.P.—Invests. & Treas.

Spencer LeRoy, III, Sr. V.P., Gen. Coun. & Secy.
Karl W. Mueller, Sr. V.P. & C.F.O.
R. Scott Rager, Sr. V.P.—Gen. Ins.
Rande K. Yeager, Sr. V.P.—Title Ins.

Consolidated Balance Sheet   As of December 31, 2010 (000 omitted)

Assets		Liabilities & Stockholders' Equity	
Investments and cash	$10,386,600	Policy liabilities & accruals	$10,239,500
Reinsurance reserves recoverable	3,262,400	Debt	475,000
Sundry assets	2,233,700	Other liabilities	1,046,800
		*Stockholders' equity	4,121,400
Total	$15,882,700	Total	$15,882,700

*259,222,360 shares common stock outstanding.

Consolidated Income Statement

Years Ended Dec. 31	Thousands — — — — —		Per Share [a] — — — — —		Common Stock Price Range [a] Calendar Year
	Net Revenues	Net Income	Diluted Earnings	Cash Dividends	
2010 [b]	$4,102,700	$ 30,100	$ 0.13	$0.69	$15.50—10.02
2009	3,803,600	(99,100)	(0.42)	0.68	12.85— 7.24
2008	3,237,700	(558,300)	(2.41)	0.67	16.50— 7.39
2007	4,091,000	272,400	1.17	0.63	23.51—13.73
2006	3,794,200	464,800	1.99	0.59	23.50—20.20

[a] Restated to reflect all stock dividends or splits declared through December 31, 2009.
[b] Includes results from PMA Capital Corporation from date of acquisition, October 1, 2010.

Transfer Agent & Registrar: Wells Fargo Shareholder Services

General Counsel:	Spencer LeRoy, III, Sr. V.P.	Traded (Symbol):	NYSE (ORI)
Investor Relations:	Aldo C. Zucaro, Chm.	Stockholders:	2,629 (R)
Human Resources:	Charles Strizak, Dir.	Employees:	8,000
Auditors:	KPMG LLP	Annual Meeting:	In May

Old Second Bancorp, Inc.

37 South River Street, Aurora, Illinois 60507

Telephone: (630) 892-0202   **www.oldsecond.com**

Old Second Bancorp, Inc. is a bank holding company that provides community banking and trut business services. Its services include demand, savings, time deposit, individual retirement, and Keogh deposit accounts; commercial, industrial, consumer, and real estate lending, including installment loans, farm loans, lines of credit, and overdraft checking; safe deposit operations; and trust services. The company has one bank subsidiary: Old Second National Bank. The company provides services through 27 banking locations and one commercial loan production office located in Cook, Kane, Kendall, DeKalb, DuPage, LaSalle, and Will counties. In 2008, the company purchased Heritage Banc, Inc. Incorporated in Delaware in 1981.

Directors (In addition to indicated officers)

Edward Bonifas	William Meyer
Barry Finn	Gerald Palmer
William Kane	James Carl Schmitz
John Ladowicz	

Officers (Directors*)

*William B. Skoglund, Chm., Pres. & C.E.O.
*James Eccher, Exec. V.P. & C.O.O.; Pres. &
　C.E.O.—Old Second Natl. Bank

*J. Douglas Cheatham, Exec. V.P. & C.F.O.

Consolidated Balance Sheet   As of December 31, 2010 (000 omitted)

Assets		Liabilities & Stockholders' Equity	
Cash & cash equivalents	$ 98,758	Deposits	$1,908,528
Securities	148,647	Short-term borrowings	4,141
Loans, net	1,613,821	Other liabilities	127,294
Net premises & equipment	54,640	*Stockholders' equity	83,958
Other assets	208,055		
Total	$2,123,921	Total	$2,123,921

*13,911,475 shares common stock outstanding.

Consolidated Income Statement

Years Ended Dec. 31	Thousands — — — —		Per Share — — — —		Common Stock Price Range Calendar Year
	Total Income	Net Income	Net Income	Cash Dividends	
2010	$151,591	$(113,187)	$(8.03)	$0.02	$ 7.30— 0.69
2009	175,697	(69,869)	(5.04)	0.10	13.31— 3.55
2008	193,200	11,824	0.86	0.63	29.38—10.65
2007	187,596	23,972	1.89	0.59	30.92—25.81
2006	170,736	23,656	1.75	0.55	33.20—29.06

Transfer Agent & Registrar: Old Second Bancorp, Inc.
Corporate Counsel: Barack Ferrazzano Kirschbaum
　　　　　　　　　　　& Nagelberg LLP
Investor Relations: J. Douglas Cheatham, C.F.O.
Human Resources: Robert DiCosola
Info. Tech.: Greg Baugher

Auditors: Plante & Moran PLLC
Traded (Symbol): NASDAQ (OSBC)
Stockholders: 1,084 (R)
Employees: 522
Annual Meeting: In May

Orbitz Worldwide, Inc.

500 West Madison Street, Suite 1000, Chicago, Illinois 60661
Telephone: (312) 894-5000   **www.orbitz.com**

Orbitz Worldwide, Inc. is a leading global online travel company that uses innovative technology to enable leisure and business travelers to research, plan, and book a broad range of travel products and services. Customers have access to a comprehensive set of products including air, hotels, vacation packages, car rentals, cruises, travel insurance, and destination services from suppliers worldwide. Customer brands include Orbitz, CheapTickets, ebookers, HotelClub, RatesToGo, the Away Network, Asia Hotels, and corporate travel brand Orbitz for Business. Incorporated in New Jersey in 1999.

Directors (In addition to indicated officers)

Jeff Clarke, Chm.	Jill A. Greenthal
Martin J. Brand	William J.G. Griffith, IV
Mark S. Britton	Kristina M. Leslie
Robert L. Friedman	Jaynie Miller Studenmund
Bradley T. Gerstner	

Officers (Directors*)

*Barney Harford, C.E.O.	Russell C. Hammer, Sr. V.P. & C.F.O.
Michael J. Nelson, Pres.—Partner Svcs. Grp.	Roger Liew, Sr. V.P. & Chf. Technology Off.
Tamer Tamar, Pres.—ebookers	Christopher K. Orton, Sr. V.P. & Chf. Mktg. Off.
Samuel L. Fulton, Sr. V.P.—Retail	Thomas L. Kram, Grp. V.P. & Chf. Acct. Off.

Consolidated Balance Sheet   As of December 31, 2010 (000 omitted)

Assets		Liabilities & Stockholders' Equity	
Current assets	$ 188,425	Current liabilities	$ 422,791
Trademarks & trade names	128,431	Other liabilities	604,059
Goodwill, net	677,964	*Stockholders' equity	189,853
Other assets	221,883		
Total	$1,216,703	Total	$1,216,703

*102,342,860 shares common stock outstanding.

Consolidated Income Statement

Years Ended Dec. 31	Thousands — — — —		Per Share — — — —		Common Stock Price Range [a] Calendar Year
	Net Revenue	Net Income	Diluted Earnings	Cash Dividends	
2010	$757,000	$ (58,000)	$(0.58)	$0.00	$ 7.86—3.56
2009	738,000	(337,000)	(4.01)	0.00	8.11—1.10
2008	870,000	(299,000)	(3.58)	0.00	8.99—2.00
2007	859,000	(42,000)[b]	(0.51)[b]	0.00	15.00—7.53
2006 [c]	242,000	(25,000)			
2006 [d]	510,000	(121,000)			

[a] Initial public offering completed July 20, 2007.
[b] Reflects period from July 18, 2007 through December 31, 2007.
[c] Successor company, from August 23, 2006 through December 31, 2006.
[d] Predecessor company, from January 1, 2006 through August 22, 2006.

Transfer Agent & Registrar:	American Stock Transfer & Trust Co.		
General Counsel:	James P. Shaughnessy, Sr. V.P.	Traded (Symbol):	NYSE (OWW)
Investor Relations:	Melissa Hayes	Stockholders:	51 (R)
Human Resources:	James P. Shaughnessy, Sr. V.P.	Employees:	1,400
Auditors:	Deloitte & Touche LLP	Annual Meeting:	In June

Packaging Corporation of America

1900 West Field Court, Lake Forest, Illinois 60045

Telephone: (847) 482-3000   **www.packagingcorp.com**

Packaging Corporation of America (PCA) is the fifth largest producer of containerboard and corrugated products in the United States in terms of production capacity. PCA produced approximately 2.4 million tons of containerboard and shipped about 31.0 billion square feet of corrugated products in 2010. The company operates four containerboard mills and 67 corrugated products manufacturing plants throughout the United States. The company's converting operations produce a wide variety of corrugated packaging products, including conventional shipping containers used to protect and transport manufactured goods. The company also produces multi-color boxes and displays with strong visual appeal that help to merchandise the packaged product in retail locations. The company is also a large producer of meat boxes and wax-coated boxes for the agricultural industry. PCA is highly integrated and converts approximately 80% of the containerboard it produces into finished corrugated containers for sale to local and national customers. Incorporated in Delaware in 1999.

Directors (In addition to indicated officers)

Cheryl K. Beebe
Henry F. Frigon
Hasan Jameel
Samuel M. Mencoff

Roger B. Porter
Thomas S. Souleles
James D. Woodrum

Officers (Directors*)

*Paul T. Stecko, Chm.
*Mark W. Kowlzan, C.E.O.
Thomas A. Hassfurther, Exec. V.P.—Corrugated Prods.
Thomas W.H. Walton, Sr. V.P.—Sales & Mktg., Corrugated Prods.

Richard B. West, Sr. V.P. & C.F.O.
Stephen T. Calhoun, V.P.—Hum. Res.
Charles J. Carter, V.P.—Containerboard Mill Oper.
Kent A. Pflederer, V.P., Gen. Coun. & Secy.

Consolidated Balance Sheet As of December 31, 2010 (000 omitted)

Assets		Liabilities & Stockholders' Equity	
Current assets	$ 798,041	Current liabilities	$ 405,558
Net property, plant & equipment	1,337,986	Long-term debt	549,099
Goodwill	38,854	Deferred items	9,190
Other assets	49,393	Other liabilities	251,426
		*Stockholders' equity	1,009,001
Total	$2,224,274	Total	$2,224,274

*102,308,231 shares common stock outstanding.

Consolidated Income Statement

Years Ended Dec. 31	Thousands — — — — —		Per Share — — — —		Common Stock Price Range Calendar Year
	Net Sales	Net Income	Diluted Earnings	Cash Dividends	
2010	$2,435,606	$205,435	$2.00	$0.60	$27.08—20.00
2009	2,147,589	265,895	2.60	0.60	24.18— 9.66
2008	2,360,493	135,609	1.31	1.20	28.74—10.95
2007	2,316,006	170,066	1.61	1.05	31.88—21.87
2006	2,187,046	125,032	1.20	1.00	24.23—20.19

Transfer Agent & Registrar: Computershare Investor Services

General Counsel:	Kent Pflederer, V.P.	Traded (Symbol):	NYSE (PKG)
Investor Relations:	Barbara Sessions	Stockholders:	88 (R)
Human Resources:	Stephen T. Calhoun, V.P.	Employees:	8,100
Info. Tech.:	Robert A. Schneider, V.P.	Annual Meeting:	In May
Auditors:	Ernst & Young LLP		

Park Bancorp, Inc.

5400 South Pulaski Road, Chicago, Illinois 60632

Telephone: (773) 582-8616 **www.parkfed.com**

Park Bancorp, Inc. is the bank holding company for Park Federal Savings Bank. The bank attracts retail deposits from the general public and invests those deposits together with funds generated from operations, primarily in fixed-rate, one- to four-family residential mortgage loans and securities. The bank invests on a limited basis in multi-family mortgage, commercial real estate, construction, land, and consumer loans. The bank conducts its operations through its main office, two branches located in Chicago, and one branch in Westmont. The company's real estate development wholly owned subsidiaries, PBI Development Corporation and GPS Development Corporation, are currently inactive. Incorporated in Delaware in 1996.

Directors (In addition to indicated officers)

Robert W. Krug
John J. Murphy

Victor H. Reyes
Paul Shukis

Officers (Directors*)

*David A. Remijas, Chm. & C.E.O.
*Richard J. Remijas, Jr., Pres. & C.O.O.

Victor E. Caputo, C.F.O., Treas. & Secy.
Paul J. Lopez, Sr. V.P. & Chf. Lending Off.

Consolidated Balance Sheet As of December 31, 2010 (000 omitted)

Assets		Liabilities & Stockholders' Equity	
Cash & cash equivalents	$ 19,018	Deposits	$148,797
Securities	30,031	Securities	2,600
Net loans	135,559	FHLB advances	39,800
Net premises & equipment	9,018	Other liabilities	2,569
Other assets	18,163	*Stockholders' equity	18,023
Total	$211,789	Total	$211,789

*1,193,174 shares common stock outstanding.

Consolidated Income Statement

Years Ended Dec. 31	Thousands — — — —		Per Share — — — —		Common Stock Price Range Calendar Year
	Total Income	Net Income	Basic Earnings	Cash Dividends	
2010	$ 9,905	$(5,355)	$(4.50)	$0.00	$ 7.30— 3.25
2009	10,835	(4,275)	(3.63)	0.00	10.95— 2.85
2008	12,015	(2,367)	(2.02)	0.40	26.97— 5.00
2007	12,783	(117)	(0.10)	0.72	35.00—23.42
2006	12,950	0	0.00	0.72	36.00—31.10

Transfer Agent & Registrar: Registrar and Transfer Company
Corporate Counsel: Vedder Price, P.C. Traded (Symbol): NASDAQ Capital (PFED)
Investor Relations: Richard J. Remijas, Jr., Pres. Stockholders: 194 (R)
Human Resources: Richard J. Remijas, Jr., Pres. Employees: 57
Info. Tech.: Maureen Schiesser, V.P. Annual Meeting: In May
Auditors: Crowe Horwath LLP

PCTEL, Inc.

471 Brighton Drive, Bloomingdale, Illinois 60108
Telephone: (630) 372-6800   www.pctel.com

PCTEL, Inc. designs and develops software-based radios for wireless network optimization and develops and distributes innovative antenna solutions. Customers include public and private carriers, wireless infrastructure providers, wireless equipment distributors, value added resellers, and other original equipment manufacturers. PCTEL's SeeGull® scanning receivers, receiver-based products, and CLARIFY® interference management solutions are used to measure, monitor, and optimize cellular networks. The company also designs, distributes, and supports innovative antenna solutions for public safety applications, unlicensed and licensed wireless broadband, fleet management, network timing, and other global positioning systems (GPS) applications. Its portfolio includes a broad range of WiMAX antennas, WiFi antennas, Land Mobile Radio antennas, and GPS antennas that serve innovative applications in telemetry, RFID, WiFi, fleet management, and mesh networks. In January 2010, PCTEL acquired Sparco Technologies Inc., a wireless local area network (WLAN) products and services company based in San Antonio, Texas. PCTEL Secure, a joint venture with Eclipse Design Technologies that the company entered into in January 2011, designs Android-based, secure communication products. Incorporated in California in 1994; reincorporated in Delaware in 1998.

Directors (In addition to indicated officers)

Richard C. Alberding	Giacomo Marini
Brian J. Jackman	John R. Sheehan
Steven D. Levy	Carl A. Thomsen

Officers (Directors*)

*Martin H. Singer, Ph.D., Chm. & C.E.O.	Varda Goldman, V.P. & Gen. Coun.
John Schoen, C.F.O.	Tony Kobrinetz, V.P.—Technology & Oper.
Jeffrey A. Miller, Sr. V.P.—Sales & Mktg.	David Neumann, V.P.—Gbl. RFS Sales
Rod Bothwell, V.P.—Sourcing & Qual.	

Consolidated Balance Sheet As of December 31, 2010 (000 omitted)

Assets		Liabilities & Stockholders' Equity	
Current assets	$ 90,659	Current liabilities	$ 11,799
Net property & equipment	11,088	Long-term liabilities	2,111
Long-term invest. securities	9,802	*Stockholders' equity	116,655
Other intangible assets	8,865		
Other assets	10,151		
Total	$130,565	Total	$130,565

*18,285,784 shares common stock outstanding.

Consolidated Income Statement

Years Ended Dec. 31	Thousands — — — — —		Per Share — — — — —		Common Stock Price Range Calendar Year
	Revenues	Net Income	Diluted Earnings	Cash Dividends	
2010	$69,254	$ (3,456)	$(0.20)	$0.00	$ 7.07—4.88
2009	56,002	(4,483)	(0.26)	0.00	7.19—3.83
2008	76,927	38,297 a	1.99 a	0.50	11.53—3.73
2007	69,888	6,031 b	0.28 b	0.00	11.00—6.59
2006	76,768	(10,019) a	(0.48) a	0.00	11.64—7.44

a Includes income from discontinued operations of $37,138,000 ($1.93 per diluted share) in 2008 and $1,029,000 ($0.05 per diluted share) in 2006.
b Includes loss from discontinued operations of $82,000.

Transfer Agent & Registrar: Wells Fargo Shareowner Services

General Counsel:	Varda Goldman, V.P.	Traded (Symbol):	NASDAQ (PCTI)
Investor Relations:	John Schoen, C.F.O.	Stockholders:	46 (R)
Auditors:	Grant Thornton LLP	Employees:	345
		Annual Meeting:	In June

Princeton National Bancorp, Inc.

606 South Main Street, Princeton, Illinois 61356-2080
Telephone: (815) 875-4444   www.pnbc-inc.com

Princeton National Bancorp, Inc., is a single-bank holding company which operates a full service commercial banking and trust business in north central Illinois (Bureau, DeKalb, Grundy, Kane, Kendall, LaSalle, Marshall, McHenry, Will, and contiguous counties) through its wholly owned subsidiary, Citizens First National Bank. The bank, which was organized in 1865, conducts its business through 21 offices in 17 communities. The bank's services consist primarily of commercial, real estate, and agricultural lending; consumer deposit and financial services; and trust, brokerage, insurance, and farm management services, which it provides to individuals, businesses, and governmental bodies. Principal consumer services the bank offers are demand, savings, and time deposit accounts; home mortgage loans; installment loans; and brokerage services. Incorporated in Delaware in 1981.

Directors (In addition to indicated officers)

Craig O. Wesner, Chm.
Gretta E. Bieber
Gary C. Bruce
Sharon L. Covert

John R. Ernat
Mark Janko
Stephen W. Samet

Officers (Directors*)

*Thomas D. Ogaard, Pres. & C.E.O.
*Todd D. Fanning, Exec. V.P. & C.O.O.
Rodney Stickle, Sr. V.P. & & C.F.O.

Laura C. Anderson, V.P.—Internal Audit
Lou Ann Birkey, V.P.—Inv. Rel. & Corp. Secy.
Toni Milnes, V.P.—Risk Mgt.

Consolidated Balance Sheet As of December 31, 2010 (000 omitted)

Assets		Liabilities & Stockholders' Equity	
Cash & cash equivalents	$ 43,880	Total deposits	$ 962,961
Investment securities	260,939	Borrowings	71,559
Loans, net	674,348	Other liabilities	5,090
Premises & equipment	26,901	*Stockholders' equity	56,861
Other assets	90,403		
Total	$1,096,471	Total	$1,096,471

*3,325,941 shares common stock outstanding.

Consolidated Income Statement

Years Ended Dec. 31	Thousands — — — —		Per Share — — — —		Common Stock
	Total Income	Net Income	Basic Earnings	Cash Dividends [a]	Price Range Calendar Year
2010	$61,058	$(16,979)	$(5.52)	$0.00	$11.50— 2.73
2009	69,980	(21,126)	(6.76)	0.70	23.06— 9.70
2008	70,415	7,326	2.22	1.12	29.75—22.05
2007	72,857	6,770	2.04	1.08	33.72—23.04
2006	63,771	6,488	1.93	1.05	35.45—32.02

[a] Declared.

Transfer Agent & Registrar: Princeton National Bancorp, Inc.

General Counsel:	Howard & Howard	Traded (Symbol):	NASDAQ (PNBC)
Investor Relations:	Lou Ann Birkey, V.P.	Stockholders:	758 (R)
Human Resources:	Jill Smith, Sr. V.P.	Employees:	352
Auditors:	BKD, LLP	Annual Meeting:	In May

PrivateBancorp, Inc.

120 South LaSalle Street, Chicago, Illinois 60603
Telephone: (312) 564-2000   **www.theprivatebank.com**

PrivateBancorp, Inc. is a registered bank holding company which, through its subsidiary The PrivateBank & Trust Company, provides customized business and personal financial services to middle-market commercial and commercial real estate companies as well as business owners, executives, entrepreneurs and families. PrivateBank operates through 34 offices located in 10 states serving the greater Atlanta, Chicago, Cleveland, Denver, Des Moines, Detroit, Kansas City, Milwaukee, and St. Louis metro areas.

Directors (In addition to indicated officers)

Norman R. Bobins	Cheryl Mayberry McKissack	Collin Roche
Robert F. Coleman	James B. Nicholson	William R. Rybak
James M. Guyette	Edward W. Rabin, Jr.	Alejandro Silva

Officers (Directors*)

*Ralph B. Mandell, Chm. Emeritus
*Larry D. Richman, Pres. & C.E.O.
Alan S. Adams, Managing Dir., Head of Community Banking
Karen B. Case, Exec. Managing Dir., Pres.—Commer. Real Estate
Jennifer R. Evans, Managing Dir., Gen. Coun. & Secy.
Kristine R. Garrett, Managing Dir., Head of PrivateWealth
Bruce R. Hague, Exec. Managing Dir., Pres—Natl. Commer. Banking
John D. Heiberger, Managing Dir.—Risk Mgt.

Bruce S. Lubin, Exec. Managing Dir., Pres.—Illinois Commer. & Specialty Banking
Robert W. Frentzel, Managing Dir.—Specialized Ind.
Jeffrey D. Steele, Managing Dir.—Specialized Ind.
C. Brant Ahrens, Managing Dir. & C.O.O.
Elizabeth (Bess) Cummings, Managing Dir. & C.I.O.
Kevin M. Killips, Managing Dir. & C.F.O.
Joan A. Schellhorn, Managing Dir. & Chf. Hum. Res. Off.
Kevin J. Van Solkema, Managing Dir. & Chf. Credit Off.
Leonard E. Wiatr, Managing Dir., Chf. Risk Off.
James F. Turner, Managing Dir.—Commer. Real Estate

Consolidated Balance Sheet As of December 31, 2010 (000 omitted)

Assets		Liabilities & Stockholders' Equity	
Cash & cash equivalents	$ 654,088	Deposits	$10,535,429
Securities	1,881,786	Short-term borrowings	118,561
Net loans	8,891,536	Long-term debt	414,793
Covered assets, net	381,876	Other liabilities	168,928
Net property & equipment	40,975	*Equity	1,227,910
Goodwill	94,621		
Other assets	520,739		
Total	$12,465,621	Total	$12,465,621

*Common stock: voting—67,139,000 shares outstanding; non-voting—3,536,000 shares outstanding.

Consolidated Income Statement

Years Ended Dec. 31	Thousands — — — — —		Per Share — — — — —		Common Stock Price Range Calendar Year
	Total Income [a]	Net Income	Diluted Earnings	Cash Dividends	
2010	$601,171	$(12,090)	$(0.17)	$0.04	$17.96— 8.85
2009	550,182	(42,506)	(0.95)	0.04	33.00— 8.33
2008	446,699	(93,491)	(3.16)	0.30	49.50—20.41
2007	334,198	11,028	0.49	0.30	42.51—25.41
2006	280,473	37,846	1.76	0.24	47.51—34.82

[a] Interest income plus non-interest income.

Transfer Agent & Registrar: Computershare Investor Services
Corporate Counsel: Vedder, Price P.C.
Investor Relations: Tracy Kessner, Assoc. Managing Dir.
Human Resources: Joan A. Schellhorn, Chf. Hum. Res. Off.
Info. Tech.: James Bennett, C.T.O.

Auditors: Ernst & Young LLP
Traded (Symbol): NASDAQ (PVTB)
Stockholders: 498 (R)
Employees: 1,060
Annual Meeting: In May

Richardson Electronics, Ltd.

40W267 Keslinger Road, P.O. Box 393, LaFox, Illinois 60147-0393

Telephone: (630) 208-2200   www.rell.com

Richardson Electronics, Ltd. is a leading global provider of engineered solutions, power grid and microwave tubes and related consumables, and customized display solutions, serving customers in the radio frequency (RF) and microwave communications, military, marine, aviation, industrial, scientific, and medical markets. The company delivers engineered solutions for its customers' needs through design-in support, systems integration, prototype design and manufacturing, testing, logistics, and aftermarket technical service and repair. Products include semiconductor fabrication equipment, electron tubes, microwave generators, and visual technology solutions. These products are used to control, switch or amplify electrical power signals, or are used as display devices in a variety of industrial, commercial, and communication applications. Richardson's customers include industrial users, original equipment manufacturers, repair service organizations, and other distributors. The company operates through two business units: Electron Device Group and Canvys. In March 2011, Richardson Electronics completed the sale of the assets and certain liabilities of its RF, Wireless and Power Division to Arrow Electronics, Inc. The company maintains 36 locations worldwide. Incorporated in Illinois in 1947; reincorporated in Delaware in 1986.

Directors (In addition to indicated officers)

Scott Hodes
Ad Ketelaars
John R. Peterson

Harold L. Purkey
Samuel Rubinovitz

Officers (Directors*)

*Edward J. Richardson, Chm., Pres., C.E.O. & C.O.O.
Kyle C. Badger, Exec. V.P., Gen. Coun. & Secy.
Wendy Diddell, Exec. V.P.—Corp. Dev.
Kathleen S. Dvorak, Exec. V.P., C.F.O. & Chf. Strat. Off.

Kathleen M. McNally, Sr. V.P.—Mktg. Oper. & Customer Support
James M. Dudek, Jr., Corp. Cont. & Chf. Acct. Off.

Consolidated Balance Sheet As of May 28, 2011 (000 omitted)

Assets		Liabilities & Stockholders' Equity	
Current assets	$288,188	Current liabilities	$ 75,304
Net property, plant & equipment	5,216	Other liabilities	14,577
Other assets	20,650	*Stockholders' equity	224,173
Total	$314,054	Total	$314,054

*14,809,000 shares common and 2,952,000 shares Class B common stock outstanding.

Consolidated Income Statement [a]

Years Ended Abt. May 31	Thousands — — — — Net Sales	Net Income	Per Share — — — — Diluted Earnings	Cash Dividends	Common Stock Price Range Fiscal Year
2011	$158,867	$ 90,074	$ 4.95	$0.11	$13.82—8.00
2010	135,372	16,095	0.92	0.08	12.35—2.84
2009	141,190	(12,164)	(0.69)	0.08	7.00—2.47
2008 [b]	192,206	(8,426)	(0.48)	0.12	9.90—3.59
2007 [c]	187,355	40,679	2.35	0.16	10.30—6.58

[a] Certain prior year amounts have been restated to reflect the sale of RF, Wireless and Power Division on March 1, 2011.
[b] Includes a $9,200,000 goodwill impairment charge, employee termination-related charges of approximately $3,300,000, and inventory obsolescence charges of $1,900,000 and $900,000 in the DSG and RF, Wireless & Power Division, respectively.
[c] Includes retirement of long-term debt expenses of $2,500,000, loss of $2,400,000 (net of tax) from discontinued operations, and a $2,900,000 severance expense. Also includes an after-tax gain of $41,600,000 from the sale of the Security Systems Division and a gain of $4,000,000 on the sale of two buildings and land.

Transfer Agent & Registrar: IST Shareholder Services

General Counsel:	Kyle C. Badger, Exec. V.P.	Traded (Symbol):	NASDAQ (RELL)
Investor Relations:	Kathleen S. Dvorak, C.F.O.	Stockholders:	817 Class A; 18 Class B (R)
Human Resources:	Kathleen S. Dvorak, C.F.O.	Employees:	295
Info. Tech.:	Kathleen S. Dvorak, C.F.O.	Annual Meeting:	In October
Auditors:	Ernst & Young LLP		

RLI Corp.

9025 North Lindbergh Drive, Peoria, Illinois 61615
Telephone: (309) 692-1000 **www.rlicorp.com**

RLI Corp. is a holding company which, through its subsidiaries, underwrites selected property and casualty insurance and marine insurance. The company offers specialty insurance products designed to meet specific insurance needs of niche groups that are underserved by the insurance industry or to provide them with a type of product not generally offered by other companies. The principal specialty insurance coverages written by the company are commercial property, general liability, personal and commercial umbrella, commercial transportation liability, and contract and miscellaneous surety bonds. In addition, the company writes professional liability, employer's excess indemnity, in-home business owners coverage, directors' and officers' liability, and commercial fidelity and crime coverage. Major subsidiaries include RLI Insurance Company, Mt. Hawley Insurance Company, and RLI Indemnity Company. The company maintains offices throughout the United States, operating in all 50 states, the District of Columbia, and Puerto Rico. In April 2011, RLI acquired Contractors Bonding and Insurance Company, a Seattle-based insurance company specializing in surety bonds and related niche property and casualty insurance products. Incorporated in Delaware in 1984 as the successor to an Illinois corporation which was incorporated in 1965; reincorporated in Illinois in 1993.

Directors (In addition to indicated officers)

Kaj Ahlmann
Barbara R. Allen
John T. Baily

Jordan W. Graham
Gerald I. Lenrow
Charles M. Linke

F. Lynn McPheeters
Robert O. Viets

Officers (Directors*)

*Jonathan E. Michael, Chm., Pres. & C.E.O.
Joseph E. Dondanville, Sr. V.P. & C.F.O.
Craig W. Kliethermes, Sr. V.P.—Risk Svcs.
Todd W. Bryant, V.P. & Cont.
Seth A. Davis, V.P.—Internal Audit
Carol J. Denzer, V.P. & C.I.O.
Donald J. Driscoll, V.P.—Claims

Jeffrey D. Fick, V.P.—Hum. Res.
Aaron H. Jacoby, V.P.—Corp. Dev.
Daniel O. Kennedy, V.P., Gen. Coun. & Corp. Secy.
John E. Robison, Treas. & Chf. Invest. Off.
Michael J. Stone, Pres. & C.O.O.—RLI Ins. & MH Ins. Cos.

Consolidated Balance Sheet As of December 31, 2010 (000 omitted)

Assets		Liabilities & Stockholders' Equity	
Investments & accrued income	$1,817,636	Unpaid losses & settlement exp.	$1,173,943
Ceded unearned premiums	62,631	Unearned premiums	301,537
Reins. balances recov. on unpaid		Reinsurance balances payable	23,851
losses/sett. exp.	354,163	Bonds payable	100,000
Net property & equipment	18,370	Other liabilities	123,885
Premiums & reinsurance balances		*Stockholders' equity	791,376
receivable	107,391		
Other assets	154,401		
Total	$2,514,592	Total	$2,514,592

*20,964,540 shares common stock outstanding.

Consolidated Income Statement

Years Ended Dec. 31	Thousands — — — —		Per Share — — — —		Common Stock Price Range Calendar Year
	Total Revenue	Net Income	Diluted Earnings	Cash Dividends	
2010	$583,424	$127,432	$6.00	$8.15 a	$61.09—49.91
2009	546,552	93,845	4.32	1.08	61.17—43.13
2008	561,012	78,676	3.60	0.99	66.61—44.64
2007	652,345	175,867	7.30	0.87	60.82—51.00
2006	632,708	134,639	5.27	0.75	57.41—45.16

a Includes special dividend of $7.00 per share paid on December 29, 2010.

Transfer Agent & Registrar: Wells Fargo Shareowner Services

General Counsel:	Daniel O. Kennedy, V.P.	Traded (Symbol):	NYSE (RLI)
Investor Relations:	John E. Robison, Treas.	Employees:	670
Human Resources:	Jeffrey D. Fick, V.P.	Annual Meeting:	In May
Info. Tech.:	Carol J. Denzer, C.I.O.		
Auditors:	KPMG LLP		

Rubicon Technology, Inc.

900 East Green Street, Bensenville, Illinois 60106

Telephone: (847) 295-7000   **www.rubicon-es2.com**

Rubicon Technology, Inc. is an advanced electronic materials provider that develops, manufactures, and sells monocrystalline sapphire and other innovative crystalline products for light-emitting diodes (LEDs), radio frequency integrated circuits (RFICs), blue laser diodes, optoelectronics, and other optical applications. LEDs grown on Rubicon sapphire products are used in applications such as small displays for mobile devices; flashes for digital cameras; backlighting units for displays used in notebook computers, desktop monitors, and LCD televisions; public display signs; automotive lights; traffic signals; and general and specialty lighting. In addition, Rubicon has developed sapphire products that are used for Silicon-on-Sapphire (SoS) RFICs, as well as products for military, aerospace, sensor, and other applications. Principal customers are wafer polishing companies and semiconductor device manufacturers. Incorporated in Delaware in 2001.

Directors (In addition to indicated officers)

Don N. Aquilano, Chm.   Michael E. Mikolajczyk
Donald R. Caldwell   Raymond J. Spencer

Officers (Directors*)

*Raja M. Parvez, Pres. & C.E.O.   William F. Weissman, C.F.O., Treas. & Secy.

Consolidated Balance Sheet As of December 31, 2010 (000 omitted)

Assets		Liabilities & Stockholders' Equity	
Total current assets	$122,231	Total current liabilities	$ 14,648
Net property & equipment	82,511	*Stockholders' equity	192,094
Investments	2,000		
Total	$206,742	Total	$206,742

*22,960,669 shares common stock outstanding.

Consolidated Income Statement

Years Ended Dec. 31	Thousands — — — — —		Per Share [a] — — — —		Common Stock
	Revenue	Net Income [b]	Diluted Earnings [b]	Cash Dividends	Price Range [a] Calendar Year
2010	$77,362	$ 29,111	$ 1.28	$0.00	$35.90—14.50
2009	19,808	(9,630)	(0.48)	0.00	22.00— 3.12
2008	37,838	4,355	0.19	0.00	34.94— 2.50
2007	34,110	(68,413)	(27.22)	0.00	25.75—14.00
2006	20,752	(36,619)[c]	(146.57)		

[a] Stock began trading on November 16, 2007.
[b] Available to common stockholders.
[c] On January 1, 2006, the company adopted FSP150-5 and recorded approximately $221,000 as a cumulative effect of change in accounting principle.

Transfer Agent & Registrar: American Stock Transfer & Trust Co.

General Counsel:	McGuire Woods LLP	Traded (Symbol):	NASDAQ (RBCN)
Investor Relations:	William F. Weissman, C.F.O.	Stockholders:	25 (R)
Auditors:	Grant Thornton LLP	Employees:	250
		Annual Meeting:	In June

John B. Sanfilippo & Son, Inc.

1703 North Randall Road, Elgin, Illinois 60123

Telephone: (847) 289-1800   www.jbssinc.com

John B. Sanfilippo & Son, Inc. is one of the nation's leading suppliers of branded and private label nut and dried fruit products. The company processes, packages, markets, and distributes shelled nuts and inshell nuts that sell under a variety of private labels and under the company's Fisher® and Sunshine Country® brand names. The company also markets and distributes, and often manufactures or processes, a diverse product line of food and snack items that includes peanut butter, natural snacks and trail mixes, sunflower seeds, and sesame snack products. John B. Sanfilippo & Son sells its products to retailers, wholesalers, industrial users for food manufacturing, food service companies, and international customers. The company maintains production facilities in Illinois, Georgia, California, North Carolina, and Texas. In May 2010, the company acquired Orchard Valley Harvest, Inc., one of the nation's leading suppliers of branded and private label nut and dried fruit products in the produce category. Incorporated in Delaware in 1979 as the successor by merger to an Illinois corporation that was incorporated in 1959.

Directors (In addition to indicated officers)

Jasper B. Sanfilippo, Chm. Emer.	Ellen Connelly Taaffe
Timothy R. Donovan	Mathias A. Valentine
Gov. Jim Edgar	Daniel M. Wright

Officers (Directors*)

*Jeffrey T. Sanfilippo, Chm. & C.E.O.	Walter R. Tankersley, Jr., Sr. V.P.—Industrial Sales
*Jasper B. Sanfilippo, Jr., Pres., C.O.O. & Asst. Secy.	Howard Brandeisky, V.P.—Global Mktg. & Innovation
*Michael J. Valentine, C.F.O., Grp. Pres. & Secy.	Jose Cabanin, V.P.—Intl. Sales
James A. Valentine, C.I.O.	Brenda Cannon, V.P.—Food Safety/Qual.
Michael G. Cannon, Sr. V.P.—Corp. Oper.	Christopher Gardier, V.P.—Cons. Sales
Thomas J. Fordonski, Sr. V.P.—Hum. Res.	John H. Garoni, V.P.—Foodservice Sales
Everardo Soria, Sr. V.P.—Pecan Oper. & Procurement	William R. Pokrajac, V.P.—Risk Mgt. & Inv. Rel.
Robert J. Sarlls, Sr. V.P.—Cons. Sales, Strat. & Bus. Dev.	Herbert J. Marros, Dir.—Fin. Reporting & Taxation
	Frank Pellegrino, V.P.—Fin. & Corp. Cont.

Consolidated Balance Sheet As of June 30, 2011 (000 omitted) (unaudited)

Assets		Liabilities & Stockholders' Equity	
Current assets	$177,251	Current liabilities	$111,914
Net property, plant & equipment	153,692	Long-term liabilities	56,167
Other assets	20,845	*Stockholders' equity	183,707
Total	$351,788	Total	$351,788

*10,770,359 average shares common stock outstanding.

Consolidated Income Statement

Years Ended Abt. June 30	Thousands — — — — Net Sales	Net Income	Per Share — — — — Diluted Earnings	Cash Dividends	Common Stock Price Range Fiscal Year
2011 a	$674,212	$ 2,835	$ 0.26	$0.00	$16.20—11.14
2010	561,633	14,425	1.34	0.00	17.68— 7.03
2009	553,846	6,917	0.65	0.00	10.75— 4.01
2008	541,771	(5,957)	(0.56)	0.00	12.30— 6.72
2007	540,858	(13,577)	(1.28)	0.00	16.19— 9.78

a Includes a goodwill impairment charge of $5.7 million.

Transfer Agent & Registrar:	American Stock Transfer & Trust Co.		
Corporate Counsel:	Jenner & Block; Stahl Cowen Crowley LLC	Auditors:	PricewaterhouseCoopers LLP
		Traded (Symbol):	NASDAQ (JBSS)
Investor Relations:	William R. Pokrajac, V.P.	Stockholders:	63 Common,
Human Resources:	Thomas J. Fordonski, Sr. V.P.		18 Class A (R)
Info. Tech.:	James A. Valentine, C.I.O.	Employees:	1,350
		Annual Meeting:	In November

Sara Lee Corporation
3500 Lacey Road, Downers Grove, Illinois 60515
Telephone: (630) 598-6000   www.saralee.com

Sara Lee Corporation is a global manufacturer and marketer of high-quality brand-name products for consumers throughout the world. Well-known brand names include Sara Lee, Ball Park, Hillshire Farm, Jimmy Dean, Douwe Egberts, State Fair, and Senseo. As of August 2011, the company is in the process of divesting its North American refrigerated dough, North American fresh bakery, international bakery, and remaining household and body care businesses. In January 2011, Sara Lee Corporation announced that it will divide the company into two independent, publicly-held companies. One company will focus on the North American retail meat and foodservice businesses. The second company will focus on the international coffee and tea businesses. Incorporated in Maryland in 1939.

Directors (In addition to indicated officers)

Christopher B. Begley	Laurette T. Koellner	Norman R. Sorensen
Crandall C. Bowles	John D. G. McAdam, Ph.D.	Jeffrey W. Ubben
Virgis W. Colbert	Sir Ian Prosser	Cees J.A. van Lede
James S. Crown		Jonathan P. Ward

Officers (Directors*)

*Jan Bennink, Chm.
Marcel Smits, C.E.O.
Mark Garvey, Exec. V.P. & C.F.O.
Frank van Oers, Exec. V.P. & C.E.O.—Intl. Beverage & Bakery

Stephen J. Cerrone, Exec. V.P.—Hum. Res.
B. Thomas Hansson, Sr. V.P.—Strat. & Corp. Dev.
Paulette Dodson, Sr. V.P., Gen. Coun. & Secy.

Consolidated Balance Sheet As of July 2, 2011 (000 omitted)

Assets		Liabilities & Stockholders' Equity	
Current assets	$ 4,584,000	Current liabilities	$ 4,122,000
Net property, plant & equipment	1,648,000	Long-term debt	1,936,000
Goodwill	811,000	Other liabilities	1,501,000
Other assets	1,099,000	Minority interest in subsidiaries	29,000
Noncurrent assets held for sale	1,391,000	*Stockholders' equity	1,945,000
Total	$9,533,000	Total	$9,533,000

*587,099,794 shares common stock outstanding.

Consolidated Income Statement [a]

Years Ended Abt. June 30	Thousands — — — —		Per Share — — — —		Common Stock Price Range Fiscal Year
	Net Sales	Net Income	Diluted Earnings	Cash Dividends	
2011	$8,681,000	$1,296,000	$ 2.06	$ 0.46	$20.26—13.22
2010 [b]	8,339,000	527,000	0.73	0.44	15.08— 9.17
2009	8,366,000	380,000	0.52	0.44	15.07— 6.80
2008	8,650,000	(64,000)	(0.11)	0.42	17.54—12.15
2007	7,853,000	502,000	0.68	0.50	18.15—14.08

a From continuing operations. The amounts shown include the impact of certain significant items. Significant items may include, but are not limited to: exit activities, asset and business dispositions, impairment charges, transformation charges, Project Accelerate charges, spin-off related costs, settlement and curtailment gains or losses and various significant tax matters.
b 53 weeks.

Transfer Agent & Registrar: BNY Mellon Shareowner Services
General Counsel: Paulette Dodson, Sr. V.P.
Investor Relations: Robin Jansen, V.P.
Human Resources: Stephen J. Cerrone, Exec. V.P.
Info. Tech.: Anne Teague, C.I.O.
Auditors: PricewaterhouseCoopers LLP

Traded (Symbol): NYSE, CSE, LON (SLE)
Stockholders: 59,926 (R)
Employees: 21,000
Annual Meeting: In October

Schawk, Inc.

1695 South River Road, Des Plaines, Illinois 60018
Telephone: (847) 827-9494   **www.schawk.com**

Schawk, Inc., is one of the world's largest independent brand image solutions companies, serving the consumer products packaging, retail, pharmaceutical, and advertising markets. The company delivers a broad range of digital premedia graphic services (strategic, creative, and executional) through more than 150 locations in 18 countries across North America, Europe, Asia, and Australia. Schawk designs, creates, and manages image and text for reproduction to exact specifications for a variety of media, including packaging for consumer products, point-of-sale displays, and other promotional and advertising materials. In November 2010, the company acquired Real Branding, a digital marketing agency with offices in San Francisco and New York. Founded in 1953 and incorporated in Illinois in 1965; reincorporated in Delaware in 1972.

Directors (In addition to indicated officers)

Leonard S. Caronia
Stanley N. Logan
Judith W. McCue

John T. McEnroe
Michael G. O'Rourke
Hollis W. Rademacher

Officers (Directors*)

*Clarence W. Schawk, Chm.
*David A. Schawk, Pres. & C.E.O.
*A. Alex Sarkisian, Exec. V.P., C.O.O. & Secy.
Timothy J. Cunningham, Exec. V.P. & C.F.O.
Chuck Dale, Exec. V.P.—Gbl. Oper.

Christopher Splan, Exec. V.P.—Bus. Dev.
Brad Wills, Exec. V.P.—Intl. Oper.
Eric Ashworth, Chf. Strat. Off.
Ronald J. Vittorini, Gen. Coun.

Consolidated Balance Sheet   As of December 31, 2010 (000 omitted)

Assets		Liabilities & Stockholders' Equity	
Current assets	$162,992	Current liabilities	$119,822
Net property & equipment	48,684	Long-term debt	37,080
Goodwill	193,626	Deferred items	9,135
Other assets	44,557	Other liabilities	19,696
		*Stockholders' equity	264,126
Total	$449,859	Total	$449,859

*25,761,334 shares common stock outstanding.

Consolidated Income Statement

Years Ended Dec. 31	Thousands — — — — Net Sales	Net Income [a]	Per Share — — — — Diluted Earnings [a]	Cash Dividends	Common Stock Price Range Calendar Year
2010	$460,626	$ 32,420	$ 1.25	$0.20	$21.24—12.18
2009	452,446	19,497	0.78	0.06	13.82— 5.18
2008	494,184	(60,006) [b]	(2.24) [b]	0.13	18.61— 9.92
2007 [c]	544,409	30,598	1.10	0.13	24.71—13.53
2006 [c]	546,118	25,949	0.95	0.13	26.22—15.11

[a] From continuing operations.
[b] Includes selling, general, and administrative expenses of $148,600,000, as well as $48,000,000 impairment of goodwill charges, $10,400,000 restructuring charges, $7,300,000 pension withdrawal expenses, expenses similiar to which were not recorded for 2007.
[c] Restated to correct an error in the financial statements for the year ended Dec. 31, 2002.

Transfer Agent & Registrar: Computershare Investor Services
Corporate Counsel: Vedder Price P.C.
Investor Relations: Timothy Allen, V.P.
Human Resources: Carol Campagnolo, Sr. V.P.
Info. Tech.: Gary Rietz, C.I.O.
Auditors: Ernst & Young LLP

Traded (Symbol): NYSE (SGK)
Stockholders: 990 (R)
Employees: 3,200
Annual Meeting: In May

Sears Holdings Corporation

3333 Beverly Road, Hoffman Estates, Illinois 60179

Telephone: (847) 286-2500   **www.searsholdings.com**

Sears Holdings Corporation is a broadline retailer with approximately 4,038 full-line and specialty stores in the United States and Canada. The company operates through its subsidiaries, including Sears Roebuck and Co. and Kmart Corporation. Sears Holdings sells proprietary branded merchandise under brand names that include: Kenmore, Craftsman, DieHard, and Lands' End. Other company trademarks and service marks include: The Great Indoors, Canyon River Blues, Apostrophe, and Covington. The company is also the largest provider of home services in the U.S., with more than 11 million service calls made annually. In June 2011, the company's subsidiary, Orchard Supply Hardware Stores Corporation, filed a registration statement with the Securities and Exchange Commission in connection with Sears Holdings Corporation's plan to spin off its interest in Orchard. Incorporated in Delaware in 2005.

Directors (In addition to indicated officers)

Edward S. Lampert, Chm.
William C. Kunkler, III
Steven T. Mnuchin

Ann N. Reese
Emily Scott
Thomas J. Tisch

Officers (Directors*)

*Louis J. D'Ambrosio, Pres. & C.E.O.
Robert A. Schriesheim, Exec. V.P. & C.F.O.
Michael Castleman, V.P. & Int. Pres.—Kenmore, Craftsman & DieHard
John D. Goodman, Exec. V.P.—Apparel & Home
Edgar O. Huber, C.E.O. & Pres. of Lands' End
W. Bruce Johnson, Exec. V.P.—Off-Mall Bus. & Supply Chain

Dave A. Drobny, Sr. V.P., Gen. Coun. & Corp. Secy.
William R. Harker, Sr. V.P.
William K. Phelan, Sr. V.P., Acting C.F.O., Cont. & Chf. Acct. Off.
Sam Solomon, Sr. V.P. & Pres.—Tools

Consolidated Balance Sheet As of January 29, 2011 (000 omitted)

Assets		Liabilities & Stockholders' Equity	
Current assets	$11,535,000	Current liabilities	$ 8,618,000
Net property & equipment	7,365,000	Long-term debt	2,663,000
Goodwill	1,392,000	Other liabilities	4,373,000
Intangible assets	3,139,000	Noncontrolling interest	103,000
Other assets	837,000	*Stockholders' equity	8,511,000
Total	$24,268,000	Total	$24,268,000

*109,000,000 shares common stock outstanding.

Consolidated Income Statement [a]

Years Ended Abt. Jan. 31	Thousands — — — —		Per Share — — — —		Common Stock Price Range Fiscal Year
	Revenues	Net Income	Diluted Earnings	Cash Dividends	
2010	$43,326,000	$ 133,000	$1.19	$0.00	$125.42— 59.21
2009	44,043,000	235,000	1.99	0.00	106.06— 34.27
2008	46,770,000	53,000	0.42	0.00	112.80— 26.80
2007	50,703,000	826,000	5.70	0.00	195.18— 84.72
2006 [b]	53,016,000	1,492,000	9.58	0.00	182.38—115.95

[a] The periods presented here were impacted by significant items which affected the comparability of amounts reflected in these selected data. Please refer to the company's SEC filings for details.
[b] 53 weeks.

Transfer Agent & Registrar: Computershare Investor Services

General Counsel:	Dave A. Drobny, Sr. V.P.	Traded (Symbol):	NASDAQ (SHLD)
Investor Relations:	William K. Phelan, Sr. V.P.	Stockholders:	16,320 (R)
Human Resources:	William R. Harker, Sr. V.P.	Employees:	312,000
Auditors:	Deloitte & Touche LLP	Annual Meeting:	In May

SigmaTron International, Inc.

2201 Landmeier Road, Elk Grove Village, Illinois 60007
Telephone: (847) 956-8000   **www.sigmatronintl.com**

SigmaTron International, Inc. is an independent provider of electronic manufacturing services, which include printed circuit board assemblies and completely assembled (boxbuild) electronics products. Customers for the company's products include those in the consumer electronics, life sciences, semiconductor, gaming, industrial electronics, fitness, telecommunications, automotive, and home appliance industries. Included among the wide range of services that the company offers its customers are manual and automatic assembly and testing of customer products; material sourcing and procurement; design, manufacturing, and test engineering support; warehousing and shipment services; and assistance in obtaining product approvals from governmental and other regulatory bodies. The company provides these services through an international network of facilities located in North America and Asia. Incorporated in Delaware in 1993.

Directors (In addition to indicated officers)

Barry R. Horek
Bruce J. Mantia
Thomas W. Rieck

Paul J. Plante
Dilip S. Vyas

Officers (Directors*)

*Gary R. Fairhead, Pres. & C.E.O.
*Linda K. Frauendorfer, C.F.O., V.P.—Fin., Treas. & Secy.
Gregory A. Fairhead, Exec. V.P.; Asst. Secy.
Rajesh B. Upadhyaya, Exec. V.P.—West Coast Oper.
Daniel P. Camp, V.P.—Acuña Oper.
Curtis Campbell, V.P. of Sales—West Coast Oper.
Hom-Ming Chang, V.P.—China Oper.

Yousef M. Heidari, V.P.—Eng.
Donald G. Madsen, V.P.—Cust. Svc. Union City Oper.
Dennis P. McNamara, V.P.—Eng.
Stephen H. McNulty, V.P.—Sales
Thomas F. Rovtar, V.P.—Info. Technology
John P. Sheehan, V.P.—Dir. of Supply Chain; Asst. Secy.
Keith D. Wheaton, V.P.—Bus. Dev. West Coast Oper.

Consolidated Balance Sheet   As of April 30, 2011 (000 omitted)

Assets		Liabilities and Stockholders' Equity	
Current assets	$75,833	Current liabilities	$24,256
Net property, plant & equipment	26,189	Long-term debt	24,302
Other assets	845	Capital lease obligations	1,044
		Other liabilities	3,522
		*Stockholders' equity	49,743
Total	$102,867	Total	$102,867

*3,864,274 shares common stock outstanding.

Consolidated Income Statement

Years Ended Apr. 30	Thousands — — — —		Per Share — — — —		Common Stock Price Range Fiscal Year
	Net Sales	Net Income	Diluted Earnings	Cash Dividends	
2011	$151,728	$ 1,978	$ 0.51	$0.00	$ 8.94—4.89
2010	122,476	2,245	0.58	0.00	7.44—1.41
2009	133,745	1,956	0.51	0.00	7.29—1.27
2008 a	167,811	(6,456)	(1.69)	0.00	13.37—5.25
2007	165,909	1,698	0.44	0.00	11.00—7.11

a Includes goodwill impairment chage of $9,298,945.

Transfer Agent & Registrar: American Stock Transfer & Trust Co.

Corporate Counsel:	Howard & Howard PLLC	Traded (Symbol):	NASDAQ Capital (SGMA)
Investor Relations:	Linda K. Frauendorfer, V.P.	Stockholders:	1,406 (B)
Human Resources:	Sandy Miedema	Employees:	1,780
Info. Tech.	Thomas F. Rovtar, V.P.	Annual Meeting:	In September
Auditors:	BDO USA LLP		

Sparton Corporation

425 North Martingale Road, Suite 2050, Schaumburg, Illinois 60173-2213
Telephone: (847) 762-5800   www.sparton.com

Sparton Corporation is a provider of complex and sophisticated electromechanical devices with capabilities that include concept development, industrial design, design and manufacturing engineering, production, distribution, and field service. Primary markets that the company serves include: navigation and exploration, defense and security, medical, and complex systems. In 2010, the company completed acquisition of the contract manufacturing business of Delphi Medical Systems, LLC. In March 2011, the company completed the acquisition of the contract manufacturing business of Byers Peak, Incorporated. Both acquisitions provided Sparton Corporation with expansion into the therapeutic device market. Manufacturing facilities are located in Strongsville, Ohio; DeLeon Springs and Brooksville, Florida; and Ho Chi Minh City, Vietnam. The company is a primary supplier of sonobuoys and anti-submarine warfare devices used by the U.S. Navy and other free-world countries. Originally incorporated in 1900; reincorporated in Ohio in 1919.

Directors (In addition to indicated officers)

David P. Molfenter, Chm.	Douglas R. Schrank
James D. Fast	W. Peter Slusser
Joseph J. Hartnett	James R. Swartwout
William I. Noecker	

Officers (Directors*)

*Cary B. Wood, Pres. & C.E.O.	Jake Rost, V.P./Gen. Mgr.—Medical
Gregory A. Slome,Sr. V.P. & C.F.O.	Duane K. Stierhoff, V.P./Gen. Mgr.—Medical
Gordon B. Madlock, Sr. V.P.—Operations	Device Oper.
Michael W. Osborne, Sr. V.P.—Bus. Dev.	James M. Lackemacher, V.P/Gen. Mgr.—
Steven M. Korwin, Sr. V.P.—Qual., Eng. & Info. Sys.	Defense & Security Sys.
Lawrence R. Brand, V.P.—Hum. Res.	Robert L. Grimm II, V.P. & Gen. Mgr.—Complex Sys.

Consolidated Balance Sheet   As of June 30, 2011 (000 omitted)

Assets		Liabilities & Stockholders' Equity	
Current assets	$ 93,411	Current liabilities	$ 42,088
Net property & equipment	11,395	Environmental remediation	3,763
Goodwill	7,472	Long term debt	1,670
Other assets	10,331	Pension liability	41
		*Stockholders' equity	75,047
Total	$122,609	Total	$122,609

*10,236,484 shares common stock outstanding.

Consolidated Income Statement

| Years Ended June 30 | Thousands — — — — — | | Per Share — — — — — | | Common Stock |
	Net Sales	Net Income	Diluted Earnings[a]	Cash Dividends	Price Range Fiscal Year
2011 [a]	$203,352	$ 7,461	$ 0.73	$0.00	$10.22—4.78
2010	173,977	7,440	0.75	0.00	6.74—2.60
2009	221,871	(15,753)	(1.61)	0.00	4.15—1.35
2008	229,805	(13,138)	(1.34)	0.00	7.37—3.59
2007	200,086	(7,769)	(0.79)	0.00	8.99—6.94

[a] Includes operating results of the medical businesses acquired from Delphi Medical Systems, LLC and Byers Peak, Incorporated from dates of acquisition: August 2010 and March 2011, respectively.

Transfer Agent & Registrar: IST Shareholder Services

Investor Relations:	Gregory A. Slome, C.F.O.	Traded (Symbol):	NYSE (SPA)
Human Relations:	Lawrence R. Brand, V.P.	Stockholders:	448 (R)
Info. Tech.	Steven M. Korwin, Sr. V.P.	Employees:	1,013
Auditors:	BDO USA, LLP	Annual Meeting:	In October

Standard Parking Corporation

900 North Michigan Avenue, Suite 1600, Chicago, Illinois 60611-1542
Telephone: (312) 274-2000   www.standardparking.com

Standard Parking Corporation is a leading national provider of parking facility management and ground transportation services. The company provides on-site management services at multi-level and surface parking facilities for all major markets of the parking industry and manages more than one million parking spaces in hundreds of cities across the United States and Canada. Clients include some of the nation's largest private and public owners, managers, and developers of major office buildings, residential properties, commercial properties, shopping centers, and other retail properties, sports and special event complexes, hotels, hospitals, and medical centers. The company also provides ancillary services, including valet parking, as well as on-street parking enforcement and meter collections. As of December 2010, Standard Parking Corporation managed nearly 2,100 parking facility locations in approximately 341 cities, operated 25 parking-related service centers serving 64 airports, and operated a fleet of approximately 540 shuttle buses. Incorporated in Delaware in 1981. Reincorporated in 2004.

Directors (In addition to indicated officers)

Robert S. Roath, Chm.
Charles L. Biggs

Karen M. Garrison
Michael J. Roberts

Officers (Directors*)

*James A. Wilhelm, Pres. & C.E.O.
G. Marc Baumann, Exec. V.P., C.F.O. & Treas.
Thomas L. Hagerman, Exec. V.P. & C.O.O.
Gerard M. Klaisle, Exec. V.P. & Chf. Hum. Res. Off.
John Ricchiuto, Exec. V.P.—Oper.
Robert N. Sacks, Exec. V.P., Gen. Coun. & Secy.

Edward E. Simmons, Exec. V.P.—Oper.
Steven A. Warshauer, Exec. V.P.—Oper.
Michael K. Wolf, Exec. V.P., Chf. Admin. Off. & Assoc. Gen. Coun.
Daniel R. Meyer, Sr. V.P., Corp. Cont. & Asst. Treas.
Michael E. Swartz, Sr. V.P.—Admin. Svcs.

Consolidated Balance Sheet As of December 31, 2010 (000 omitted)

Assets		Liabilities & Stockholders' Equity	
Current assets	$ 64,098	Current liabilities	$ 84,639
Net leaseholds & equipment	16,839	Long-term borrowings, excluding	
Goodwill	132,196	current portion	97,229
Other assets	42,499	Other liabilities	36,961
		*Stockholders' equity	36.803
Total	$255,632	Total	$255,632

*15,775,645 shares common stock outstanding.

Consolidated Income Statement

Years Ended Dec. 31	Thousands — — — — —		Per Share a — — — — —		Common Stock Price Range a Calendar Year
	Total Revenue	Net Income	Diluted Earnings	Cash Dividends	
2010	$721,143	$16,840	$1.06	$0.00	$20.04—14.61
2009	695,494	14,092	0.90	0.00	20.31—13.90
2008	700,760	19,045	1.07	0.00	23.74—15.09
2007	621,721	17,373	0.90	0.00	24.98—15.82
2006	605,945	35,751	1.75	0.00	20.00— 9.60

a Restated to reflect a 2-for-1 stock split in January 2008.

Transfer Agent & Registrar: Continental Stock Transfer & Trust Co.
General Counsel: Robert N. Sacks, Exec. V.P.   Traded (Symbol): NASDAQ (STAN)
Investor Relations: G. Marc Baumann, Exec. V.P.   Stockholders: 3,785 (R)
Human Resources: Gerard M. Klaisle, Exec. V.P.   Employees: 11,971
Info. Tech.: Keith Evans, Sr. V.P.   Annual Meeting: In April
Auditors: Ernst & Young LLP

Stepan Company

Edens Expressway and Winnetka Road, Northfield, Illinois 60093

Telephone: (847) 446-7500   www.stepan.com

Stepan Company is a major manufacturer of specialty and intermediate chemicals used in a broad range of industries. Stepan has three reportable segments: surfactants, polymers, and specialty products. Stepan produces surfactants, which are the key ingredient in consumer and industrial cleaning compounds. Manufacturers of detergents, shampoos, lotions, toothpaste, and cosmetics depend on surfactants to achieve the foaming and cleaning qualities required of their products. Surfactants are also used in lubricating ingredients and emulsifiers for spreading agricultural products. Stepan also produces germicidal quaternary compounds, as well as other specialty products that are often custom-made to meet individual needs, such as flavors, emulsifiers, and solubilizers used in the food and pharmaceutical industries. The company is also a principal supplier of phthalic anhydride, a commodity chemical intermediate which is used in polyester resins, alkyd resins, and plasticizers. Polyols and polyurethane foam systems sold by the company are used in plastics, building materials, and refrigeration industries. Stepan utilizes a network of modern production facilities located in North and South America, Europe, the Philippines, and China. In June 2011, the company acquired several product lines of Lipid Nutrition B.V., a part of Loders Croklaan B.V. The acquired product lines will be integrated into Stepan's Food and Health Specialties business, which will be renamed Stepan Lipid Nutrition. Incorporated in Illinois in 1940; reincorporated in Delaware in 1959.

Directors (In addition to indicated officers)

Michael R. Boyce
Joaquin Delgado

Gregory E. Lawton
Edward J. Wehmer

Officers (Directors*)

*F. Quinn Stepan, Chm.
*F. Quinn Stepan, Jr., Pres. & C.E.O.
James E. Hurlbutt, V.P. & C.F.O.
Scott C. Mason, V.P.—Supply Chain
Frank Pacholec, V.P.—Res. & Dev.;
    Corp. Sustainability Off.
Gregory Servatius, V.P.—Hum. Res.

John V. Venegoni, V.P. & Gen. Mgr.—
    Surfactants
Robert J. Wood, V.P. & Gen. Mgr.—Polymers
H. Edward Wynn, V.P., Gen. Coun. & Secy.
Kathleen O. Sherlock, Asst. Gen. Coun. & Asst.
    Secy.

Consolidated Balance Sheet As of December 31, 2010 (000 omitted)

Assets		Liabilities & Stockholders' Equity	
Current assets	$427,826	Current liabilities	$205,627
Net property, plant & equipment	353,585	Long-term debt	159,963
Other assets	30,020	Deferred income taxes	5,154
		Other liabilities	87,616
		Minority interest	3,580
		*Stockholders' equity	349,491
Total	$811,431	Total	$811,431

*10,105,748 shares common stock outstanding.

Consolidated Income Statement

Years Ended Dec. 31	Thousands — — — — Net Sales	Net Income	Per Share — — — — Diluted Earnings	Cash Dividends	Common Stock Price Range Calendar Year
2010	$1,431,122	$65,427	$5.90	$0.98	$79.75—45.99
2009	1,276,382	63,049	5.84	0.90	67.98—22.80
2008	1,600,130	37,172	3.52	0.85	60.82—27.75
2007	1,329,901	15,118	1.50	0.83	35.00—25.14
2006	1,172,583	6,670	0.63	0.81	33.00—25.05

Transfer Agent & Registrar: Computershare Investor Services

General Counsel:	H. Edward Wynn, V.P.	Traded (Symbol):	NYSE, CSE (SCL)
Investor Relations:	James E. Hurlbutt, C.F.O.	Stockholders:	1,327 (R)
Human Resources:	Gregory Servatius, V.P.	Employees:	1,768
Info. Tech.:	Richard Lindquist	Annual Meeting:	In May
Auditors:	Deloitte & Touche LLP		

Stericycle, Inc.

28161 North Keith Drive, Lake Forest, Illinois 60045

Telephone: (847) 367-5910   www.stericycle.com

Stericycle, Inc. is a business services company that specializes in protecting people and reducing risk. Services include medical waste disposal and sharps disposal management, product recalls and retrievals, OSHA compliance training, pharmaceutical recalls and medical device returns, hazardous waste disposal, healthcare integrated waste stream management, pharmaceutical waste disposal, medical safety product sales, and high volume notification services. Stericycle serves over 485,000 customers throughout the United States, Canada, Mexico, Argentina, Brazil, Chile, Ireland, Japan, Romania, Portugal, and the United Kingdom. The company has a fully integrated, national medical waste management network, including 136 processing/collection centers and 129 additional transfer and collection sites. Customers include hospitals, blood banks, and pharmaceutical manufacturers, as well as outpatient clinics, medical and dental offices, long-term and sub-acute care facilities, veterinary offices, municipalities, and retail pharmacies. In April 2011, Stericycle completed its acquisition of Healthcare Waste Solutions, Inc., a portfolio company of Altaris Capital Partners, LLC. Incorporated in Delaware in 1989.

Directors (In addition to indicated officers)

Thomas D. Brown
Rod F. Dammeyer
William K. Hall
Jonathan T. Lord, M.D.

John Patience
James W. P. Reid-Anderson
Jack W. Schuler
Ronald G. Spaeth

Officers (Directors*)

*Mark C. Miller, Chm. & C.E.O.
Michael J. Collins, Exec. V.P. & Pres.—
    Return Mgt. Svcs.

Richard T. Kogler, Exec. V.P. & C.O.O.
Frank J.M. ten Brink, Exec. V.P. & C.F.O.
Charles A. Alutto, Pres.—Stericycle USA

Consolidated Balance Sheet As of December 31, 2010 (000 omitted)

Assets		Liabilities & Stockholders' Equity	
Current assets	$ 368,688	Current liabilities	$ 308,489
Net property, plant & equipment	267,971	Other liabilities	1,250,184
Goodwill	1,595,764	Minority interest	31,925
Other assets	406,600	*Stockholders' equity	1,048,425
Total	$2,639,023	Total	$2,639,023

*85,242,387 shares common stock outstanding.

Consolidated Income Statement

| Years Ended Dec. 31 | Thousands — — — — | | Per Share — — — — | | Common Stock |
	Revenues	Net Income	Diluted Earnings[a]	Cash Dividends	Price Range [a] Calendar Year
2010	$1,439,388	$207,879[b]	$2.39[b]	$0.00	$81.78—51.16
2009	1,177,736	175,691[c]	2.03[c]	0.00	58.10—45.82
2008	1,083,679	148,708	1.68	0.00	64.77—48.83
2007	932,767	118,378	1.32	0.00	61.87—36.59
2006	789,637	105,270	1.16	0.00	37.81—28.64

[a] Adjusted to reflect a 2-for-1 stock split in May 2007.
[b] Includes $8.9 million of acquisition-related expenses; $5.2 million of restructuring and plant closure costs; litigation settlement expense of $0.5 million; $1.8 million gain in sale of assets; and $1.2 million benefit due to a net release of prior years' tax reserves. The net effect of these adjustments negatively impacted diluted earnings per share by $0.13.
[c] Includes $6.8 million of after-tax transactional expenses related to acquisitions, and $1.0 million of after-tax restructuring costs for regulated returns management services business, partially offset by $1.8 million benefit due to a net release of the prior years' tax reserves. The net effect of these transactions negatively impacted diluted earnings per share by $0.06.

Transfer Agent & Registrar: Wells Fargo Shareowner Services

Corporate Counsel:	Johnson & Colmar	**Traded (Symbol):**	NASDAQ (SRCL)
Investor Relations:	Frank ten Brink, Exec. V.P.	**Stockholders:**	154 (R)
Auditors:	Ernst & Young LLP	**Employees:**	9,078
		Annual Meeting:	In May

Strategic Hotels & Resorts, Inc.

200 West Madison Street, Suite 1700, Chicago, Illinois 60606-3415
Telephone: (312) 658-5000   **www.strategichotels.com**

Strategic Hotels & Resorts, Inc. is a real estate investment trust (REIT) that is an owner and asset manager of upscale and luxury hotels and resorts. As of July 2011, the company's portfolio consisted of 17 properties totaling 7,762 rooms located in North America and Europe. The properties include large convention hotels, business hotels, and resorts, which are managed by internationally known hotel management companies. Properties included in the company's portfolio operate under the following brands: Fairmont®, Four Seasons®, Hyatt®, InterContinental®, Loews®, Marriott®, Ritz-Carlton®, and Westin®. Incorporated in Maryland in 2004.

Directors (In addition to indicated officers)

Raymond L. Gellein, Jr., Chm.
Robert P. Bowen
Kenneth Fisher
James A. Jeffs

Richard D. Kincaid
David M.C. Michels
William A. Prezant
Eugene F. Reilly

Officers (Directors*)

*Laurence S. Geller, Pres. & C.E.O.
Richard J. Moreau, Exec. V.P.—Asset Mgt.
Diane M. Morefield, Exec. V.P. & C.F.O.

Stephen M. Briggs, Sr. V.P.—Chf. Acct. Off.
Paula C. Maggio, Sr. V.P., Secy. & Gen. Coun.

Consolidated Balance Sheet As of December 31, 2010 (000 omitted)

Assets		Liabilities & Shareholders' Equity	
Cash & cash equivalents	$ 78,842	Accounts payable & accrued exp.	$ 266,773
Restricted cash & cash equivalents	34,618	Mortgages & other debt payable	1,118,281
Net property & equipment	1,835,451	Bank credit facility	28,000
Goodwill	40,359	Deferred gains on sale of hotels	3,930
Investment in joint ventures	18,024	Other liabilities	99,988
Accounts receivable, net	35,250	Minority interests	25,082
Deferred items	7,443	*Shareholders' equity	620,262
Other assets	112,329		
Total	$2,162,316	Total	$2,162,316

*151,305,314 shares common stock outstanding.

Consolidated Income Statement

Years Ended Dec. 31	Thousands — — — —		Per Share — — — —		Common Stock Price Range Calendar Year
	Total Revenues[a]	Net Revenues[a]	Basic Earnings[ab]	Cash Dividends	
2010	$686,293	$(230,800)	$(2.41)	$0.00	$ 6.97— 1.84
2009	655,256	(246,433)	(3.45)	0.00	3.07— 0.61
2008	841,291	(317,486)	(4.25)	0.72	16.90— 0.77
2007	873,879	68,771	0.94	0.96	24.35—16.15
2006	626,969	122,719	0.03	0.92	23.56—18.43

[a] Restated to reflect the retrospective application of new accounting guidance related to noncontrolling interests and convertible debt instruments.
[b] (Loss) income per common share from continuing operations—basic.

Transfer Agent & Registrar: BNY Mellon Shareowner Services
General Counsel:	Paula C. Maggio, Sr. V.P.	Traded (Symbol):	NYSE (BEE)
Investor Relations:	Diane M. Morefield, C.F.O.	Stockholders:	81 (R)
Auditors:	Deloitte & Touche LLP	Employees:	43
		Annual Meeting:	In May

SunCoke Energy, Inc.

1011 Warrenville Road, 6th Floor, Lisle, Illinois 60532

Telephone: (630) 824-1000   **www.suncoke.com**

SunCoke Energy, Inc. is the largest independent producer of high-quality metallurgical coke in the Americas. Metallurgical coke is a principal raw material in the integrated steelmaking process. The company owns and operates four metallurgical cokemaking facilities in the United States, with an additional facility scheduled to be completed in the second half of 2011, and also operates one cokemaking facility in Brazil. SunCoke Energy currently sells approximately 3.6 million tons of metallurgical coke per year to its three primary customers in the United States: ArcelorMittal, United States Steel Corporation, and AK Steel Corporation. In January 2011, the company acquired Harold Keene Coal Co., Inc. and its affiliated companies. SunCoke Energy's mining operations consist of 13 active underground mines and one active surface and highwall mine in Russell and Buchanan Counties, Virginia and McDowell County, West Virginia. Effective July 21, 2011, SunCoke Energy was spun-off from Sunoco, Inc., and became a separate, publicly traded company. Sunoco owns approximately 83.4 percent of SunCoke Energy. Incorporated in Delaware in 2010.

Directors (In addition to indicated officers)

Alvin "Al" Bledsoe
Robert J. Darnall
Stacy L. Fox
Peter B. Hamilton

Michael J. Hennigan
Brian P. MacDonald
Charmian Uy
Dennis Zeleny

Officers (Directors*)

*Frederick A. Henderson, Chm. & C.E.O.
Michael J. Thomson, Pres. & C.O.O.
Denise R. Cade, Sr. V.P., Gen. Coun. & Secy.
Matthew McGrath, Sr. V.P.—Corp. Strat. &
  Bus. Dev.

Mark Newman, Sr. V.P. & C.F.O.
Michael S. White, Sr. V.P.—Oper.
James M. Mullins, V.P.—Coal Oper.
Thomas E. White, V.P.—Commer. Oper.
Fay West, V.P. & Cont.

Consolidated Balance Sheet As of December 31, 2010 (000 omitted)

Assets		Liabilities & Stockholders' Equity	
Current assets	$ 192,448	Total current liabilities	$1,055,724
Net property & equipment	1,180,208	Other liabilities	233,401
Other assets	345,810	Noncontrolling interest	59,800
		Stockholders' equity	369,541
Total	$1,718,466	Total	$1,718,466

Consolidated Income Statement

Years Ended Dec. 31	Thousands — — — — —		Per Share [a] — — — —		Common Stock Price Range [a] Calendar Year
	Total Revenues	Net Income [b]	Diluted Earnings [b]	Cash Dividends	
2010	$1,326,593	$139,199	$1.38 [c]	$0.00	
2009	1,144,986	189,684			
2008	840,251	113,904			
2007 [d]	519,709	30,450			
2006 [d]	527,996	36,793			

[a] Stock began trading on July 21, 2011.
[b] Attributable to net parent investment/SunCoke Energy, Inc. stockholders.
[c] Pro forma.
[d] Unaudiited.

Transfer Agent & Registrar: Computershare Investor Services

General Counsel:	Denise R. Cade, Sr. V.P.	Traded (Symbol):	NYSE (SXC)
Investor Relations:	Mark Newman, Sr. V.P.	Stockholders:	NA
Auditors:	Ernst & Young LLP	Employees:	1,180
		Annual Meeting:	To be determined

SXC Health Solutions Corp.

2441 Warrenville Road, Suite 610, Lisle, Illinois 60532-3642

Telephone: (630) 577-3100   **www.sxc.com**

SXC Health Solutions Corp. (formerly Systems Xcellence Inc.) is a leading provider of pharmacy benefit management (PBM) services and healthcare information technology (HCIT) solutions to the healthcare benefit management industry. Product offerings and solutions combine a wide range of applications and PBM services designed to assist customers in reducing the cost and managing the complexity of their prescription drug programs. Customers include pharmacy benefit managers, managed care organizations, self-insured employer groups, unions, third party healthcare plan administrators, and state and federal government entities. The company's PBM services include electronic point-of-sale pharmacy claims management, retail pharmacy network management, mail service pharmacy claims management, specialty pharmacy claims management, Medicare Part D services, benefit design consultation, preferred drug management programs, drug review and analysis, consulting services, data access, and reporting and information analysis. The company also owns a mail service pharmacy and a specialty service pharmacy. In December 2010, SXC Health Solutions completed its acquisition of MedfusionRx, LLC, a leading independent specialty pharmacy provider. Founded in 1993; incorporated in the Yukon Territory, Canada; present name adopted in 2007.

Directors (In addition to indicated officers)

Terrence C. Burke   Anthony R. Masso
Steven Cosler   Philip R. Reddon
William J. Davis   Curtis J. Thorne

Officers (Directors*)

*Mark A. Thierer, Chm., Pres. & C.E.O.   Joel Saban, Exec. V.P.—Pharmacy Oper.
Jeffrey Park, Exec. V.P. & C.F.O.   Clifford Berman, Sr. V.P., Gen. Coun. &
John Romza, Exec. V.P.—Res. & Dev.; Chf.   Corp. Secy.
  Technology Off.

Consolidated Balance Sheet As of December 31, 2010 (000 omitted)

Assets		Liabilities & Stockholders' Equity	
Current assets	$517,054	Current liabilities	$237,450
Net property & equipment	20,896	Deferred income taxes	15,111
Goodwill	220,597	Other liabilities	10,492
Other assets	57,762	*Stockholders' equity	553,256
Total	$816,309	Total	$816,309

*61,602,997 shares common stock outstanding.

Consolidated Income Statement

Years Ended Dec. 31	Thousands — — — — —		Per Share a — — — — —		Common Stock
	Revenue	Net Income	Diluted Earnings	Cash Dividends	Price Range ab Calendar Year
2010	$1,948,389	$64,735	$1.03	$0.00	$45.78—22.61
2009	1,438,634	46,061	0.86	0.00	28.08— 7.81
2008 c	862,939	15,113	0.32	0.00	9.42— 4.93
2007	93,171	13,146	0.30	0.00	15.69— 5.73
2006	80,923	13,647	0.35	0.00	12.63— 7.80

a Adjusted to reflect a 2-for-1 stock split on September 17, 2010, effected in the form of a stock dividend.
b Stock began trading June 13, 2006.
c Includes results of operations of National Medical Health Card Systems, Inc., since date of acquisition, April 30, 2008.

Transfer Agent & Registrar: CIBC Mellon Trust Company

General Counsel:	Cliff Berman, Sr. V.P.	Traded (Symbol):	NASDAQ (SXCI); TSX (SXC)
Investor Relations:	Tony Perkins, Sr. Dir.	Stockholders:	23,925 (R)
Auditors:	KPMG LLP	Employees:	1,216
		Annual Meeting:	In May

Taylor Capital Group, Inc.

9550 West Higgins Road, Rosemont, Illinois 60018

Telephone: (847) 653-7978   www.taylorcapitalgro

Taylor Capital Group, Inc. is a bank holding company that derives virtually all of its revenue
subsidiary, Cole Taylor Bank. Taylor Capital currently operates nine banking centers through
Chicago metropolitan area and its operations extend to many states across the country. The cor
focuses on closely held businesses and the people who own and manage them and provides a range
of products and services concentrated in the areas of commercial banking, asset-based lending,
commercial real estate lending, residential mortgage lending, and personal banking. Incorporated in
Delaware in 1996.

Directors (In addition to indicated officers)

Jeffrey W. Taylor, V. Chm.
Ronald L. Bliwas
C. Bryan Daniels
Ronald D. Emanuel
M. Hill Hammock
Elzie Higginbottom
Michael H. Moskow

Louise O'Sullivan
Melvin E. Pearl
Shepherd G. Pryor, IV
Harrison I. Steans
Jennifer W. Steans
Richard W. Tinberg

Officers (Directors*)

*Bruce W. Taylor, Chm.
*Mark A. Hoppe, Pres. & C.E.O.

Randall T. Conte, C.F.O. & C.O.O.
Lawrence G. Ryan, Exec. V.P. & Chf. Lending Off.

Consolidated Balance Sheet As of December 31, 2010 (000 omitted)

Assets		Liabilities & Stockholders' Equity	
Cash & cash equivalents	$ 81,329	Total deposits	$3,026,906
Investment securities	1,254,477	Other borrowings	511,008
Loans, net	2,969,790	Notes payable & FHLB advances	505,000
Net premises & equipment	15,890	Other liabilities	232,139
Other assets	162,368	*Stockholders' equity	208,801
Total	$4,483,854	Total	$4,483,854

*17,877,708 shares common stock outstanding.

Consolidated Income Statement

Years Ended Dec. 31	Thousands — — — — —		Per Share — — — — —		Common Stock Price Range Calendar Year
	Total Income	Net Income [a]	Diluted Earnings	Cash Dividends	
2010	$281,199	$ (79,278)	$ (5.27)	$0.00	$18.05— 7.82
2009	253,621	(43,033)	(4.10)	0.00	11.50— 2.64
2008	216,885	(143,358)	(13.72)	0.10	21.60— 5.10
2007	243,770	(9,570)	(0.89)	0.40	39.45—19.70
2006	237,265	46,163	4.12	0.28	43.18—28.61

[a] Applicable to common stockholders.

Transfer Agent & Registrar: Computershare Investor Services

Investor Relations:	Christina Hachikian, V.P.	Traded (Symbol):	NASDAQ (TAYC)
Human Resources:	Mary Ceas, Grp. Sr. V.P.	Stockholders:	174
Info. Tech.:	Clio Mulryne, Grp. Sr. V.P.	Employees:	591
Auditors:	KPMG LLP	Annual Meeting:	In May

hone and Data Systems, Inc.

North LaSalle Street, Suite 4000, Chicago, Illinois 60602

Telephone: (312) 630-1900   **www.teldta.com**

Telephone and Data Systems, Inc. (TDS) provides wireless, local and long-distance telephone and broadband service nationwide through its wireless and wireline businesses. As of December 2010, TDS served approximately 7.2 million customers. U.S. Cellular, a majority-owned subsidiary, is the nation's sixth-largest wireless provider, offering a comprehensive range of wireless services and products and networks to more than six million customers. TDS Telecom, a wholly owned subsidiary, provides voice, broadband, and video services to residential and business customers. The company also conducts printing and distribution services through its majority-owned subsidiary, Suttle-Straus, Inc. Incorporated in Iowa in 1968; reincorporated in Delaware in 1998.

Directors (In addition to indicated officers)

Walter C.D. Carlson, Chm.
Letitia G. Carlson, M.D.
Prudence E. Carlson
Clarence A. Davis
Donald C. Nebergall

Christopher O'Leary
George W. Off
Mitchell H. Saranow
Gary L. Sugarman
Herbert S. Wander

Officers (Directors*)

*LeRoy T. Carlson, Jr., Pres. & C.E.O.
*Kenneth R. Meyers, Exec. V.P. & C.F.O.
Douglas D. Shuma, Sr. V.P. & Corp. Cont.
Kurt B. Thaus, Sr. V.P. & C.I.O.
Scott H. Williamson, Sr. V.P.—Acquisitions & Corp. Dev.
Douglas W. Chambers, V.P. & Asst. Corp. Cont.
Kevin C. Gallagher, V.P. & Corp. Secy.

David D. Gillman, Asst. Cont.—Tax
Joseph R. Hanley, V.P.—Tech. Plan. & Svcs.
C. Theodore Herbert, V.P.—Hum. Res.
Frieda E. Ireland, V.P.—Internal Audit
Kenneth M. Kotylo, V.P.—Acquisitions & Corp. Dev.
Jane W. McCahon, V.P.—Corp. Rel.
Peter L. Sereda, V.P. & Treas.
Byron A. Wertz, V.P.—Corp. Dev.

Consolidated Balance Sheet As of December 31, 2010 (000 omitted)

Assets		Liabilities & Stockholders' Equity	
Current assets	$1,596,076	Current liabilities	$ 810,633
Net property & equipment	3,558,334	Long-term debt	1,499,862
Investments	2,528,486	Deferred liabilities & credits	990,360
Other assets	79,623	Preferred stock & minority interests	647,742
		*Stockholders' equity	3,813,922
Total	$7,762,519	Total	$7,762,519

*49,895,000 shares common; 47,531,000 shares special common; and 6,510,000 shares Series A common stock outstanding.

Consolidated Income Statement [a]

Years Ended Dec. 31	Thousands — — — —		Per Share — — — —		Common Stock
	Operating Revenues	Net Income [b]	Diluted Earnings [b]	Cash Dividends	Price Range [c] Calendar Year
2010	$4,986,829	$143,856	$1.36	$0.45	$37.91—34.96
2009	5,019,943	188,965	1.72	0.43	35.98—22.01
2008	5,091,388	88,496	0.76	0.41	66.19—21.24
2007	4,822,471	385,267	2.86	0.39	73.67—53.02
2006	4,364,180	161,255	1.37	0.37	55.22—35.14

[a] Certain prior year amounts have been revised to correct overstatement of service revenues and understatement of sales tax liabilities, and other errors.
[b] Attributable to TDS shareholders.
[c] TDS's Special Common Shares (TDS.S) were first issued in a stock dividend on May 13, 2005. TDS.S price range: 2010: $32.27—25.17; 2009: $31.17—21.89; 2008: $58.30—22.18; 2007: $68.65—48.28; 2006: $50.76—33.95.

Transfer Agent & Registrar: Computershare Investor Services
Corporate Counsel: Sidley Austin LLP
Investor Relations: Jane W. McCahon, V.P.
Human Resources: C. Theodore Herbert, V.P.
Info. Tech.: Kurt B. Thaus, Sr. V.P. & C.I.O.
Auditors: PricewaterhouseCoopers LLP

Traded (Symbol): NYSE (TDS);
(TDS.S)
Stockholders: 1,582 (R)
Employees: 12,400
Annual Meeting: In May

THE PRIVATEBANK GUIDE

Tellabs, Inc.

One Tellabs Center, 1415 West Diehl Road, Naperville, Illinois 60563
Telephone: (630) 798-8800   www.tellabs.com

Tellabs, Inc. designs, develops, markets, and services communications equipment for use by telecommunications service providers. The company operates in three segments: Broadband, Transport, and Services. Products include solutions for next-generation optical networking, managed access, carrier-class data, and voice-quality enhancement. Customers include wireline, wireless, and cable operators, as well as government agencies. The company has approximately 51 locations worldwide. Major subsidiaries include: Tellabs Operations, Inc.; Tellabs International, Inc.; Tellabs Oy; and Tellabs Denmark. With the December 2009 acquisition of WiChorus, Inc., a supplier of industry-leading infrastructure products for the mobile Internet, Tellabs entered a large and fast growing market with a purpose-built 4G mobile-network solution for WiMax and Long Term Evolution (LTE) networks. Incorporated in Illinois in 1975; reincorporated in Delaware in 1992.

Directors (In addition to indicated officers)

Bo Hedfors
Frank Ianna
Linda Wells Kahangi
Michael E. Lavin

Stephanie Pace Marshall, Ph.D.
William F. Souders
Jan H. Suwinski
Vincent H. Tobkin

Officers (Directors*)

*Michael J. Birck, Chm. & Co-Founder
*Robert W. Pullen, Pres. & C.E.O.
John M. Brots, Exec. V.P.—Global Oper.
Roger J. Heinz, Exec. V.P.—Global
 Sales & Svcs.
Daniel P. Kelly, Exec. V.P.—Global Prods.

Rizwan Khan, Exec. V.P.—Global Mktg.
Dr. Vikram Saksena, Exec. V.P. & Chf. Tech. Off.
James M. Sheehan, Exec. V.P., Chf. Admin. Off.,
 Gen. Coun. & Secy.
Timothy J. Wiggins, Exec. V.P. & C.F.O.
Rehan Jalil, Sr. V.P.—Mobile IP & Internet

Consolidated Balance Sheet As of December 31, 2010 (000 omitted)

Assets		Liabilities & Stockholders' Equity	
Current assets	$1,912,800	Current liabilities	$ 663,100
Net property, plant & equipment	269,300	Other liabilities	78,300
Goodwill	204,900	*Stockholders' equity	1,861,500
Other assets	215,900		
Total	$2,602,900	Total	$2,602,900

*362,501,548 shares common stock outstanding.

Consolidated Income Statement

Years Ended Abt. Dec. 31	Thousands — — — —		Per Share — — — —		Common Stock Price Range Calendar Year
	Revenue	Net Income	Diluted Earnings	Cash Dividends	
2010	$1,642,300	$ 155,600	$ 0.41	$0.08	$ 9.45—5.68
2009	1,525,700	113,600	0.29	0.00	7.70—3.52
2008	1,729,000	(930,100) [a]	(2.32) [a]	0.00	7.21—3.10
2007	1,913,400	65,000	0.15	0.00	13.67—6.55
2006	2,041,200	194,100 [b]	0.43 [b]	0.00	17.28—8.84

[a] Includes a non-cash goodwill impairment charge of $988,300,000.
[b] Includes restructuring and other charges of $8,000,000.

Transfer Agent & Registrar: Computershare Investor Services
General Counsel: James Sheehan, Chf. Admin. Off. Traded (Symbol): NASDAQ (TLAB)
Investor Relations: Tom Scottino, Sr. Mgr.   Stockholders: 5,818 (R)
Human Resources: James Sheehan, Chf. Admin. Off. Employees: 3,413
Auditors: Randall T. Conte, C.F.O. & C.O.O. Annual Meeting: In May
         Ernst & Young LLP

Telular Corporation

311 South Wacker Drive, Suite 4300, Chicago, Illinois 60606

Telephone: (312) 379-8397   www.telular.com

Telular Corporation develops products and services that utilize wireless networks to provide data and voice connectivity among people and machines. The company creates solutions based on the development of specialized wireless terminals that work in conjunction with software systems to provide integrated event monitoring and reporting services for machine-to-machine (M2M) applications to improve process efficiency in areas such as supply chain management, security monitoring, meter reading, vehicle tracking, and many other commercial and industrial situations. The company's two major lines of business are Telguard products and services for security dealers and TankLink products and services for logistics management of tank vessels. In addition to its Chicago, Illinois headquarters, Telular has a research and development center in Atlanta, Georgia, regional sales and technical support offices in Atlanta and Miami, Florida, and a warehouse and shipping center in Wheeling, Illinois. Subsidiaries are Telular International, Inc., Telular-Adcor Security Products, Inc., and TankLink Communications, Inc. Incorporated in Delaware in 1993.

Directors (In addition to indicated officers)

Larry J. Ford, Chm.
Lawrence S. Barker
Betsy Bernard

Brian J. Clucas
Jeffrey Jacobowitz
M. Brian McCarthy

Officers (Directors*)

*Joseph A. Beatty, Pres. & C.E.O.
George S. Brody, Sr. V.P.—Terminals &Telguard®
Jonathan M. Charak, Sr. V.P., C.F.O. & Secy.
Jerry Deutsch, Sr. V.P.—Mfg. & Oper.

Robert L. Deering, Cont., Treas. & Chf. Acct. Off.
Christopher Bear, V.P.—Prod. Dev.
Patrick Kuchevar, V.P.—Sales & Svcs., TankLink
Shawn Welsh, V.P.—Mktg. & Bus. Dev.

Consolidated Balance Sheet As of September 30, 2010 (000 omitted)

Assets		Liabilities & Stockholders' Equity	
Current assets	$40,181	Current liabilities	$ 6,135
Net property & equipment	2,169	Other liabilities	529
Intangibles & other assets	39,201	*Stockholders' equity	74,887
Total	$81,551	Total	$81,551

*14,871,889 shares common stock outstanding.

Consolidated Income Statement

Years Ended Sept. 30	Thousands — — — —		Per Share — — — —		Common Stock Price Range Fiscal Year
	Total Revenue	Net Income	Basic Earnings	Cash Dividends	
2010	$47,354	$ 38,121	$ 2.55	$0.00	$5.14—2.33
2009	47,194	1,866	0.11	0.00	3.52—1.14
2008 a	66,154	(1,379)	(0.07)	0.00	8.59—1.99
2007 a	74,507	(1,946)	(0.11)	0.00	7.50—2.00
2006	45,706	(11,818)	(0.70)	0.00	4.15—1.71

a The fixed cellular product (FCP) segment was abandoned effective June 30, 2008. As a result, this segment has been segregated and classified as discontinued operations and amounts for all periods presented have been restated to reflect this classification.

Transfer Agent & Registrar: Registrar and Transfer Company

Investor Relations:	Jonathan M. Charak, Sr. V.P., C.F.O. & Secy.	Traded (Symbol):	NASDAQ (WRLS)
		Stockholders:	204 (R); 4,455 (B)
Human Resources:	Tiffany Voltz	Employees:	83
Auditors:	Grant Thornton LLP	Annual Meeting:	In February

Tenneco Inc.

500 North Field Drive, Lake Forest, Illinois 60045
Telephone: (847) 482-5000   www.tenneco.com

Tenneco Inc., formerly Tenneco Automotive Inc., is a world leader in designing, manufacturing, and marketing ride control and emission control systems and products. The company's value-added technologies provide quieter, cleaner, and safer transportation. Tenneco serves original equipment manufacturers and repair and replacement markets, or aftermarkets, worldwide through leading brands such as Monroe®, Rancho®, and Clevite® Elastomers; Fric Rot™ ride control products; and Walker®, Fonos™, Gillet™, and DynoMax® emission control products. As an automotive parts supplier, the company designs, manufactures, markets, and sells individual component parts for vehicles and groups of components that are combined as modules or systems within vehicles. Incorporated in Delaware in 1996. Present name adopted in 2005.

Directors (In addition to indicated officers)

Charles W. Cramb
Dennis J. Letham
Roger B. Porter
David B. Price, Jr.

Paul T. Stecko
Mitsunobu Takeuchi
Jane L. Warner

Officers (Directors*)

*Gregg M. Sherrill, Chm. & C.E.O.
*Hari N. Nair, C.O.O.
Kenneth R. Trammell, Exec. V.P. & C.F.O.
Neal A. Yanos, Exec. V.P.—N. Amer.
Brent J. Bauer, Sr. V.P. & Gen. Mgr.—N. Amer. Original Equip. Emission Control
Michael J. Charlton, Sr. V.P.—Global Supply Chain Mgt. & Mfg.
Josep M. Fornos, Sr. V.P.—Eur., South Amer. & India
James D. Harrington, Sr. V.P., Gen. Coun. & Corp. Secy.
Timothy E. Jackson, Sr. V.P. & Chf. Tech. Off.
Barbara A. Kluth, Sr. V.P.—Global Hum. Res.
Maritza Gibbons, V.P.—Strat. Plan. & Bus. Dev.

Patrick Guo, V.P. & Managing Dir.—China
H. William Haser, V.P. & C.I.O.
Jeff Jarrell, V.P. & Managing Dir.—Japan
John E. Kunz, V.P.—Tax & Treas.
Paul D. Novas, V.P. & Cont.
Enrique Orta, V.P. & Gen. Mgr.—Eur. Original Equip. Emission Control
Jane Ostrander, V.P.—Global Commun.
Sandro Paparelli, V.P. & Gen. Mgr.—Eur. Original Equip. Ride Control
Kevin Swint, V.P. & Gen. Mgr.—N. Amer. Original Equip. Ride Control
Guillermo Minuzzi, Managing Dir.—South Amer.

Consolidated Balance Sheet As of December 31, 2010 (000 omitted)

Assets		Liabilities & Stockholders' Deficit	
Current assets	$1,790,000	Current liabilities	$1,468,000
Net property, plant & equipment	1,050,000	Long-term debt	1,160,000
Other assets	327,000	Deferred items	181,000
		Other liabilities	311,000
		Minority interest	51,000
		*Stockholders' deficit	(4,000)
Total	$3,167,000	Total	$3,167,000

*59,208,103 shares common stock outstanding.

Consolidated Income Statement

Years Ended Dec. 31	Thousands — — — —		Per Share — — — —		Common Stock Price Range Calendar Year
	Net Sales	Net Income	Diluted Earnings	Cash Dividends	
2010	$5,937,000	$ 39,000	$ 0.63	$0.00	$43.71—17.17
2009	4,649,000	(73,000)	(1.50)	0.00	19.78— 0.67
2008	5,916,000	(415,000)	(8.95)	0.00	30.41— 1.31
2007	6,184,000	(5,000)	(0.11)	0.00	37.73—23.04
2006	4,682,000	49,000	1.05	0.00	27.55—19.61

Transfer Agent & Registrar: Wells Fargo Shareowner Services
General Counsel: James D. Harrington, Sr. V.P.   Traded (Symbol): NYSE, CSE (TEN)
Investor Relations: Linae Golla, Exec. Dir.   Stockholders: 19,691 (R)
Human Resources: Barbara A. Kluth, Sr. V.P.   Employees: 22,000
Info. Tech.:   H. William Haser, C.I.O.   Annual Meeting: In May
Auditors: PricewaterhouseCoopers LLP

Titan International, Inc.

2701 Spruce Street, Quincy, Illinois 62301

Telephone: (217) 228-6011   www.titan-intl.com

Titan International, Inc. and its subsidiaries hold the unique position of manufacturing both wheels and tires for its target markets. A leading manufacturer in the off-highway industry, Titan produces a broad range of specialty products to meet the needs of original equipment manufacturers and aftermarket customers in the agricultural, earthmoving/construction, and consumer markets. Titan's earthmoving/construction market inlues wheels and tires supplied to the mining industry, and the consumer market includes products for all0terrain vehicles and recreational/utility trailers. Incorporated in Illinois in 1983.

Directors (In addition to indicated officers)

Erwin H. Billig, V. Chm.
J. Michael A. Akers
Richard M. Cashin, Jr.

Albert J. Febbo
Mitchell I. Quain
Anthony L. Soave

Officers (Directors*)

*Maurice M. Taylor, Jr., Chm. & C.E.O.
Kent W. Hackamack, Exec. V.P.—
  Corp. Dev.

Cheri T. Holley, V.P., Gen. Coun. & Secy.
Jim Allen, V.P.—Sales
Paul G. Reitz, C.F.O.

Consolidated Balance Sheet As of December 31, 2010 (000 omitted)

Assets		Liabilities & Stockholders' Equity	
Current assets	$487.940	Current liabilities	$ 92,353
Net property, plant & equipment	248,054	Long-term debt	373,564
Other assets	51,476	Other long-term liabilities	43,238
		*Stockholders' equity	278,315
Total	$787,470	Total	$787,470

*35,366,727 shares common stock outstanding.

Consolidated Income Statement

Years Ended Dec. 31	Thousands — — — — —		Per Share a — — — — —		Common Stock Price Range a Calendar Year
	Total Income	Net Income	Diluted Earnings	Cash Dividends	
2010	$ 881,591	$ 358	$(0.01)	$0.20	$19.86— 7.15
2009	727,599	(24,645)	(0.71)	0.20	11.44— 3.05
2008	1,036,700	13,337	0.38	0.18	37.77— 5.40
2007	837,021	(7,247)	(0.23)	0.16	35.29—19.90
2006	679,454	5,144	0.21	0.28	20.85—16.20

a Adjusted to reflect a 5-for-4 stock split in 2008.

Transfer Agent & Registrar: BNY Mellon Shareowner Services

General Counsel: Cheri T. Holley, V.P.

Auditors: PricewaterhouseCoopers LLP

Traded (Symbol):	NYSE (TWI)
Stockholders:	8,800 (B)
Employees:	2,400
Annual Meeting:	In May

Tootsie Roll Industries, Inc.

7401 South Cicero Avenue, Chicago, Illinois 60629

Telephone: (773) 838-3400   **www.tootsie.com**

Tootsie Roll Industries, Inc. has been engaged in the manufacture and sale of candy since 1896. The company's products include the brand names Tootsie Roll, Tootsie Pop, Charms Blow-Pop, Mason Dots, Andes, Sugar Daddy, Charleston Chew, Dubble Bubble, Razzles, Caramel Apple jPop, Junior Mints, Cella's Chocolate-Covere Cherries, and Nik-L-Nip. The company's products are distributed through approximately 100 candy and grocery brokers and by the company itself to approximately 15,000 customers throughout the United States. These customers include wholesale distributors of candy and groceries, supermarkets, variety stores, dollar stores, chain grocers, drug chains, cooperative grocery associations, warehouse and membership club stores, vending machine operators, the U.S. military, and fundraising charitable organizations. The company's manufacturing facilities are located in Chicago; Cambridge, Massachusetts; Delavan, Wisconsin; Covington, Tennessee; Hazelton, Pennsylvania; Concord, Ontario, Canada; and Mexico City, Mexico. Incorporated in Virginia in 1919.

Directors (In addition to indicated officers)

Richard P. Bergeman   Barre A. Seibert
Lana Jane Lewis-Brent

Officers (Directors*)

*Melvin J. Gordon, Chm. & C.E.O.   John P. Majors, V.P.—Physical Distrib.
*Ellen R. Gordon, Pres. & C.O.O.   John W. Newlin, Jr., V.P.—Mfg.
 Thomas E. Corr, V.P.—Mktg. & Sales   Barry P. Bowen, Treas. & Asst. Secy.
 G. Howard Ember, Jr., V.P.—Fin. & C.F.O.   Richard F. Berezewski, Cont.

Consolidated Balance Sheet As of December 31, 2010 (000 omitted)

Assets		Liabilities & Stockholders' Equity	
Current assets	$237,591	Current liabilities	$ 58,505
Net property, plant & equipment	215,492	Deferred income taxes	48,743
Trademarks	175,024	Other liabilities	84,181
Other assets	232,276	*Stockholders' equity	668,954
Total	$860,383	Total	$860,383

*35,988,000 shares common and 20,399,00 shares Class B common stock outstanding.

Consolidated Income Statement

Years Ended Dec. 31	Thousands — — — —		Per Share a — — — —		Common Stock Price Range Calendar Year
	Net Sales	Net Income	Basic Earnings	Cash Dividends	
2010	$517,149	$53,714	$0.94	$0.32	$29.84—23.34
2009	495,592	53,878	0.93	0.32	28.06—19.46
2008	492,051	39,315	0.67	0.32	31.35—21.45
2007	492,742	51,914	0.87	0.32	32.69—23.55
2006	495,990	66,011	1.09	0.32	33.26—26.35

a Adjusted for annual 3% stock dividends.

Transfer Agent & Registrar: American Stock Transfer & Trust Company
General Counsel: ,Becker Ross, LLP   Traded (Symbol): NYSE (TR)
Investor Relations: Barry P. Bowen, Treas.   Stockholders: 18,000, common;
Auditors: PricewaterhouseCoopers LLP   5,000 Class B (B)
                                             Employees: 2,200
                                             Annual Meeting: In May

TreeHouse Foods, Inc.

2021 Spring Road, Suite 600, Oak Brook, Illinois 60523
Telephone: (708) 483-1300   www.treehousefoods.com

TreeHouse Foods, Inc. is a food manufacturing company that markets to the retail and food service industries through Bay Valley Foods, E.D. Smith, Sturm Foods, and S.T. Specialty. Products include non-dairy powdered coffee creamer, canned soup, salad dressings and sauces, sugar-free drink mixes and sticks, instant oatmeal and not cereals, macaroni and cheese, skillet dinners and other side dishes and salads; salsa and Mexican sauces, jams and pie fillings under the E.D. Smith brand name, pickles and related products, infant feeding products, and other food products including aseptic sauces, refrigerated salad dressings, and liquid non-dairy creamer. In March 2010, the company acquired Sturm Foods, a manufacturer of hot cereal and soft drink mixes. In October 2010, the company acquired S.T. Specialty Foods, Inc., a manufacturer of macaroni and cheese and skillet dinners. Incorporated in Delaware in 2005.

Directors (In addition to indicated officers)

George V. Bayly	Ann M. Sardini
Diana S. Ferguson	Gary D. Smith
Dennis F. O'Brien	Terdema L. Ussery, II
Frank J. O'Connell	David B. Vermylen

Officers (Directors*)

*Sam K. Reed, Chm., Pres. & C.E.O.
Dennis F. Riordan, Exec. V.P. & C.F.O.
Thomas E. O'Neill, Exec. V.P., Gen. Coun., Chf. Admin. Off. & Corp. Secy.
Harry J. Walsh, Exec. V.P. & Pres.—Bay Valley Foods, LLC

Sharon M. Flanagan, Sr. V.P.—Strat.
Erik T. Kahler, Sr. V.P.—Corp. Dev.
Alan T. Gambrel, Sr. V.P.—Hum. Res. & C.A.O.—Bay Valley Foods, LLC

Consolidated Balance Sheet As of December 31, 2010 (000 omitted)

Assets		Liabilities & Stockholders' Equity	
Current assets	$ 440,803	Current liabilities	$ 203,360
Property, plant & equipment	386,191	Long-term debt	976,452
Goodwill	1,076,321	Deferred taxes	194,917
Other assets	487,933	Other liabilities	38,553
		*Stockholders' equity	977,966
Total	$2,391,248	Total	$2,391,248

*35,440,000 shares common stock outstanding.

Consolidated Income Statement

Years Ended Dec. 31	Thousands — — — — —		Per Share — — — —		Common Stock Price Range Calendar Year
	Net Sales	Net Income	Diluted Earnings	Cash Dividends	
2010	$1,817,024	$90,919	$2.51	$0.00	$53.30—36.84
2009	1,511,653	81,314	2.48	0.00	40.38—24.28
2008	1,500,650	28,224	0.90	0.00	31.61—19.24
2007	1,157,902	41,622	1.33	0.00	32.59—21.15
2006	939,396	44,856	1.43	0.00	33.20—18.42

Transfer Agent & Registrar: BNY Mellon Shareowner Services
General Counsel: Thomas E. O'Neill, Sr. V.P.
Investor Relations: P. I. Aquino
Human Resources: Alan T. Gambrel, Sr. V.P.
Info. Tech.: Rob Hanlon, V.P.—Info. Tech.
Auditors: Deloitte & Touche LLP

Traded (Symbol): NYSE (THS)
Stockholders: 4,128 (R)
Employees: 4,000
Annual Meeting: In April

Ulta Salon, Cosmetics & Fragrance, Inc.

1000 Remington Boulevard, Suite 120, Bolingbrook, Illinois 60440

Telephone: (630) 410-4800 www.ulta.com

Ulta Salon, Cosmetics & Fragrance, Inc. is the largest beauty retailer that provides one-stop shopping for prestige, mass, and salon products and salon services in the United States. The company provides affordable indulgence to its customers by combining the product breadth, value, and convenience of a beauty superstore with the distinctive environment and experience of a specialty retailer. Ulta offers a unique combination of over 20,000 prestige and mass beauty products across the categories of cosmetics, fragrance, haircare, skincare, bath and body products, and salon styling tools, as well as salon haircare products. The company also offers full-service salons in all of its stores. As of July 30, 2011, Ulta operated 415 stores in 42 states. The company also distributes its products through the Company's website: www.ulta.com. Incorporated in Delaware in 1990.

Directors (In addition to indicated officers)

Dennis K. Eck, Chm.
Hervé J.F. Defforey
Robert F. DiRomualdo
Charles Heilbronn

Lorna E. Nagler
Charles J. Philippin
Kenneth T. Stevens

Officers (Directors*)

*Chuck Rubin, Pres. & C.E.O.
Gregg R. Bodnar, C.F.O. & Asst. Secy.
Kimberley Grayson, Sr. V.P. & Chf. Mktg. Off.
Robert S. Guttman, Sr. V.P., Gen. Coun. & Secy.

Cynthia Payne, Sr. V.P.—Store Ops.
Vincent A. Scarfone, Sr. V.P.—Hum. Res.
Janet Taake, Sr. V.P.—Mdse.

Consolidated Balance Sheet As of January 29, 2011 (000 omitted)

Assets		Liabilities & Stockholders' Equity	
Current assets	$404,389	Current liabilities	$163,357
Net property & equipment	326,099	Deferred rent	134,572
		Other liabilities	30,026
		*Stockholders' equity	402,533
Total	$730,488	Total	$730,488

*60,202,000 shares common stock outstanding.

Consolidated Income Statement

Years Ended Abt. Jan. 31	Thousands — — — —		Per Share — — — —		Common Stock Price Range [a] Fiscal Year
	Net Sales	Net Income	Diluted Earnings	Cash Dividends	
2011	$1,454,838	$71,030	$1.16	$0.00	$37.85—17.29
2010	1,222,771	39,356	0.66	0.00	21.61— 4.29
2009	1,084,646	25,268	0.43	0.00	15.92— 5.76
2008 [a]	912,141	25,335	0.48	0.00	35.43—12.50
2007 [b]	755,113	22,543	0.45	0.00	

[a] Initial public offering: October 25, 2007.
[b] 53 weeks.

Transfer Agent & Registrar: American Stock Transfer & Trust Co.

General Counsel: Robert S. Guttman, Sr. V.P.
Investor Relations: Gregg R. Bodnar, C.F.O.
Human Resources: Vincent A. Scarfone, Sr. V.P.
Auditors: Ernst & Young LLP

Traded (Symbol): NASDAQ (ULTA)
Stockholders: 141 (R)
Employees: 4,000 Full Time; 7,700 Part Time
Annual Meeting: In June

United Continental Holdings, Inc.

77 West Wacker Drive, Chicago, Illinois, 60601

Telephone: (312) 997-8000   www.united.com

United Continental Holdings, Inc. is the holding company for United Airlines and Continental Airlines. The company was formed on October 1, 2010, when Continental Airlines, Inc. merged with a wholly owned subsidiary of UAL Corporation. Together with United Express, Continental Express, and Continental Connection, United Continental Holdings operates a total of approximately 5,800 flights a day to destinations throughout the Americas, Europe, and Asia from hubs in Chicago, Cleveland, Denver, Guam, Houston, Los Angeles, New York, San Francisco, Tokyo, and Washington, D.C. United and Continental will continue to operate separately under United Continental Holdings, Inc. until receipt of a single operating certificate from the Federal Aviation Administration, which they expect to receive by the end of 2011. United and Continental are members of Star Alliance which offers more than 21,200 daily flights to 181 countries worldwide. In July 2011, the company announced that Mileage Plus will be the loyalty program for both United Airlines and Continental Airlines beginning in 2012. Incorporated in Delaware in 1968.

Directors (In addition to indicated officers)

Glenn F. Tilton, Chm.	Jane C. Garvey	James J. O'Connor
Kirbyjon H. Caldwell	Walter Isaacson	Laurence E. Simmons
Carolyn Corvi	Henry L. Meyer III	David J. Vitale
Stephen R. Canale	Wendy J. Morse	John H. Walker
W. James Farrell	Oscar Munoz	Charles Yamarone

Officers (Directors*)

*Jeffery A Smisek, Pres. & C.E.O.
Michael P. Bonds, Exec. V.P.—Hum. Rel. & Labor Rel.
Jim Compton, Exec. V.P. & Chf. Revenue Off.
Jeffrey T. Foland, Exec. V.P. & Pres., Mileage Plus Holdings, LLC

Nene Foxhall, Exec. V.P—Communic. & Gov. Aff.
Peter D. McDonald, Exec. V.P. & C.O.O.
Zane Rowe, Exec. V.P. & C.F.O.
Brett J. Hart, Sr. V.P., Gen. Coun. & Secy.

Consolidated Balance Sheet As of December 31, 2010 (000 omitted)

Assets		Liabilities & Stockholders' Deficit	
Current assets	$ 12,045,000	Current liabilities	$12,645,000
Net property & equipment	16,945,000	Long-term liabilities	12,470,000
Other assets	10,608,000	Other liabilities	12,756,000
		*Stockholders' deficit	1,727,000
Total	$39,598,000	Total	$39,598,000

*327,922,565 shares common stock outstanding.

Consolidated Income Statement

Years Ended Dec. 31	Thousands — — — — —		Per Share — — — — —		Common Stock Price Range [a] Calendar Year
	Operating Revenues	Net Income	Diluted Earnings	Cash Dividends	
2010 [b]	$34,013,000	$ 854,000	$ 2.35	$0.00	$29.75—12.13
2009 [b]	28,608,000	(708,000)	(2.51)	0.00	

[a] UAL common stock began trading on the NYSE on October 1, 2010. Prior to that date, UAL common stock was listed on the NASDAQ Global Select Market under the symbol UAUA.

[b] Includes pro forma results from the first quarter of 2009 through the third quarter of 2010, and actual results for the fourth quarter of 2010.

Transfer Agent & Registrar: Computershare Investor Services

General Counsel: Brett J. Hart, Sr. V.P.

Investor Relations: Tyler Reddien, Managing Dir.

Human Resources: Michael P. Bonds, Exec. V.P.

Info. Tech.: Robert Edwards, Sr. V.P. & C.I.O.

Auditors: Ernst & Young LLP

Traded (Symbol): NYSE (UAL)

Stockholders: 28,600 (R)

Employees: 86,852

Annual Meeting: In June

United States Cellular Corporation

8410 West Bryn Mawr Avenue, Suite 700, Chicago, Illinois 60631-3486

Telephone: (773) 399-8900 **www.uscc.com**

United States Cellular Corporation provides a comprehensive range of wireless services and products to more than 6.1 million customers in five geographic market areas in 26 states. The company believes that it is the sixth largest wireless operating company in the United States as of December 31, 2010. U.S. Cellular is a majority-owned subsidiary of Telephone and Data Systems. Incorporated in Delaware in 1983.

Directors (In addition to indicated officers)

LeRoy T. Carlson, Jr., Chm.	Ronald E. Daly
James Barr III	Paul-Henri Denuit
LeRoy T. Carlson	Harry J. Harczak, Jr.
Walter C.D. Carlson	Gregory P. Josefowicz
J. Samuel Crowley	

Officers (Directors*)

*Mary N. Dillon, Pres. & C.E.O.
Steven T. Campbell, Exec. V.P.—Fin., C.F.O. & Treas.
Carter S. Elenz, Exec. V.P.—Cust. Svcs.
Alan D. Ferber, Exec. V.P., Chf. Strategy & Brand Officer
Michael S. Irizarry, Exec. V.P.—Chf. Tech. Off.
*Kenneth R. Meyers, Chf. Acct. Off.
Jeffrey J. Childs, Exec. V.P. & Chf. Hum. Res. Off.
Rochelle J. Boersma, V.P.—Agt. Effectiveness
Thomas P. Catani, V.P.—Sales, East Reg.

R. Lynn Costlow, V.P.—Customer Svcs.
John M. Cregier, V.P.—Info. Tech.
John C. Gockley, V.P.—Legal & Reg. Affs.
Jeffrey S. Hoersch, V.P.—Fin. Plan. & Analysis
Katherine L. Hust, V.P.—Sales, Mid. Cent. Reg.
Denise M. Hutton, V.P.—Org. Learning
David Kimbell, V.P.—Mktg.
Kevin R. Lowell, V.P.—Natl. Network Oper.
Edward Perez, V.P.—Mktg. & Sales Oper.
Ljubica Petrich, V.P. & Cont.
Thomas S. Weber, V.P.—Fin. Strat.
Nick B. Wright, V.P.—Sales, West. Reg.

Consolidated Balance Sheet As of December 31, 2010 (000 omitted)

Assets		Liabilities & Stockholders' Equity	
Current assets	$1,109,624	Current liabilities	$ 665,995
Net property & equipment	2,615,072	Long-term debt	867,941
Investments	2,158,547	Deferred items	864,718
Other assets & deferred charges	50,367	Minority interest	54,373
		*Stockholders' equity	3,480,583
Total	$5,933,610	Total	$5,993,610

*52,541,000 shares common and 33,006,000 shares Series A common stock outstanding.

Consolidated Income Statement

Years Ended Dec. 31	Thousands — — — —		Per Share — — — —		Common Stock Price Range Calendar Year
	Service Revenues	Net Income [a]	Diluted Earnings [a]	Cash Dividends	
2010	$4,177,681	$132,324	$1.53	$0.00	$ 50.24—33.84
2009	4,213,880	206,372	2.37	0.00	47.95—29.62
2008	4,242,554	33,140	0.38	0.00	85.85—27.18
2007	3,939,751	309,324	3.50	0.00	104.74—67.70
2006	3,472,817	178,082	2.02	0.00	70.42—49.49

a Attributable to U.S. Cellular shareholders.

Transfer Agent & Registrar: Computershare Investor Services

Corporate Counsel:	Sidley Austin LLP	Traded (Symbol):	NYSE (USM)
Investor Relations:	Jane McCahon, V.P.	Stockholders:	355 (R)
Human Resources:	Jeffrey J. Childs, Exec. V.P.	Employees:	8,700
Info. Tech.:	John Cregier, V.P.	Annual Meeting:	In May
Auditors:	PricewaterhouseCoopers LLP		

THE PRIVATEBANK GUIDE

United Stationers Inc.

One Parkway North Boulevard, Suite 100, Deerfield, Illinois 60015-2559
Telephone: (847) 627-7000   **www.unitedstationers.com**

United Stationers Inc. is a wholesale distributor of business products that stocks a line of approximately 100,000 products, including technology products, traditional office products, office furniture, janitorial and breakroom supplies, and industrial supplies. The company's network of 64 distribution centers ships these items to more than 25,000 reseller customers. Customers include independent office products dealers; contract stationers; office products superstores; computer products resellers; office furniture dealers; mass merchandisers; mail order companies; sanitary supply, paper, and foodservice distributors; drug and crocery store chains; health-care distributors; e-commerce merchants; oil field, welding supply, and industrial/MRO distributors; and other independent distributors. Incorporated in Delaware in 1981.

Directors (In addition to indicated officers)

Frederick B. Hegi, Jr., Chm.
Robert B. Aiken, Jr.
William M. Bass
Jean S. Blackwell
Daniel J. Connors

Charles K. Crovitz
Roy W. Haley
Benson P. Shapiro
Jonathan P. Ward
Alex D. Zoghlin

Officers (Directors*)

*P. Cody Phipps, Pres. & C.E.O.
S. David Bent, Sr. V.P. & C.I.O.
Ronald C. Berg, Sr. V.P.—Supply Chain
Eric A. Blanchard, Sr. V.P., Gen. Coun. & Secy.
Patrick T. Collins, Sr. V.P.—Sales
Timothy P. Connolly, Pres.—Ops. & Logistic Svcs.
Jeffrey G. Howard, Sr. V.P.—Natl. Accounts & Channel Mgt.

Barbara J. Kennedy, Sr. V.P.—Hum. Res.
Fareed A. Khan, Sr. V.P. & C.F.O.
Joseph R. Templet, Sr. V.P.—Trade Dev.
Robert J. Kelderhouse, V.P. & Treas.
Kenneth M. Nickel, V.P., Cont. & Chf. Acct. Off.
Stephen A. Schultz, Grp. Pres.—Lagasse & ORS Nasco
Todd Shelton, Pres.—United Stationers Supply

Consolidated Balance Sheet   As of December 31, 2010 (000 omitted)

Assets		Liabilities & Stockholders' Equity	
Current assets	$1,365,406	Current liabilities	$ 614,753
Net property, plant & equipment	135,301	Long-term debt	435,000
Goodwill, net	328,581	Other liabilities	99,112
Other assets	79,735	*Stockholders' equity	759,598
Total	$1,908,663	Total	$1,908,663

*23,093,861 shares common stock outstanding.

Consolidated Income Statement

Years Ended Dec. 31	Thousands — — — —		Per Share — — — —		Common Stock Price Range Calendar Year
	Net Sales	Net Income	Diluted Earnings	Cash Dividends	
2010	$4,832,237	$112,757	$4.67	$0.00	$67.22—53.58
2009	4,710,291	100,985	4.19	0.00	58.03—18.49
2008	4,986,878	98,414	4.13	0.00	57.14—28.39
2007	4,646,399	107,195	3.83	0.00	70.82—45.79
2006	4,546,914	132,213[a]	4.21[a]	0.00	56.01—44.77

[a] Includes $6,000,000 in restructuring and other charges, partially offset for $4,100,000 reversal of previously established restructuring reserves; and $60,600,000 ($1.21 per diluted share) in one-time favorable benefits from product content syndication program and certain marketing program changes.

Transfer Agent & Registrar: Wells Fargo Shareowner Services

General Counsel:	Eric A. Blanchard, Sr. V.P.	Traded (Symbol):	NASDAQ GS (USTR)
Investor Relations:	Mary Disclafani	Stockholders:	541 (R)
Human Resources:	Barbara J. Kennedy, Sr. V.P.	Employees:	5,950
Info. Tech.:	S. David Bent, C.I.O.	Annual Meeting:	In May
Auditors:	Ernst & Young LLP		

USG Corporation

550 West Adams Street, Chicago, Illinois, 60661-3676
Telephone: (312) 436-4000   www.usg.com

USG Corporation, through its subsidiaries, is a leading manufacturer and distributor of building materials. The company is North America's leading producer of gypsum wallboard, joint compound and an array of related products for the construction and remodeling industries. USG is also a global leader in the manufacture of ceiling suspension systems. L&W Supply Corporation, a wholly owned subsidiary, is the leading distributor of gypsum wallboard and other building materials in the United States. Brand names include: SHEETROCK®, DUROCK®, and FIBEROCK®. Gypsum rock is mined or quarried at 13 company-owned locations in North America, and USG manufactures products at 39 plants located throughout the United States, Canada, and Mexico. Incorporated in Delaware in 1984.

Directors (In addition to indicated officers)

Jose Armario	Brian A. Kenney
Lawrence M. Crutcher	Richard P. Lavin
W. Douglas Ford	Steven F. Leer
Gretchen R. Haggerty	Marvin E. Lesser
William H. Hernandez	

Officers (Directors*)

*William C. Foote, Chm.
*James S. Metcalf, Pres. & C.E.O.
Stanley L. Ferguson, Exec. V.P. & Gen. Coun.
Richard H. Fleming, Exec. V.P. & C.F.O.
Christopher R. Griffin, Exec V.P—Ops.
Brian J. Cook, Sr. V.P.—Hum. Res.
Dominic A. Dannessa, Sr. V.P. & Chf. Tech. Off.
Brendan J. Deely, Sr. V.P.; Pres. & C.E.O.—L&W
  Supply Corp.

D. Rick Lowes, Sr. V.P.—Bus. Dev. & Oper. Svcs.
William J. Kelley, V.P. & Cont.
Karen L. Leets, V.P. & Treas.
Mary A. Martin, V.P. & Assoc. Gen. Coun.
Ellis A. Regenbogen, V.P., Corp. Secy. & Assoc.
  Gen. Coun.
Jeffrey P. Rodewald. V.P.—Empl. Ben., Safety
  & Corp. Svcs.
Jennifer F. Scanlon, V.P. & Pres., USG International

Consolidated Balance Sheet As of December 31, 2010 (000 omitted)

Assets		Liabilities & Stockholders' Equity	
Current assets	$1,437,000	Current liabilities	$ 529,000
Net property, plant & equipment	2,266,000	Long-term debt	2,301,000
Other assets	234,000	Other liabilities	638,000
		*Stockholders' equity	619,000
Total	$4,087,000	Total	$4,087,000

*102,876,000 shares common stock outstanding.

Consolidated Income Statement

Years Ended Dec. 31	Thousands — — — —		Per Share [a] — — — —		Common Stock Price Range [a] Calendar Year
	Net Sales	Net Income	Diluted Earnings	Cash Dividends	
2010	$2,939,000	$(405,000)	$(4.03)	$0.00	$25.59—11.21
2009	3,235,000	(787,000)	(7.93)	0.00	19.88— 4.16
2008	4,608,000	(463,000)	(4.67)	0.00	40.25— 5.50
2007 [b]	5,202,000	77,000	0.79	0.00	58.74—34.69
2006 [b]	5,810,000	297,000	4.46	0.00	93.71—43.68

[a] Restated to reflect effect of rights offering that concluded in July 2006.
[b] Restated to adjust for change in accounting method.

Transfer Agent & Registrar: Computershare Investor Services
General Counsel: Stanley L. Ferguson, Exec. V.P. Traded (Symbol): NYSE, CSE (USG)
Investor Relations: Brian P. Moore, Sr. Dir.   Stockholders: 2,994 (R)
Human Resources: Brian J. Cook, Sr. V.P.   Employees: 9,250
Info. Tech.: Dominic A. Dannessa, Sr. V.P. Annual Meeting: In May
Auditors: Deloitte & Touche LLP

VASCO Data Security International, Inc.

1901 South Meyers Road, Suite 210, Oakbrook Terrace, Illinois 60181
Telephone: (630) 932-8844   www.vasco.com

VASCO Data Security International, Inc. provides strong authentication and e-signature solutions, specializing in online accounts, identies, and transactions. VASCO serves a customer base of approximately 10,000 companies in more than 100 countries, including 1,700 international financial institutions. VASCO's product and service lines include: VACMAN, a core authentication platform; IDENTIKEY, an authentication server; aXs GUARD, an authentication appliance; DIGIPASS, a suire of e-signature software products; and DIGIPASS as a Service (DPS) that offers on-demand identity and transaction security. The company's international headquarters is located in Glattbrugg, Switzerland. Incorporated in Delaware in 1997.

Directors (In addition to indicated officers)

Michael P. Cullinane   Jean K. Holley
John N. Fox, Jr.   John R. Walter

Officers (Directors*)

*T. Kendall Hunt, Chm. & C.E.O.   Clifford K. Bown, Exec. V.P. & C.F.O.
Jan Valcke, Pres. & C.O.O.

Consolidated Balance Sheet As of December 31, 2010 (000 omitted)

Assets		Liabilities & Stockholders' Equity	
Current assets	$122,654	Current liabilities	$ 25,765
Net property & equipment	4,771	Other liabilities	683
Goodwill, net	12,772	*Stockholders' equity	116,493
Other assets	2,744		
Total	$142,941	Total	$142,941

*37,640,000 shares common stock outstanding.

Consolidated Income Statement

Years Ended Dec. 31	Total Revenues	Net Income [a]	Per Share — — — — Diluted Earnings [a]	Cash Dividends	Common Stock Price Range Calendar Year
2010	$107,963	$10,806	$0.28	$0.00	$ 9.00— 5.76
2009	101,695	11,862	0.31	0.00	10.60— 3.85
2008	132,977	24,291	0.64	0.00	27.48— 6.64
2007	119,980	20,963	0.55	0.00	44.25—11.71
2006	76,062	12,587	0.33	0.00	12.49— 6.88

[a] From continuing operations.

Transfer Agent & Registrar: Illinois Stock Transfer Company
Corporate Counsel: Katten Muchin Rosemann LLP   Traded (Symbol):   NASDAQ (VDSI)
Auditors: KPMG LLP   Stockholders: 75 (R)
                                                      Employees: 342
                                                      Annual Meeting: In June

Ventas, Inc.

111 South Wacker Drive, Suite 4800, Chicago, Illinois 60606
Telephone: (312) 660-3800 **www.ventasreit.com**

Ventas, Inc. is a real estate investment trust (REIT) with a geographically diverse portfolio of seniors housing and healthcare properties in the United States and Canada. Its diverse portfolio of more than 1,300 assets in 47 states (including the District of Columbia) and two Canadian provinces consists of seniors housing communities, skilled nursing facilities, hospitals, medical office buildings, and other properties. Through its Lillibridge subsidiary, Ventas provides management, leasing, marketing, facility development, and advisory services to highly rated hospitals and health systems throughout the United States. In May 2011, the company acquired substantially all of the real estate assets of Atria Senior Living Group, Inc. In July 2011, Ventas completed its acquisition of Nationwide Health Properties, Inc., creating one of the largest publicly traded REITs and the leading healthcare REIT by equity value. Incorporated in Kentucky in 1983; commenced operations in 1985; and reorganized as a Delaware corporation in 1987.

Directors (In addition to indicated officer)

Douglas Crocker II
Richard I. Gilchrist
Ronald G. Geary
Jay M. Gellert
Matthew J. Lustig
Robert D. Paulson

Robert D. Reed
Sheli Z. Rosenberg
Glenn J. Rufrano
James D. Shelton
Thomas C. Theobald

Officers (Director*)

*Debra A. Cafaro, Chm. & C.E.O.
Raymond J. Lewis, Pres.
*Douglas M. Pasquale, Sr. Advisor
Todd W. Lillibridge, Exec. V.P.—Med.
  Property Oper.
T. Richard Riney, Exec. V.P., Chf. Admin. Off.,
  Gen. Coun. & Corp. Secy.

Richard A. Schweinhart, Exec. V.P. & C.F.O.
John D. Cobb, Sr. V.P. & Chf. Invest. Off.
Vincent M. Cozzi, Sr. V.P.—Med. Property Oper.
Timothy A. Doman, Sr. V.P.—Asset Mgt.
Julie Dreixler, Sr. V.P.—Hum. Res.
Robert J. Brehl, Chf. Acct. Off. & Cont.

Consolidated Balance Sheet As of December 31, 2010 (000 omitted)

Assets		Liabilities & Stockholders' Equity	
Net real estate investments	$5,444,114	Total liabilities	$3,367,816
Cash & cash equivalents	21,812	Minority interest	3,479
Other assets	292,095	*Stockholders' equity	2,386,726
Total	$5,758,021	Total	$5,758,021

*157,265,000 shares common stock outstanding.

Consolidated Income Statement [a]

| Years Ended Dec. 31 | Thousands — — — — | | Per Share— — — — | | Common Stock |
	Total Revenues	Net Income [bc]	Diluted Earnings [b]	Cash Dividends	Price Range Calendar Year
2010	$1,016,867	$246,167	$1.56	$2.14	$56.20—40.36
2009	931,575	266,495	1.74	2.05	44.91—19.13
2008	919,145	222,603	1.59	2.05	52.00—17.31
2007	752,720	273,681	2.22	1.90	47.97—31.38
2006	397,951	131,154	1.25	1.58	42.40—29.54

[a] Updated to comply with SFAS numbers 144, 160, and 51, and APB 14-1.
[b] Attributable to common stockholders.
[c] Funds from operations (Normalized FFO), in thousands: 2010: $453,981; 2009: $409,045; 2008: $379,469; 2007: $327,136; 2006: $254,878.

Transfer Agent & Registrar:	Wells Fargo Shareowner Services		
Corporate Counsel:	Willkie Farr & Gallagher LLP	Traded (Symbol):	NYSE (VTR)
Investor Relations:	David J. Smith	Stockholders:	2,900 (R)
Human Resources:	Julie Dreixler, Sr. V.P.	Employees:	263
Auditors:	Ernst & Young LLP	Annual Meeting:	In May

Walgreen Co.

200 Wilmot Road, Deerfield, Illinois 60015
Telephone: (847) 914-2500   www.walgreens.com

Walgreen Co. is in the retail drugstore business, selling prescription and proprietary drugs, and also carrying additional product lines such as cosmetics, toiletries, food and beverages, and general merchandise, and providing photofinishing services. At August 31, 2011, the company operated 8,210 facilities in 50 states and the District of Columbia, Puerto Rico, and Guam. Walgreen drugstores serve more than 5.9 million customers daily and fill one in five retail prescriptions in America. Pharmacy services include retail, specialty, infusion, medical facility, long-term care, and mail service, along with pharmacy benefit solutions and respiratory services. These services are offered to individuals, employers, managed care organizations, health systems, and pharmacy benefit managers. Walgreen's Take Care Health Systems subsidiary is a manager of worksite health centers and in-store convenient care clinics, with more than 700 locations throughout the U.S. The company's online presence, Walgreens.com, receives 15 million visits per month. Incorporated in Illinois in 1909.

Directors (In addition to indicated officers)

Alan G. McNally, Chm.
David J. Brailer, MD
Steven A. Davis
William C. Foote
Mark P. Frissora

Ginger L. Graham
Nancy M. Schlichting
David Y. Schwartz
Alejandro Silva
James A. Skinner

Officers (Directors*)

*Gregory D. Wasson, Pres. & C.E.O.
Kermit Crawford, Pres.—Pharm.
Hal F. Rosenbluth, Pres.—Health & Wellness
Mark A. Wagner, Pres.—Comm. Svcs. Mgmt.
Thomas J. Sabatino, Exec. V.P., Gen. Coun. & Secy.
Wade D. Miquelon, Exec. V.P. & C.F.O.

Sona Chawla, Pres.—E-Commerce
Mia M. Scholz, Sr. V.P., Cont., and Chf. Acct. Off.
Timothy J. Theriault, Sr. V.P. & C.I.O.
Kathleen Wilson-Thompson, Sr. V.P. & Chf. Hum. Res. Off.
W. Bryan Pugh, V.P.—Merchandising
Robert G. Zimmerman, Sr. V.P. & Chf. Strat. Off.

Consolidated Balance Sheet   As of August 31, 2011 (000 omitted, unaudited)

Assets		Liabilities & Stockholders' Equity	
Current assets	$12,322,000	Current liabilities	$ 8,083,000
Net property & equipment	11,526,000	Long-term debt	2,396,000
Other assets	3,606,000	Other liabilities	2,128,000
		*Stockholders' equity	14,847,000
Total	$27,454,000	Total	$27,454,000

*924,500,000 average diluted shares common stock outstanding.

Consolidated Income Statement

Years Ended Aug. 31	Thousands — — — — —		Per Share — — — — —		Common Stock Price Range Fiscal Year
	Net Sales	Net Earnings	Diluted Earnings	Cash Dividends [a]	
2011[b]	$72,184,000	$2,714,000	$2.94	$0.75	$45.18—27.69
2010	67,420,000	2,091,000	2.12	0.59	40.37—26.36
2009	63,335,000	2,006,000	2.02	0.48	36.04—21.03
2008	59,034,000	2,157,000	2.17	0.40	47.93—31.39
2007	53,762,000	2,041,000	2.03	0.33	51.60—39.91

[a] Cash dividends declared.
[b] Unaudited.

Transfer Agent & Registrar: Wells Fargo Shareowner Services

General Counsel:	Dana I. Green, Exec. V.P.	Auditors:	Deloitte & Touche LLP
Investor Relations:	Rick J. Hans, Div. V.P.	Traded (Symbol):	NYSE, NASDAQ, CSE (WAG)
Human Resources:	Kathleen Wilson-Thompson, Sr. V.P. & Chf. H.R. Off.	Stockholders:	90,249 (R)
		Employees:	244,000
Info. Tech.:	Timothy J. Theriault, Sr. V.P.	Annual Meeting:	Second Wednesday in January

Wells-Gardner Electronics Corporation

9500 West 55th Street, Suite A, McCook, Illinois 60525-3605
Telephone: (708) 290-2100　　　　　　www.wellsgardner.com

Wells-Gardner Electronics Corporation is a global distributor and manufacturer of liquid crystal display monitors (LCDs), and other related distribution products for a variety of markets including, but not limited to, gaming machine manufacturers, casinos, coin-operated video game manufacturers, and other display integrators. The company's primary business is the distribution, design, manufacture, assembly, service, and marketing of electronics components, which consist of LCD video color monitors, gaming supplies and components. Wells-Gardner has subcontract relationships with Taiwanese electronics companies to manufacture LCD displays in China. The company's American Gaming & Electronics (AGE), is a leading parts distributor, service center, and a seller of refurbished gaming machines to the gaming markets. The company has offices in Nevada, New Jersey, Florida, and Illinois. Incorporated in Illinois in 1925.

Directors (In addition to indicated officers)

Merle H. Banta
Marshall L. Burman

Frank R. Martin

Officers (Directors*)

*Anthony Spier, Chm., Pres. & C.E.O.
James F. Brace, Exec. V.P., C.F.O.,
　　Treas. & Secy.
S. David Silk, Sr. V.P.—Bus. Dev. & Eng.

Wally Sa'd, Sr. V.P.—Sales
Renee Zimmerman, V.P. & Corp. Cont.
Laurisa Reptowski, Dir.—U.S. Oper.

Consolidated Balance Sheet As of December 31, 2010 (000 omitted)

Assets		Liabilities & Stockholders' Equity	
Current assets	$17,022	Current liabilities	$ 2,935
Net property, plant & equipment	421	Long-term debt	565
Other assets	1,506	*Stockholders' equity	15,449
Total	$18,949	Total	$18,949

*10,988,219 shares common stock outstanding.

Consolidated Income Statement

Years Ended Dec. 31	Thousands — — — —		Per Share — — — —		Common Stock Price Range Calendar Year [a]
	Net Sales	Net Income	Diluted Earnings [a]	Cash Dividends	
2010	$45,704	$ 190	$0.02	$0.00	$2.89—1.45
2009	52,526	1,097	0.10	0.00	2.97—0.33
2008	53,839	204	0.02	0.00	1.79—0.33
2007	59,308	195	0.02	0.00	4.18—1.35
2006	64,748	343	0.03	0.00	3.36—1.35

[a] Stockholders received 5 percent stock dividends in 2010, 2008, 2007, and 2006. Diluted earnings and stock prices are restated to reflect these dividends.

Transfer Agent & Registrar: StockTrans, a Broadridge Company
Corporate Counsel: Gould & Ratner, LLP
Investor Relations: James F. Brace, Exec. V.P.
Human Resources: Gene Ahner, Dir.
Auditors: Blackman Kallick, LLP

Traded (Symbol): NYSE Amex (WGA)
Stockholders: 441 (R)
Employees: 67
Annual Meeting: In May

Westell Technologies, Inc.

750 North Commons Drive, Aurora, Illinois 60504
Telephone: (630) 898-2500   www.westell.com

Westell Technologies, Inc. is a holding company for Westell, Inc. and Conference Plus, Inc. Westell, Inc. designs, distributes, markets, and services a broad range of broadband networking equipment, digital transmission, remote monitoring, power distribution, and demarcation products used by telephone companies and other telecommunications service providers. Conference Plus, Inc. is a leading global provider of audio, web, video, and IP conferencing services. In April 2011, the company sold substantially all of the assets of its Customer Networking Solutions (CNS) division (other than certain retained business and Westell's HomeCloud™ business) to NETGEAR, Inc. The company markets its products in the U.S. and Canada principally through its domestic field sales organization and selected distributors. Incorporated in Delaware in 1980; present name adopted in 1995.

Directors (In addition to indicated officers)

Kirk R. Brannock
Robert W. Foskett
James M. Froisland
Dennis O. Harris

Martin Hernandez
Eileen A. Kamerick
Robert C. Penny, III

Officers (Directors*)

*Richard S. Gilbert, Chm., Pres. & C.E.O.
Brian S. Cooper, Sr. V.P. & C.F.O.
Amy Forster, Sr. V.P. & Chf. Acct. Off.
Christopher J. Shaver, Sr. V.P.—Bus. Dev. &
  Gen. Mgr.—CNS Div.

Brian Powers, V.P. & Gen. Mgr.—OSPlant Sys. Div.
Mark Skowronski, V.P.—Supply Chain Oper. & Qual.
Timothy J. Reedy, Pres. & C.E.O.—ConferencePlus

Consolidated Balance Sheet   As of March 31, 2011 (000 omitted)

Assets		Liabilities & Stockholders' Equity	
Current assets	$137,090	Current liabilities	$ 34,387
Net property & equipment	3,250	Other liabilities	7,719
Other assets	61,047	*Stockholders' equity	159,281
Total	$201,387	Total	$201,387

*54,174,144 shares Class A and 14,555,815 shares Class B common stock outstanding.

Consolidated Income Statement

Years Ended Mar. 31	Thousands — — — —		Per Share [a] — — — —		Common Stock
	Total Revenues	Net Income	Basic Earnings	Cash Dividends	Price Range [a] Fiscal Year
2011	$190,177	$ 67,936	$ 1.00	$0.00	$3.80—1.26
2010	181,485	10,327	0.15	0.00	1.88—0.27
2009	185,916	(16,684) [b]	(0.24) [b]	0.00	1.83—0.02
2008	205,729	(76,230) [b]	(1.08) [b]	0.00	2.97—1.33
2007	256,533	8,694 [c]	0.12 [c]	0.00	4.15—1.84

[a] Class A common stock.
[b] Includes loss from discontinued operations, net of tax, of $206,000 in 2009 and $1,456,000 ($0.02 per share) in 2008.
[c] Includes income from discontinued operations, net of tax, of $773,000 ($0.01 per share).

Transfer Agent & Registrar: IST Shareholder Services

Corporate Counsel:	Quarles & Brady	Traded (Symbol):	NASDAQ (WSTL)
Investor Relations:	Brian S. Cooper, Sr. V.P.	Stockholders:	656 Class A; 5 Class B (R)
Human Resources:	Sharon Hintz, Dir.	Employees:	365
Info. Tech.:	Chris Marshall, Dir.	Annual Meeting:	In September
Auditors:	Ernst & Young LLP		

WidePoint Corporation

18W100 22nd Street, Suite 104, Oakbrook Terrace, Illinois 60181
Telephone: (630) 629-0003   **www.widepoint.com**

WidePoint Corporation is a leading provider of wireless mobility management and cybersecurity solutions. the company has grown through the merger of highly specialized regional IT companies united by a common set of corporate values. Principal ares of business operations are wireless telecommunications expense management, forensic informatics, identity management, and consulting services. Wireless telecommunications expese management services are provided through on-staff experience and proven solutions for managing complex communication networks. WidePoint provides forensic laboratory information technology services to federal, state, and local law enforcement agencies throughout the United States. The company's identity management products focus on information assurance services and systems that help maintain national security and technology leadership. Consulting services include strategic planning, independent validation and verification, help desk support, training and curriculum development, business process re-engineering, and security architectural analysis. Incorporated in Delaware in 1997.

Directors (In addition to indicated officers)

Otto J. Guenther   James M. Ritter
George W. Norwood   Morton S. Taubman

Officers (Directors*)

*Steve L. Komar, Chm. & C.E.O.   Daniel E. Turissini, V.P., Chf. Tech. Off.;
*James T. McCubbin, Exec. V.P. & C.F.O.   Pres. & C.E.O.—ORC
*Ronald S. Oxley, Exec. V.P.—Sales & Mktg.   Jin Kang, Pres. & C.E.O.—iSYS

Consolidated Balance Sheet As of December 31, 2010 (000 omitted)

Assets		Liabilities	
Current assets	$17,557	Current liabilities	$10,541
Net property, plant & equipment	1,241	Long-term debt, net	564
Goodwill, net	11,330	Other liabilities	275
Other assets	4,2687	*Stockholders' equity	22,016
Total	$34,396	Total	$34,396

*62,690,873 shares common stock outstanding.

Consolidated Income Statement

Years Ended Dec. 31	Thousands — — — — —		Per Share — — — — —		Common Stock Price Range Calendar Year
	Total Revenues	Net Income	Diluted Earnings	Cash Dividends	
2010	$50,813	$6,381	$0.10	$0.00	$1.42—0.63
2009	43,344	1,410	0.02	0.00	0.70—0.18
2008	35,459	(1,090)	(0.02)	0.00	1.44—0.15
2007	14,129	(517)	(0.01)	0.00	2.42—0.70
2006	17,953	(434)	(0.01)	0.00	3.13—2.10

Transfer Agent & Registrar: American Stock Transfer & Trust Co.

Legal Counsel:	Foley & Lardner	Traded (Symbol):	NYSE Amex (WYY)
Investor Relations:	Hayden IR	Stockholders:	153 (R)
Info. Tech.:	Daniel E. Turissini, V.P.	Employees:	115
Auditors:	Moss Adams LLP	Annual Meeting:	In December

Wintrust Financial Corporation

727 North Bank Lane, Lake Forest, Illinois 60045

Telephone: (847) 615-4096   www.wintrust.com

Wintrust Financial Corporation is a financial holding company that operates 15 community bank sub-sidiaries that are located in the greater Chicago and southern Wisconsin market areas. Wintrust also operates non-bank subsidiaries including one of the largest commercial insurance premium finance companies operating in the United States; a company providing short-term accounts receivable financ-ing and value-added outsourced administrative services to the temporary staffing services industry; companies engaging primarily in the origination and purchase of residential mortgages for sale into the secondary market throughout the United States; and companies providing wealth management services including broker-dealer, money management, advisory, trust, and estate services. As of August 2011, the company operated 95 banking offices. In July 2011, Wintrust signed a definitive agreement to acquire Elgin State Bancorp, Inc. Incorporated in Illinois as North Shore Community Bancorp, Inc. in 1992; present name adopted in 1996.

Directors (In addition to indicated officers)

Peter D. Crist, Chm.	Bert A. Getz, Jr.	Albin F. Moschner
Allan E. Bulley, Jr.	H. Patrick Hackett, Jr.	Thomas J. Neis
Bruce K. Crowther	Scott K. Heitmann	Hollis W. Rademacher
Joseph F. Damico	Charles H. James, III	Ingrid S. Stafford

Officers (Directors*)

*Edward J. Wehmer, Pres. & C.E.O.	Timothy S. Crane, Exec. V.P.
David A. Dykstra, Sr. Exec. V.P., C.O.O., Secy. & Treas.	John S. Fleshood, Exec. V.P.—Risk Mgt.
	Richard B. Murphy, Exec. V.P. & Chf. Credit Off.
James H. Bishop, Exec. V.P.	David L. Stoehr, Exec. V.P. & C.F.O.
Lloyd M. Bowden, Exec. V.P.—Tech.	Thomas P. Zidar, Exec. V.P.—Wealth Mgt.

Consolidated Balance Sheet   As of December 31, 2010 (000 omitted)

Assets		Liabilities & Stockholders' Equity	
Cash & due from banks	$ 153,690	Deposits	$ 10,803,673
Federal funds sold	18,890	Junior subordinated debentures	249,493
Deposits with banks, interest-bearing	865,575	FHLB advances	423,500
Securities	1,583,588	Other liabilities	1,066,941
Net loans	9,820,336	*Stockholders' equity	1,436,549
Net property & equipment	363,696		
Other assets	1,174,381		
Total	$13,980,156	Total	$13,980,156

*31,991,579 shares common stock outstanding.

Consolidated Income Statement

Years Ended Dec. 31	Thousands — — — —		Per Share — — — —		Common Stock Price Range Calendar Year
	Net Revenue	Net Income	Diluted Earnings	Cash Dividends	
2010	$607,996	$63,329	$1.02	$0.18	$44.93—27.79
2009	629,523	73,069	2.18	0.27	33.87— 9.70
2008	344,245	20,488	0.76	0.36	44.90—15.37
2007	341,493	55,653	2.24	0.32	50.00—31.81
2006	339,926	66,493	2.56	0.28	59.64—45.08

Transfer Agent & Registrar: IST Stockholder Services

Investor Relations:	David A. Dykstra, Sr. Exec. V.P.	Traded (Symbol):	NASDAQ GS (WTFC)
Human Resources:	Michael Cherwin, Sr. V.P.	Stockholders:	1,505 (R)
Info. Tech.:	Lloyd M. Bowden, Exec. V.P.	Employees:	2,588
Auditors:	Ernst & Young LLP	Annual Meeting:	In May

WMS Industries Inc.

800 South Northpoint Boulevard, Waukegan, Illinois 60085

Telephone: (847) 785-3000   www.wms.com

WMS Industries Inc. designs, manufactures, and distributes games, video, and mechanical reel-spinning gaming machines and video lottery terminals to authorized customers in legal gaming venues world-wide. WMS sells products outright or leases products, primarily on a participation basis, through its gaming operations business. Substantially all of its gaming machines are manufactured at its facility in Waukegan, Illinois. The company conducts business through its wholly owned subsidiaries, including WMS Gaming Inc., Orion Financement Company B.V., and Systems in Progress GmbH, which market products under the WMS, WMS Gaming, Orion Gaming, and SiP trademarks. The company's products are installed in all of the major regulated gaming jurisdictions in the U.S., as well as in more than 100 international gaming jurisdictions. Incorporated in Delaware in 1974.

Directors (In addition to indicated officers)

Robert J. Bahash
Patricia M. Nazemetz
Louis J. Nicastro
Neil D. Nicastro
Edward W. Rabin, Jr.

Ira S. Sheinfeld
Bobby L. Siller
William J. Vareschi, Jr.
Keith R. Wyche

Officers (Directors*)

*Brian R. Gamache, Chm. & C.E.O.
Orrin J. Edidin, Pres.
Scott D. Schweinfurth, Exec. V.P., C.F.O.
 & Treas.
Kenneth Lochiatto, Exec. V.P. & C.O.O.

Larry J. Pacey, Exec. V.P.—Gbl. Prods. & Chf.
 Innovation Off.
Kathleen J. McJohn, V.P., Gen. Coun. & Secy.
John P. McNicholas, Jr.—V.P., Cont. & Chf.
 Acct. Off.

Consolidated Balance Sheet   As of June 30, 2011 (000 omitted)

Assets		Liabilities & Stockholders' Equity	
Current assets	$ 497,500	Current liabilities	$ 152,400
Net property, plant & equipment	171,500	Other liabilities	38,000
Other assets	377,300	*Stockholders' equity	855,900
Total	$1,046,300	Total	$1,046,300

*56,800,000 shares common stock outstanding.

Consolidated Income Statement

Years Ended June 30	Thousands— — — — Total Revenues	Net Income	Per Share — — — — Diluted [a] Earnings	Cash Dividends	Common Stock Price Range [a] Fiscal Year
2011	$783,300	$ 81,000	$1.37	$0.00	$48.75—28.09
2010	765,100	112,900	1.88	0.00	51.77—35.59
2009	706,400	92,200	1.59	0.00	35.60—15.48
2008	650,100	67,500	1.15	0.00	40.78—24.61
2007	539,800	48,900	0.86	0.00	31.20—16.40

[a] Adjusted to reflect a 3-for-2 stock split on May 7, 2007, effected in the form of a stock dividend.

Transfer Agent & Registrar: American Stock Transfer & Trust Co.

Corporate Counsel:	Blank Rome LLP	Traded (Symbol):	NYSE (WMS)
Investor Relations:	William Pfund, V.P.	Stockholders:	705 (R)
Human Resources:	Janice Rike, Sr. V.P.	Employees:	1,764
Chf. Tech. Off.:	Laurie Lasseter, Sr. V.P.	Annual Meeting:	In December
Auditors:	Ernst & Young LLP		

Zebra Technologies Corporation

475 Half Day Road, Suite 500, Lincolnshire, Illinois 60069

Telephone: (847) 634-6700   www.zebra.com

Zebra Technologies Corporation offers a broad range of innovative technology solutions to identify, track, and manage critical assets. The Specialty Printing Group designs and sells devices that print variable information, bar coded labels, RFID tags, receipts, and ID cards on demand at the point of issuance for customers in manufacturing, retail, health care, service organizations, and governments. Applications include such operations as inventory control, automated warehousing, just-in-time manufacturing, health care record tracking, and baggage handling. The Enterprise Solutions Group employs state-of-the-art software and hardware solutions to track, manage, and optimize high-value assets, equipment, and people across the world's largest supply chains. These operations include tracking containers through ports, optimizing parts for manufacturing, and managing ground support at airports. Incorporated in Illinois in 1969; reincorporated in Delaware in 1991.

Directors (In addition to indicated officers)

Michael A. Smith, Chm.
Richard L. Keyser
Andrew K. Ludwick

Ross W. Manire
Robert J. Potter, Ph.D.

Officers (Directors*)

*Anders Gustafsson, C.E.O.
*Gerhard Cless, Exec. V.P.
Michael C. Smiley, C.F.O.
Hugh K. Gagnier, Sr. V.P.—Oper.,
   Spec. Printing Grp.
Philip Gerskovich, Sr. V.P.—Corp. Dev.

Jim Kaput, Sr. V.P., Gen Couns. & Secy.
Todd R. Naughton, V.P.—Fin. & Chf. Acct. Off.
Joanne Townsend, V.P.—Hum. Res.
Michael H. Terzich, Sr. V.P.—Gbl. Sales &
   Mktg., Spec. Printing Grp.
Donald F. O'Shea, V.P. & C.I.O.

Consolidated Balance Sheet As of December 31, 2010 (000 omitted)

Assets		Liabilities & Stockholders' Equity	
Current assets	$476,304	Current liabilities	$136,051
Net property, plant & equipment	88,983	Other liabilities	12,781
Goodwill	151,933	*Stockholders' equity	730,032
Other intangibles	49,706		
Other assets	111,938		
Total	$878,864	Total	$878,864

*55,711,325 shares common stock outstanding.

Consolidated Income Statement

Years Ended Dec. 31	Thousands — — — — —		Per Share — — — — —		Common Stock
	Net Sales	Net Income	Diluted Earnings	Cash Dividends	Price Range Calendar Year
2010	$956,848	$101,778	$ 1.77	$0.00	$39.31—24.14
2009	803,585	47,104	0.79	0.00	28.87—16.00
2008	976,700	(38,421)	(0.60)	0.00	38.47—16.18
2007	868,279	110,113	1.60	0.00	42.50—32.93
2006	759,524	70,946 a	1.00 a	0.00	47.97—29.23

a Includes one-time adjustment, increasing income by $1,319,000 ($0.02 per diluted share), net of taxes, related to the adoption of SFAS No. 123(R), using the modified retrospective approach.

Transfer Agent & Registrar: BNY Mellon Shareowner Services

General Counsel:	Jim Kaput, V.P.	Traded (Symbol):	NASDAQ (ZBRA)
Investor Relations:	Douglas A. Fox, V.P. & Treas.	Stockholders:	237 (R)
Human Resources:	Joanne Townsend, V.P.	Employees:	2,750
Info. Tech.:	Donald F. O'Shea, C.I.O.	Annual Meeting:	In May
Auditors:	Ernst & Young LLP		

Index and Rankings

Index to Operations by Product Classification
Based on the North American Industry Classification System (NAICS)

111998 **All Other Miscellaneous Crop Farming**
Abbott Laboratories
Lifeway Foods, Inc.
John B. Sanfilippo & Son, Inc.

212312 **Crushed and Broken Limestone Mining and Quarrying**
Continental Materials Corporation

212319 **Other Crushed and Broken Stone Mining and Quarrying**
Oil-Dri Corporation of America

212321 **Construction Sand and Gravel Mining**
Continental Materials Corporation

212324 **Kaolin and Ball Clay Mining**
Oil-Dri Corporation of America

212325 **Clay and Ceramic and Refractory Minerals Mining**
AMCOL International Corporation

221111 **Hydroelectric Power Generation**
Exelon Corporation
NiSource, Inc.

221112 **Fossil Fuel Electric Power Generation**
Exelon Corporation

221113 **Nuclear Electric Power Generation**
Exelon Corporation

221122 **Electric Power Distribution**
Exelon Corporation

221210 **Natural Gas Distribution**
Exelon Corporation
Integrys Energy Group, Inc.
Nicor Inc.
NiSource, Inc.

237130 **Power and Communication Line and Related Structures Construction**
MYR Group Inc.

237990 **Other Heavy and Civil Engineering Construction**
Great Lakes Dredge & Dock Corporation

311211 **Flour Milling**
Archer-Daniels-Midland Company
Corn Products International, Inc.

311221 **Wet Corn Milling**
Archer-Daniels-Midland Company
Corn Products International, Inc.

311222 **Soybean Processing**
Archer-Daniels-Midland Company

311223 **Other Oilseed Processing**
Archer-Daniels-Midland Company

311312 **Cane Sugar Refining**
Archer-Daniels-Midland Company

311330 **Confectionery Manufacturing from Purchased Chocolate**
John B. Sanfilippo & Son, Inc.
Tootsie Roll Industries, Inc.

311421 **Fruit and Vegetable Canning**
TreeHouse Foods, Inc.

311510 **Dairy Product (except Frozen) Manufacturing**
TreeHouse Foods, Inc.

311511 **Fluid Milk Manufacturing**
Lifeway Foods, Inc.

311513 **Cheese Manufacturing**
Kraft Foods Inc.
Lifeway Foods, Inc.

311514 **Dry, Condensed, and Evaporated Dairy Product Manufacturing**
Mead Johnson Nutrition Company

311612 **Meat Processed from Carcasses**
Sara Lee Corporation

311811 **Retail Bakeries**
BAB, Inc.

311821 **Cookie and Cracker Manufacturing**
Kraft Foods Inc.

311911 **Roasted Nuts and Peanut Butter Manufacturing**
John B. Sanfilippo & Son, Inc.

311919 **Other Snack Food Manufacturing**
John B. Sanfilippo & Son, Inc.

311920 **Coffee and Tea Manufacturing**
Kraft Foods Inc.
Sara Lee Corporation

311941 **Mayonnaise, Dressing, and Other Prepared Sauce Manufacturing**
TreeHouse Foods, Inc.

311999 **All Other Miscellaneous Food Manufacturing**
Kraft Foods Inc.
TreeHouse Foods, Inc.

312140 **Distilleries**
Fortune Brands Inc.

314999 **All Other Miscellaneous Textile Product Mills**
IDEX Corporation
MFRI, Inc.

322121 **Paper (except Newsprint) Mills**
KapStone Paper & Packaging Corp.
Packaging Corporation of America

322130 **Paperboard Mills**
KapStone Paper & Packaging Corp.
Packaging Corporation of America

323110 **Commercial Lithographic Printing**
R.R. Donnelley & Sons Company

323118 **Blankbook, Looseleaf Binder, and Device Manufacturing**
ACCO Brands Corporation

323121 **Tradebinding and Related Work**
R.R. Donnelley & Sons Company

323122 **Prepress Services**
R.R. Donnelley & Sons Company
Schawk, Inc.

325110 **Petrochemical Manufacturing**
Stepan Company

325131 **Inorganic Dye and Pigment Manufacturing**
Nalco Holding Company

325211 **Plastics Material and Resin Manufacturing**
AMCOL International Corporation
Stepan Company

325311 Nitrogenous Fertilizer Manufacturing
CF Industries Holdings, Inc.

325312 Phosphatic Fertilizer Manufacturing
CF Industries Holdings, Inc.

325411 Medicinal and Botanical Manufacturing
Abbott Laboratories

325412 Pharmaceutical Preparation Manufacturing
Abbott Laboratories
Acura Pharmaceuticals Inc.
Akorn, Inc.
Horizon Pharma, Inc.
Hospira, Inc.

325414 Biological Product (except Diagnostic) Manufacturing
BioSante Pharmaceuticals, Inc.

325520 Adhesive Manufacturing
USG Corporation

325613 Surface Active Agent Manufacturing
Stepan Company

325998 All Other Miscellaneous Chemical Product and Preparation Manufacturing
Nalco Holding Company

326113 Unsupported Plastics Film and Sheet (except Packaging) Manufacturing
ACCO Brands Corporation
Material Sciences Corporation

326121 Unsupported Plastics Profile Shape Manufacturing
ACCO Brands Corporation
Aptargroup, Inc.
Brunswick Corporation
Illinois Tool Works Inc.
USG Corporation

326130 Laminated Plastics Plate, Sheet, and Shape Manufacturing
ACCO Brands Corporation
Material Sciences Corporation

326299 All Other Rubber Product Manufacturing
The Female Health Company

327320 Ready-Mix Concrete Manufacturing
Continental Materials Corporation

327420 Gypsum Product Manufacturing
USG Corporation

331000 Primary Metal Manufacturing
Nanophase Technologies Corporation

331111 Iron and Steel Mills (Including Coke Ovens)
SunCoke Energy, Inc.

331422 Copper Wire (except Mechanical) Drawing
Coleman Cable Inc.

331492 Secondary Smelting, Refining, and Alloying of Nonferrous Metal (except Copper and Aluminum)
Nanophase Technologies Corporation

331521 Nonferrous Metal Foundries
Broadwind Energy, Inc.

332115 Crown and Closure Manufacturing
Aptargroup, Inc.

332117 Powder Metallurgy Part Manufacturing
Aptargroup, Inc.

332212 Hand and Edge Tool Manufacturing
Deere & Company
Federal Signal Corporation

332439 Other Metal Container Manufacturing
AAR CORP.
Caterpillar Inc.
IDEX Corporation
Navistar International Corporation

332710 Machine Shops
MFRI, Inc.

332722 Bolt, Nut, Screw, Rivet, and Washer Manufacturing
Chicago Rivet & Machine Co.
Illinois Tool Works Inc.

332812 Metal Coating, Engraving (except Jewelry and Silverware), and Allied Services to Manufacturers
Material Sciences Corporation

332813 Electroplating, Plating, Polishing, Anodizing, and Coloring
Material Sciences Corporation

332912 Fluid Power Valve and Hose Fitting Manufacturing
AAR CORP.
Lawson Products, Inc.

333111 Agriculture, Construction, and Mining Machinery Manufacturing
Caterpillar Inc.
Deere & Company
Dover Corporation
Titan International, Inc.

333120 Construction Machinery Manufacturing
Caterpillar Inc.
Deere & Company
Dover Corporation
Titan International, Inc.

333131 Mining Machinery and Equipment Manufacturing
Caterpillar Inc.

333293 Printing Machinery and Equipment Manufacturing
Zebra Technologies Corporation

333294 Food Product Machinery Manufacturing
John Bean Technologies Corp.
The Middleby Corporation

333313 Office Machinery Manufacturing
ACCO Brands Corporation

333319 Other Commercial and Service Industry Machinery Manufacturing
John Bean Technologies Corp.
Manitex International, Inc.
The Middleby Corporation

333411 Air Purification Equipment Manufacturing
Fuel Tech, Inc.
W.W. Grainger, Inc.
MFRI, Inc.

333412 Industrial and Commercial Fan and Blower Manufacturing
Fuel Tech, Inc.

333414 Heating Equipment (except Warm Air Furnaces) Manufacturing
Continental Materials Corporation

333415 Air-Conditioning and Warm Air Heating Equipment and Commercial and Industrial Refrigeration Equipment Manufacturing
Continental Materials Corporation
The Middleby Corporation

333511 **Industrial Mold Manufacturing**
Federal Signal Corporation

333513 **Machine Tool (Metal Forming Types) Manufacturing**
Chicago Rivet & Machine Co.

333611 **Turbine and Turbine Generator Set Units Manufacturing**
Caterpillar Inc.

333612 **Speed Changer, Industrial High-Speed Drive, and Gear Manufacturing**
Illinois Tool Works Inc.

333618 **Other Engine Equipment Manufacturing**
Brunswick Corporation
Caterpillar Inc.
Deere & Company

333911 **Pump and Pumping Equipment Manufacturing**
IDEX Corporation

333912 **Air and Gas Compressor Manufacturing**
IDEX Corporation

333992 **Welding and Soldering Equipment Manufacturing**
Illinois Tool Works Inc.

334111 **Electronic Computer Manufacturing**
Motorola Solutions, Inc.

334113 **Computer Terminal Manufacturing**
Molex Incorporated
Wells-Gardner Electronics Corporation

334119 **Other Computer Peripheral Equipment Manufacturing**
Zebra Technologies Corporation

334210 **Telephone Apparatus Manufacturing**
Cobra Electronics Corporation
Motorola, Inc.
Tellabs, Inc.
Telular Corporation
Westell Technologies, Inc.

334220 **Radio and Television Broadcasting and Wireless Communications Equipment Manufacturing**
Anixter International Inc.
Cobra Electronics Corporation
Federal Signal Corporation
Littelfuse, Inc.
Methode Electronics, Inc.
Molex Incorporated
Motorola Mobility Holdings, Inc.
Motorola Solutions, Inc.
PCTEL, Inc.
Richardson Electronics, Ltd.
SigmaTron International, Inc.
Tellabs, Inc.
Telular Corporation
Wells-Gardner Electronics Corporation

334290 **Other Communications Equipment Manufacturing**
Cobra Electronics Corporation
Federal Signal Corporation
Tellabs, Inc.

334310 **Audio and Video Equipment Manufacturing**
Wells-Gardner Electronics Corporation

334411 **Electron Tube Manufacturing**
Richardson Electronics, Ltd.

334412 **Bare Printed Circuit Board Manufacturing**
SigmaTron International, Inc.

334413 **Semiconductor and Related Device Manufacturing**
Richardson Electronics, Ltd.
Rubicon Technology
SigmaTron International, Inc.

334415 **Electronic Resistor Manufacturing**
Methode Electronics, Inc.

334417 **Electronic Connector Manufacturing**
Methode Electronics, Inc.
Molex Incorporated

334419 **Other Electronic Component Manufacturing**
Cabot Microelectronics Corporation
Rubicon Technology
Sparton Corporation

334510 **Navigational, Measuring, Electromedical, and Control Instruments Manufacturing**
Baxter International Inc.

334514 **Totalizing Fluid Meter and Counting Device Manufacturing**
Cobra Electronics Corporation
Landauer, Inc.
SigmaTron International, Inc.

335110 **Electric Lamp Bulb and Part Manufacturing**
Lime Energy Co.

335311 **Power, Distribution, and Specialty Transformer Manufacturing**
Littelfuse, Inc.

335313 **Switchgear and Switchboard Apparatus Manufacturing**
Littelfuse, Inc.
Methode Electronics, Inc.
Molex Incorporated
Tellabs, Inc.

335314 **Relay and Industrial Control Manufacturing**
Littelfuse, Inc.
Methode Electronics, Inc.

335921 **Communication and Energy Wire and Cable Manufacturing**
Coleman Cable Inc.

335931 **Current-Carrying Wiring Device Manufacturing**
Littelfuse, Inc.
Methode Electronics, Inc.
Molex Incorporated

336111 **Automobile Manufacturing**
Federal Signal Corporation
Navistar International Corporation

336211 **Motor Vehicle Body Manufacturing**
Navistar International Corporation

336399 **All Other Motor Vehicle Parts Manufacturing**
Manitex International, Inc.
Tenneco Inc.

336411 **Aircraft Manufacturing**
The Boeing Company
Northstar Aerospace Inc.

336412 **Aircraft Engine and Engine Parts Manufacturing**
AAR CORP.

336413 **Other Aircraft Parts and Auxiliary Equipment Manufacturing**
Northstar Aerospace Inc.

336414 **Guided Missile and Space Vehicle Manufacturing**
The Boeing Company

336510 **Railroad Rolling Stock Manufacturing**
FreightCar America, Inc.

336612 **Boat Building**
Brunswick Corporation

339111 **Laboratory Apparatus and Furniture Manufacturing**
Baxter International Inc.

339914 **Costume Jewelry and Novelty Manufacturing**
CTI Industries Corporation

339920 **Sporting and Athletic Goods Manufacturing**
Brunswick Corporation

339950 **Sign Manufacturing**
Federal Signal Corporation

421110 **Automobile and Other Motor Vehicle Wholesalers**
LKQ Corporation

421120 **Motor Vehicle Supplies and New Parts Wholesalers**
Lawson Products, Inc.

421140 **Motor Vehicle Parts (Used) Wholesalers**
LKQ Corporation

421210 **Furniture Wholesalers**
United Stationers Inc.

421220 **Home Furnishing Wholesalers**
Fortune Brands Home & Security, Inc.

421330 **Roofing, Siding, and Insulation Material Wholesalers**
USG Corporation

421420 **Office Equipment Wholesalers**
United Stationers Inc.

421430 **Computer and Computer Peripheral Equipment and Software Wholesalers**
United Stationers Inc.

421440 **Other Commercial Equipment Wholesalers**
The Middleby Corporation

421450 **Medical, Dental, and Hospital Equipment and Supplies Wholesalers**
Baxter International Inc.

421460 **Ophthalmic Goods Wholesalers**
Akorn, Inc.

421510 **Metal Service Centers and Offices**
A.M. Castle & Co.

421520 **Coal and Other Mineral and Ore Wholesalers**
A.M. Castle & Co.

421610 **Electrical Apparatus and Equipment, Wiring Supplies, and Construction Material Wholesalers**
Anixter International Inc.
W.W. Grainger, Inc.
Littelfuse, Inc.

Molex Incorporated
Richardson Electronics, Ltd.

421620 **Electrical Appliance, Television, and Radio Set Wholesalers**
Cobra Electronics Corporation

421690 **Other Electronic Parts and Equipment Wholesalers**
Anixter International Inc.
Motorola, Inc.
Richardson Electronics, Ltd.

421710 **Hardware Wholesalers**
Chicago Rivet & Machine Co.
Lawson Products, Inc.

421720 **Plumbing and Heating Equipment and Supplies (Hydronics) Wholesalers**
W.W. Grainger, Inc.

421730 **Warm Air Heating and Air-Conditioning Equipment and Supplies Wholesalers**
W.W. Grainger, Inc.

421740 **Refrigeration Equipment and Supplies Wholesalers**
The Middleby Corporation

421830 **Industrial Machinery and Equipment Wholesalers**
W.W. Grainger, Inc.
Lawson Products, Inc.

421860 **Transportation Equipment and Supplies (except Motor Vehicle) Wholesalers**
AAR CORP.

422120 **Stationery and Office Supplies Wholesalers**
OfficeMax Incorporated
United Stationers Inc.

422210 **Drugs and Druggists' Sundries Wholesalers**
Baxter International Inc.

422450 **Confectionery Wholesalers**
Kraft Foods Inc.
John B. Sanfilippo & Son, Inc.
Tootsie Roll Industries, Inc.

422690 **Other Chemical and Allied Products Wholesalers**
Stepan Company

422820 **Wine and Distilled Alcoholic Beverage Wholesalers**
Beam Inc.

423690 **Other Electronic Parts and Equipment Merchant Wholesalers**
LKQ Corporation

441310 **Automotive Parts and Accessories Stores**
Midas, Inc.

442110 **Furniture Stores**
OfficeMax Incorporated

445310 **Beer, Wine, and Liquor Stores**
Walgreen Co.

446110 **Pharmacies and Drug Stores**
Walgreen Co.

446120 **Cosmetics, Beauty Supplies, and Perfume Stores**
Ulta Salon Cosmetics & Fragrance Inc.

452110 **Department Stores**
Sears Holdings Corporation

453210 Office Supplies and Stationery Stores
OfficeMax Incorporated

481111 Scheduled Passenger Air Transportation
United Continental Holdings, Inc.

483113 Coastal and Great Lakes Freight Transportation
GATX Corporation
Nicor Inc.

484121 General Freight Trucking, Long-Distance, Truckload
AMCOL International Corporation
United Stationers Inc.

486210 Pipeline Transportation of Natural Gas
Nicor Inc.

486910 Pipeline Transportation of Refined Petroleum Products
GATX Corporation

488210 Support Activities for Rail Transportation
GATX Corporation

488510 Freight Transportation Arrangement
Echo Global Logistics, Inc.
Hub Group, Inc.

492110 Couriers
United Continental Holdings, Inc.

493110 General Warehousing and Storage
GATX Corporation

511120 Periodical Publishers
R.R. Donnelley & Sons Company

511140 Database and Directory Publishers
Morningstar, Inc.

511210 Software Publishers
Morningstar, Inc.
SXC Health Solutions Corp.

517110 Wired Telecommunications Carriers
Consolidated Communications Holdings, Inc.
Neutral Tandem Inc.
Telephone and Data Systems, Inc.

517210 Cellular and Other Wireless Telecommunications
Neutral Tandem Inc.
United States Cellular Corporation

517211 Paging
Telephone and Data Systems, Inc.
United States Cellular Corporation

518210 Data Processing, Hosting, and Related Services
R.R. Donnelley & Sons Company

522110 Commercial Banking
First Bankers Trustshares, Inc.
First Busey Corporation
First Midwest Bancorp, Inc.
First Robinson Financial Corporation
Northern States Financial Corporation
Northern Trust Corporation
Old Second Bancorp, Inc.
Princeton National Bancorp, Inc.
PrivateBancorp, Inc.
Taylor Capital Group, Inc.
Wintrust Financial Corporation

522120 Savings Institutions
BankFinancial Corporation
First Clover Leaf Financial Corp.
Great American Bancorp, Inc.
MB Financial, Inc.
Northern States Financial Corporation
Park Bancorp, Inc.

522210 Credit Card Issuing
Discover Financial Services
Old Second Bancorp, Inc.

522220 Sales Financing
Caterpillar Inc.
Deere & Company
GATX Corporation
Navistar International Corporation

522291 Consumer Lending
Discover Financial Services

522292 Real Estate Credit
First Midwest Bancorp, Inc.
First Robinson Financial Corporation
Old Second Bancorp, Inc.
Park Bancorp, Inc.
PrivateBancorp, Inc.

523110 Investment Banking and Securities Dealing
Calamos Asset Management, Inc.
First Busey Corporation
National Holdings Corporation

523120 Securities Brokerage
Calamos Asset Management, Inc.

523130 Commodity Contracts Dealing
National Holdings Corporation

523210 Securities and Commodity Exchanges
CME Group Inc.
CBOE Holdings, Inc.

523920 Portfolio Management
The Allstate Corporation
Calamos Asset Management, Inc.
Horace Mann Educators Corporation

523930 Investment Advice
Morningstar, Inc.

524113 Direct Life Insurance Carriers
The Allstate Corporation
Aon Corporation
CNA Financial Corporation
Deere & Company
Horace Mann Educators Corporation
Kemper Corporation
Old Republic International Corporation

524114 Direct Health and Medical Insurance Carriers
CNA Financial Corporation
Kemper Corporation

524126 Direct Property and Casualty Insurance Carriers
The Allstate Corporation
Aon Corporation
CNA Financial Corporation
CNA Surety Corporation
Horace Mann Educators Corporation
Kemper Corporation
Navistar International Corporation
Old Republic International Corporation
RLI Corp.

524127 Direct Title Insurance Carriers
Old Republic International Corporation

524210 Insurance Agencies and Brokerages
Aon Corporation
Arthur J. Gallagher & Co.
Kemper Corporation
RLI Corp.

524292 Third Party Administration of Insurance and Pension Funds
SXC Health Solutions Corp.

525910 Open-End Investment Funds
Calamos Asset Management, Inc.

525930 Real Estate Investment Trusts
Equity Lifestyle Properties, Inc.
Equity Residential
First Industrial Realty Trust, Inc.
General Growth Properties, Inc.
Inland Real Estate Corporation
Strategic Hotels & Resorts, Inc.
Ventas Inc.

531110 Lessors of Residential Buildings and Dwellings
Inland Real Estate Corporation
Ventas Inc.

531120 Lessors of Nonresidential Buildings (except Miniwarehouses)
Inland Real Estate Corporation

531210 Offices of Real Estate Agents and Brokers
First Busey Corporation
Inland Real Estate Corporation
Jones Lang LaSalle Incorporated

533110 Lessors of Nonfinancial Intangible Assets (except Copyrighted Works)
BAB, Inc.

541380 Testing Laboratories
Landauer, Inc.

541512 Computer Systems Design Services
Anixter International Inc.
Envestnet, Inc.
Orbitz Worldwide, Inc.
PCTEL, Inc.
SigmaTron International, Inc.
VASCO Data Security International, Inc.
WidePoint Corporation

541611 Administrative Management and General Management Consulting Services
APAC Customer Services, Inc.
Huron Consulting Group Inc.
Navigant Consulting, Inc.
WidePoint Corporation

541612 Human Resources and Executive Search Consulting Services
General Employment Enterprises, Inc.
Heidrick & Struggles International, Inc.

541613 Marketing Consulting Services
Mattersight Corporation

541618 Other Management Consulting Services
Huron Consulting Group Inc.
InnerWorkings, Inc.

541710 Research and Development in the Physical, Engineering, and Life Sciences
Allscripts Healthcare Solutions, Inc.
The Boeing Company

541910 Marketing Research and Other Public Opinion Polling
Morningstar, Inc.

541990 Other Professional, Scientific, and Technical Services
Envestnet, Inc.
Morningstar, Inc.

551111 Offices of Bank Holding Companies
BankFinancial Corporation
First Bankers Trustshares, Inc.
First Busey Corporation
First Clover Leaf Financial Corp.
First Midwest Bancorp, Inc.
First Robinson Financial Corporation
Great American Bancorp, Inc.
MB Financial, Inc.
Northern States Financial Corporation
Northern Trust Corporation
Old Second Bancorp, Inc.
Park Bancorp, Inc.
Princeton National Bancorp, Inc.
PrivateBancorp, Inc.
Taylor Capital Group, Inc.
Wintrust Financial Corporation

551112 Offices of Other Holding Companies
The Allstate Corporation
Aon Corporation
Archer-Daniels-Midland Company
Calamos Asset Management, Inc.
CF Industries Holdings, Inc.
CME Group Inc.
CNA Financial Corporation
Consolidated Communications Holdings, Inc.
Continental Materials Corporation
DeVry Inc.
Exelon Corporation
GATX Corporation
General Employment Enterprises, Inc.
Horace Mann Educators Corporation
MFRI, Inc.
The Middleby Corporation
Morton's Restaurant Group, Inc.
MYR Group Inc.
Nalco Holding Company
Navistar International Corporation
Nicor Inc.
Old Republic International Corporation
RLI Corp.
Sears Holdings Corporation
Telephone and Data Systems, Inc.
Tellabs, Inc.
Tootsie Roll Industries, Inc.
United Continental Holdings, Inc.
USG Corporation
Walgreen Co.
WMS Industries Inc.

561310 Employment Placement Agencies
Heidrick & Struggles International, Inc.
General Employment Enterprises, Inc.

561320 Temporary Help Services
General Employment Enterprises, Inc.

561422 Telemarketing Bureaus
APAC Customer Services, Inc.

561599 All Other Travel Arrangement and Reservation Services
Orbitz Worldwide, Inc.

562211 Hazardous Waste Treatment and Disposal
Heritage-Crystal Clean Inc.
Stericycle, Inc.

562910 Remediation and Other Waste Management Services
Heritage-Crystal Clean Inc.

611210 **Junior Colleges**
Career Education Corporation
DeVry Inc.

611310 **Colleges, Universities, and Professional Schools**
Career Education Corporation
DeVry Inc.

611410 **Business and Secretarial Schools**
Career Education Corporation
DeVry Inc.

611420 **Computer Training**
Career Education Corporation
DeVry Inc.

713120 **Amusement Arcades**
WMS Industries Inc.

713950 **Bowling Centers**
Brunswick Corporation

722110 **Full-Service Restaurants**
Cosi, Inc.
McDonald's Corporation
Morton's Restaurant Group, Inc.

722211 **Limited-Service Restaurants**
McDonald's Corporation

811111 **General Automotive Repair**
Midas, Inc.

812112 **Beauty Salons**
Ulta Salon Cosmetics & Fragrance,Inc.

812921 **Photofinishing Laboratories (except One-Hour)**
Walgreen Co.

812930 **Parking Lots and Garages**
Standard Parking Corporation

Industrial, Retail, Transportation, Utility, Insurance, REITs, and Other Diversified Financial Companies

Company	Rank by Sales or Revenues '10	'09	Sales or Revenues (000 Omitted)	Rank by Assets '10	'09	Assets (000 Omitted)	Year End
Archer-Daniels-Midland Company	1	3	80,676,000	14	11	31,028,000	06/11
Walgreen Co.	2	2	72,184,000	16	15	27,454,000	08/10
The Boeing Company	3	1	64,306,000	3	3	68,565,000	12/10
Kraft Foods Inc.	4	5	49,207,000	2	2	95,289,000	12/10
Sears Holdings Corporation	5	4	43,326,000	18	16	24,268,000	01/11
Caterpillar Inc.	6	6	42,588,000	4	4	64,020,000	12/10
Abbott Laboratories	7	8	35,166,721	6	6	59,462,266	12/10
United Continental Holdings, Inc.	8	9	34,013,000	10	19	39,598,000	12/10
The Allstate Corporation	9	7	31,400,000	1	1	130,874,000	12/10
Deere & Company	10	10	26,004,600	9	9	43,266,800	10/10
McDonald's Corporation	11	11	24,075,000	13	12	31,975,200	12/10
Exelon Corporation	12	12	18,644,000	8	7	52,240,000	12/10
Illinois Tool Works Inc.	13	13	15,870,376	21	21	16,250,273	12/10
Baxter International Inc.	14	14	12,843,000	20	20	17,489,000	12/10
Navistar International Corporation	15	15	12,145,000	26	26	9,730,000	10/10
Motorola Mobility Holdings, Inc	16	16	11,460,000	35	34	6,204,000	12/10
R.R. Donnelley & Sons Company	17	17	10,018,900	28	28	9,083,200	12/10
CNA Financial Corporation	18	18	9,209,000	7	5	55,331,000	12/10
Sara Lee Corporation	19	19	8,681,000	27	27	9,533,000	06/11
Aon Corporation	20	21	8,512,000	15	17	28,982,000	12/10
Discover Financial Services	21	20	8,241,217	5	8	60,784,968	11/10
Motorola Solutions, Inc.	22	24	7,871,000	17	14	25,577,000	12/10
W.W. Grainger, Inc.	23	27	7,182,158	45	43	3,904,377	12/10
OfficeMax Incorporated	24	23	7,150,007	44	42	4,078,929	12/10
*Fortune Brands Inc.	25	25	7,141,500	24	24	12,675,300	12/10
Dover Corporation	26	28	7,132,648	30	30	8,562,894	12/10
NiSource, Inc.	27	26	6,422,000	19	18	19,938,800	12/10
Tenneco Inc.	28	32	5,937,000	49	49	3,167,000	12/10
Anixter International Inc.	29	30	5,472,100	50	51	2,933,300	12/10
Integrys Energy Group, Inc.	30	22	5,203,200	25	25	9,816,800	12/10
Telephone and Data Systems, Inc.	31	29	4,986,829	32	31	7,762,519	12/10
United Stationers Inc.	32	31	4,832,237	65	63	1,908,663	12/10
Corn Products International, Inc.	33	37	4,367,000	41	48	5,071,000	12/10
Nalco Holding Company	34	36	4,250,500	40	39	5,223,700	12/10
United States Cellular Corporation	35	33	4,177,681	37	35	5,993,610	12/10
Old Republic International Corp.	36	35	4,102,700	23	23	15,882,700	12/10
CF Industries Holdings, Inc.	37	47	3,965,000	29	55	8,758,500	12/10
Hospira, Inc.	38	34	3,917,200	36	37	6,046,300	12/10
Molex Incorporated	39	40	3,587,334	46	45	3,597,852	06/11
Hyatt Hotels Corporation	40	38	3,527,000	33	32	7,243,000	12/10
Brunswick Corporation	41	44	3,403,300	52	50	2,678,000	12/10
Mead Johnson Nutrition Company	42	43	3,141,600	60	60	2,293,100	12/10
CME Group Inc.	43	46	3,003,700	11	10	35,046,100	12/10
USG Corporation	44	39	2,939,000	43	41	4,087,000	12/10
Jones Lang LaSalle Incorporated	45	48	2,925,613	48	47	3,349,861	12/10
General Growth Properties, Inc.	46	42	2,823,486	12	13	32,367,379	12/10
Kemper Corporation	47	41	2,743,400	31	29	8,358,500	12/10
Nicor Inc.	48	45	2,709,800	42	40	4,496,500	12/10
LKQ Corporation	49	50	2,469,881	59	61	2,299,509	12/10
Packaging Corporation of America	50	49	2,435,606	61	58	2,224,274	12/10

Company	Rank by Sales or Revenues '10	'09	Sales or Revenues (000 Omitted)	Rank by Assets '10	'09	Assets (000 Omitted)	Year End
DeVry Inc.	51	51	2,182,371	66	64	1,850,503	06/11
Career Education Corporation	52	53	2,124,236	69	65	1,560,856	12/10
Aptargroup, Inc.	53	52	2,076,719	64	62	2,032,718	12/10
Equity Residential	54	54	1,966,849	22	22	16,184,194	12/10
SXC Health Solutions Corp.	55	60	1,948,389	80	86	816,309	12/10
Arthur J. Gallagher & Co.	56	56	1,864,200	47	44	3,596,000	12/10
Hub Group, Inc.	57	59	1,833,737	89	88	629,407	12/10
TreeHouse Foods, Inc.	58	58	1,817,024	57	68	2,391,248	12/10
AAR CORP.	59	62	1,775,782	68	67	1,703,727	05/11
Tellabs, Inc.	60	57	1,642,300	54	52	2,602,900	12/10
IDEX Corporation	61	61	1,513,073	58	59	2,381,695	12/10
Ulta Salon, Cosmetics & Fragrance, Inc.	62	65	1,454,838	86	92	730,488	01/11
Stericycle, Inc.	63	55	1,439,388	53	56	2,639,023	12/10
Stepan Company	64	63	1,431,122	81	87	811,431	12/10
ACCO Brands Corporation	65	64	1,330,500	73	72	1,149,600	12/10
SunCoke Energy, Inc.	66	67	1,326,593	67	66	1,718,466	12/10
GATX Corporation	67	66	1,204,900	39	38	5,442,400	12/10
Ventas, Inc.	68	69	1,016,867	38	36	5,758,021	12/10
Horace Mann Educators Corp.	69	68	974,711	34	33	7,005,541	12/10
Zebra Technologies Corporation	70	72	956,848	76	77	878,864	12/10
A.M. Castle & Co.	71	71	943,706	95	90	529,352	12/10
Titan International, Inc.	72	76	881,591	84	82	787,470	12/10
John Bean Technologies Corp.	73	70	880,400	92	94	582,200	12/10
AMCOL International Corporation	74	79	852,538	82	83	799,093	12/10
WMS Industries Inc.	75	73	783,300	75	74	1,046,300	06/11
KapStone Paper & Packaging Corp.	76	83	782,676	87	84	719,727	12/10
Orbitz Worldwide, Inc.	77	75	757,000	71	69	1,216,703	12/10
Federal Signal Corporation	78	74	726,500	85	81	764,500	12/10
Standard Parking Corporation	79	80	721,143	106	106	255,632	12/10
The Middleby Corporation	80	82	719,121	77	79	873,172	12/10
Coleman Cable Inc.	81	90	703,763	99	102	341,111	12/10
Navigant Consulting, Inc.	82	77	703,660	78	78	869,035	12/10
Great Lakes Dredge & Dock Corp.	83	85	686,900	88	85	698,825	12/10
Strategic Hotels & Resorts, Inc.	84	81	686,293	62	53	2,162,316	12/10
John B. Sanfilippo & Son, Inc.	85	87	674,212	98	98	351,788	06/10
Allscripts Healthcare Solutions, Inc.	86	78	613,309	56	73	2,418,587	05/11
Littelfuse, Inc.	87	95	608,021	90	93	621,129	12/10
Accretive Health, Inc.	88	89	606,294	105	123	262,619	12/10
Huron Consulting Group Inc.	89	86	604,600	83	80	788,983	12/10
MYR Group Inc.	90	84	597,077	97	99	380,148	12/10
RLI Corp.	91	88	583,424	55	54	2,514,592	12/10
Morningstar, Inc.	92	93	555,351	74	75	1,086,302	12/10
Tootsie Roll Industries, Inc.	93	92	517,149	79	76	860,383	12/10
Heidrick & Struggles Int'l, Inc.	94	97	513,236	94	96	545,027	12/10
Equity Lifestyle Properties, Inc.	95	91	511,361	63	57	2,048,395	12/10
InnerWorkings, Inc.	96	99	482,212	104	103	279,925	12/10
Schawk, Inc.	97	94	460,626	96	97	449,859	12/10
CBOE Holdings, Inc.	98	96	437,104	107	89	254,112	12/10
Methode Electronics, Inc.	99	100	428,215	100	101	334,744	05/11
Echo Global Logistics, Inc.	100	107	426,374	119	117	161,548	12/10
Cabot Microelectronics Corp.	101	104	408,201	93	95	571,7560	09/10
Consolidated Comm. Holdings, Inc.	102	98	383,400	72	70	1,209,546	12/10
Calamos Asset Management, Inc.	103	105	326,039	91	91	589,246	12/10
APAC Customer Services, Inc.	104	103	325,958	116	115	163,165	12/10
Lawson Products, Inc.	105	102	316,780	108	105	236,384	12/10
Morton's Restaurant Group, Inc.	106	106	296,100	111	110	201,814	12/10
First Industrial Realty Trust, Inc.	107	101	288,541	51	46	2,750,054	12/10

Company	Rank by Sales or Revenues '10	'09	Sales or Revenues (000 Omitted)	Rank by Assets '10	'09	Assets (000 Omitted)	Year End
Addus HomeCare Corporation	108	108	271,732	114	111	166,924	12/10
Oil-Dri Corporation of America	109	110	226,755	118	114	173,393	12/10
MFRI, Inc.	110	111	218,598	115	113	163,275	01/11
Northstar Aerospace	111	112	216,985	120	112	152,046	12/10
Sparton Corporation	112	116	203,352	125	121	122,609	06/11
Neutral Tandem Inc.	113	117	199,826	101	104	315,527	12/10
Midas, Inc.	114	114	192,400	109	109	229,700	12/10
Westell Technologies, Inc.	115	115	190,177	112	120	201,387	03/11
Inland Real Estate Corporation	116	118	167,029	70	71	1,254,841	12/10
Richardson Electronics, Ltd.	117	120	158,867	102	107	314,054	05/11
SigmaTron International, Inc.	118	121	151,728	130	125	102,867	04/11
FreightCar America, Inc.	119	109	142,889	103	100	310,643	12/10
Material Sciences Corporation	120	119	137,624	126	122	113,931	02/11
Broadwind Energy, Inc.	121	113	136,896	113	108	183,506	12/10
Landauer, Inc.	122	129	114,367	121	119	150,696	09/10
Continental Materials Corporation	123	124	114,284	134	128	79,561	12/10
Heritage-Crystal Clean, Inc.	124	128	112,118	131	134	89,572	12/10
National Holdings Corporation	125	123	110,952	146	144	17,380	09/10
Cobra Electronics Corporation	126	125	110,520	135	129	74,354	12/10
Cosi, Inc.	127	122	109,699	141	138	31,351	12/10
VASCO Data Security Int'l, Inc.	128	126	107,963	122	116	142,941	12/10
Envestnet, Inc.	129	130	98,052	123	130	141,868	12/10
Manitex International, Inc.	130	136	95,875	128	126	105,517	12/10
Lime Energy Co.	131	133	95,718	132	131	86,276	12/10
Mattersight Corporation	132	127	88,100	136	132	66,190	12/10
Akorn, Inc.	133	131	86,409	127	133	111,116	12/10
Fuel Tech, Inc.	134	132	81,795	129	127	103,203	12/10
Rubicon Technology, Inc.	135	143	77,362	110	124	206,742	12/10
PCTEL, Inc.	136	135	69,254	124	118	130,565	12/10
Lifeway Foods, Inc.	137	134	63,543	137	135	52,029	12/10
WidePoint Corporation	138	139	50,813	139	141	34,396	12/10
CTI Industries Corporation	139	140	47,748	140	140	32,861	12/10
Telular Corporation	140	138	47,354	133	136	81,551	09/10
Wells-Gardner Electronics Corp.	141	137	45,704	144	142	18,949	12/10
Chicago Rivet & Machine Co.	142	142	28,521	143	143	23,659	12/10
The Female Health Company	143	141	22,222	145	145	18,368	09/10
General Employ. Enterprises, Inc.	144	144	11,917	148	148	9,889	09/10
Nanophase Technologies Corp.	145	145	9,461	147	146	13,483	12/10
Acura Pharmaceuticals, Inc.	146	146	3,311	142	139	25,493	12/10
BAB, Inc.	147	147	2,914	149	149	4,071	11/10
BioSante Pharmaceuticals, Inc.	148	148	2,474	138	137	44,767	12/10
Horizon Pharma, Inc.	149	149	2,376	117	147	161,685	12/10

* In October 2011 Fortune Brands spun off Fortune Brands Home & Security, Inc. and changed its name to Beam, Inc.

Bank and Savings Institution Holding Companies

Company	Rank by Total Income '10	'09	Total Income (000 Omitted)	Rank by Assets '10	'09	Total Assets (000 Omitted)	Year End
Northern Trust Corporation	1	1	4,025,700	1	1	83,843,900	12/10
MB Financial, Inc.	2	4	615,396	4	4	10,320,364	12/10
Wintrust Financial Corporation	3	2	607,996	2	2	13,980,156	12/10
PrivateBancorp, Inc.	4	3	601,171	3	3	12,465,621	12/10
First Midwest Bancorp, Inc.	5	5	420,899	5	5	8,146,973	12/10
Taylor Capital Group, Inc.	6	6	281,199	6	6	4,483,854	12/10
First Busey Corporation	7	7	218,936	7	7	3,605,003	12/10
Old Second Bancorp, Inc.	8	8	151,591	8	8	2,123,921	12/10
BankFinancial Corporation	9	9	72,064	9	9	1,530,655	12/10
Princeton National Bancorp, Inc.	10	10	61,058	10	10	1,096,471	12/10
First Bankers Trustshares, Inc.	11	11	37,094	11	11	690,644	12/10
Northern States Financial Corporation	12	12	29,962	13	12	531,728	12/10
First Clover Leaf Financial Corp.	13	13	27,687	12	13	574,970	12/10
First Robinson Financial Corporation	14	16	10,878	15	15	208,831	03/11
Great American Bancorp, Inc.	15	14	10,464	16	16	158,060	12/10
Park Bancorp, Inc.	16	15	9,905	14	14	211,789	12/10

Glossary of Abbreviations Used in this Guide

Acct.	Accounting	Govt.	Government
Add'l.	Additional (Internet)	Hon.	Honorary, Honorable
Adm.	Admiral	Hum. Res.	Human Resources
Admin.	Administration, Administrator	Inc.	Incorporated
Adv.	Advertising	Ind.	Industries
Affs.	Affairs	Info.	Information
Ag.	Agricultural	Intl.	International
Amer.	America	Invest.	Investment
Assoc.	Associate	Inv.	Investor
Asst.	Assistant	Ins.	Insurance
Assn.	Association	Ltd.	Limited
Atty.	Attorney	Med.	Medical
Ben.	Benefits	Merch.	Merchandise, Merchandising
Bus.	Business	Metro.	Metropolitan
C.E.O.	Chief Executive Officer	Mfg.	Manufacturing
C.F.O.	Chief Financial Officer	Mgr.	Manager
C.I.O.	Chief Information Officer	Mgt.	Management
C.O.O.	Chief Operating Officer	Mktg.	Marketing
Chf.	Chief	Natl.	National
Chf. Acct. Off.	Chief Accounting Officer	Off.	Officer
Chf. Admin. Off.	Chief Administrative Officer	Oper.	Operations
Chm.	Chairman, Chairperson	Perm.	Permanent
Co. (Cos.)	Company (Companies)	Pkg.	Packaging
Comm.	Committee	Plan.	Planning
Commun.	Communication, Communications	Pres.	President
		Prin.	Principal, Principle
Commer.	Commercial	Prod. (Prods.)	Product, Production (Products)
Comp.	Compensation	Prof.	Professor, Professional
Compt.	Comptroller	Proj(s).	Project(s)
Cons.	Consumer	Prop. & Cas.	Property & Casualty
Const.	Construction	Ptnr.	Partner
Cont.	Controller	Pub.	Public
Coord.	Coordinator	Qual.	Quality
Corp.	Corporation, Corporate	Rec.	Recreation
Coun.	Counsel	Reg.	Regulatory
Ctr.	Center	Rel.	Relations
Dep.	Deputy	Res.	Research
Dev.	Development	Ret.	Retired
Dir.	Director	Secy.	Secretary
Dist.	District	Spec.	Special, Specialist, Specialty
Distr.	Distribution, Distributor	Sr.	Senior
Div.	Division, Divisional	Strat.	Strategic, Strategy
Econ.	Economic, Economics	Svcs.	Services
Educ.	Education	Sys.	System
Emer.	Emeritus	Tech.	Technical, Technician
Empl.	Employee	Trans.	Transportation
Eng.	Engineer, Engineering	Treas.	Treasurer
Envir.	Environment, Environmental	Univ.	University
Equip.	Equipment	V.	Vice
Eur.	Europe, European	V. Chm.	Vice Chairman, Vice Chairperson
Exec.	Executive		
Fin.	Finance, Financial	V.P.	Vice President
Gen.	General	WW	Worldwide
Grad.	Graduate		
Grp.	Group		

Changes from Last Year's Edition

New Listings in the 2011-2012 Edition

Broadwind Energy, Inc.
Dover Corporation
Echo Global Logistics Inc.
Fortune Brands Home & Security, Inc.
Horizon Pharma, Inc.
Motorola Mobility Holdings, Inc.
SunCoke Energy, Inc.

Name Changes

eLoyalty Corporation *to* Mattersight Corporation
Fortune Brands Inc. *to* Beam Inc.
Motorola, Inc. *to* Motorola Solutions, Inc.
UAL Corporation *to* United Continental Holdings, Inc.
Unitrin, Inc. *to* Kemper Corporation

Companies No Longer Listed

Alberto-Culver Company	Acquired by Unilever PLC.
ATC Technology Corporation	Acquired by GENCO Supply Chain Solutions, Pittsburgh, PA.
Aventine Renewable Energy Holdings, Inc.	Emerged from bankruptcy; successor company relocated headquarters to Dallas, TX.
CNA Surety Corporation	Acquired by CNA Financial Corporation.
Deerfield Capital Corp.	Merged with Commercial Industrial Financial Corp. (CIFC) with headquarters in New York.
Diamond Management & Technology Consultants, Inc.	Acquired by PricewaterhouseCoopers LLP.
Gardner Denver, Inc.	Headquarters moved to Wayne, PA.
Hewitt Associates, Inc.	Acquired by Aon Corporation.
NovaMed, Inc.	Acquired by H.I.G. Capital.
optionsXpress Holdings, Inc.	Acquired by Charles Schwab Corp.
Pactive Corporation	Acquired by Reynolds Group Holdings Limited.
Playboy Enterprises	Completed a transition to private ownership.
RC2 Corporation	Acquired by TOMY Company, Ltd.
Rewards Network Inc.	Acquired and taken private by Equity Group Investments.
Smurfit-Stone Container Corporation	Acquired by Rock-Tenn Company.